The Landmark Trust Handbook

Contents

Map and Landmarks by size	Inside front cover
Foreword	2

Introduction
Landmark: Champion of Buildings	4
Sir John Smith CH CBE (1923–2007)	6
Keeping History Alive	8
Never Beyond Rescue	10
Where We Need Your Help Now	13
Buildings Rescued by Our Supporters	14
How You Can Support Us	17
The Sublime, the Beautiful and the Picturesque	18
A Brief History of Rooms	20
History to Live In	22
Booking Information	24

Landmarks in Britain	25
Lundy	202
Landmarks in Italy	216
The Landmark Trust USA	224
People	231
Acknowledgments	232

Left: Sixteenth-century wall painting at Margells, Devon.

CLARENCE HOUSE

Sir John Smith's creation, the Landmark Trust, was unique in the 1960's. Single-handedly, he changed the course of conservation in this country by finding a practical use and viable future for small and often idiosyncratic historic buildings. By breathing new life into them, Landmarks continue to be a source of enjoyment, appreciation and learning to the many thousands whose lives have been enriched by staying in, visiting or living near them.

The Landmark Trust is now an indispensable protector of this country's cultural fabric; a charity admired and respected far beyond these shores and one of which I am inordinately proud to be Patron. I am delighted to see it in such good shape to meet the undoubted challenges ahead. I wish it every conceivable success in its utterly vital conservation work.

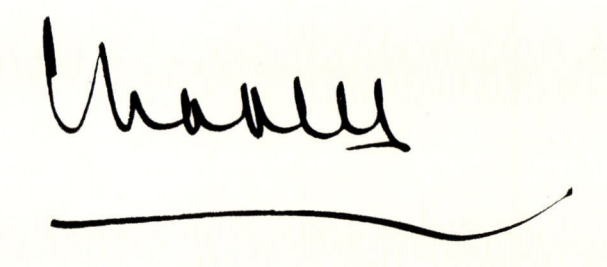

Win a £3,000 holiday

Enter our Spring Raffle by 30 April for your chance to win your dream holiday in a Landmark, whilst contributing to our current restoration projects. First prize is a holiday to the value of £3,000, and there are second prizes of £1,000 and third prizes of £300. You can buy tickets online at www.landmarktrust.org.uk/raffle.

Chris Crook

After more than 40 years, Chris Crook, our custodian at **Woodspring Priory** is retiring.

Chris has been the contact for many Landmarkers and visitors, and has worked tirelessly running the Priory's museum, maintaining the grounds, and promoting Woodspring Priory to schools and local groups.

We are enormously grateful to Chris for his long contribution to Landmark and wish him a relaxing retirement.

Chris Crook at Woodspring Priory

Landmark goes greener

Wortham Manor, Devon

As part of our continuing improvements programme, we now have a policy of installing 'greener energy' systems where possible. Technological advances mean that heat is now captured more efficiently, so that ground- and air-source heat pumps can be used to heat radiators, rather than just underfloor heating as previously. Heat pumps typically provide triple the heat output per unit of energy consumed, enabling us to reduce our carbon footprint as well as saving on heating costs (the payback period can be as short as seven years). At **Wortham Manor** an air-source heat pump has replaced an oil-fired boiler and night storage heaters (the great hall retains its traditional heating, a massive open fireplace). At isolated **Woodspring Priory**, a new heat pump has replaced a Liquid Propane Gas boiler.

Flying trees at Crownhill Fort

Unchecked growth of self-seeded trees at **Crownhill Fort** long predated our involvement there but had been a cause of concern for a while. Some trees were in danger of being blown over and damaging the Fort's fabric; elsewhere roots were already beginning to affect the Fort's structures, especially the Chemin de Ronde where roots had broken through.

The felling team at Crownhill Fort, Devon

However, the steep surrounding ditch, nearby houses and proximity of the A38 made the felling and removal extremely hazardous. After a bat survey, full risk assessment and extensive consultation including with English Heritage, it was agreed that one major felling campaign would be the least damaging approach, with further lower-level vegetation clearances to follow. Early February saw some dramatic scenes at Crownhill. Over two days, 200 tonnes of felled timber were lifted off the site by helicopter, at a rate of a journey every few minutes. Not surprisingly, this generated considerable interest locally and this Palmerstonian fort now stands properly revealed once more. See our website for photographs of the work.

The Landmark Trust
Shottesbrooke Maidenhead Berkshire SL6 3SW
Bookings 01628 825925   Office 01628 825920   Website www.landmarktrust.org.uk

Printed on an FSC certified mixed sources paper containing 50% recovered waste and 50% virgin fibre.

Charity registered in England & Wales 243312 and Scotland SC039205

The Silver Darlings & the Shore Cottages

The Shore Cottages, Caithness

Publicity for our appeal for the Shore Cottages at Berriedale in Caithness received a welcome boost last Autumn through association with a Scottish touring theatre production of Neil Gunn's epic tale of the herring fishery, *The Silver Darlings*, which vividly portrays the triumphs and disasters of families like those who lived and fished from the Shore Cottages. Thanks to this and a great number of supporters, we have now raised £227,316 towards the total project cost of £600,000. Eight private individuals so far have very generously become Guardians, each contributing £6,000 or 1% of the total cost. If we are to rescue these evocative remnants of Scotland's past, we urgently need more donations of any size. You can donate quickly and easily on our website, or to find out more on becoming a Guardian, please contact Anna Clayton on 01628 825920 or aclayton@landmarktrust.org.uk.

BTCV volunteers at Astley Castle

Get involved

Gentle consolidation [of the] fabric of Astley Castle [...] details of the archi[tecture...] are plenty of oppo[rtunities...] project. We are al[so looking] for Conservation [volunteers] and undergrowth. [...] Friends and Patro[ns...] a chance to learn [...] If you fancy some[thing...] our website soon [for...] design a new knot garden for the castle site. The downloadable entry pack [...] of knot gardens and their planting. All this is made possible by the generou[s...]

To find out how to volunteer at Astley, visit our website or contact Kasia Ho[...]

Handbook

The 23rd edition of the Landmark Trust Handbook* features 190 historic buildings available to stay in – follies, castles, towers, banqueting houses, cottages and other unusual buildings. Through the building entries and a collection of articles, the Handbook traces our architectural heritage from the 12th to the 20th century.

The 232-page Handbook costs just £10 plus postage and packing. The Handbook cost is refundable against your first booking or you may wish to use the refund voucher to make [a] donation to support Landmark's [w]ork in rescuing historic buildings.

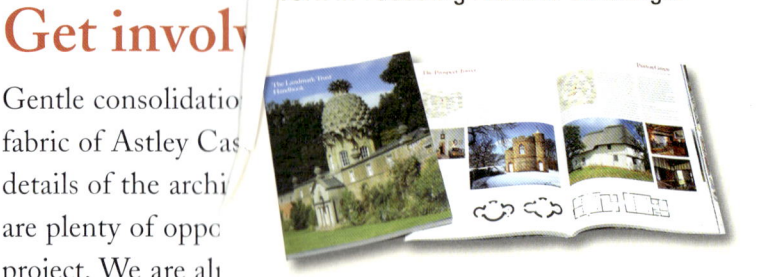

Order your Handbook
- Online at **www.landmarktrust.org.uk**
- Booking Office on **01628 825925**
- Or complete the form overleaf and return it to The Landmark Trust, Shottesbrooke, Maidenhead, Berkshire SL6 3SW

*Published in October 2008

You can make donations online securely and quickly at www.landmarktrust.

Projects & Restoration

Lundy 40th Appeal

The response so far to our call for help has been wonderful, with a little over £56,000 donated from various sources. However, we need this generosity to continue in order to be able to secure a sustainable future for Lundy.

The money raised to date will help us to fund the maintenance of footpaths and drystone walls, and continue to control invasive rhododendron. We plan to replace the island's main fresh water tank and enhance the visitor information point to improve the understanding of Lundy and its delicate ecosystems but we urgently need further help for this.

Repairing a dry stone wall near Stoneycroft, Lundy

Please support Lundy by donating now at www.landmarktrust.org.uk, or by calling the Development Office on 01628 825920.

G.I. Hopley contractors repointing Cowside

Reviving Cowside

Cowside in Upper Wharfedale has now been re-roofed with traditional stone slates and largely repointed, although this year's deep snowfalls inevitably brought work to a halt for several weeks and delayed the programme of works. Meanwhile, the seventeenth-century wall paintings known to exist beneath later paint in the parlour have been protected. We must curb our impatience to uncover and decode them fully until works are more advanced and humidity levels in the house have stabilised later in the year. Vernacular wall paintings are a great rarity in Yorkshire: all that can be said for now is that they appear to be two monochrome Biblical texts in rectangular cartouches. As Spring begins to creep up the wild and beautiful Dales, work will once more gather momentum. Check the website for updates on progress at Cowside.

Become a Landmark Patron

It is ten years since we launched the Landmark Patrons and during this time their vital support has contributed over £1.3 million in total to a variety of projects, for which we are extremely grateful. Our Patrons continue to play a crucial role and in return for their support they receive benefits such as early booking privileges and opportunities to see work in progress. The annual subscription is £1,000 (joint £1,500) and Life Patronage is £10,000 (joint £15,000).

For further information or to become a Patron please contact Anna Clayton on 01628 825920 or visit our website.

Award-winning conservation

Clavell Tower, Dorset

In October, Clavell Tower at Kimmeridge Bay in Dorset was announced as the winner of the RICS Conservation Award for 2009, which recognises excellence in conservation and construction. Already a regional finalist, Clavell Tower had to beat international competition for this accolade, of which we are very proud. The judges praised in particular the high standard of craftsmanship and detail involved in dismantling and reconstructing the tower, whose spectacular setting now makes it one of our most popular buildings.

...s Landmark in France

...ter Edward VIII, Duke of Windsor, gave up his throne in 1936 to marry his adored American divorcée, Wallis Simpson, the couple led a sociable existence at the heart of European café society. They also had use of 4 rue du Champ d'Entraînement in the Bois de Boulogne, but Le Moulin de la Tuilerie was the only house they ever owned.

Here, both were happy. The converted eighteenth-century ...ill house itself was the ...in house, and the outbuildings ...re charmingly converted into ...itional accommodation for ...ir guests: **La Maison des Amis** ... **Le Célibataire** (loosely, the ...chelor pad). The buildings are ...strained and characteristically ...rench in style, their quiet dignity and beauty deriving from their original honest purpose and materials.

The Duke commissioned garden designer Russell Page to create an English country garden which became his pride and joy. The Duchess organised lunch parties and country house weekends, the house festooned with geraniums and with canasta on the terrace. Famous guests – Cecil Beaton, Marlene Dietrich, Richard Burton, Henry Ford and many others – came to stay. It was here, more than anywhere else, that characterised the Windsors and their fascinating existence.

Today, the place retains all its charm, and the garden its layout if not its cottage planting. Le Moulin will become a Landmark for twelve, La Maison des Amis for four and Le Célibataire for two, to be booked together or separately. Gif-sur-Yvette is just three and a half hours from St Pancras by train, perfect for a short break to explore Paris, Versailles and much more. You will, however, almost certainly want to stay for longer. La Moulin de la Tuilerie will open in Summer 2010. Please contact the Booking Office or visit our website for further information.

Russell Page designed the garden at Gif-sur-Yvette, its layout survives.

The Windsors themselves converted the outbuildings, Le Célibataire (pictured) and La Maison des Amis into additional accommodation for their guests.

Everyman books in Landmarks

We are grateful to have been offered free copies from the Everyman series for our Landmark libraries. Joseph Dent founded Everyman in 1906, as a self-taught publisher and tenth child of a Darlington housepainter who came to London with just half a crown in his pocket. Dent wanted 'a whole bookshelf of the immortals' for just a few shillings available to every reader – a democracy of purpose which fits well with our own charitable aims.

Every Landmark has its own carefully chosen library, such as this one at Howthwaite.

Hear first

To receive our regular emails including special offers and project updates, please register on our website at: www.landmarktrust.org.uk/register.

2010 Open Days

Landmark Open Days are open to all and admission is free. Please check our website for the latest information and opening times.

Anderton House, Devon
11 and 12 September

Auchinleck House, Ayrshire
5 September

Cavendish Hall, Suffolk
27 June

Clavell Tower, Dorset
11 and 12 September

Dolbelydr, Denbighshire
23 to 26 April*
10 to 14 September*

Freston Tower, Suffolk
21 to 24 May*
10 to 14 September*

The Gothic Temple, Buckinghamshire
23 May+
11 and 12 September+
3 October+

The Grange, Kent
9 April to 12 April*
10 to 14 September*

Keeper's Cottage, Bedfordshire
10 to 12 September

Morpeth Castle, Northumberland
12 September

Queen Anne's Summerhouse, Bedfordshire
11 to 13 June
10 to 12 September

The Ruin, North Yorkshire
11 and 12 September

Villa Saraceno, Vicenza
4 July

Wilmington Priory, East Sussex
7 May to 10 May*
10 to 14 September*

*On the final Open Day the Landmark will only be open in the morning from 10am to 1pm.

+Please note that there is a National Trust admission charge to Stowe Gardens.

We are currently planning further Open Days. Check our website for more information.

Le Moulin de la Tuilerie lau

In 2007 Landmark received an invitation from France's coastal conservancy agency, the Conservatoire du littoral, to help them provide a new future for threatened historic buildings they have acquired on stretches of coastline they buy to protect from development, an aim similar to that of the National Trust's Enterprise Neptune.

The courtyard at Le Moulin de la Tuilerie. The main residence, Le Moulin, is to the left, with the gardens beyond.

Landmark France (as we have called this new initiative) is now working actively with the Conservatoire on two projects, with others in the pipeline. For this we have set up Landmark France as a charitable entity in France (known as an *Association Loi 1901*), through valuable *pro bono* advice from international law practice, Lovells LLB, and accountancy firm, Mazars.

The restorations will be mostly funded by the Conservatoire with Landmark advising and paying for a minority share of costs, for which we will fundraise in France.

However, the historic place with which we now launch Landmark France comes from another source. About a year ago, the owners of an important site in a spectacularly beautiful setting contacted us for help with its future. This was **Le Moulin de la Tuilerie** (more prosaically in English, the Tile Mill) at Gif-sur-Yvette, a pretty town just 45 minutes south west of central Paris by direct train. Here, the suburbs of Paris finally melt into true countryside in the lovely Vallée de la Haute Chevreuse. The buildings and location are worthy destinations in themselves, but what sets them apart is that Le Moulin de la Tuilerie was formerly the country retreat of the Duke and Duchess of Windsor, who took up residence in Paris when the French government offered them tax-free status after the Second World War.

The Duke and Duchess of Windsor in the garden at Gif-sur-Yvette in 1966

Anniversary for Chopin

Composer Frédéric Chopin was born 200 years ago and was fêted in British society under the wing of his pupil and friend, Jane Stirling. Jane's brother Charles owned **Gargunnock House** (for sixteen) and it is said this formed part of the composer's tour of country house soirées, the 1848 Broadwood piano there being bought especially for the composer.

Gargunnock House, Central Scotland

Stargazing

It gets ever harder to see the stars against the night-time glow of our towns and cities. Galloway Forest Park, however, has recently been named the UK's first Dark Sky Park, for the superb visibility of the constellations there. **Glenmalloch Lodge** stands at the edge of the Park, with **Castle of Park** and **Old Place of Monreith** close by. Keen stargazers can find near equivalent conditions at **Appleton Water Tower**, **Nicolle Tower** and **Fort Clonque**, and on **Lundy**.

Appleton Water Tower, Norfolk

Keeping up appearances

Landmark is constantly working to keep its buildings up to scratch. A major refurbishment has just taken place at **Tixall Gatehouse**, with repairs to its fine exterior stonework and roof terrace. We have also installed new bathrooms, new heating and hot water systems, redecorated and improved insulation. The furnishings have also been revisited, making this magical building an altogether cosier place to stay. **Knowle Hill** (pictured on front cover) and **Castle of Park** have also been brightened by redecoration and refurnishing, so now is a particularly good time to visit (or re-visit) these lovely Landmarks.

Tixall Gatehouse, Derbyshire

World Heritage Sites

Just three examples of the UK's many World Heritage Sites within easy reach of Landmarks.

Castles and town walls of King Edward in Gwynedd

The Bath Tower occupies a part of the fortified town wall, built by Edward I to protect Caernarfon. The castles and fortified towns of North Wales constitute some of the finest and best preserved examples of medieval military architecture in Europe.

The Bath Tower, Caernarfon

Frontiers of the Roman Empire

The Pineapple, **Gargunnock House** and **Hill House** are all within easy reach of the Antonine Wall, and **Brinkburn Mill**, **Coop House** and **Causeway House** are close to Hadrian's Wall. At different times, both walls protected the northernmost limits of the Roman Empire in Britain.

Cornwall and West Devon mining landscape

The ruins of engine houses, foundries and ports still litter this pock-marked landscape which at one time supplied the world with copper and arsenic.

Danescombe Mine is one such site, where Landmark accommodation has been created within an old engine house. **Whiteford Temple**, **Endsleigh**, **Lower Porthmeor** and **Frenchman's Creek** are all also close to many of the sites.

See the full list on our website.

Landmark Holidays

Letter from the Director

Landmark has always been centred in the UK, and always will be, but we have a presence abroad in Italy, and in the USA through our sister charity there. However a Landmark in a new country constitutes a red letter day. Le Moulin de la Tuilerie near Paris, the country home of the Duke and Duchess of Windsor after the abdication, is beautiful and atmospheric, and a place to fascinate British and French Landmarkers alike.

Peter Pearce at the opening of Queen Anne's Summerhouse with English Heritage's Greg Luton.

This excitement, of course, will not be allowed to disturb the momentum of our work in this country, where we have just opened the wonderful Pugin gatehouse at Oxenford in Surrey. We will also open in May the most magnificent bequest we have ever received, Cavendish Hall in Suffolk, the gift of Mrs Pamela Matthews and accompanied by a donation of £1 million to create a new large Landmark. This could hardly be bettered as an example of the value of a bequest to us, whether of a building or money, but every bequest however large and small is equally gratefully received - and valued.

Peter Pearce, Director

Cavendish Hall, an outstanding legacy

Cavendish Hall, Suffolk

As a little girl, Pamela Matthews fell in love with this charming Regency country house in rural Suffolk, not far from Newmarket (where her ex-cavalry officer father was Starter at the racecourse). Years later, her second husband, journalist and writer Tom Matthews, bought it for her. Mrs Matthews wanted others to enjoy the house, and so left it to Landmark in her will, adding a very generous endowment. The house has been beautifully redecorated according to its period, and much else done to make it comfortable for the 21st century – new kitchen, bathrooms, heating and wiring. The grounds too have been re-landscaped. Cavendish Hall can be booked from May and sleeps up to twelve people.

For further information on making a bequest to Landmark, please contact Emma Seymour on 01628 825920 or email eseymour@landmarktrust.org.uk.

Oxenford Gatehouse: another gem by A W N Pugin

Oxenford was once owned by Waverley Abbey and later by the Viscounts Midleton of Peper Harow. In 1843, the 5th Viscount Midleton commissioned A W N Pugin to design a gatehouse, barn and outbuildings in 'the Abbey Style'. The Picturesque scene that resulted is rightly judged among Pugin's best work. Today's owners of the still-working farm at Oxenford had no use for the Grade II* listed gatehouse and approached Landmark to let it on their behalf. We have been closely involved with the restoration works and, newly landscaped too, the gatehouse now stands revealed next to ancient fishponds as a masterpiece of the Gothic Revival. Its rural setting belies its proximity to London, a very special weekend retreat for up to four people.

Oxenford Gatehouse, Surrey

Booking Office 01628 825925   Monday to Friday 9am - 6pm and Saturday 10am - 4pm

Landmark News

The Landmark Trust newsletter Issued twice yearly Spring 2010

Five new Landmarks open in 2010

In 2010 we will add another five buildings to Landmark's collection illustrating the breadth and richness of our architectural past. **Oxenford Gatehouse** near Elstead in Surrey (for up to four people) was designed by A W N Pugin and opened in January. With its Picturesque profile and setting and furnishings carefully chosen to evoke Pugin's distinctive style, we are confident it will prove as popular as **The Grange**, our other building designed by Pugin.

Cavendish Hall in Suffolk (for up to twelve people) is a lovely Regency country house that came to us as an exceptionally generous bequest from Mrs Pamela Matthews. An endowment has allowed us to refurbish and refurnish the house, and bookings are already open. Cavendish Hall will welcome its first visitors in May.

With the other three buildings, Landmark embarks on an exciting new initiative, extending our activities into France. The internationally known site is called **Le Moulin de la Tuilerie** at Gif-sur-Yvette, south west of Paris, and was the former country residence of the Duke and Duchess of Windsor. Set at the mouth of a beautiful valley designated a *Parc regional*, yet less than an hour from central Paris by direct train, these Landmarks are a fitting introduction to Landmark in France. Turn to pages 4 and 5 to find out more.

Oxenford Gatehouse, Surrey

The Landmark Trust is a building preservation charity that rescues historic buildings at risk for everyone to enjoy, giving them a new life by letting them for inspiring holidays.

Inside

3 Keeping up appearances

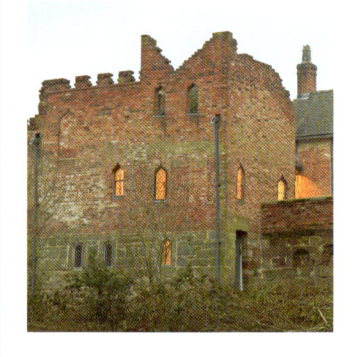

4 Landmark launches in France

7 Get involved at Astley Castle

The Landmark Trust

R Baeggli
Baselstrasse 25A
Po Box 666
Riehen
CH 4125
Switzerland

9 April 2010

255458-LMT/433814-LMT
ROW

Dear Baeggli

Thank you for your recent purchase of the Landmark Trust Handbook which is enclosed with a Price List and our latest Newsletter. You have also been sent a £10 refund voucher to cover the cost of the Handbook which can be used against a stay in one of our 190 historic buildings.

Full details of our buildings are also available on our website, complete with photographs, maps and floorplans. You can search availability online and provisionally reserve your holiday in a Landmark. We will then contact you by telephone to confirm the details and take payment.

If you have any queries about staying in one of our buildings please do not hesitate to contact our Booking Office. They are open between 9am and 6pm, Monday to Friday and 10am to 4pm on Saturday. Please call on 01628 825925 or email bookings@landmarktrust.org.uk

I hope we can welcome you to a Landmark soon.

Yours sincerely

Victoria O'Keeffe
Booking Office

The Landmark Trust Shottesbrooke Maidenhead Berkshire SL6 3SW
Patron HRH The Prince of Wales   *Chairman* Martin Drury CBE   *Director* Peter Pearce FRICS
Charity registered in England & Wales 243312 *and Scotland* SC039205

Bookings 01628 825925   *Office* 01628 825920   *Facsimile* 01628 825417   *Website* www.landmarktrust.org.uk

The Landmark Trust

Important Information

The Handbook and Price List are as accurate as we can make them when they go to press. However, our ongoing maintenance programmes mean that changes to the facilities in the buildings do occur and these are noted below. Please contact the Booking Office on 01628 825925 for further details.

HOWTHWAITE
Until the 12 March 2009, Howthwaite will only sleep 7 and will have two bathrooms and no shower room.

DISHWASHERS
Purton Green now has a dishwasher.

SHOWERS
At present Ingestre Pavilion does not have a shower room on the ground floor

AVAILABILITY LISTS
Availability is updated daily on the Landmark website http://www.landmarktrust.org.uk.

ARRIVAL AND DEPARTURE TIMES
Arrival time is 4pm. Departure time is by 10am in every Landmark building. Early arrivals and late departures prevent our housekeepers from preparing properties for the next arrivals. Please plan your journeys to respect these times.

October 2008

The Landmark Trust Shottesbrooke Maidenhead Berkshire SL6 3SW
Patron HRH The Prince of Wales   *Chairman* Martin Drury CBE   *Director* Peter Pearce FRICS
Charity registered in England & Wales 243312 *and Scotland* SC039205

Bookings 01628 825925   *Office* 01628 825920   *Facsimile* 01628 825417   *Website* www.landmarktrust.org.uk

Cavendish Hall

Cavendish, Suffolk

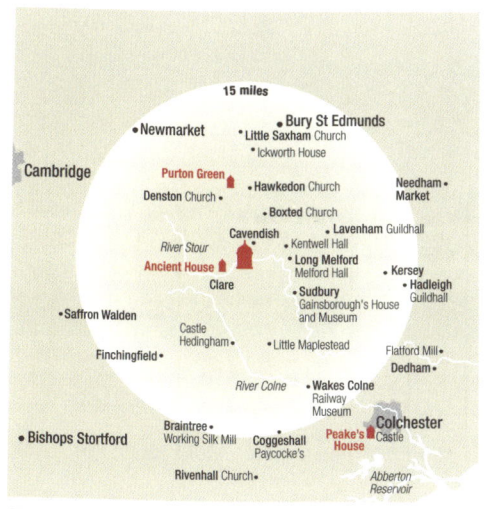

New Landmark

For up to 12 people
Open fire
Open grounds
Adjacent parking

Cavendish Hall is a Regency country house of great charm, set in a small well-timbered park on the outskirts of a timeless village deep in the countryside loved by John Constable. It came to us through the exceptional generosity of its last owner, Pamela Matthews, who had lived here as a child in the 1920s. In 1964 she married as her second husband T.S. (Tom) Matthews, a distinguished American journalist, writer and former editor of *Time* magazine. Knowing that she had always loved the house, he bought it for her.

Cavendish Hall has played no part in national events, but it is one of those solid and gracious country houses that enrich the local scene and help define the tone of our ancient villages, both through its residents and those who have worked for them. It has inspired happy times, affection and deep loyalty.

Built circa 1800, Cavendish Hall was bought in the 1830s by Dr John Yelloly, sometime physician to George IV. The Yelloly family owned it for over a century, and for most of this time it was let to a succession of tenants, the sort of honest middling gentry who people the novels of Austen and Trollope.

The Matthews themselves were a colourful and interesting couple. T.S. Matthews, a prolific author in his own right, counted among his friends some of the great literary figures of the twentieth century, including Robert Graves and T.S. Eliot.

Thanks to Pamela Matthews' wish that as many people as possible should enjoy the house she loved so much, Cavendish Hall offers the chance to experience life in a house such as Jane Austen might have known, with a well-stocked library that evokes the house's twentieth-century connections as much as its Regency origins.

Cavendish Hall before refurbishment.

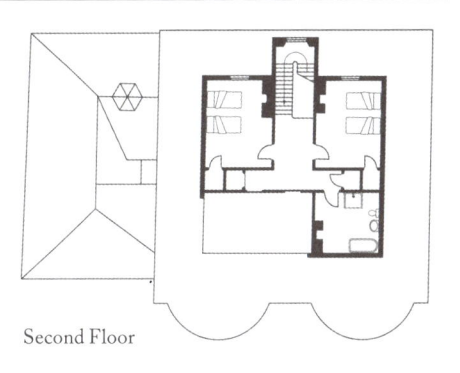

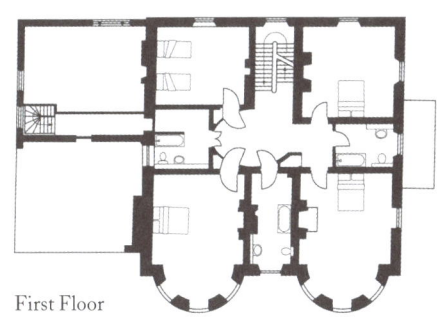

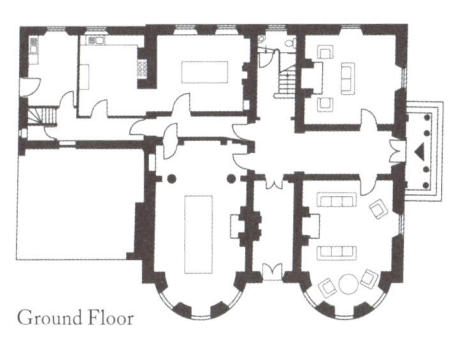

Second Floor

First Floor

Ground Floor

The Landmark Trust

Booking Office **01628 825925**
Overseas **+44 1628 825925**

Office **01628 825920**
Fax **01628 825417**

Website **www.landmarktrust.org.uk**
Email **bookings@landmarktrust.org.uk**

Cavendish Hall
Cavendish, Suffolk

New Landmark

Prices for 2010

Prices shown are per property for the period stated and not per person

Sleeps	Beds	Facilities	4 Jan to 7 Feb			8 Feb to 28 Mar			29 Mar to 31 Mar	1 Apr to 5 Apr	6 Apr to 8 Apr	9 Apr to 15 Apr			16 Apr to 29 Apr		
			Short Stays		Weeks	Short Stays		Weeks		Easter		Short Stays		Weeks	Short Stays		Weeks
			Start Fri 3 nights	Start Mon 4 nights	Start Fri or Mon 7 nights	Start Fri 3 nights	Start Mon 4 nights	Start Fri or Mon 7 nights	Start Mon 3 nights	Start Thurs 5 nights	Start Tues 3 nights	Start Fri 3 nights	Start Mon 4 nights	Start Fri or Mon 7 nights	Start Fri 3 nights	Start Mon 4 nights	Start Fri or Mon 7 nights
12	3T 3D	🛏x2 🛁x2 🚿 📺 🔥 ❄ 🐕	1227	1024	1801	1914	1385	2640	1039	3045	1737	2261	1746	3206	2019	1560	2863

30 Apr to 3 May	4 May to 6 May	7 May to 27 May			28 May to 31 May	1 Jun to 3 Jun	4 Jun to 8 Jul			9 Jul to 26 Aug			27 Aug to 30 Aug	31 Aug to 2 Sep	3 Sep to 28 Oct			29 Oct to 19 Dec			20 Dec to 22 Dec	23 Dec to 29 Dec	30 Dec to 3 Jan
May BH		Short Stays		Weeks	Spr BH		Short Stays		Weeks	Short Stays		Weeks	Aug BH		Short Stays		Weeks	Short Stays		Weeks		Xmas	New Year
Start Fri 4 nights	Start Tues 3 nights	Start Fri 3 nights	Start Mon 4 nights	Start Fri or Mon 7 nights	Start Fri 4 nights	Start Tues 3 nights	Start Fri 3 nights	Start Mon 4 nights	Start Fri or Mon 7 nights	Start Fri 3 nights	Start Mon 4 nights	Start Fri or Mon 7 nights	Start Fri 4 nights	Start Tues 3 nights	Start Fri 3 nights	Start Mon 4 nights	Start Fri or Mon 7 nights	Start Fri 3 nights	Start Mon 4 nights	Start Fri or Mon 7 nights	Start Mon 3 nights	Start Thurs 7 nights	Start Thurs 5 nights
2458	1225	2102	1624	2981	2520	1673	2510	1854	3491	2630	2237	3893	2861	1635	2285	1679	3171	1454	1162	2093	1035	4377	3718

Stogursey Castle, Somerset

Landmark: Champion of Buildings

The Landmark Trust is the champion of threatened small historic buildings, rescuing and then repairing them with care and faithfulness to their history before offering them as inspiring places to stay in or visit. This Handbook contains 190 such stories of redemption, places where you can now have what Sir John Smith, Landmark's Founder, memorably called 'an experience of a mildly elevating kind'.

Landmark offers through these buildings essential space for reflection, appreciation of beauty and interest around us, understanding the significance of place, and refreshment of spirit. Our restored buildings known as 'Landmarks' are, to quote a Landmarker, 'good for the soul'. Historic buildings and their stories become ever more valued in today's world where disorientating change makes history a touchstone.

Perhaps surprisingly in an age when restoring historic buildings has become a national passion, we continue to receive enquiries about threatened buildings at the rate of two or three a week, of which to our sadness we can only ever attempt a few. Neglect, disinterest, ignorance of quality, obstinate refusal to accept economic reality, unsympathetic neighbours, and difficult access all require of us determination, persistence, patience and a dogged refusal to give up on wonderful buildings for which we are often the champion of last resort.

There is something quintessentially traditional about Landmarks as places to stay. No two are the same, even though all come equipped with modern comforts, and each surprises and delights in a different way. We would rather ask you to accept, even relish, their eccentricities rather than spoil them and so mask their characters. Their extraordinary and gratifying popularity suggests a vote of confidence in this regard. Thus, while we have done our best to make each warm and comfortable, Landmarks

Peter Pearce at Silverton Park Stables.

may involve an outdoor and starlit trip to the bathroom, ancient doors and windows which no longer fit perfectly, doorways of a height for Tudors, and stone steps eroded by centuries of passing feet.

Staying in Landmarks is about the fun of discovery. Many find the experience addictive, writing in our Logbooks of the many they have stayed in and forming part of an informal club which anyone, from any walk of life, may 'join' without the need for membership. You simply become a Landmarker when you turn the key in the lock of your first Landmark of, we hope, many.

Landmarks in the early 21st century are undergoing an unprecedented campaign to update and improve them, not least because our early restorations again need attention. The development of more effective technologies for cost effective green power generation will help heat and light future Landmarks. We are breaking new ground architecturally as well; in our planned scheme at Astley Castle, new and modern architecture will brace and steady the crumbling ancient walls to create the Landmark accommodation within. Despite these responses to the modern world, however, the backbone of Landmark's work will always be painstaking conservation by craftsmen versed in working with traditional methods and materials, based on exacting historical research.

Friendless historic buildings find a champion in the Landmark Trust. It takes courage and a sense of adventurousness not to be daunted by the challenges that some of them present but Landmark has never lacked either. It takes, too, a sense of romance – for what are ancient places if not romantic? These beautiful, often eccentric buildings cast their shafts of light on the pages of this country's history. They help you to step into the shoes for a short while of someone who has lived another life in another time.

Peter Pearce, Director

The restoration of Silverton Park Stables, Devon, was completed in 2008.

Left: Fragments of a classical frieze from the long demolished main house were found in undergrowth and are now displayed in the Landmark.

Middle left: The view along the old carriage drive towards Silverton Park Stables.

Bottom left: Reclaimed pitch pine boards from the London Docklands being laid.

Bottom right: The old tack room is now a triple bedroom, complete with reproductions of the original tack pegs.

Middle right: The windows on the west elevation overlook the old walled garden.

Top right: Martin Drury and Peter Pearce discuss the cornice repairs.

www.landmarktrust.org.uk

Sir John Smith CH CBE
1923–2007

Founder of the Landmark Trust

As a member of the National Trust's Executive Committee in the 1960s Sir John Smith helped to save many of the furnished country houses that are now safely in its hands. He admired the National Trust, but realised that because it could only take on buildings which were endowed, many were slipping through the net.

'There are many minor, but handsome buildings of all kinds,' he wrote, 'into whose construction went much thought and care, which are part of our history and which contribute greatly to the scene; but whose original use has disappeared and which cannot be preserved from vandals, demolition or decay unless a new use and a source of income can be found for them'.

These characteristically measured and simple words reveal much about the man: his sense of history, his interest in the forlorn and unfashionable, his respect for the qualities of thought and care, his appreciation of the role of buildings in creating the distinctive landscape of Britain and the attributes, not usually combined in a conservationist, of vision, practicality and financial acumen. They were also the genesis of the Landmark Trust.

The Landmark Trust was founded in 1965 on the simple, but new idea that people would pay for the privilege of becoming the temporary owner of an interesting old building and that the income generated would fund its maintenance. It was an idea that quickly caught on. Today, the Landmark Trust owns or leases 190 buildings, including 23 on Lundy and four in Italy. Some, like Palladio's Villa Saraceno are bigger and grander than anything John Smith had in mind at the beginning, but all were under threat when they were acquired and it is the glorious variety of the buildings now listed in this Handbook that rejoices the hearts of those who may do no more than thumb its pages and dream.

Church Cottage, the first Landmark, opened in 1967.

In the early years the money was provided by the Manifold Trust, set up by John and his wife, Christian, in 1962. While the Landmark Trust reflected the romantic side of John's complex personality, the Manifold Trust was the product of his head for business. As deputy governor of Royal Exchange Assurance, he had noticed that by buying long leases a few years before expiry a substantial income could be generated for a charitable trust. The result was what he described as 'a cataract of gold' for the Landmark Trust in its early years and for other charitable causes that were close to his heart.

Buildings had intrigued John since childhood and as a young man he had thoughts of becoming an architect. But, in founding the Landmark Trust he had a wider purpose. He wanted to open people's eyes to their surroundings, to kindle new interests, to win support for his conviction that conservation is not a reactionary force but essential to mankind's survival, and to provide time and space for contemplation of 'what is being done to this planet and its occupants'. In this, as in much else, he was ahead of his time.

John had a quick and probing mind, acute powers of observation and a sardonic wit. He relished the odd and the absurd, and his wide interests and formidable memory made him an engaging companion. He was intensely loyal to those who served him, but dismissive of officialdom and relentless in his hostility to those he felt were unappreciative of his efforts. In his make-up there was an obsessive quality which made him exacting and hard to please, but it was this same quality, expressed through attention to detail and a conviction that like-minded people would respond to his prescription for an enjoyable, mind-broadening experience, that has given the Landmark Trust its distinctive tone.

It is the task of those who carry on his work to maintain that distinctive tone in the face of daily pressure to conform to the priorities of other interests. It is a task we relish and in taking it up we honour his memory and, with the many thousands of people who stay in or visit Landmarks each year and on behalf of those who will do so in years to come, we give thanks for his incomparable legacy.

Martin Drury, Chairman

Sir John Smith CH CBE

Keeping History Alive

Landmark's work is focussed on making sure that the buildings of the past continue not just to exist, but to thrive, so passing on the inspiration inherent in our shared history. In a busy modern world, Landmark's buildings offer not just somewhere to stay but also a chance to pause, and to reflect on our place in space and time.

The buildings we take on are mostly those that would be lost without our help, left so derelict and decayed that they have passed beyond a rational commercial decision to save them. Landmark is different. We believe that if a historic building is worth saving, we can convince others too, and that the wider social value of these buildings justifies the one-off effort of raising money for their restoration.

Through their use as Landmarks, our buildings are history to live in. Staying in a Landmark, you will encounter a beautiful and atmospheric place to use as your own, a depth of experience beyond that possible as a day visitor. You will also find, if you care to, information to enhance your time there.

Each building has its own History Album, an illustrated account of the history of the place, the events it has witnessed and the people who have known it. The album also includes an account of Landmark's own intervention in the building's history through the restoration process, and of some of the traditional craft skills this has involved. We take seriously the responsibility of keeping these skills alive.

Each building also has its own small library, a bookcase stocked with relevant and wide-ranging books, as if by an interested and knowledgeable private host.

This enjoyment and inspiration inherent in our buildings is not restricted to those who stay there. The very survival of these buildings enriches our surroundings, but we also work hard to make sure a deeper appreciation of their significance is available to everyone, through the information and visits we provide.

Young visitors to an Open Day explore the history of Luttrell's Tower, Hampshire.

Each year, we run a programme of free Open Days for the general public, a combination of grant-aided buildings open regularly throughout the year and a revolving selection of our other buildings. Details of these Open Days can be found on our website. At all our Open Days, summaries of the building's history for children as well as adults are always available at no charge. Several buildings have museum rooms, again opened without charge, (Woodspring Priory, The Grange, Auchinleck House, The White House) and others have information boards for the general public (as at Clavell Tower). Detailed guide books are available for some of our larger buildings or sites (Goddards, Old Campden House, The Grange, Auchinleck House, Woodspring Priory and Villa Saraceno).

Lectures are given every year, either on specific projects or on our work in general, both to specialist audiences and the wider community. On specific projects, we may work with local colleges and schools: at Clavell Tower, we ran an education programme for four local schools and provided on-site training for students from Weymouth College. Similar initiatives will take place for Queen Anne's Summerhouse.

We have always maintained careful archives on our buildings, backed by research, and this information is available to all who enquire. Our website provides universal access to our work and direct contact with Landmark's staff.

All this wider activity is our way of making sure that as many people as possible share in our buildings.

Like pebbles thrown back into the pool of time, Landmark's buildings spread ripples of inspiration and enjoyment throughout the country. The best way to experience them will always be to stay in them. Two beliefs lie at the heart of Landmark's work: one is our commitment to the act of saving good buildings against the odds, the other is our belief in the importance of making exceptional buildings available to everyone, to discover what it is to live in a beautiful and atmospheric place as if it were your own.

No two Landmarks are alike, and the chances are that each one you stay in will provide an experience you will remember for the rest of your life.

Top: Schoolchildren from four local schools visited Clavell Tower, Dorset, as part of an education programme run prior to its dismantling and rebuilding.

Above: An Open Day at Ingestre Pavilion, Staffordshire.

Top right: Crownhill Fort, Devon, an extensive Victorian fort, is regularly open to the public.

Middle right: Food that would have been eaten in a 17th-century banqueting house was displayed during an Open Day at Old Campden House, Gloucestershire.

Bottom right: 20,000 people visit Lundy each year either on day trips or by staying in one of the 23 Landmarks. Many arrive on the *MS Oldenburg*.

Never Beyond Rescue

In a nation that places as much emphasis on its history as ours, it may seem strange that historic buildings remain at risk. Yet this is still the case: the flow of buildings suggested to Landmark as being in need of our help remains constant, well over a hundred each year, from a wide range of sources all over the country.

The three or four restorations we complete each year are therefore only a fraction of those buildings in need, our activity limited in practice by our team's resources and the funds we can raise. Often the more desperate a building's situation, the more likely we are to become involved in its future. Our criteria relate to intangibles as well as physical dereliction, requiring the buildings that come into our care to be in some sense significant, with the potential to enrich the lives not just of those who stay in them, but also of those who visit them, read about them or pass by them.

Before any of this can take effect in the restored buildings, practical skills must be brought into play. We strive to ensure that Landmark's restorations are carried out to the highest standards of conservation practice, guided by certain principles. We aim to repair rather than renew. We respect alterations and additions that are part of a building's character, but not slavishly. If later, inferior work obscures a finer original, or decay has gone beyond even our commitment to repair, we will sometimes seek permission to reverse or remove later changes. We do not make changes based on speculation or try to disguise our work by ageing it artificially. We respect our buildings and their settings; occasionally, rather than resort to unseemly alteration, we may trust in our visitors' sense of adventure and ask them to adapt to the building rather than the reverse.

After Landmark's Trustees have decided to take a building on, there is always a pause while

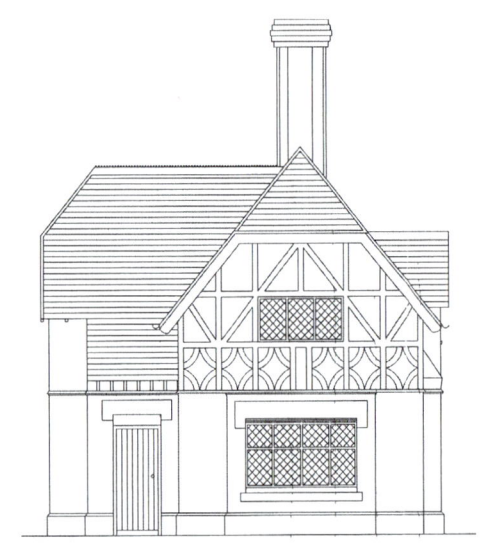

Keeper's Cottage, Bedfordshire.

funds are raised for its restoration, the building is analysed and researched, detailed plans are drawn up and necessary permissions sought (a high proportion of Landmarks are listed). Sometimes it can take years just to agree a lease.

The execution of a restoration relies on the skill of the craftsmen and women involved. We usually employ local architects and contractors. A belief in the importance of keeping traditional craft skills alive underpins all our work. This approach also emphasises traditional materials, honestly used: lime mortars to ensure healthy permeability; oak, pine and other traditional woods in good joinery; bespoke iron for door and window fittings; glass selected to replicate the liveliness of earlier production techniques.

We also believe in the need to ensure that such traditional skills remain vigorous and are passed forward. We therefore encourage our contractors to employ apprentices in key conservation-based trades when working on our buildings.

Every project brings satisfactions large and small of such skills successfully applied. At Silverton Park Stables, it was the lines of cast iron harness pegs and push-button latches, replicated from surviving originals by a local blacksmith, and the steady application of a wooden frame known as a 'horse' to run in the high-level cornice moulding in lime render around the parapet. At Clavell Tower, in a traditional on-site workshop known as the bankers' shed, stonemasons wielded chisel and mallet to reproduce the fine quatrefoil piercings, just as they would have done when the first tower was built.

Astley Castle, Warwickshire.

Clavell Tower, Dorset

Left: The bankers' shed at Clavell Tower, Dorset.

Top: At The Grange, Kent, the roof had to be entirely replaced.

Above: Causeway House, Northumberland, being rethatched in heather.

Such attention to detail also extends to buildings that have been in our care for longer, sometimes through maintenance, sometimes in returning to correct or improve earlier solutions when funds become available. Causeway House, near Hadrian's Wall, is a rare surviving example of a heather thatched building. In 2007, it needed re-thatching, requiring us to seek out both the heather and a thatcher who could work it. Clytha Castle, one of our earliest projects, came to us in 1974 clad in a cement render. This continued to cause problems because of damp penetration, and we have had successive campaigns to replace it with a breathable lime render (the sand used producing a lovely, self-coloured, pinkish render). In 2007, this replacement was completed, together with a reorganisation of the accommodation there. Similarly, we returned to Alton Station in 2008, to incorporate the atmospheric waiting room block into the Landmark.

This careful approach extends beyond the fabric to the finishes of our buildings. The vibrant blue in the main room of The Ruin is based on the original copper-based paint, identified through paint analysis. At The Grange Augustus Pugin's personal wallpaper was reproduced. At Auchinleck House the decorative ceiling was repaired using *papier mâché*. Many of our curtains, specially screen-printed, reveal a motif identified from the building's history. No two projects are the same, and their execution involves a wide range of professional skills, whether in-house or commissioned from outside.

By the time the restoration is complete, the building will have come far from the neglected and probably derelict state in which we found it. Many people will, in some way, have contributed to or participated in its rescue. There is no other organisation with a comparable track record in rescuing historic buildings at risk. No two projects are ever the same and each brings its own challenges, but long years of experience give us the confidence to trust that a way can be found to bring each building safely to completion and then to a successful future as a Landmark, whatever the obstacles encountered along the way. With your help, we hope we can continue to rise to the challenges yet to come.

Where We Need Your Help Now

The Shore Cottages, Berriedale, Caithness
This humble row of herring fishermen's cottages embodies much of the history of Caithness over the past 200 years. Now derelict, left without mains water or electricity and accessed only by a footbridge, the cottages were abandoned in the 1950s.

Cowside, Langstrothdale, North Yorkshire
Cowside is special both as an unaltered, late seventeenth-century vernacular farmstead and for its remote setting deep in Upper Wharfedale. As with many buildings we have rescued in the past, remoteness has led to decline.

Warder's Tower, near Biddulph, Staffordshire
From the outside Warder's Tower looks deceptively solid but in fact the structure is deteriorating rapidly. Built in 1829 the tower was both a home to the estate gamekeeper and an eyecatcher in a designed landscape.

Astley Castle, near Nuneaton, Warwickshire
Astley Caste is a site of national significance dating back to the Saxon period. It has been owned by three English Queens and witnessed events that have shaped our history, but its condition is now extremely fragile and Landmark is its final hope.

Lundy, Bristol Channel
Lundy is one of the most important sites for nature conservation in the UK but it is only through donations to The Lundy Fund that we can continue to protect this unique environment.

Belmont, Lyme Regis, Dorset
This handsome Georgian villa is important for being the home of two renowned past residents, Mrs Eleanor Coade, the inventor of an artificial cast stone, and more recently the author John Fowles.

Buildings Rescued by Our Supporters

Glenmalloch Lodge, Dumfries & Galloway
Cost of restoration: £315,600
Funded by: Individual supporters including Patrons; Historic Scotland; trusts and foundations; and unrestricted fundraising income*
Opened as a Landmark: September 2007

Philanthropy through architecture is nothing new. In the 1830s, Harriet, Countess of Galloway, built this diminutive schoolroom near Newton Stewart to educate twenty-five poor girls in reading, arithmetic and needlework. It is a typical example of the picturesque model architecture of its time. Today, its remoteness in a wide and beautiful glen is part of its charm, but more recently had led to its decline, leaving it derelict and stranded, without water or electricity, inhabited only by barn owls and swallows.

Glenmalloch Lodge before restoration (above) and after restoration (top).

New life as a Landmark provides an ideal solution for buildings in such remote settings. Thanks to our many supporters, we were able to restore and re-roof it with Cumbrian slates in traditional diminishing courses. The local whinstone and warm pink sandstone quoins were repointed. To include a bathroom, a small extension was put on at the rear, the mason mimicking the decorative galleting known locally as 'mouse's ladders' around its openings. The new electrical supply has been buried, and water comes from the burn. Painting the cottage in the Cumloden estate green was timed around the fledging of the swallows' brood; the barn owls have fine new nesting boxes in nearby woods.

Clavell Tower before restoration (above) and during restoration (above right).

Silverton Park Stables before restoration (left) and during restoration (below).

Clavell Tower, Dorset
Cost of restoration: £899,833
Funded by: Heritage Lottery Fund; Country Houses Foundation; other trusts and foundations; Dorset County Council; individual supporters including Patrons; and unrestricted fundraising income*
Opened as a Landmark: September 2008

Clavell Tower was about to fall off a Dorset cliff. In a uniquely radical intervention for Landmark, we recorded this nineteenth-century folly stone by stone, and then dismantled and rebuilt it further from the cliff's edge. The tower will continue to stand as sentinel and beacon, enjoyed not just by those who stay in it but also by the thousands who every year walk this glorious sweep of the Coastal Path.

Silverton Park Stables, Devon
Cost of restoration: £1,134,410
Funded by: An anonymous private donor; funds from a bequest from Diana Wray Bliss; Garfield Weston Foundation; other trusts; and numerous individual supporters
Opened as a Landmark: June 2008

Acquired in 1987 and funded entirely from private sources, Silverton Park Stables is an example of Landmark's persistence in unlocking even the most intractable restoration challenge and converting the most unlikely spaces into inspirational places to stay. This monumental stable block was left unfinished by its ambitious patron, the 4th Earl of Egremont in 1845. Today, it has new life and purpose as a Landmark that evokes collegiate as much as equestrian activity, set around its cobbled quadrangle.

Keeper's Cottage, Shuttleworth, Bedfordshire
Cost of restoration: £435,900
Funded by: An anonymous individual supporter; English Heritage; The Shuttleworth Trust; and funds from a bequest from Diana Wray Bliss
Opened as a Landmark: March 2007

This small grouping was once the powerhouse of one of the great Edwardian shooting estates. Our restoration of the derelict cottage also included its kennel block and gave a rare chance to reconstruct the collapsed outbuildings of a model gamekeeper's establishment of the 1870s, following the original plans found in the local Record Office.

Stoker's Cottage, Stretham, Cambridgeshire
Cost of restoration: £80,100
Funded by: An anonymous individual supporter; and unrestricted fundraising income*
Opened as a Landmark: February 2008

Landmark cherishes its ability to help with the humble as much as the grand, and also to lend a hand to smaller organisations with complementary aims. This tiny cottage was built in 1840 for a toll keeper and then stoker for the Stretham Old Engine, housed next door to keep fenland flooding at bay. By taking on the cottage, we enable the small local trust who care for the Old Engine to concentrate on their main purpose.

*Unrestricted fundraising income includes legacies, raffle income and the subscriptions of Friends and Patrons.

Keeper's Cottage before restoration (above left) and after restoration (above).

Stoker's Cottage before restoration (left) and after restoration (below).

How You Can Support Us

The Landmark Trust relies on the generosity of many individuals and grant-giving bodies to rescue and secure the future of buildings at risk and ensure the unique environment of Lundy can remain accessible to all. We are immensely grateful for every donation we receive and would like to thank our supporters for their continued generosity.

There are many ways you can help us while also getting closer to Landmark's work. We run appeals to support each project, which are vital to their funding and you can make a donation at any time including online at **www.landmarktrust.org.uk/donate**. Regular donations to Landmark are invaluable to help us to react quickly and giving us a Direct Debit for as little as £5 a month is an easy way to help us fill funding gaps.

Remember us in your will
Legacies are vital in helping us save fine buildings before it is too late. Those who make bequests leave lasting memorials of happy times spent in Landmarks. We can also accept buildings as legacies, whether or not they become Landmarks. Any gift you leave us, large or small, makes a real difference and will be used to preserve our special buildings and places for future generations to enjoy. If you would like to receive our legacy guide, please call the Development Office.

Friends of the Landmark Trust
Landmark Friends are enthusiasts who support our work and enjoy visiting and staying in Landmarks, and meeting other Landmarkers. As a Friend you will receive the Handbook and the Friends' newsletter, and, for an additional charge, can attend Friends' receptions and house parties. The annual subscription is £50 per person or £40 by annual Direct Debit. Individual Life membership is £500.

Freston Tower, Suffolk, was given to Landmark by Claire Hunt who wished it to have a secure future.

Patrons of the Landmark Trust
Landmark Patrons make an important contribution to the rescue and restoration of historic buildings and in doing so help preserve traditional craft skills and materials. As a Patron you will receive benefits including: early booking privileges; invitations to see work in progress and finished projects; an annual opportunity to meet our Director; an advance copy of the Handbook; and acknowledgement of your Patronage in our Report and Accounts. The annual individual subscription is £1,000 (joint £1,500); monthly Direct Debits can be set up. Life Patronage is £10,000 (joint £15,000).

Project Guardians
Some of our fundraising projects have Guardians' schemes, which enable donors to become closely involved with that project. For example, in return for a gift of £6,000 the Guardians of Cowside will enjoy a number of benefits including exclusive visits to Cowside with members of the Landmark team and taking part in discussions on the project.

To support our work or to find out more, please contact the Development Office on 01628 825920, email **fundraising@landmarktrust.org.uk** or visit **www.landmarktrust.org.uk/supporting**.

A Friends' reception at Woodspring Priory, Somerset.

The Sublime, the Beautiful and the Picturesque

Several of the buildings in Landmark's care are survivors of a time when people's appreciation of the beauties of their native landscapes was quickened by comparison with others further afield, and when, much like us today, they turned back to pastures closer to home.

Two hundred and fifty years ago, the European Grand Tour was the equivalent of today's gap year. A tour of the sites and architecture of Europe was seen as the essential final stage of a wealthy young man's education. It gave him experience of the world and, more than, a passing introduction to the glories of European art and architecture.

Often the travellers returned captivated, laden with antiquities and paintings, and determined to capture on their own estates some of the splendours of landscape and architecture they had encountered abroad. From the 1750s, theorists like Edmund Burke also began to instruct tourists on how to respond to what they saw on their travels. A landscape or building might be considered Beautiful or – more to Burke's taste – it might be Sublime, evoking a more personal reaction, a 'delicious terror' from its awe-inspiring and dramatic appearance.

As the century wore on, travellers increasingly sought such responses closer to home. They visited ruined monasteries and abbeys, revelling in the melancholy emotions evoked. Many came to gaze on Rosslyn Castle or its chapel, staying or being refreshed at Collegehill House, next door. Wild natural landscapes like the Lake District (where Howthwaite overlooks the Wordsworths' Dove Cottage) were sought out. Landowners also took it upon themselves to manipulate responses to their own estates through building follies and features.

These small buildings in the landscape are among the building types most likely to be left

Rosslyn Castle, near Edinburgh.

stranded by modern life and so are often compelling cases for Landmark's care. They become some of our best-loved buildings.

The Gothic Temple at Stowe (1741) and Culloden Tower (1746) are early essays in landscape embellishment, each carrying a political message and less concerned with evoking an emotional response than, for example, The Ruin at Hackfall (by 1767). The Ruin manages to combine the Beautiful and the Sublime. Its design is almost certainly based on a watercolour by Robert Adam, done on his own Grand Tour to Rome in the 1750s. A smooth and Classical front elevation gives onto a terrace suspended above a rocky gorge, enough in itself to trigger awe, but towering above are three craggy and fragmentary domes, as if of some crumbling ruin. It is a fine building to be in, but also to admire from Aislabie's carefully designed vistas in Hackfall Gardens (newly restored).

Robin Hood's Hut (also built in 1767) is a gentler variation on a similar theme, at Halswell, another famous garden of its time. Here, a thatched hermit's cottage confronts you, the delicious thrill perhaps provided by the thought that a hairy hermit might emerge to greet you. An elegant umbrello provides contrast on the other side, with wide views of calm Somerset skies and levels, a fine example of a Beautiful landscape.

Both buildings, however, also begin to represent a new aesthetic – the Picturesque. This lay between the two poles of Beautiful and Sublime, defined rather loosely by William Gilpin as 'that particular kind of beauty, which is agreeable in a picture'. Landmark examples of this picture book appeal would be Swiss Cottage at Endsleigh (1815), a chalet seemingly transported from the Alps to perch on a heavily wooded gorge above the winding River Tamar, or Warder's Tower, a current project in Staffordshire, where both tower and artificially created reservoirs help enhance a naturally Picturesque landscape.

The Picturesque would infiltrate much of Victorian architecture through pattern books and model architecture, but these were more utilitarian buildings than the delightfully *dilettante* creations of eighteenth-century landscape enthusiasts. They were gentlemen of leisure; appropriate, then, that their buildings should now be the perfect spots to feed our own appreciation of their landscapes, at our own leisure.

Right: Robin Hood's Hut, Somerset.

Below and bottom right: The Ruin, North Yorkshire and the watercolour by Robert Adam on which it is likely to be based.

Eighteenth-century Theories of Aesthetics

The Beautiful: based on universal values of harmony, regularity and smoothness. Unthreatening – an Italian lake.

The Sublime: a psychological reaction, emphasising spiritual values and emotional response. Appreciated disharmony and irregularity in landscape and architecture for the 'delicious terror,' the sense of awe and physical and metaphysical peril they could evoke.

The Picturesque: the appreciation and manipulation of a landscape to provide the proportions and satisfactions of viewing it as a picture.

www.landmarktrust.org.uk 19

A Brief History of Rooms

Landmark's collection of buildings, currently stretching from c.1250 (Purton Green) to 1972 (Anderton House), allows the evolution of domestic houses to be traced across seven centuries. The gradual development of floorplans in the home had a direct influence on how households lived in them, shaping our relationships as well as increasing our comfort.

This evolution of floorplans lies at the heart of so-called vernacular architecture, the building styles of everyday people in their own regions, developing organically over the centuries, using the materials to hand and largely oblivious to 'taste'.

The hall
Our earliest homes were single storey 'halls', open to the roof timbers (like Purton Green). The hearth was in the middle; the smoke escaped through a hole in the roof. Roof dimensions depended on the spans feasible from local trees. Everyone in the household – family, servants and labourers if such there were – lived, ate and slept in the hall.

The screens passage
During the Middle Ages the hall began to evolve. A 'high' and a 'low' end developed. The master sat at the 'high' end, lit by a large window and facing the body of the hall. At the other end, a wooden partition or 'screen' kept out the draughts from two external doors, creating a cross passage. Beyond this passage was the service area of the house, usually with two doors leading into the 'buttery' and the 'pantry' (The Old Hall, Wortham Manor, Plas Uchaf).

The hall offered little privacy, so the next stage was the addition of private chambers for the head of the household – parlours, solars – above the service rooms or as an extension to the 'high' end.

Chimneys and staircases
Then came revolutionary developments: chimneys and staircases. The smoke hood was a transitional form, a timber-framed insertion at one end of the hall, still above an open hearth. Builders in stone areas, however, started to imitate the brick-built chimneystacks of higher status owners.

Many medieval houses were adapted by adding an external chimneystack to an outside

The 'low' end of the hall at New Inn, Suffolk.

How Floorplans Evolved

The shaded areas indicate later extensions. Such changes can also be traced on other plans for individual buildings in this Handbook.

The hall
The simple central hall survives at Purton Green (c.1250) in Suffolk.

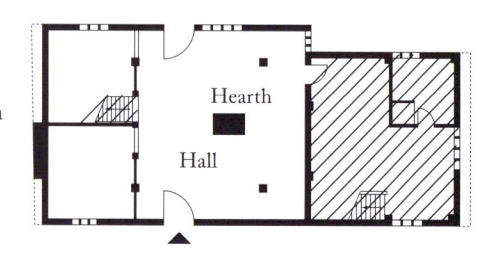

The screens passage
Plas Uchaf in Powys (1435) has the remnants of a screens passage. Its huge fireplace was added later.

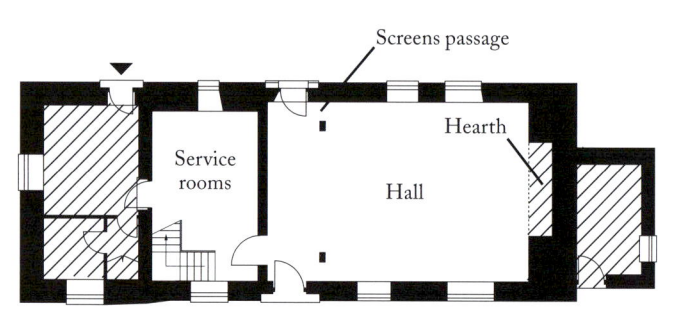

wall, as at Monkton Old Hall, and by inserting an extra floor into the roofspace of the hall (Wortham and Gurney Manors). New houses such as Dolbelydr (1578) might include a first floor from the start, here reached by a spiral wooden staircase squeezed in beside a flue incorporated within the external wall. For the first time, this served hearths heating the first as well as ground floor rooms. The screens passage and service rooms remained, for now.

Corridors and lobby entries

The possibilities for how a simple rectangular space could be lived in now multiplied. By placing the chimneystack centrally in the house, more heat could be captured and the opportunity provided for back-to-back hearths, heating rooms to either side on both floors (Manor Farm, Hawker's Cottages, Pond Cottage). The staircase could be placed behind the stack, and a draught-free lobby entrance created at the front.

As the first floor became used entirely for bedrooms, corridors were inserted to meet greater expectations of privacy (Manor Farm).

All these developments occured within local craft traditions. It was only in the nineteenth century that such traditions began to break down with the advent of professionally trained architects. Yet even the most recent Landmark, Anderton House, draws inspiration from a vernacular form, the Devon longhouse (Sanders).

Traces of more ancient forms survive in our buildings then, if you know where to look. Next time you stay in a vernacular Landmark, perhaps you too will pause to think how our forebears might have moved through the rooms you relax in today.

Top left: The hall at the heart of Purton Green dates from around 1250.

Top: Wortham Manor, Devon. A later floor was inserted into its fine medieval hall.

Above: The screens passage with service rooms beyond at Manor Farm, Norfolk.

Chimneys and staircases
Dolbelydr in Denbighshire (1578) still has a hall, but was heated by a massive chimneystack, and has a floor above, originally reached by a spiral staircase.

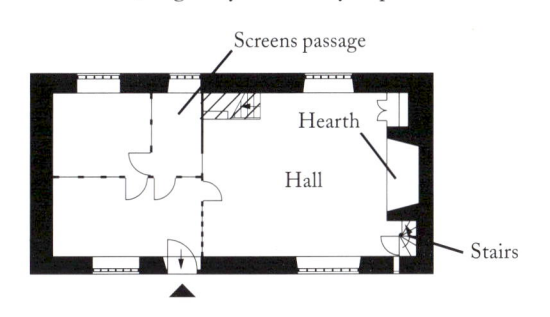

Corridors and lobby entries
At Manor Farm in Norfolk (*c.*1600), the chimneystack is enclosed with multiple hearths opening off it. The screens passage persists, the staircase is still a spiral and there is also an original first floor corridor.

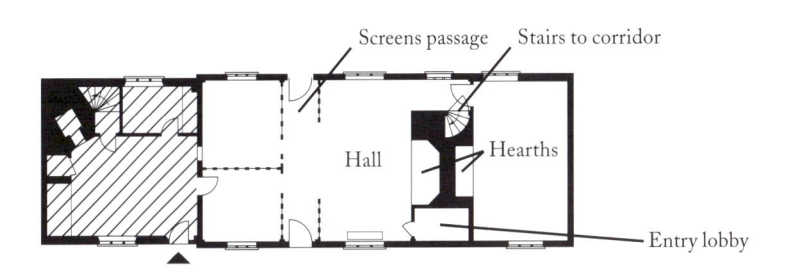

History to Live In

What will it be like to stay in a Landmark? Our visitors tell us that no two stays are the same, and it is our aim that every Landmark should be memorable and uplifting. The buildings in our care are of all types, sizes and dates, something to delight everybody. Our hope is that everyone may find some present enjoyment in these places of the past.

Memorable stays in unusual buildings
Each Landmark is a unique survivor from our past. Not all our buildings started life as domestic buildings and much thought goes into how best to convert each to its new use. Occasionally, its character or needs will result in an unusual configuration of the accommodation, in a way that we nevertheless judge will be novel and perhaps entertaining for the duration of your stay.

Somewhere to feel at home
Landmarks feel lived-in, the sort of places that welcome you in and then quietly surprise you by the inspiration they offer. Our furniture is carefully chosen to fit happily with its surroundings – most of it is old, simple and good, but sometimes with an unexpected flourish.

The rugs and carpets will probably have seen use elsewhere, being of a quality to last, but the curtains will often have been specially designed for the building. The pictures too usually have a special reason for hanging where they do. Everything works together to provide a memorable and comfortable setting in which to spend your time.

A place to talk and eat together
With no television our visitors enjoy just spending time together, whether in front of an open fire with a good book, chatting around the dining table or completing the jigsaw puzzle provided of the building. Virtually every Landmark has a private area in which to sit out. Many have sizeable gardens and several have spectacular views or battlements to be looked over.

Some Landmarkers come with the intention of exploring the local area but find they never venture further than the bottom of the garden. For those wanting to go further a field we provide a specially made, large-scale walking map and information on things to do in the local area. A Logbook is there for you to record your discoveries for the benefit of those who stay next.

History to discover undisturbed
While some choose to stay in our buildings simply because they are wonderful places to be, we have always found that many of our visitors want to know more about the place they are in. For each Landmark, our Historian writes a History Album, a careful but readable account of the building, its history and past inhabitants, and a description of its restoration. There will be a bookcase containing the sort of relevant and interesting books you might expect from a well-read host, as well as those standard reference books you sometimes need to get the most out of a good walk or conversation.

In booking a Landmark you will find yourself for a short time the owner of a fine old building. Sleeping under its roof you can study it at leisure, be there early and late, in all lights and weathers and gain an understanding of why and how its builders made it as they did.

Equipment in Landmarks

A stay cannot be relaxing unless the facilities we take for granted in modern life can be relied upon. Our kitchens are well-equipped and all have a wide and standard range of utensils. Even in the smallest buildings, there will be provision for two extra place settings beyond those who are sleeping there. We aim to make our kitchens sociable places, not somewhere to banish the cook, and an increasing number of buildings have dishwashers, freezers and washing machines.

Making sure it all runs smoothly

Every Landmark has a Housekeeper who will make it ready for you. Often, they have known the building longer than we have and all take great pride in their work. They can be invisible if you wish, but are also useful sources of local knowledge and our Logbooks testify to how much they can add to our visitors' stay.

A fresh window on life

Landmarks offer a chance to step off the treadmill of modern life in surroundings that spring from our past but enrich our futures. Many of our visitors return again and again, finding in each Landmark stay a source of inspiration, refreshment and, often, new knowledge and interest. History meets the present day, and the encounter is, usually, highly satisfactory.

Facing page: Cloth Fair, London.
Top: Margells, Devon.
Above: Manor Farm, Norfolk.
Far right: Ingestre Pavillion, Staffordshire.

www.landmarktrust.org.uk

Booking Information

All the buildings in this Handbook can be booked for anything from a short break over a weekend to longer stays of up to three weeks. The fold-out map at the front of the Handbook helps you see at a glance where each Landmark is located and how many people it can accommodate.

Each building has its own detailed entry in the Handbook and the floor plans are there to help you understand its layout as you plan your stay. To help identify the less self-explanatory symbols, please see the panel on the far right. After the location of each building, a grid reference is given which relates to the fold-out map at the front of the Handbook. For each Landmark, there is a map with a fifteen-mile circle centred on the Landmark to indicate other places that might interest you in the area. The number each Landmark can accommodate is found below the map. Where, for example, it shows 4+2, this indicates that two of the beds are not part of the main building or are of lesser status than the other available beds.

Towels and bed linen are provided, and beds made up in advance. The beds themselves, however ancient the bed head, have modern mattresses, blankets and pillows. A baby's travel cot is usually provided, though not its bed linen.

Causeway House, Northumberland.

Gurney Manor, Somerset.

Landmarks are all fully heated, either by central heating or night storage heaters. Wherever possible, our buildings also have open fires or a woodstove. Logs or coal will be easily available locally. During colder months, you may wish to bring an extra jumper or two and hot water bottles for some buildings, as indicated in the Price List.

Well-behaved dogs are welcome in all Landmarks except those where the problems or temptations are too great; this too can be checked in the Handbook entries. Mentioned only because people sometimes ask, children are welcome in all our buildings.

Prices and additional information are given in the Price List. Our Booking Office staff are always happy to answer any questions you may have about a specific building, as well as advise on availability and take your booking. Availability is updated daily on our website.

Changes do occasionally take place in a building and therefore it is essential to use the current Landmark Trust Handbook and Price List when choosing your Landmark. Our booking conditions may also be found in the Price List.

We very much look forward to welcoming you to a Landmark soon.

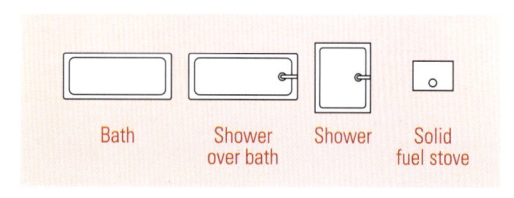

Bath   Shower over bath   Shower   Solid fuel stove

Booking Office enquiries
01628 825925
Overseas **+44 1628 825925**

General enquiries **01628 825920**
Email **bookings@landmarktrust.org.uk**

The Landmark Trust
Shottesbrooke
Maidenhead
Berkshire SL6 3SW
United Kingdom

Charity registered in England & Wales 243312 and Scotland SC039205

www.landmarktrust.org.uk

Landmarks in Britain

Goddards, Surrey

Abbey Gatehouse

Tewkesbury, Gloucestershire [I5]

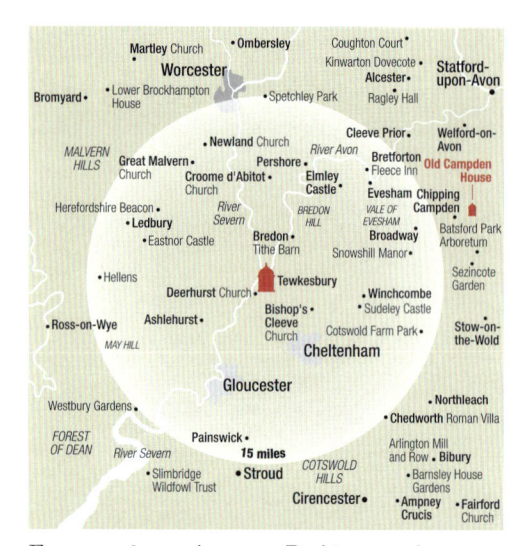

For up to 2 people
Solid fuel stove
Parking nearby
Steep staircases

Other Landmarks in Tewkesbury:
St Mary's Lane

Set between the Malvern and Cotswold's hills with all they have to offer, Tewkesbury itself is an ancient and exceptional town. Its abbey church alone is worth making the journey for. Along the main street and in the narrow lanes running off it, medieval and Tudor buildings blend pleasantly with those of later centuries. In one of these lanes, St Mary's, is another Landmark, a stocking knitter's cottage.

Abbey Gatehouse, which we lease from the trust that guards the surroundings of the abbey, is a grand building of about 1500, restored in 1849 by J. Medland. His work was thorough but skilful – indeed it is difficult to tell now just how much of the stonework he renewed. The gatehouse has only one room, a very fine one on the first floor. At one end of this we have built a gallery, rather like an organ case. Inside there is everything you need but do not want to see and on its top you sleep, close under the moulded beams of the roof, painted the same colours as the vault of the abbey choir. The soaring west window of the abbey rises only a few yards from your door, as you dwell in the 'lodging over the great gate'.

From the logbook

Wonderful to wake up in the morning with the sunlight illuminating the angel corbel.

Being a lapsed choirboy, I found the Evensong Service very moving.

The best things for us were the absolute peace, privacy and the Abbey Church itself.

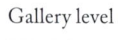

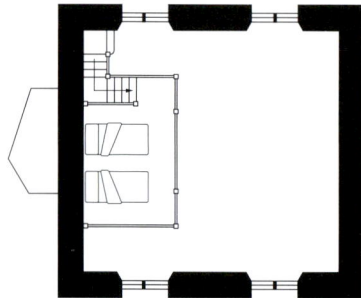

26 The Landmark Trust Handbook

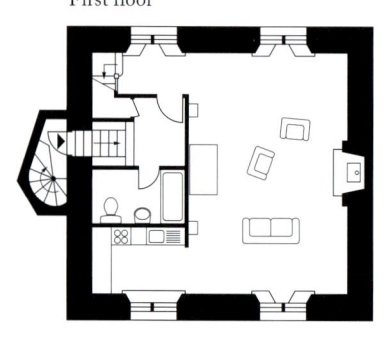

Alton Station

Alton, Staffordshire [G5]

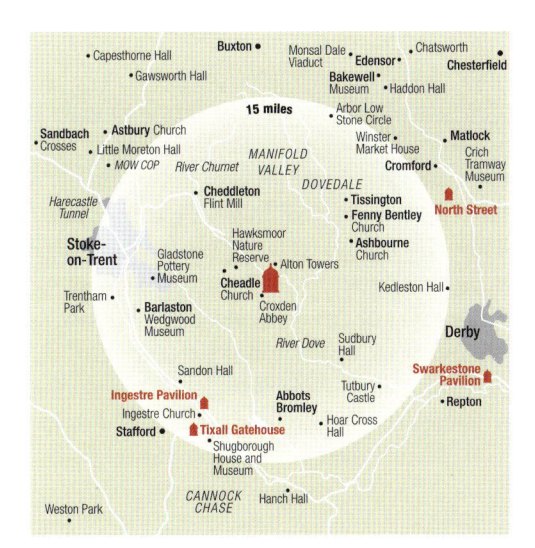

For up to 8 people
Open grounds
Parking nearby
Steep staircase
Dogs allowed

This is the only Italianate railway station in Staffordshire, a notable example of a vanishing class of building. We were indeed grateful to the County Council for conveying it to us in 1970. The railway has gone; but in its heyday the platforms took 12-coach excursion trains from the Potteries.

Its architect was probably H.A. Hunt, an architect-engineer who designed other stations on this line, which opened in 1849. Built by the North Staffordshire Railway (the 'Knotty') to a befitting standard for the Earl of Shrewsbury, then owner of Alton Towers, it stands in marvellous surroundings, both beautiful and interesting. Alton Castle, reconstructed by Pugin, rises out of the trees across the valley of the Churnet. Alton Towers itself, with its famous garden, lies immediately behind.

In 2008, nearly forty years after we took the station on, we realised our ambition to integrate the waiting room building into the Landmark accommodation. You will now cook in a small private waiting room, the main waiting room being reserved for a suitably long table around which to while away your time in front of a fire, amid remnants of former days of railway glory. A double bedroom has been made in the ticket office, while the rest of you will sleep in the stationmaster's house.

During our original work on the house, a disused flue was found to have been blocked with porters' waistcoats; and the plumbing we installed produced at first a strange chuffing sound – doubtless the yearning of this house for the sound and smell of great engines wreathed in steam.

From the logbook
Lovely week in a wonderful station playing 'railway children'

Ground floor

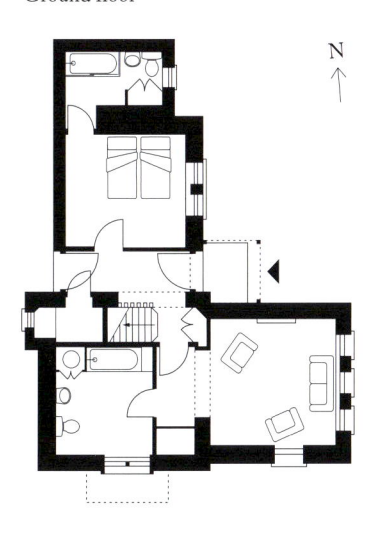

Stationmaster's House

First floor

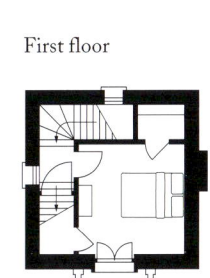

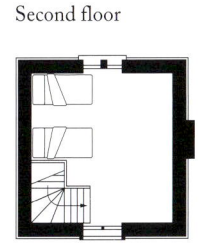

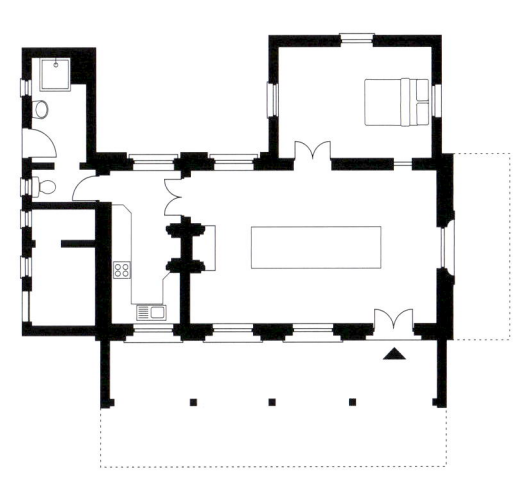

Second floor

Station Waiting Room

www.landmarktrust.org.uk

The Ancient House

Clare, Suffolk [H8]

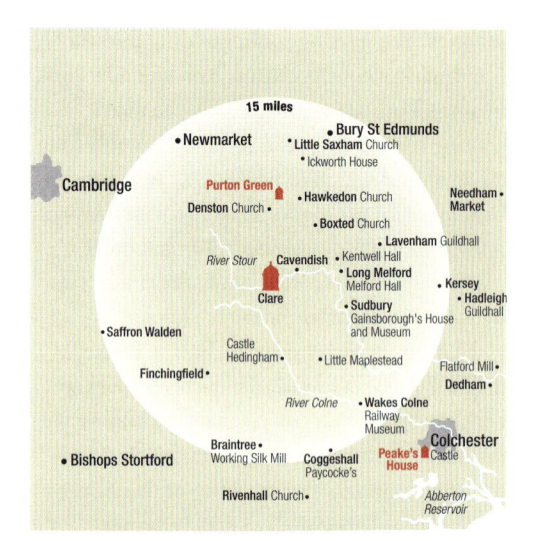

For up to 2 people
Open fire
Small enclosed garden

Parking on street
Steep staircase
Sloping floors
Dogs allowed

Standing at the south-west corner of St Peter and St Paul's churchyard, the Ancient House is a picturesque medieval timber-framed building in this remarkably unspoilt market town. Its elaborate pargeting (raised plaster decoration), so distinctive a form of vernacular decoration in East Anglia, bears the date '1473', and is one of the most celebrated examples of this art in the country. Alec Clifton-Taylor, in *The Pattern of English Building*, mentions watching two elderly pargeters working on repairs there with a compound of lime and sand, horsehair and horse fat. The house incorporates a handsome moulded timber ceiling in the ground floor chamber and elaborately carved oriel windows there and in the first floor bedroom. Staying here you will have an enviable close-up view of the great wool church and keep time by the chimes of its clock.

A local farmer, Charles W. Byford, acquired the Ancient House in the early 1930s to prevent its removal to the United States and it was subsequently given to Clare Parish Council. The Council invited us to create a Landmark here while they maintain a museum in half of the building, thus together safeguarding the future of the house. Close by is Clare Priory, founded for the Austin Friars in 1248, the earliest house of the order in England, and The Cliftons, a building whose exuberant sixteenth-century brick chimneys are richly decorated with circular shafts, Tudor patterns and star tops. Beyond there is a wealth of little-changed Suffolk villages to discover, with some of the country's finest Tudor brickwork.

From the logbook
It never ceases to amaze me that feeling you get when you walk into a Landmark for the first time – is this all for me?

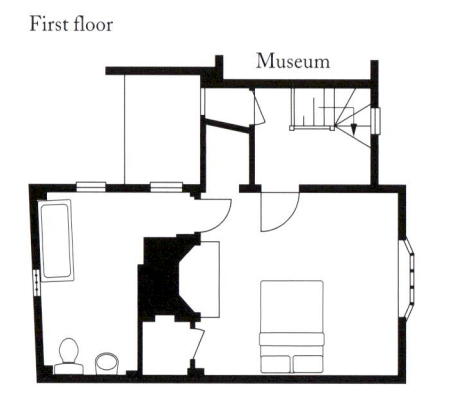

Ground floor

First floor

28   The Landmark Trust Handbook

Anderton House

Goodleigh, Devon [J3]

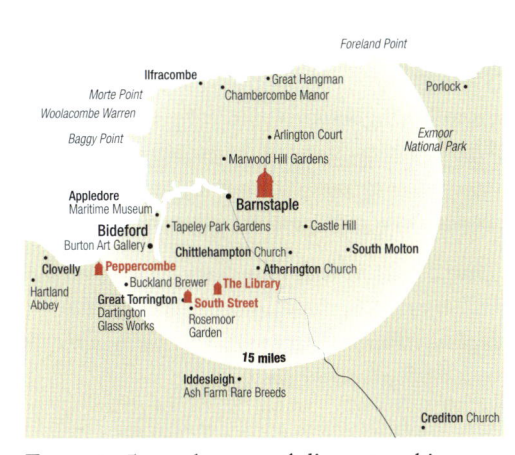

For up to 5 people
Enclosed garden
Adjacent parking
Dogs allowed

Buildings of any age can find themselves at risk. As a building designed by a living architect, Anderton House was a new departure for us when we acquired it in 2000. We chose it for all the reasons we usually apply to older buildings. For all its modernity, Anderton House is as much at home in the rolling Devon landscape it overlooks as the longhouses which inspired its profile. It is an exceptional example of uncompromisingly modern design executed in simple materials, happily caught before changing tastes had been allowed to blur its clean lines or site drainage problems to damage its fabric. It is listed Grade II*.

The Anderton family commissioned the house from Peter Aldington in 1969. It is instantly evocative of those days, with a nod to Frank Lloyd Wright in the functional treatment of the bedrooms and for Peter Aldington, 'perhaps the nearest we came to an integration of inside and outside spaces', the ultimate aim of pioneer modern architects.

The roof appears to float cleverly over the spacious open plan living area with its sliding glass walls. The house retains all its contemporary materials and detailing and is furnished to match. Here is a comfortable family home lifted to a different level of experience by the mind of an architect who is a master of his chosen idiom. Revisiting this more recent past is to be highly recommended.

Open Days are held at Anderton House annually. Please check our website for details.

From the logbook
The illusion of being outside when in never ceases to amaze.

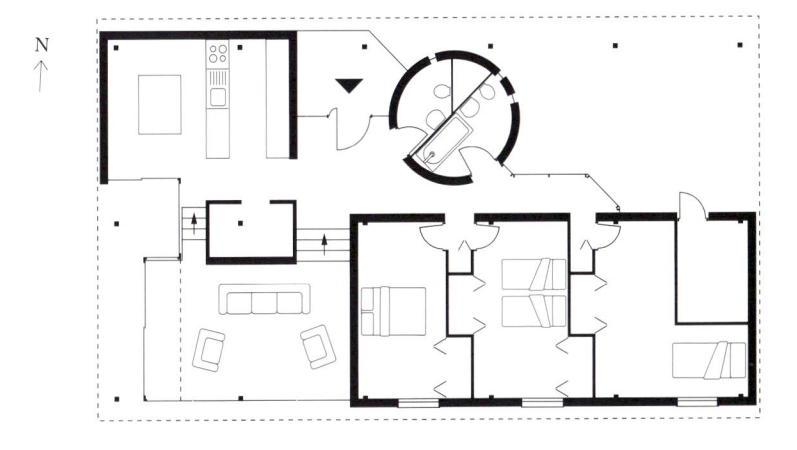

Appleton Water Tower

Sandringham, Norfolk [G8]

A public-spirited local landowner gave us a lease of this exceptional Victorian tower. There is seldom an opportunity to preserve a functional building such as this, let alone one of such quality. It was designed by Robert Rawlinson and the foundation stone was laid in July 1877 by the Princess of Wales. On the ground and first floor was a dwelling for the custodian, with a viewing room above reached by an outside stair. The flues from all the fireplaces passed through the centre of the iron tank to prevent the water from freezing – a typically Victorian idea, original, simple and practical.

From the terrace on top of the tank, which is protected by an ornate cast-iron railing, and from the room below, there is a view on all sides over miles of wide, open landscape. Here, on this exposed hilltop, you can even see a distant gleam of the Wash.

From the logbook
Much time was spent on top viewing the countryside through binoculars, watching the sun set and looking at the stars on clear nights.

Time a walk from Stiffkey to ensure you miss the incoming tide and you can go 3 miles towards Blakeney Point. We got within 51 yards of the seals without scaring them off.

Squeals of excitement as we explored the Tower.

For up to 2+2 people
Open fire
Enclosed garden
Adjacent parking
Steep staircase
Dogs allowed

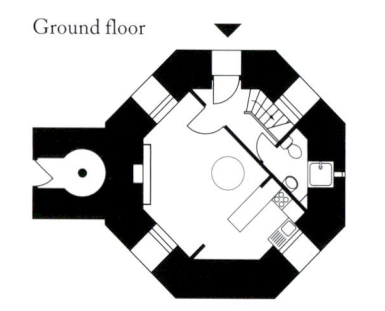

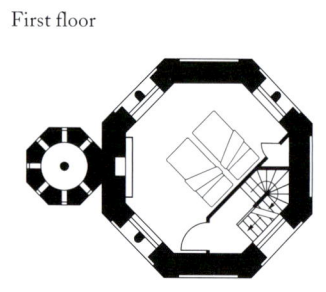

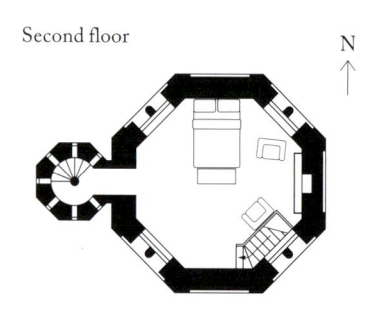

There is a bathroom on the third floor.

30 The Landmark Trust Handbook

Ascog

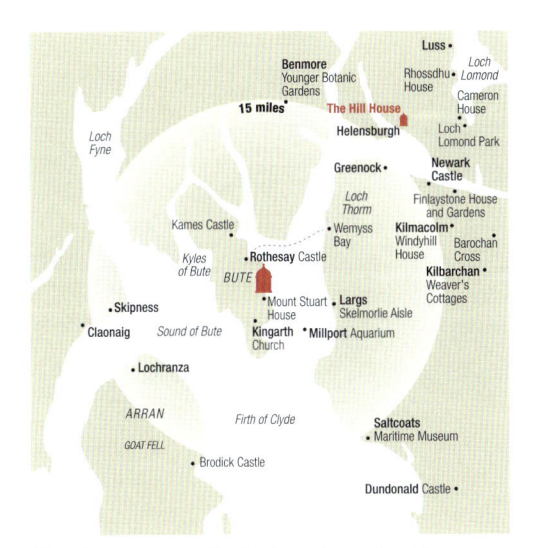

Isle of Bute, Argyll and Bute [B2]

Two houses, one for 7+2 and one for 10.

Bute has been called the Scottish Isle of Wight, and certainly Rothesay, its capital, with its Winter Garden and decorative ironwork, is reminiscent of the South Coast.

Ascog lies on the sheltered east coast of the island. Trees (especially beech) and shrubs (Charles Rennie Mackintosh drew fuchsias here) grow lushly in its mild climate. It has been gently developed as a superior resort since the 1840s, with a scattering of respectable houses above the bay. Building on the shoreline was wisely forbidden.

One such house stands in the large and secluded grounds of the old mansion house of Ascog, once home to a branch of the Stewarts. We have acquired both buildings, which stand a few hundred yards apart, each looking over its own, rather different, garden.

Ascog House is a typical laird's house of the seventeenth century, with projecting stair turret, dormer windows and crow-stepped gables. When we bought it, it was nearly, but not completely, engulfed by clumsy Victorian additions. These we removed, to restore its true proportions and dignified character. An impressive and soundly built Edwardian stair tower, on the other hand, we kept as a free-standing structure, into which we fitted an extra bedroom and bathroom.

There are frequent ferries from Wemyss Bay, less than an hour from Glasgow.

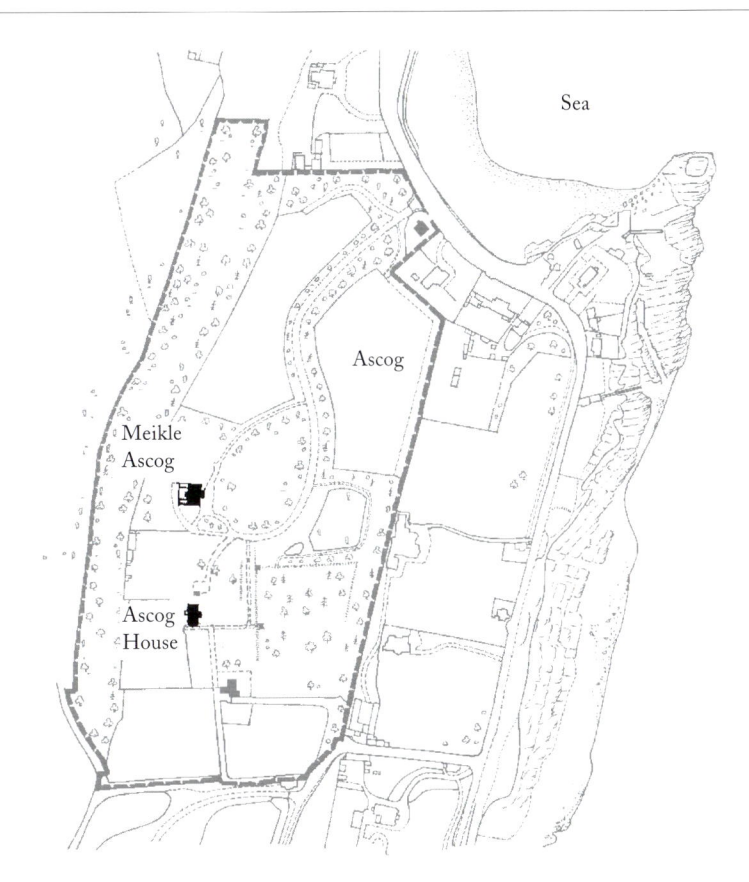

From the logbook
Loved everything – especially the swings, snowdrops, the moonlit sea, mountains and palm trees.

Our favourite walk was Stravannan Bay – we had it completely to ourselves!

Ascog

Ascog House

Seen from the front, the house's main rooms are on the first floor, reached by a wide turnpike stair. Go round behind and the rise of the ground brings them level with the garden. Inside, the arrangement of the rooms is new but there are old fireplaces, including in the kitchen a noble fragment of a magnificent carved chimney piece from an early stage in the building's history.

Most of the windows were enlarged in the usual fashion of the eighteenth century, set in deep embrasures. Those on the west look out over the old kitchen garden, now lawn, to the wooded hill behind, while those on the east overlook the old Victorian formal garden. The best view of all is from the cap house, the tiny perfect bedroom in the top of the stair turret.

For up to 7+2 people
Open fire
Large garden
Adjacent parking
Spiral staircase
Dogs allowed

Turret room

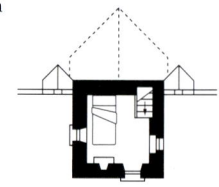

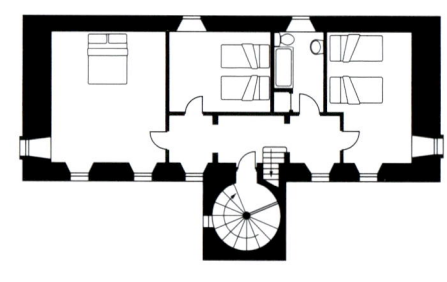

Second floor

First floor

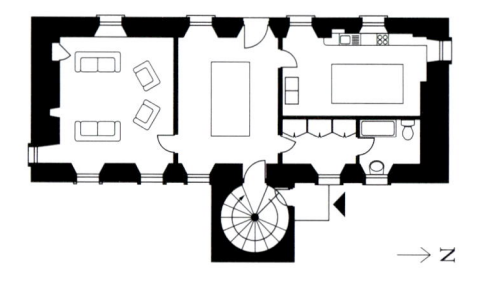

There is another twin bedroom and bathroom in Tom's Tower, 20 feet from the main house and seen on the right in the top photograph.

32   The Landmark Trust Handbook

Meikle Ascog

Meikle Ascog is what nineteenth century guide books called a neat villa. Its builder, and possibly designer, was an engineer called Robert Thom, who bought the property in 1830. Thom's greatest achievement (besides the sensitive development of Ascog) was to succeed, where engineers such as Watt and Rennie had failed, in the quest to provide Greenock with water – the loch from which it comes is named after him.

In its arrangement, his house reflects a logical and inventive personality, being laid out in the most rational way possible to achieve the most agreeable result: every room is pleasant to be in. The windows look out over a shrubbery and from the first floor you can see, framed by fine trees, the sea with the mainland beyond, where Thom made his name and his fortune.

For up to 10 people
Open fire
Large garden
Adjacent parking
Dogs allowed

First floor

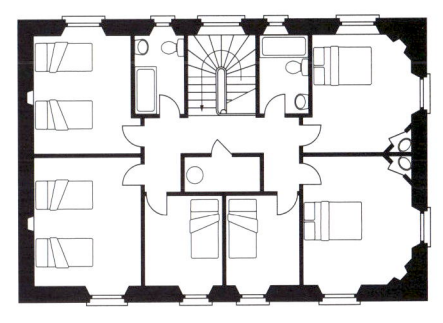

Ground floor

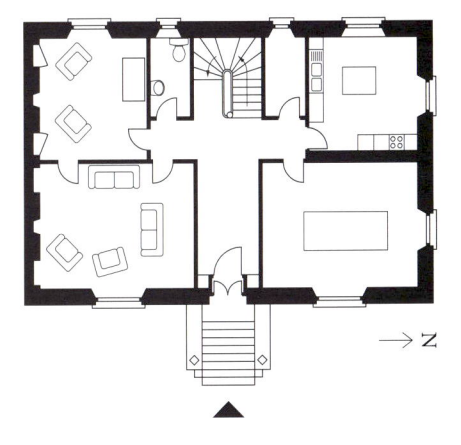

There is a further bathroom with a shower and WC in the basement.

Auchinleck House

Ochiltree, Ayrshire [B2]

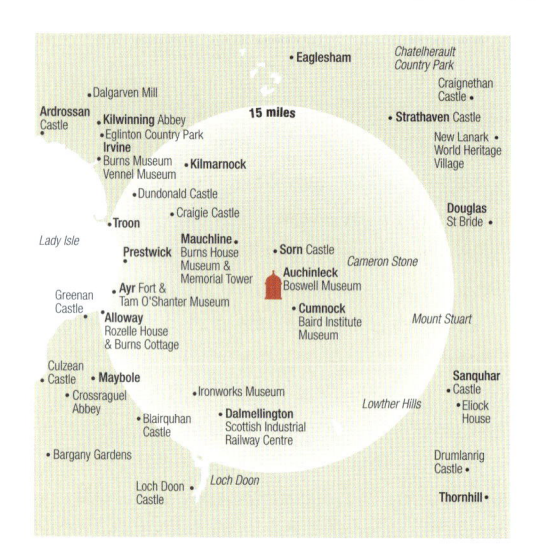

For up to 13 people
Open fire
Open grounds

Adjacent parking
Dogs allowed

Perhaps the finest example of an eighteenth-century country villa to survive in Scotland, Auchinleck House is where the renowned biographer James Boswell indulged his penchant for 'old laird and family ideas'. Built around 1760 by Boswell's father Lord Auchinleck, its architect is unknown; it seems likely that Lord Auchinleck himself had a hand in the neo-Classical design, perhaps influenced by the Adam brothers. Boswell's friend and mentor Dr. Samuel Johnson famously argued over politics with Lord Auchinleck in the library here, when they visited at the end of their tour of the Hebrides in 1773. Once inherited by Boswell, the house was host to much 'social glee', which he recorded in his *Book of Company and Liquors*.

Auchinleck House itself expresses the rich spirit of the Scottish Enlightenment, combining Classical purity in the main elevation with a baroque exuberance in the pavilions and the elaborately carved pediment. We have restored not only the house with its magnificent library looking across to Arran, but also the pavilions, the obelisks and the great bridge across the Dippol Burn, on whose picturesque banks are an ice-house and grotto.

Visitors to the house pass beneath an extract, chosen from Horace by Lord Auchinleck, carved into the pediment: *Quod petis, hic est, Est Ulubris, animus si te non deficit aequus* ('Whatever you seek is here, in this remote place, if only you have a good firm mind'). We are sure this will speak as clearly to those who stay at Auchinleck today as it did to James Boswell himself.

Open Days are held at Auchinleck House annually. Please check our website for details.

In addition, parts of the ground floor are open to the public by appointment only on Wednesday afternoons, from Easter until October. The grounds will be open throughout the spring and summer.

From the logbook
The house swallowed the children – just occasional sightings.

We recommend Scrabble using the Samuel Johnson dictionary only.

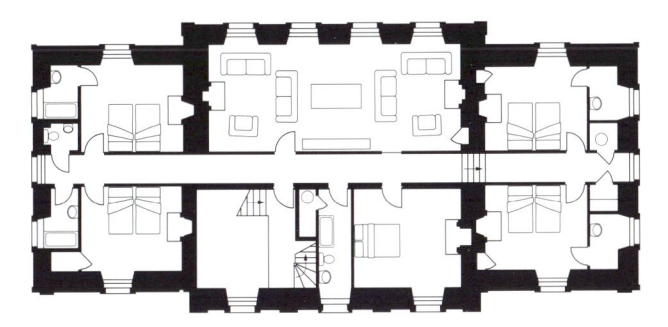

First floor

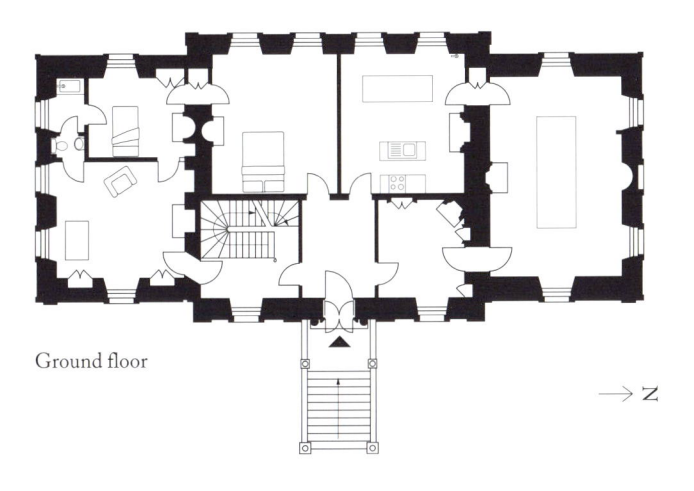

Ground floor

→ N

There is a further bathroom and also a cloakroom with WC in the basement.

www.landmarktrust.org.uk 35

The Banqueting House

Gibside, near Newcastle Upon Tyne [C5]

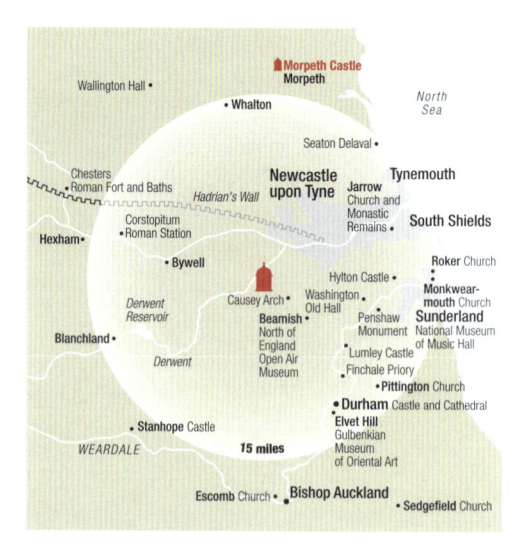

For up to 2+2 people
Solid fuel stove
Open grounds

Adjacent parking
Dogs allowed

Gibside was inherited in 1722 by George Bowes, a landowner and public figure made rich by coal. After his first wife died, he made Gibside his home and set about embellishing the park. The Banqueting House seems to have been finished by 1746. It was designed by Daniel Garrett, a former assistant of Lord Burlington's, to stand in the highest part of the park, looking over the Derwent valley.

When we first saw The Banqueting House in 1977 it was almost entirely roofless and the porch and crocketed gables had collapsed. The park, now happily transferred to the National Trust by the Earl of Strathmore and open to the public, was let to the Forestry Commission and The Banqueting House was hidden by trees.

Here was, however, an important building of most original design, part of a famous landscape. The Forestry Commission agreed to give up their lease of it and the Strathmore Estate then sold us the freehold. Most of the missing stonework was found nearby and inside we were able to save much of the plasterwork and joinery of one room. But the Great Room was just a shell: here we replaced only the main elements of Garrett's design, known from an old photograph.

The Banqueting House now stands in a grassy clearing, looking down to an octagonal pool and the valley beyond. Nearby, the Column of British Liberty rises high above the trees and a little further off lies the Gibside chapel, designed by James Paine in 1760 to hold the remains of George Bowes, ancestor of our Queen.

From the logbook
We imagined we had mastered the art of seeing through the understatements in the Handbook description. Wrong again. The Banqueting House easily exceeded all expectations.

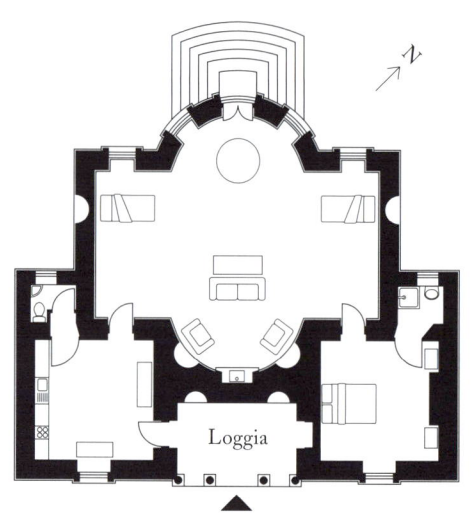

The Bath House

Near Stratford-upon-Avon, Warwickshire [H6]

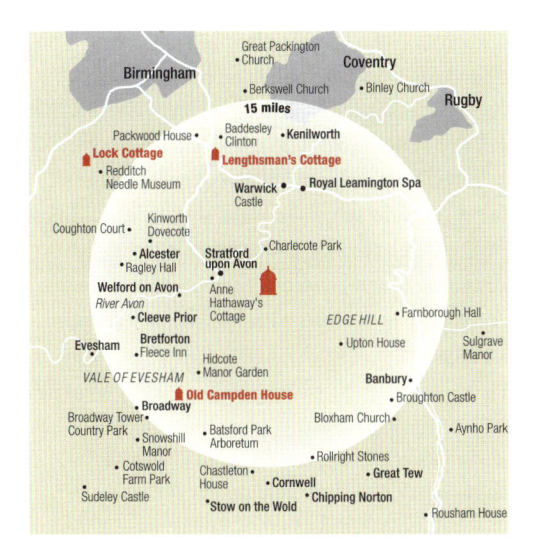

For up to 2 people
Open fire
Open grounds

Adjacent parking
Narrow steep staircases

The benefits of a cold bath were held to be almost limitless by medical opinion of the eighteenth century and many country houses were equipped with one. The Bath House here, it is thought, was designed in 1748 by the gentleman-architect Sanderson Miller for his friend Sir Charles Mordaunt. Good historical fun was had by all: the rough masonry of Antiquity, used for the bath chamber, is contrasted with the polished smoothness of the new Augustan age seen in the room above, where the bathers recovered.

Even in the upper room there is a hint of the subterranean, with a dome hung with coolly dripping icicles. Here the walls have also been frosted with shells, arranged in festoons as if 'by some invisible sea-nymph or triton for their private amusement'. This was the idea of Mrs Delany, better known for her flower pictures, who advised the Mordaunt daughters on where to find the shells. Their work was skilfully reproduced by Diana Reynell, after terrible damage by vandals.

The Bath House, at the end of a long and gated drive, has one main room to live in, but in its deep woodland setting, so near to the Forest of Arden, 'you may fleet the time carelessly, as they did in the golden world'.

From the logbook
It's possible to wake up and think one's a mermaid.

This must be the poshest bedsit in Warwickshire.

Ground floor

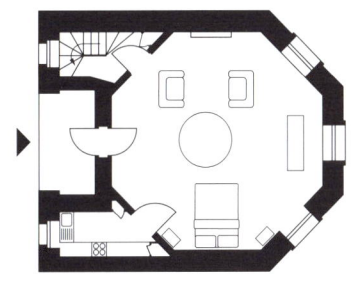

Upper level

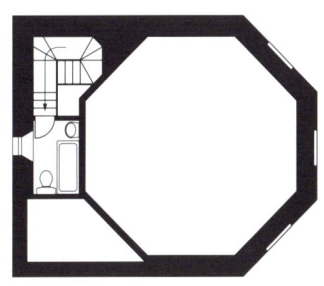

Bath Tower

Caernarfon, Gwynedd [G3]

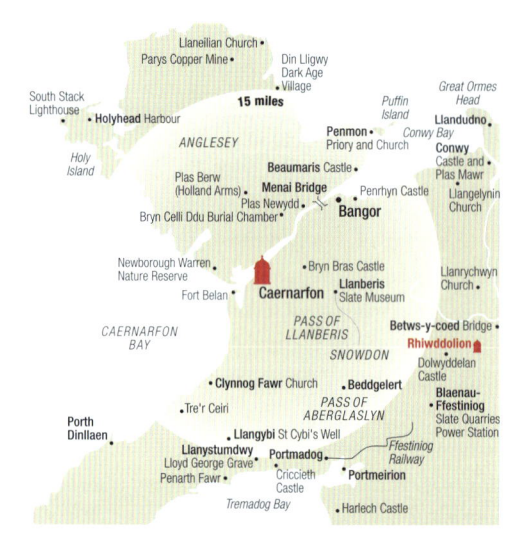

This is one of the towers of the medieval town wall, facing the Menai Strait. More recently, it was part of a Public Bath House, built in 1823 to attract tourists to the town. The present living-room was perhaps a Reading Room. Its two great windows look along the outside of the town wall in one direction, and across the Strait in the other. Here you can have your cake and eat it – the sea at your feet in front and the pleasures of an interesting town at your back.

The tower had been empty for a long time when we bought it. Both entrances are eccentric – one along a narrow alley from the street behind, the other from the sea wall. The character, and inevitably the temperature, of the spacious rooms is stamped by the thick curve of the walls. Below the sitting-room, reached by a steep spiral stair, there is a very large room in which you can sleep like soldiers of the Edwardian garrison. But if there are only two of you, you can sleep in seclusion at the top of the tower, with just the sky and the battlements.

From the logbook
A medieval atmosphere has been achieved without all the discomforts of the period.

For up to 5 people
Solid fuel stove
Roof platform

No private parking
Steep staircase

First floor

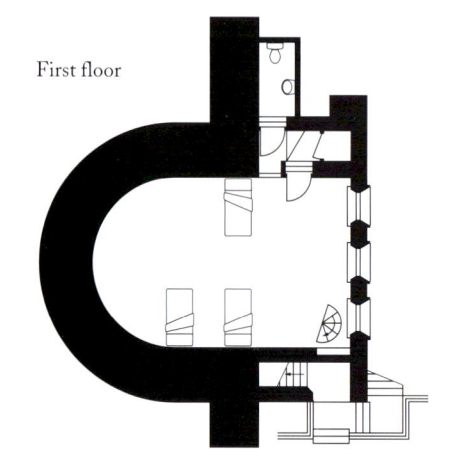

Second floor

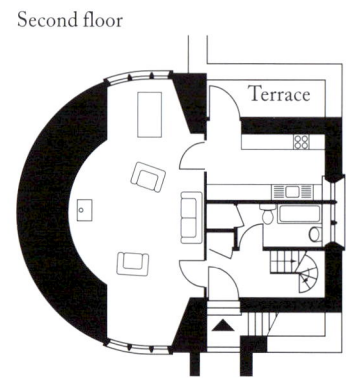

Third floor

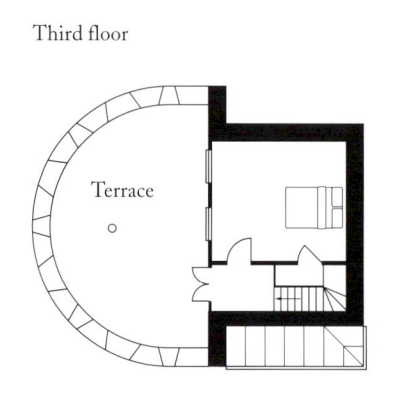

Beamsley Hospital

Near Skipton, North Yorkshire [E5]

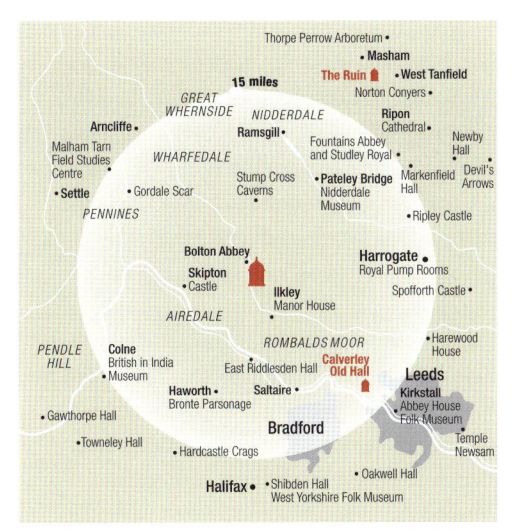

For up to 5 people
Solid fuel stove
Garden

Parking a short walk away
Dogs allowed

Almshouses are a familiar ingredient in our towns and villages, but the Hospital at Beamsley is more unusual. Set back from the conventional row of dwellings on the main road lies this circular stone building. In it were rooms for seven women, encircling a chapel, through which most of them had to pass to reach their doors, a daily encouragement to piety. Until the 1970s the little community of Mother and Sisters lived here, their lives governed by ancient, and ferociously strict, rules.

The Hospital was founded in 1593 by the Countess of Cumberland, at a time when the poor had only private charity to depend on. Her building is an Elizabethan conceit, alluding both to the six circles, or annulets, on her husband's coat of arms and to the round churches of the Templars. Her daughter, that formidable northern heroine Lady Anne Clifford, added the front range. She also furnished the chapel and, almshouses being of their nature conservative places, these fittings survive.

Finding the buildings no longer in demand, the Trustees offered them to us. The front range we have let to long-term tenants; and you can stay in the other. Using its oddly shaped rooms and repeatedly crossing the chapel is a curious experience, bringing you close to the subtle yet vigorous Elizabethan mind. And all around is Yorkshire at its highest and most unadulterated.

From the logbook
So near to so many places to see we could have stayed here for a month – so we will probably come back again and again.

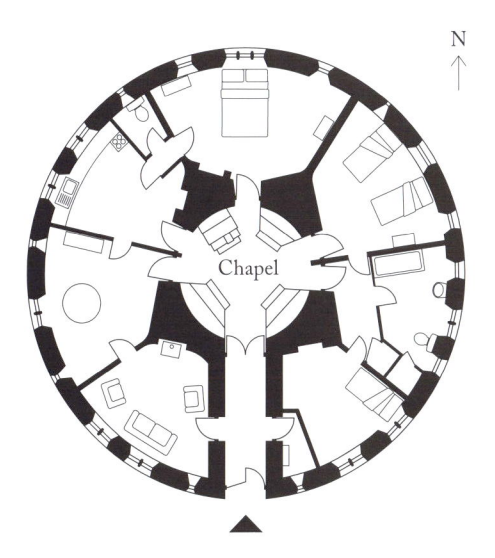

www.landmarktrust.org.uk

Beckford's Tower

Lansdown Road, Bath [J5]

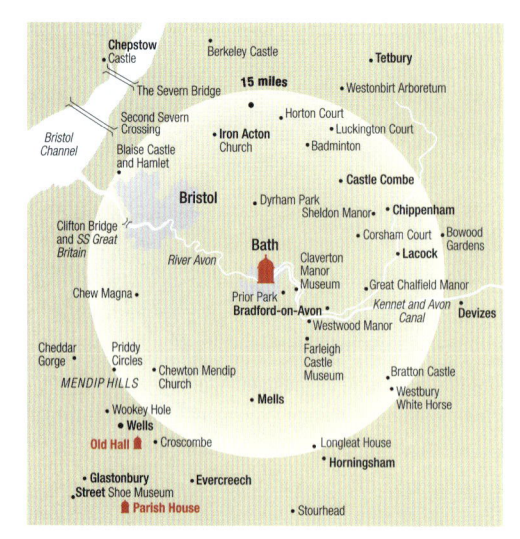

For up to 4 people
Small garden

Adjacent parking

Other Landmarks in Bath:
Elton House
Marshal Wade's House

William Beckford (1760–1844) is best known for his extraordinary Gothic folly, Fonthill Abbey in Wiltshire. Its massive central tower, 276 feet high, eventually collapsed taking most of the house with it. Forced by debt to sell Fonthill, he bought two adjacent houses in Lansdown Crescent in Bath, and was soon again pursuing his fascination with towers, building another atop the hill above. This time he chose a more sober style, Greek Revival with a hint of Tuscany.

Born immensely rich, Beckford became a collector, patron, writer and eccentric builder. But he was also indiscreet in his private life, and, cold-shouldered by English Society, he lived in Bath as a recluse. Each morning, accompanied by his dwarf and pack of spaniels, Beckford would ride up to his Tower to play with his treasures in its opulent rooms, a reminder of which can be gleaned from the Willes Maddox 'Views' of the Tower c1844, on display in the first floor museum.

After Beckford's death the Tower became a chapel and its grounds an elegant cemetery. More recently two flats, the Tower has now been repaired by the Beckford Tower Trust, who offered us the ground floor. With the proceeds of our Millennium Fund, we have made a Landmark to recreate the layout and something of the flavour of Beckford's interiors, especially in the sumptuous Scarlet Drawing Room. And like him, those who stay here can climb the fine circular staircase to the 'Belvidere' just below the elaborate, gilded lantern and enjoy, all to themselves, what Beckford called 'the finest prospect in Europe'.

The museum and the Tower (not the Landmark) will be open to the public on weekends and Bank Holiday Mondays from 10.30–5.00pm between Easter and October, and occasionally by appointment at other times.

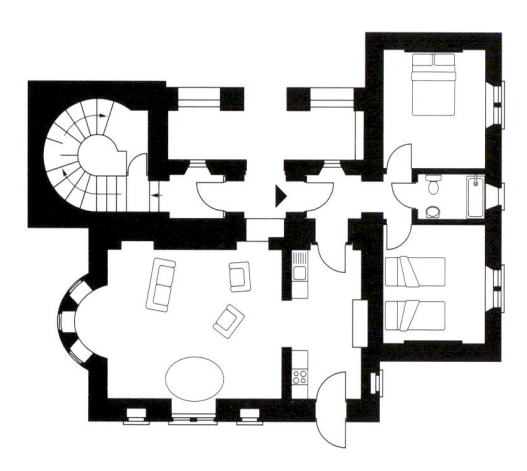

40 The Landmark Trust Handbook

Brinkburn Mill

Near Rothbury, Northumberland [C5]

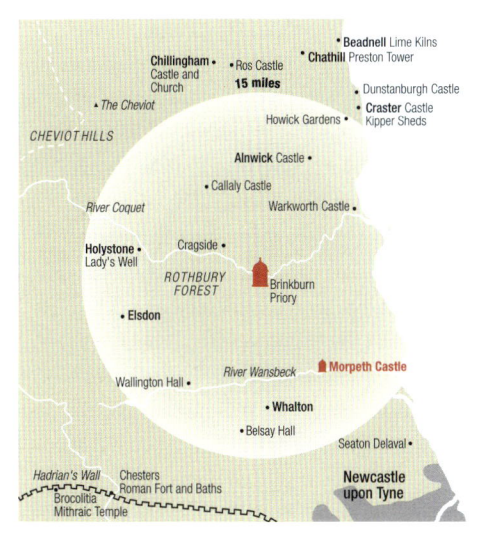

For up to 4 people
Open fire
Garden

Adjacent parking
Dogs allowed

When a priory was founded here in about 1135, the monks, with typical skill, identified one place in this otherwise steep and thickly wooded ravine where there was enough level ground for their buildings. These stood in a loop of the River Coquet, which provided, among other things, water to drive a mill.

The present mill lies at the end of a long lawn, looking back towards the pretty Gothick manor house that stands beside the soaring priory church. This mill was built in about 1800 near the site of its medieval predecessor, but was later dressed up to improve the view from the house. The wheel and grinding stones are still here, although long unused.

At the upper end of the mill, and previously separate from it, are two grander rooms. These may have been an office or perhaps a fishing lodge. One is now the sitting-room, with tall windows facing east to catch the morning sun.

Of Brinkburn's setting one historian wrote: 'This is the most deep solitude, chosen for a religious edifice, I ever yet visited'. The same can be said of the mill, reached by its own drive through the woods (once the main approach to the priory) with only the sound of the river for company. An early morning walk among the priory buildings, which are open to the public for part of the year, is recommended.

From the logbook

That old Landmark magic plus the beauty of Northumberland. As ever, Landmark comes up to and exceeds expectations. Quiet, beautiful, comfortable.

The world stopped and we got off and found a place called Brinkburn Mill.

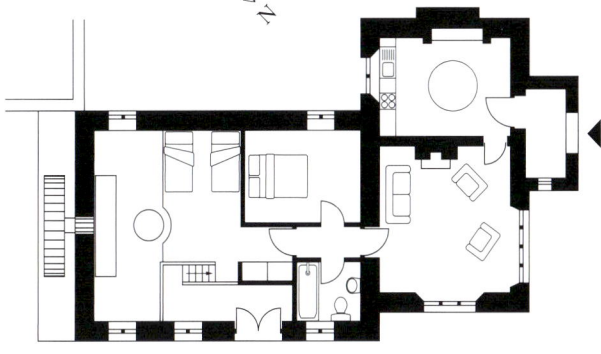

Bromfield Priory Gatehouse

Near Ludlow, Shropshire [H4]

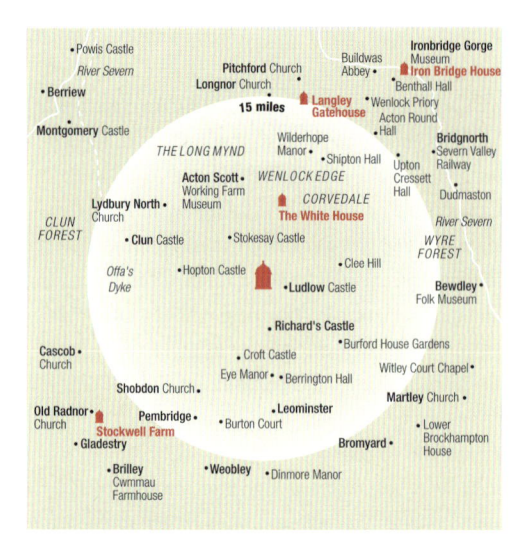

For up to 6 people
Solid fuel stove
Enclosed garden
Parking nearby
Dogs allowed
Steep staircase

The Benedictine monks of Bromfield Priory added a new stone gatehouse to their precinct before 1400. After the Dissolution a timber-framed upper storey was added to this. The room over the arch was used for the manorial court, and later, from 1836 until 1895, for the village school. A teacher's cottage was added at one end and the Gatehouse was largely done up in a Picturesque manner.

Afterwards it became, for many years, the parish reading and recreation room, complete with billiard table, and came in useful for meetings of various sorts, from the youth club to the teaching of first aid. This functional character has rubbed off on the school room itself, which is large and plain and a little formal. At one end, a chimney piece and large cupboards have been put together from an odd assortment of Jacobean carving.

Bromfield itself is an estate village and South Shropshire, with Ludlow as its capital, is deep country still. The Gatehouse now opens on to a grassy churchyard, and the estate office and yard. In front runs a private road, leading only to a few farms and to Oakly Park (the lodge was designed by C. R. Cockerell), successor to the Tudor priory house whose ruins can still be seen on the south side of the parish church.

From the logbook
A week that seemed to last for eons, full of castles, treasures and untouched countryside.

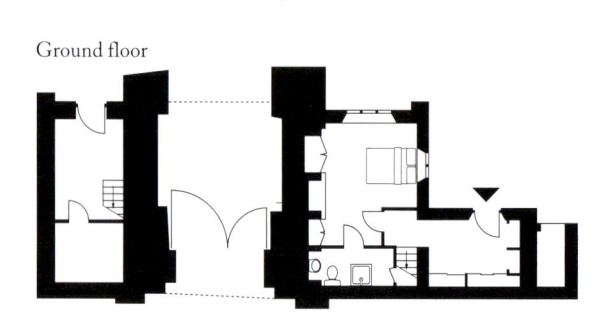

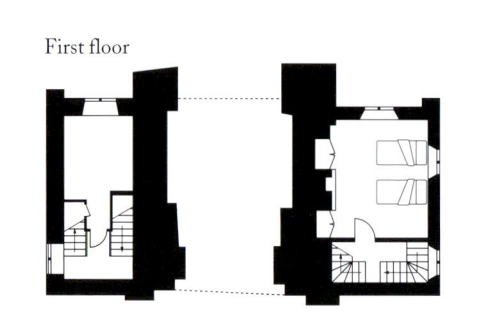

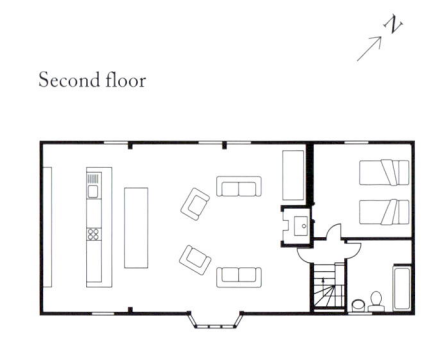

Ground floor

First floor

Second floor

Calverley Old Hall

Calverley, West Yorkshire [E5]

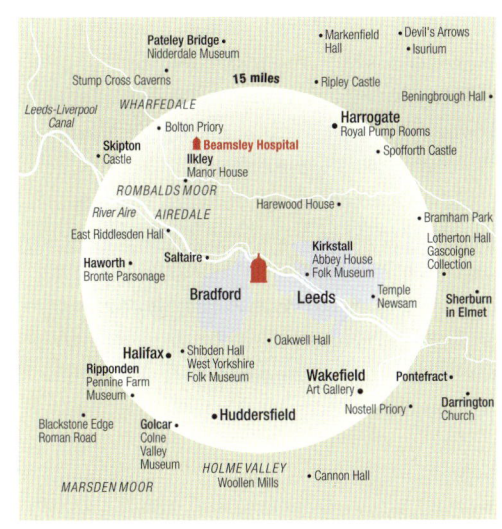

For up to 5 people
Solid fuel fire
Garden

Parking nearby
Dogs allowed

When we arrived on the scene, this ancient house, seat of the Calverley family for over 500 years, had long been divided into cottages and was about to be sold in slices. To save it from this fate, we bought the whole of it and the open ground in front.

The Calverleys were minor Yorkshire magnates, often knighted and latterly baronets. One, put to death after murdering his two eldest sons here (not in the part of the house you stay in) was the subject of a play, *The Yorkshire Tragedy*, once claimed to be by Shakespeare. Another, it is said, was the model for Sir Roger de Coverley. After the Civil War, the Calverley of the day married the heiress of Esholt Hall, nearby, and from then on the family spent most of their time there.

So Calverley Old Hall went slowly down in the world, and in 1754 was sold to the Thornhills, whose descendants sold it to us. Blackened and stony in the romantic northern manner, but still quite grand, it is now surrounded by lesser houses. We have so far repaired the chapel, the hammer-beam hall roof and one wing, the North House, in which you can stay.

The close-knit friendly life of the neighbouring streets, of corner shop and pub, soon warms all those who come to Calverley. There are many good things in the area to visit by day, before returning in the evening to ponder, under the moulded beams, on the vanished Calverleys and their once great house.

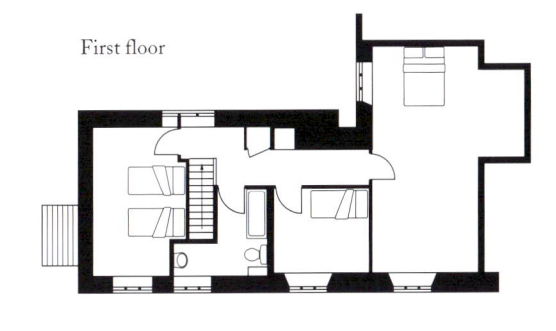

Castle of Park

Glenluce, Dumfries and Galloway [C2]

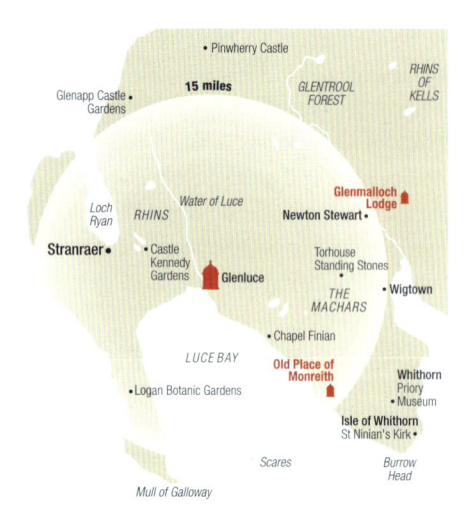

For up to 7 people
Solid fuel stove
Garden

Adjacent parking
Dogs allowed

Thomas Hay was given the lands of Park by his father, the last abbot of Glenluce, and built himself this fine new tower house in 1590. In the 1970s, after standing empty for over a century, the tower was repaired by Historic Scotland, present guardians of Glenluce Abbey. In 1990 they leased the tower to us, and we have made it habitable.

Standing, with two other houses, on a tree-fringed plateau above Luce Bay, the building is outwardly plain. Inside, it is another matter. With the walls plastered and the rooms furnished, you gain a very different impression of the life of a Jacobean laird from that given by the stony shells of so many abandoned towers.

The hall is 30 feet long, with a fine fireplace. From it the laird's private stair leads to bedrooms, each with its own privy (the potential for hide and seek is endless). The wide main stair, in its own tower, has a little room at the top called the cap house, from which you can glimpse the sea.

The eighteenth century brought larger windows to let in more light, the bright clear light of a western peninsula. There are notable gardens to visit nearby, and the rolling fields are grazed by cattle, seemingly more numerous than the human inhabitants.

From the logbook
Evocative restoration thoughtfully furnished and lit throughout – all in all, a most comfortable step back to yesteryear.

There is a single bedroom in the cap house, at the top of the stair turret.

Ground floor | First floor 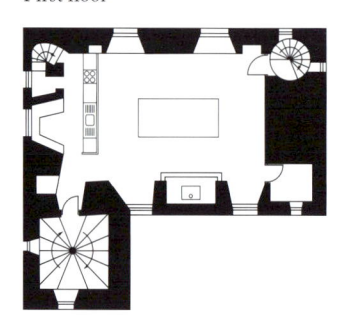 | Second floor 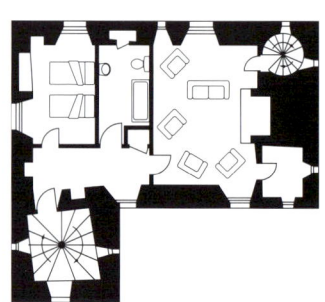 | Third floor

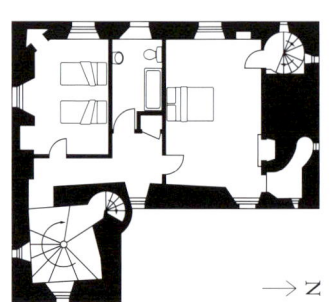

BLISSIT · THE·NA · OF · LORD·THIS
VERK VAS BEGVNT E·F ST·DAY·O ·MARCH
1530·BE·THOMAS·HAY·OF·PARK·AND
JONET·MAK·DOVEL·HIS·SPOVS

Causeway House

Bardon Mill, Northumberland [C5]

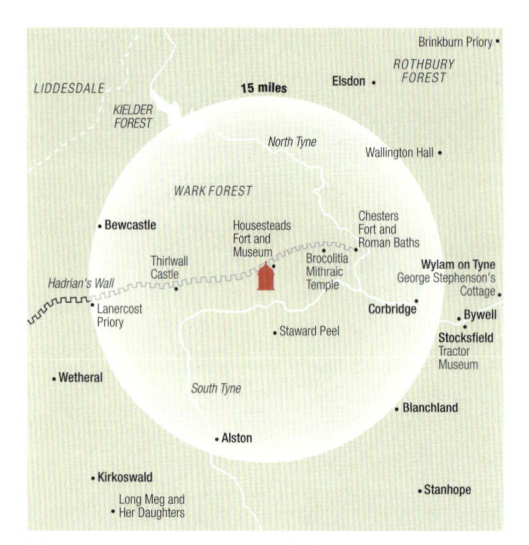

For up to 2+2 people
Enclosed garden
Gas coal fire

Adjacent parking
Dogs allowed

This is the only house in Northumberland still thatched in heather. Known locally as black thack, it was of course available in abundant supply, but was seldom used once slate became a cheap alternative in the last century. It survived here because the farmhouse, built in 1770 and never much altered, was abandoned over 20 years ago. Used as a store, its thatch was preserved beneath corrugated iron. Lorry loads of heather went into its repair, leaving a cover which is thinner and tougher than conventional thatch. Stuffed into holes in the roof we found two dresses, of about 1890, interesting examples of much worked-in clothing.

Inside, the original arrangement of living-room on one side of the cross-wall and byre on the other, with loft over, also survives. The loft is now a warm-weather bedroom, where you can sleep under the knotted tent-like thatch in a fully roofed bed.

The farm, which we own, stands in the rolling fertile land behind Hadrian's Wall. Past the front runs a Roman road, with the stump of a Roman milestone nearby, which gives visitor access within a few hundred yards to the fort and settlement of Vindolanda. Indeed few houses in Britain can have so many traces of Rome around them.

The heather thatch makes the twin bedroom harder to heat and we do not recommend this room for winter use.

From the logbook
Arrived at this lovely house, pitch black, hadn't a clue what we'd be waking up to. Daylight ... greeted by a short-eared owl sitting on the fence post

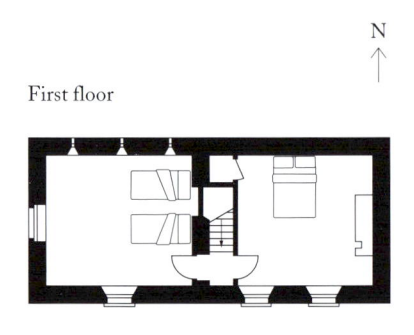

Cawood Castle

Cawood, near Selby, North Yorkshire [E6]

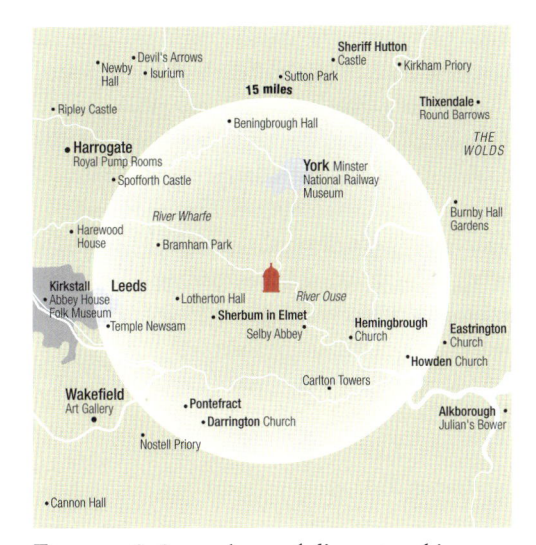

For up to 2+2 people
Solid fuel stove
Small enclosed garden
Roof platform
Adjacent parking
Extremely steep spiral staircase
Dogs allowed

This gatehouse, with the domestic wing to one side of it, is all that remains of Cawood Castle, once a stronghold of the Archbishops of York. It stands in the flat land south of York in the small town of Cawood, where there is a bridge over the Ouse. By the fifteenth century, when Archbishop Kempe built our richly decorated gatehouse with two well-proportioned rooms one over the other, it had become less of a castle and more of a palace; his Cardinal's hat, of which he was proud, appears on several of the finely carved stone shields over the archway.

Another cardinal to stay here, just once, was Thomas Wolsey: it was here that he was arrested and turned back to the South where he died soon after. Other visitors include Henry III, Edward I and Queen Margaret, Queen Isabella, and Henry VIII and Queen Catherine (Howard) – not all together, of course.

After the Civil War, Cawood was partially dismantled. In the eighteenth century the gatehouse was used as a courtroom and a respectable Georgian staircase was built to supplement the medieval spiral stair.

It was difficult to save these most historic remains because they were divided between two owners; the domestic wing, long used as a barn, was hidden by derelict farm buildings; and part of the gatehouse was in the adjoining dwelling. The first floor room, with handsome bay windows at each end, in fact contained a full-size billiard table (how ever did it get there?) manfully supporting, during all our long negotiations, a huge pile of debris from the collapsed floor above.

In the end our neighbour allowed us to truncate his house a little, and we bought and demolished the farm buildings – so that our visitors can now experience and occupy a late medieval room of the finest quality; and in it, if they like, read some history on the spot where it was made.

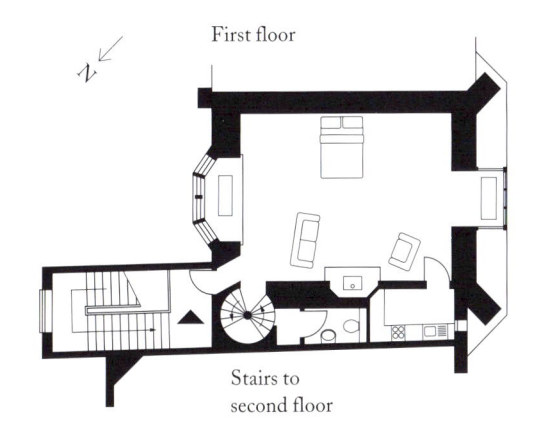

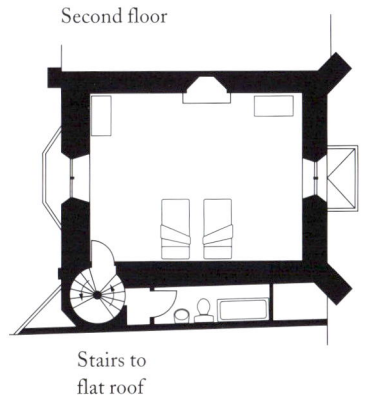

The Château

Gate Burton, Lincolnshire [F7]

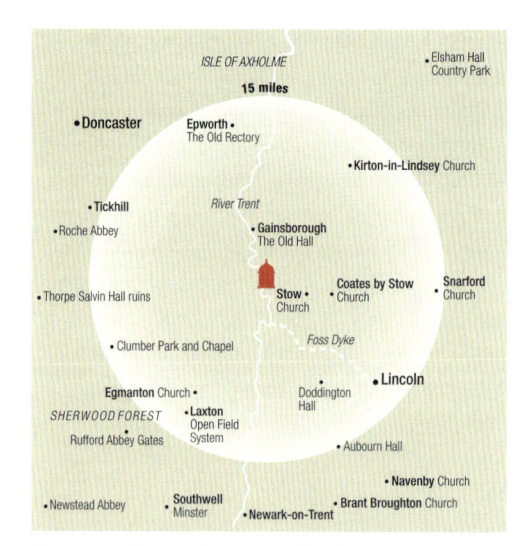

For up to 2 people
Open fire
Garden
Adjacent parking

This is the earliest recorded building by John Platt of Rotherham, designed in 1747 when he was 19 and almost his only work outside Yorkshire, where he practised and prospered for the next 50 years.

It stands on a grassy knoll above a big bend of the River Trent, on the edge of Gate Burton park. Built as a Gainsborough lawyer's weekend retreat, and later used for picnics and other mild kinds of excursion, it had since been altered and then neglected. Its present owner gave us a long lease of it.

We have restored the Château to its original elaborate and slightly French appearance, an ornament in the landscape, which shows up well from the road some distance away. John Platt must have been a talented young man, because it is difficult to realise until one is inside just how small the scale of the building is; apart from the principal room upstairs, which has a high coved ceiling, there is little space in which to swing a cat. But there are fine views across the park and up a shining reach of the River Trent, along which big slow barges, piling the water in front of them, press on towards an enormous power station, whose cooling towers steam majestically in the distance.

From the logbook

I feel like Beatrix Potter's mice, living in a very up-market doll's house.

We slept soundly only to be woken gently by the dawn chorus and bleating of lambs.

Ground floor

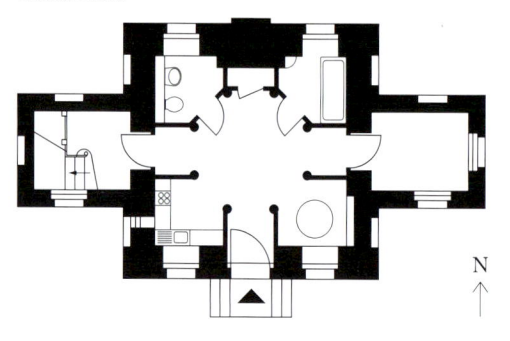

First floor

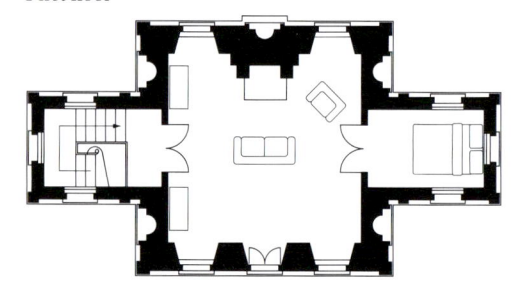

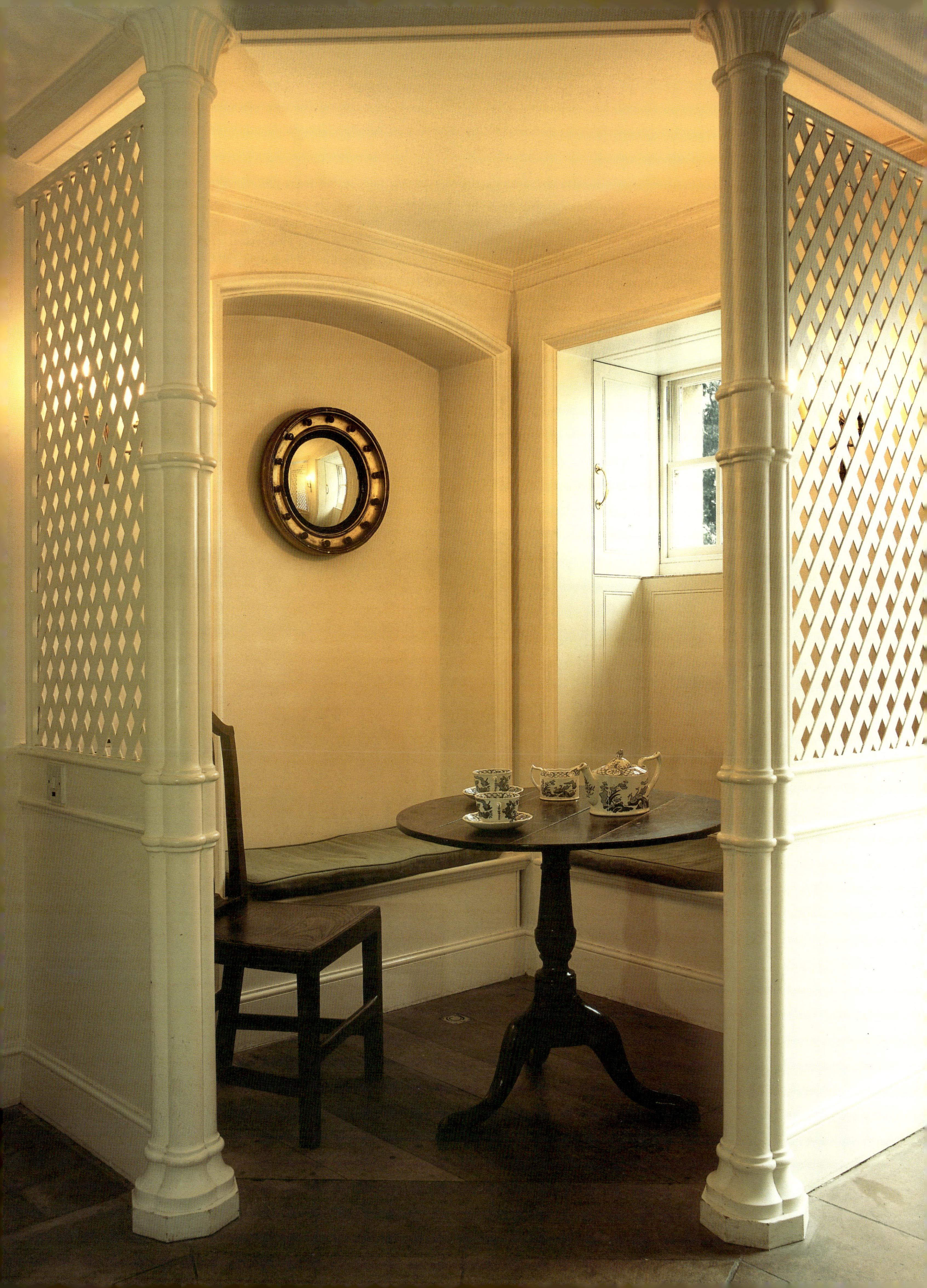

Church Cottage

Llandygwydd, Cardiganshire [I2]

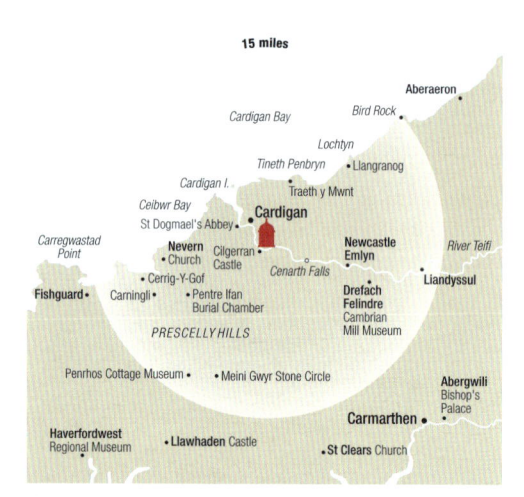

For up to 4 people
Open fire
Garden

Adjacent parking
Dogs allowed

Church Cottage is early Victorian, modestly Gothic, and made of Cilgerran slate. It was also the first Landmark acquired in 1965. The church itself, which was rebuilt in 1857 by R. J. Withers, a prolific architect and committed Ecclesiologist, was demolished in 2000, but its footprint and font remain, as does the churchyard. Our cottage was for the caretaker; it stands in a small village east of Cardigan, in a hilly, well-wooded countryside of small farms. It is also the first building we ever tackled.

Though less than a mile from the main Newcastle Emlyn to Cardigan road, Llandygwydd is quiet, although there is a small road between the cottage and the church. Plays in Cardigan are recommended; so are the coracle races on the Teifi. The south sweep of Cardigan Bay is less than ten miles away; however, the point of Church Cottage is not to dash about, but simply to be there, in this distant and unremarkable part of Wales, and feel what it is like.

From the logbook
We found lots and lots to do and never strayed outside a five mile radius from the house. Super walks and we managed to wangle a go in a coracle one evening.

We brought our dinghy and sailed on most days in Cardigan Estuary.

It was a joy to see hart's tongue ferns growing in the bank outside the bathroom window.

Ground floor

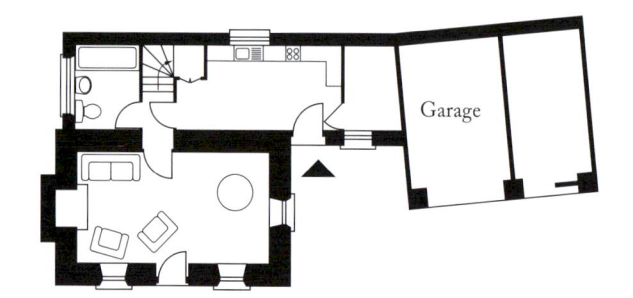

First floor

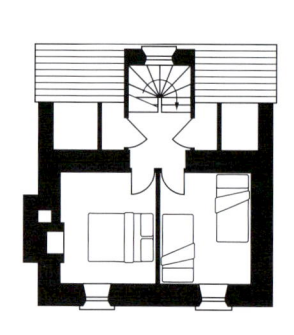

50   The Landmark Trust Handbook

Clavell Tower

Kimmeridge, near Wareham, Dorset [K5]

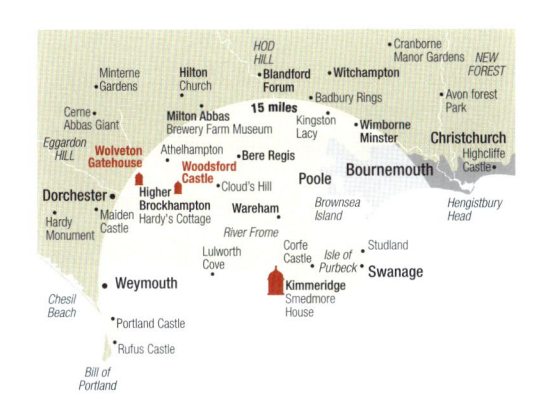

For up to 2 people
Gas coal fire
Access by steep footpath only

Parking 170 yards away at foot of cliff
Dogs allowed

Since the summer of 1830, Clavell Tower has stood sentinel on a wild and open stretch of the Dorset coast. It was built by a seventy-year-old clergyman, Reverend John Richards Clavell, who unexpectedly inherited the Smedmore Estate, on which it stands, in 1817. Why he built the tower is not clear; it has served as both folly and seamark since. With its twelve columns and pierced parapets all of local stone, a journalist reporting its completion called it 'as elegant a building as any the county of Dorset can boast of'. The young Thomas Hardy used the tower as a frontispiece for his *Wessex Poems* and courted a local coastguard's daughter here.

The geology of this coastline is at once a glory and a threat: it brought designation as a World Heritage site, but the friable Kimmeridge shales also cause gradual erosion for which there is no remedy. By 2002, Clavell Tower (which had stood empty and increasingly derelict since the Great War) was left perilously close to the edge of the crumbling cliff.

Desperate remedies were needed if it was not to be lost forever. We considered all the options, and were left with the difficult conclusion that the only feasible way to save the tower was to dismantle it and re-erect it on sounder footings, further back from the cliff's edge, carefully positioned to capture as many of its original site lines within the landscape as possible.

The result is at least as elegant as the original and has saved a well-loved local landmark, known to many who have walked the South West Coastal Path past its door. You too must walk, for ten minutes or so, up to the tower on the cliff top, leaving your car below. The effort will be worth it to stay in this unparalleled spot.

During restoration.

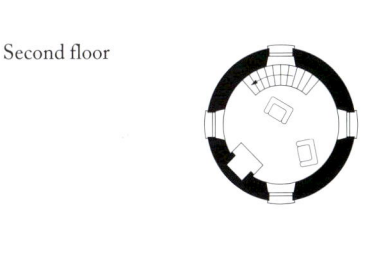

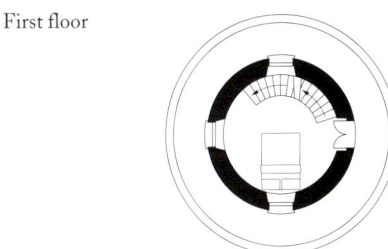

Second floor

First floor

Ground floor

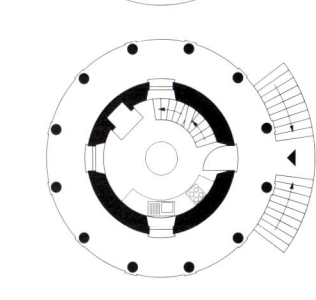

Lower Ground floor

www.landmarktrust.org.uk

Cloth Fair

Smithfield, London EC1 [J8]

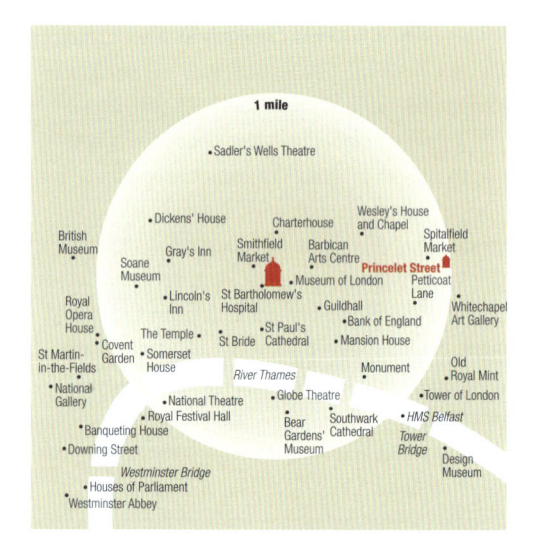

These plain Georgian houses over shops are opposite the churchyard of St Bartholomew the Great, which almost alone among City churches escaped the Great Fire of 1666. They were sold to us by the late Paul Paget, who had rescued them many years before, with No. 41, the only remaining house in the City built before the Fire. Round the corner is Smithfield market with its robust architecture, sights and smells, facing the noble buildings of St Bartholomew's Hospital. Further along Cloth Fair are new houses, bringing domestic life to this part of the City.

There is here a lingering feel of how alive the whole City of London once was before it was destroyed by money, fire and war – a place where long-established institutions, trades, houses, markets and people of all kinds were mingled together. Each of our houses has a respectable staircase, pleasant rooms and nice old joinery. No. 43 was long the home of Sir John Betjeman.

From the logbook
This house is a remarkable oasis in central London, particularly at the weekend.

History comes alive when you stay at Cloth Fair.

Cycling from Cloth Fair… puts Soho, Covent Garden and Westminster within ten minutes (and the far end of Hyde Park within twenty) so we had a lovely ride on Christmas morning down to Buckingham Palace.

No. 43
For up to 2 people
Gas coal fire
Small roof terrace
No private parking

No. 45a
For up to 4 people
Gas coal fire
No private parking

No. 45a

No. 43
First floor   Second floor

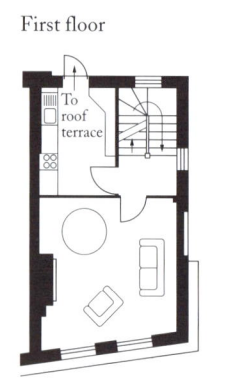

No. 45a
First floor   Second floor

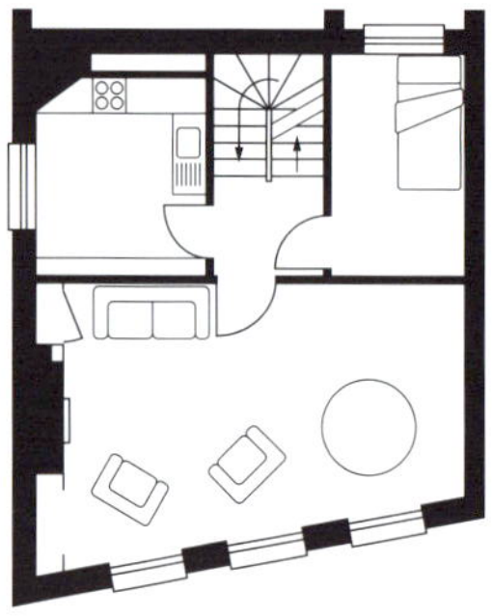

52   The Landmark Trust Handbook

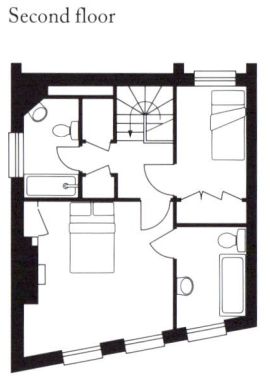

Clytha Castle

Near Abergavenny, Monmouthshire [I4]

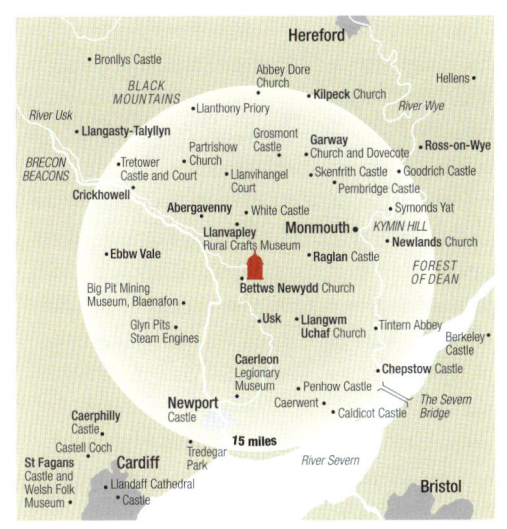

For up to 6 people
Open fire
Garden
Roof platform

Adjacent parking
Steep spiral stairs
Dogs allowed

'Erected in the year 1790 by William Jones of Clytha House, husband of Elizabeth, last surviving child of Sir William Morgan of Tredegar, it was undertaken with the purpose of relieving a mind afflicted by the loss of a most excellent wife, to the memory of whose virtues this tablet is dedicated.'

This most affecting folly, which we lease from the National Trust, stands on the summit of a small hill, at the edge of a grove of old chestnuts. It was designed by a little-known architect and garden designer, John Davenport, perhaps with help from his client. Besides being an eye-catcher, the castle was used for grand picnics and as a retreat; the square tower contains fine rooms on both floors. When we arrived it had been empty for twenty-five years and before that had housed a gamekeeper. After more than thirty years as a Landmark, we carried out a major refurbishment in 2007 and reorganised the accommodation, making the circular room in the south turret a kitchen-dining room looking out into the clearing in the woods. If you are lucky, you might just see deer, pursuing their own business in the undergrowth. We hope that the castle will continue to relieve the minds of all those who come here.

From the logbook
Seeing my daughter have the time of her life in this fairy-tale castle will live in my memory.

A perfect honeymoon destination for us; romantic and secluded.

This is our 3rd visit to Clytha and each visit is better than the last.

First floor

This bedroom is on the second floor

Turret (roofless)

Ground floor

www.landmarktrust.org.uk

The College

Week St Mary, Cornwall [K2]

For up to 5 people
Open fire
Enclosed garden

Adjacent parking
Steep staircase
Dogs allowed

When we looked at this house, on the suggestion of one of our visitors, it quickly became clear that it is only part of something that was once much larger, fragments of which appear in the walls and outbuildings around it. These, it turned out, are the remains of a remarkable school, almost the first to be founded by a woman.

Moreover, the woman who founded it, Thomasine Bonaventure, was herself remarkable. Though born here in Cornwall, she married, in turn, three London merchants, each of whom died leaving her his property. This she gave or left to charity, amongst many other benefactions, founding this school in 1506 at the place of her birth.

To oversee the building work, Thomasine appointed her first cousin, John Dinham of Wortham Manor, 12 miles away and today also a Landmark (see Wortham Manor). He remodelled his own house at about the same time, and the two buildings have much in common – notably their carved granite doorways.

Unfortunately, Thomasine also decreed that the master (with an Oxford or a Cambridge degree, and six weeks holiday a year) should pray for the souls of her husbands, a practice firmly disapproved of by the new Protestant regime; and so, as a chantry, it was dissolved two years later. Thus the College at Week St Mary, one of the oldest English schools, prosperously founded, survives only in its name, which still clings to this house more than 300 years later.

The College faces a small courtyard off the village street. Behind it a meadow slopes down to a chequer-work of little fields, and over them appears, black and afar, the high outline of Dartmoor, beyond which Thomasine ventured to such purpose.

From the logbook
Everyone should get the chance to stay in a Landmark – they're so good for the soul.

As always the logbooks have been fascinating. They record the changes to the village over the past two decades.

Ground floor

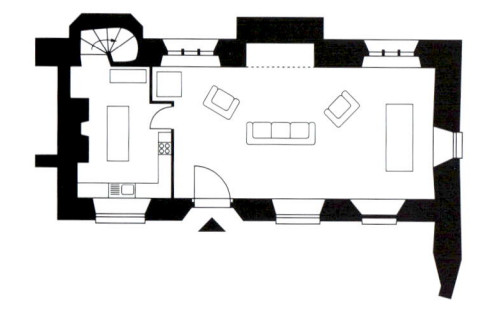

First floor

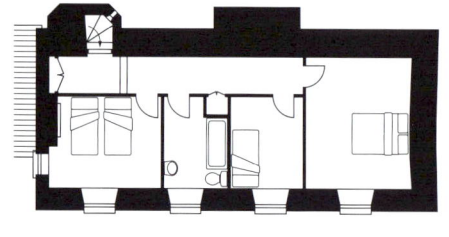

Coombe

Morwenstow, near Bude, Cornwall [K2]

Eight cottages, one for 3, four for 4, one for 5 and two for 6.

Coombe hamlet consists of a watermill, the mill house and several cottages, built among orchards round a ford on a shallow stream. It is at the junction of two wooded valleys and is half a mile from the sea at Duckpool, where a sandy beach is exposed at half tide.

Although a small and humble place, Coombe has notable connections. On the hill to the south is Stowe Barton, where the Grenville family lived for 600 years. Interesting traces remain of their great house, demolished in 1739. From soon after 1600 they owned part of Coombe, and its mill was sometimes called Stowe Mill.

Coombe is partly in the parish of Morwenstow, and its most famous vicar, the Reverend Stephen Hawker, lived here for a short time. He was the inventor (or perhaps reviver) of harvest festivals, and a moving spirit in the saving of life at sea. The Reverend Sabine Baring-Gould ('Onward Christian Soldiers') wrote a life of Hawker. We have managed to get enough copies of this book, by one famous and unusual parson about another, to put one in most of the cottages at Coombe.

We acquired the whole hamlet as part of a joint scheme with the National Trust to preserve it and its exceptional setting. It is a sheltered place, lying well back from the sea.

Almost all the surrounding land, including much of the coast (geologically one of the most impressive in Britain), belongs to the National Trust. There are long and excellent walks in all directions. The Mill itself, still with all its machinery, is a handsome and interesting stone building with a fine wheel.

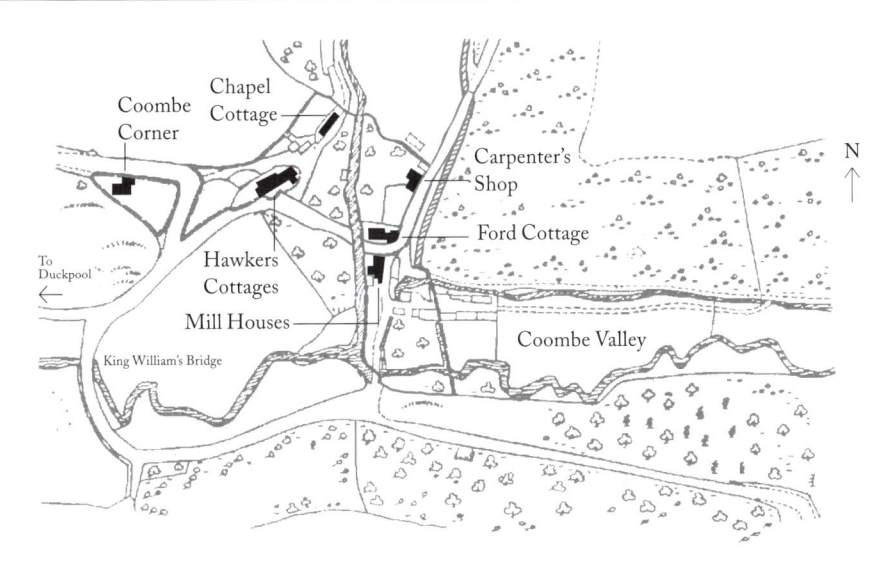

From the logbook
Silence, solitude and sea. Coombe is a truly beautiful place.

A day lasts forever here.

A wonderful week – we surfed every day at Duckpool.

Coombe

The Carpenter's Shop

The Carpenter's Shop was where a family of carpenters called Tape carried on their trade from the early nineteenth century. Much of their work must have come from the Stowe estate, which perhaps helped them put up this handsome workshop in about 1830. When we came to Coombe it had been derelict for many years.

Our architect, the late Paul Pearn, took pains to preserve its spare and functional character in the new arrangement: a large living-room open to the roof and two bedrooms leading off a gallery, reached by a spiral stair. The living-room has a slate floor and an open fire, formerly the forge. The doors open on to a large old orchard leading down to the stream.

For up to 4 people
Open fire
Shared orchard garden
Adjacent parking
Narrow spiral staircase
Dogs allowed

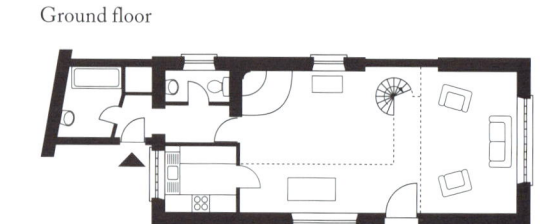

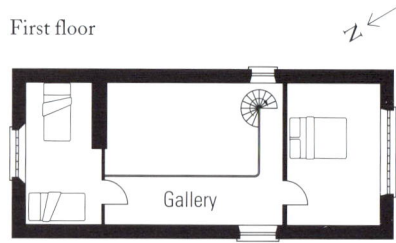

Ground floor

First floor

Chapel Cottage

Chapel Cottage takes its name from the former Bible Christian meeting room, which is now its living-room. Made of timber, it arrived in Coombe in about 1860 on wheels, which are still there under the front. These movable 'iron chapels' as they were known could be bought second-hand, which must have suited the pockets of the farm workers who made up the congregation. Once here, it was given a slate roof but fell out of use soon after 1900 and was later divided up and a bungalow added at one end. We restored the chapel itself, putting back its sash windows and timber lining, and improved the appearance and interior of the addition. It is very well placed – a little above the rest of Coombe, looking across the valley over the top of one of the orchards.

For up to 4 people
Solid fuel stove
Small garden
Parking nearby
Dogs allowed

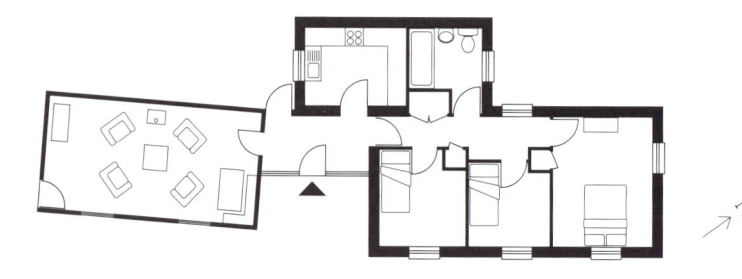

Coombe Corner

Coombe Corner was built on a hillside above the rest of the village in the 1930s. With its painted weatherboarding and large windows it represents a completely different approach to building, and to living, to the solid old houses of Coombe itself. Here life is all about enjoyment of the weather, of the Cornish coast, of the view, in a way that could scarcely be imagined by ordinary hard-working people even 50 years earlier. Simple bungalow it is, but made with discretion, forcing itself on no one. We bought it to round off our ownership of Coombe and to ensure that it was not replaced by something less well-mannered, an all too likely possibility.

For up to 6 people
Solid fuel stove
Garden
Adjacent parking
Dogs allowed

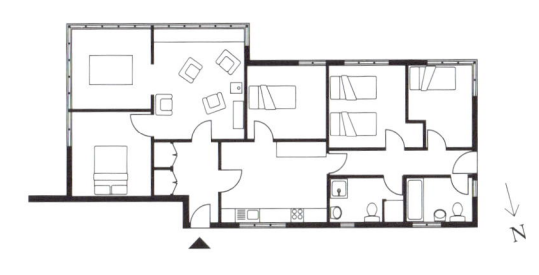

Ford Cottage

Ford Cottage is an extremely old cottage of cob and thatch on the edge of the stream, close to Mill House. Teas used to be served here. It has a large high living-room with a slate floor and solid fuel stove. It opens on to a large orchard at the back, running alongside the stream.

For up to 2+2 people
Solid fuel stove
Shared orchard garden
Adjacent parking
Dogs allowed

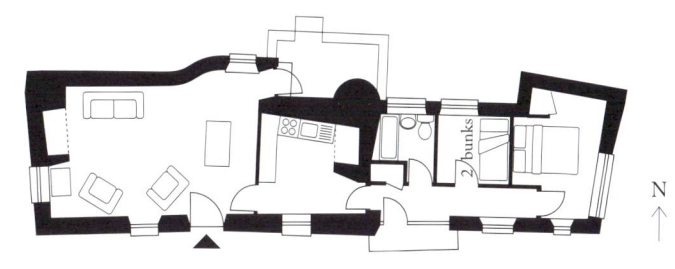

Coombe

Hawkers Cottages

Hawkers Cottages are a pair of stone, cob and thatched cottages, named after the famous Vicar of Morwenstow, who lived here briefly. The bedroom in No. 1, with a window in the form of a cross, is said to have been his study. No. 2 is slightly larger and has a handsome living-room with a slate floor and a particularly splendid old cupboard made by the carpenter at Coombe. The small gardens in front of both cottages are sheltered and pretty.

From the logbook
The clocks changed last weekend but we didn't find out till Wednesday.

No. 1
for up to 5 people

No. 2
for up to 6 people

Solid fuel stove
Small gardens
Adjacent parking
Dogs allowed

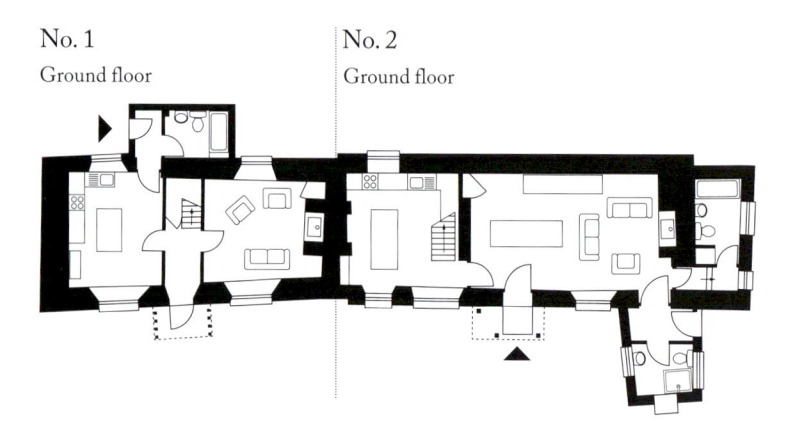

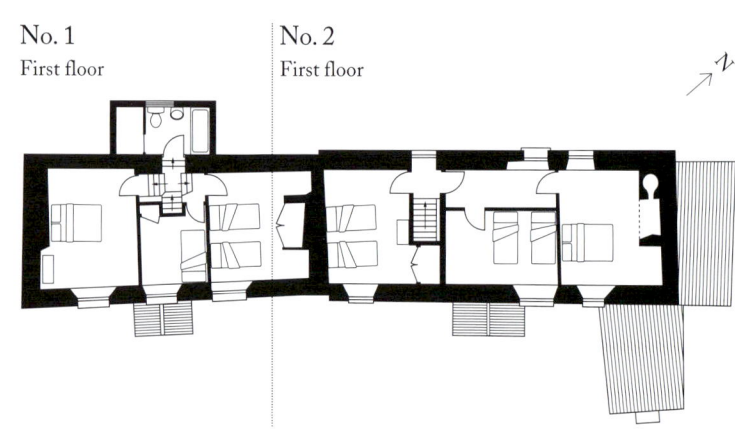

No. 1

No. 2

No. 1
Ground floor

No. 2
Ground floor

No. 1
First floor

No. 2
First floor

Mill House

Mill House dates from before 1700, with later additions, and is divided into two. It is mainly built of stone, with patches of cob, a massive chimney and a thatched and slated roof. The Tape family, living here at the turn of the twentieth century, was a large and musical one, whose children would sing in the evenings or play on the piano, the cornet and the violin. The sitting-room of No. 1, with its wide fireplace, has changed very little since that time. A shallow stream, which you can sit and watch or wade in, runs past a cobbled terrace at the back.

From the logbook
A kingfisher stopped by for breakfast.

We got colour on our faces on a day-trip to Lundy, which is highly recommended.

No. 1
for up to 4 people

No. 2
for up to 3 people

Open fire
Small outside terrace
Adjacent parking
Dogs allowed

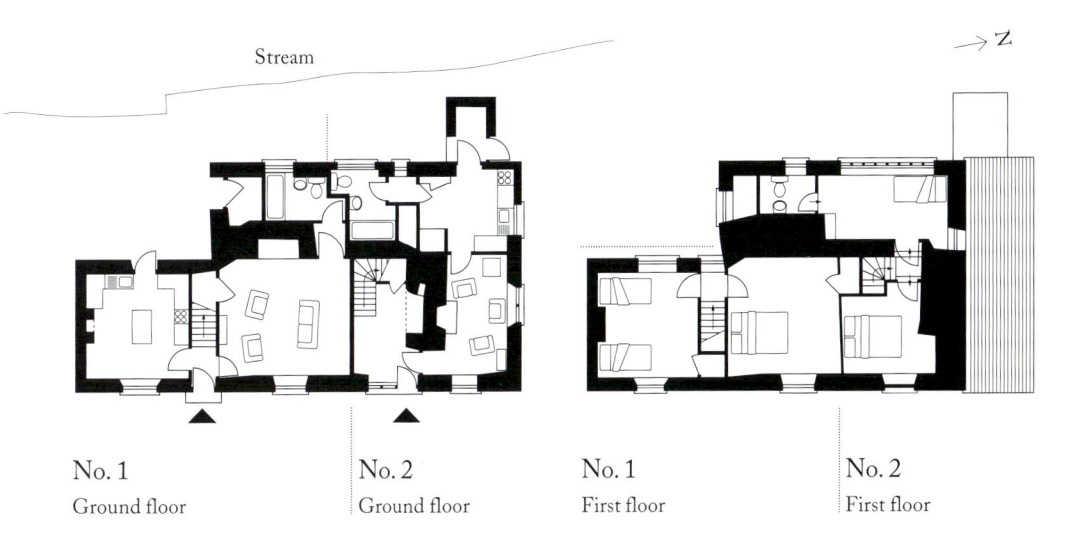

No. 1

No. 2

No. 1 Ground floor | No. 2 Ground floor | No. 1 First floor | No. 2 First floor

Coop House

Netherby, Near Carlisle [C4]

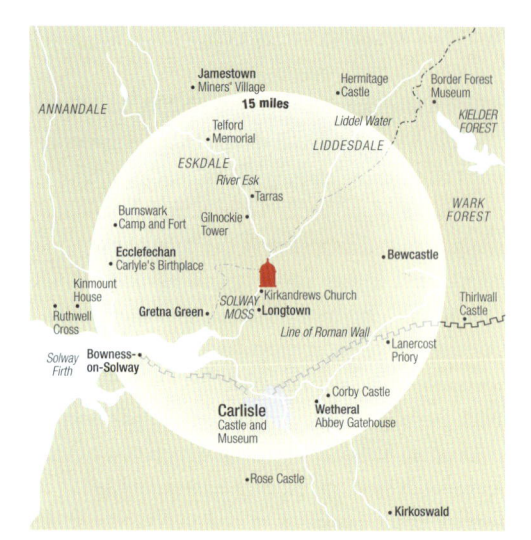

For up to 3 people
Solid fuel stove
Garden

Narrow spiral
staircase

This building serves to remind us of a progressive landowner's efforts in a remote and beautiful place. It stands on the bank of the River Esk, on a high unfenced platform once at the end of a stone weir, in front of which coops or traps were set to catch salmon. The weir was just one of many improvements made to his estate by Dr Robert Graham of Netherby in the 1760s and '70s. Another was to build this summerhouse as an ornament in the landscape around Netherby Hall and as a place to enjoy the river.

Coop House was to prove the more lasting. The river broke up the weir and only blocks of masonry are left, strewn on the river bed. It had in any case annoyed the Scots upstream who, deprived of their salmon catch, marched on Netherby in force – a scene described by Sir Walter Scott in *Redgauntlet*.

Having been for some time an estate cottage, Coop House was given up in 1936 as too remote. By the 1980s it had partly fallen down. The Grahams, who still own Netherby, gave us a lease, and we have laid a long and many-gated track and rebuilt its polygonal main room. With its three windows, this room is designed for watching the Esk as it flows past, sometimes gentle, sometimes in spate. Your nearest neighbours, a little way upstream on the opposite bank, are a pele tower and a graceful Georgian church. Behind are watermeadows, with the imposing pile of Netherby Hall in the distance.

From the logbook
The river is a wonderful companion.

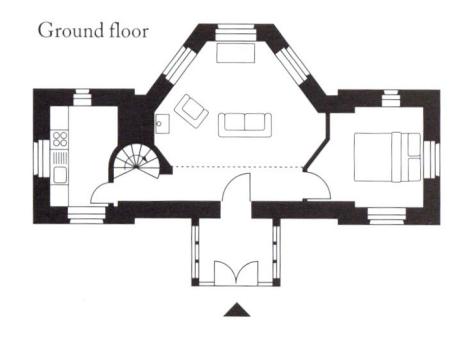

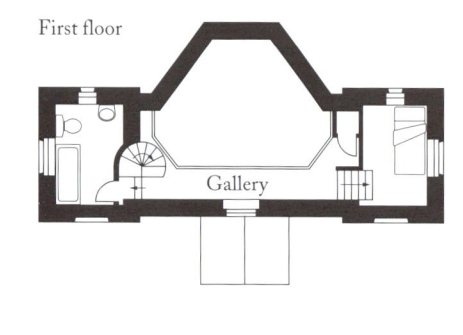

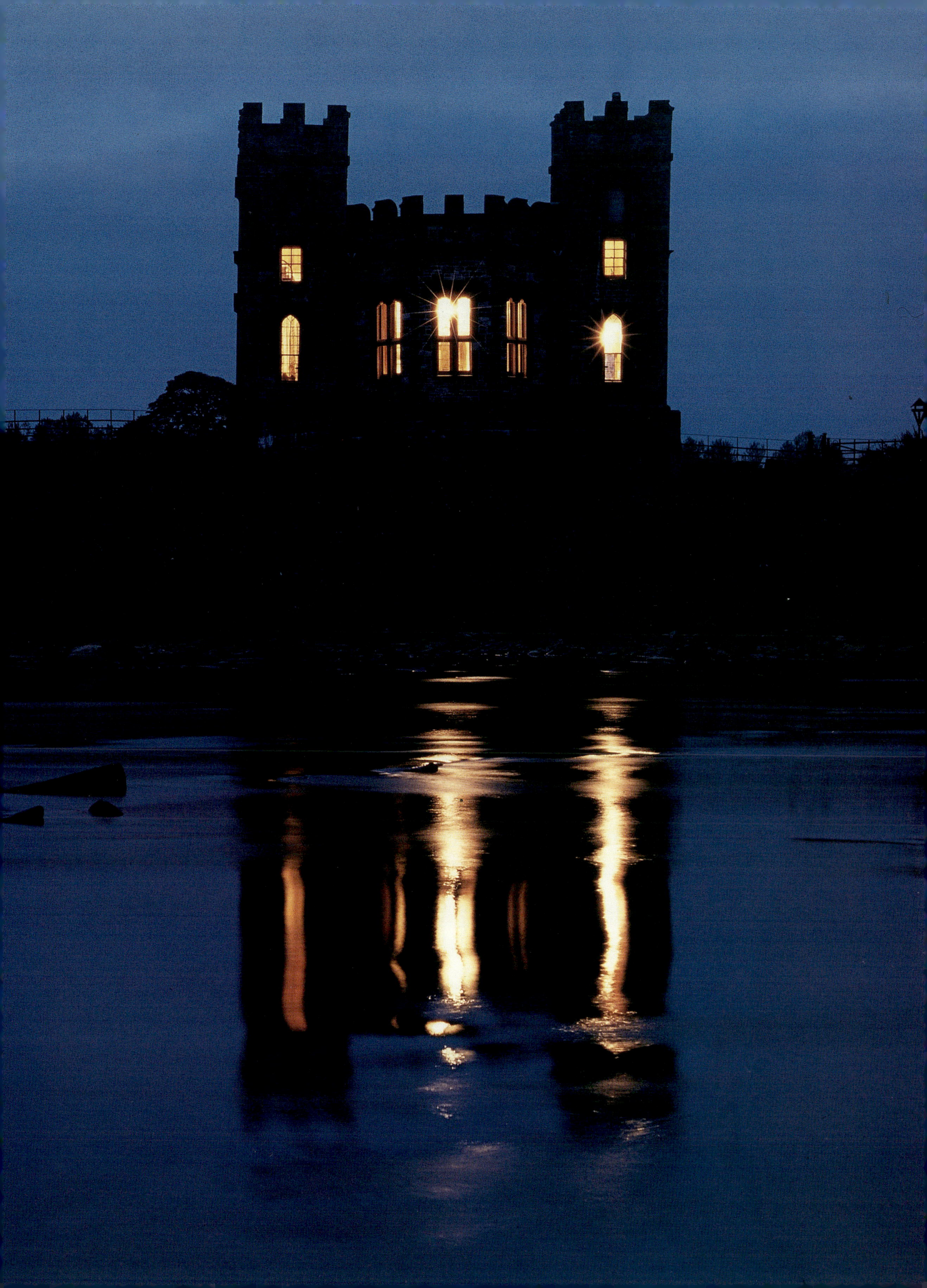

Crownhill Fort

Plymouth, Devon [L3]

For up to 8 people
Enclosed grounds
Open fire
Adjacent parking

In the 1860s it was decided to protect naval bases such as Plymouth from attack by land as well as by sea. A chain of forts was built, with Crownhill in the key position in the north of the city. It is now one of only two large works of this kind in the country to remain in good condition.

From a distance, the Fort blends with the hilltop, defended not by walls but by steep earth ramparts. These enfold the central parade ground, around which are handsome quarters for up to 300 men. For further protection, the buildings and many of the emplacements for 32 large guns have turf roofs, some restored by us. Outside the ramparts is a deep dry ditch, 30 feet wide at the bottom, which could be covered by protective fire from a *chemin de ronde* and six three-storey caponiers, reached from inside the fort by long tunnels.

Since acquiring the Fort in 1987, we have done major work to grounds, weaponry and buildings, many of which are now let to small businesses. In 1995 the Fort was opened to the public for the first time; and in 1998 it was once again armed with a Moncrieff Disappearing Gun, the only working example in the world.

Crownhill fascinates the enthusiast and the novice alike. It is also a remarkably pleasant place to be. The Officers' Quarters in which you stay face south, the kitchen with a large window and a commanding view of the comings and goings. Above all, you have the free run of this spectacular structure of stone and earth.

From the logbook
We only went outside the gate once and that was just to take photos of the gatehouse.

300 feet of shiny polished floor and sock clad kids!

The Fort is open to the public on specific weekends throughout the summer. It is also open all year round for groups by appointment, corporate and private hire, including weddings, and occupied on a daily basis by a range of small businesses.

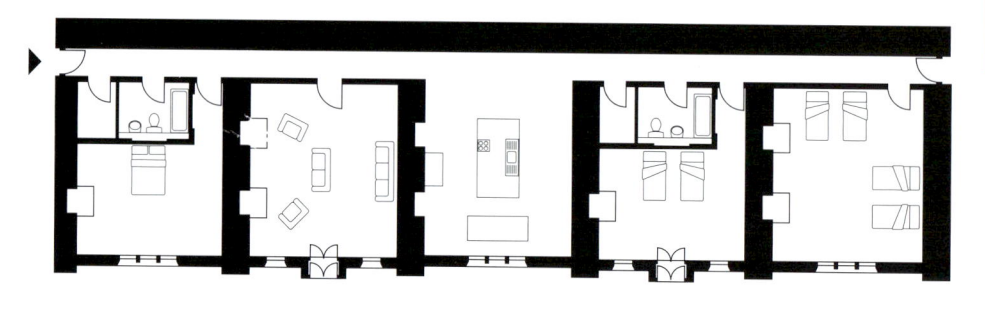

Culloden Tower

Richmond, North Yorkshire [D5]

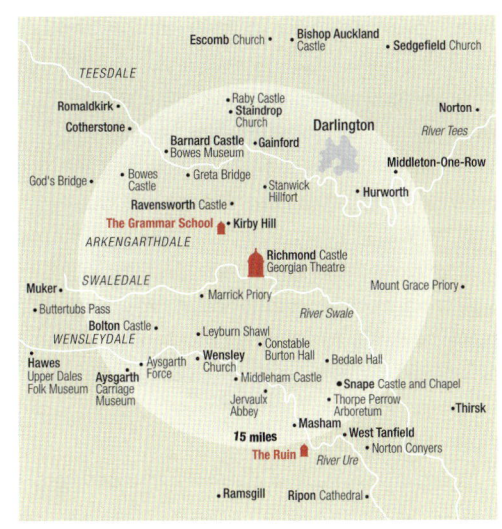

For up to 4 people
Solid fuel stove
Small fenced garden
Roof platform

Parking nearby
Steep spiral staircase
Dogs allowed

This tower was built in 1746 by John Yorke, MP for Richmond, and named to mark the final establishment of Hanoverian rule after the defeat of the Jacobites in the same year. It stands in the park of his long-demolished house, at the edge of a steep slope above the River Swale, on the site of an old pele tower. It was probably designed by Daniel Garrett, also architect of The Banqueting House.

Inside are to be found, one above the other, two tall octagonal rooms, flooded with daylight and of the highest quality. The carving and plaster work of the lower is in a Gothic style, while that of the upper is Classical. Here you will sleep under what must be our grandest bedroom ceiling, worth all the 66 steps you must climb to reach it.

Neglect and vandals had done a great deal of damage by the time we bought the tower, but old photographs and salvaged fragments made restoration possible. It is difficult to imagine, certainly to find, a more romantic situation, looking over the trees of this park with the sight and sound of the Swale hurrying over its rocks and stones below; and with the particularly handsome town of Richmond, which has an eighteenth-century theatre and much more besides, a few hundred yards away.

From the logbook
To have a whole Tower to ourselves – along with an unexpected and amazing roof – was perfect!

The Tower is wonderful – like staying in a large Wedgwood vase…

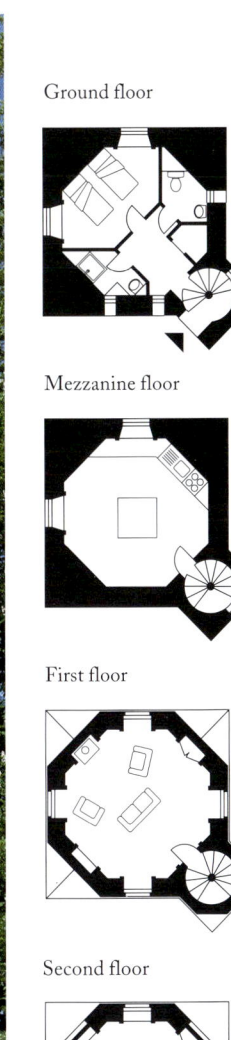

Ground floor

Mezzanine floor

First floor

Second floor

www.landmarktrust.org.uk

Danescombe Mine

Calstock, Cornwall [L3]

For up to 4 people
Solid fuel stove
Wooden decking

Adjacent parking
Steep open staircases
Dogs allowed

These are the monumental buildings of the old Cotehele Consols' copper and arsenic mine. They are unusually well built, handsome and complete, and stand by a stream in a steep wooded valley leading down to the Tamar. We have taken a long lease of them from the National Trust and have consolidated and repaired them, so that it is possible to stay here in comfort and study at close quarters the tremendous past of the Devon and Cornish mines. It was a dreadful but romantic trade which enriched among others the Dukes of Bedford and the family of William Morris.

The engine house, which we have made habitable, is strongly built of the Killas stone in which the lodes occur. It used to contain a rotary beam engine with a 40-inch cylinder driving a Taylor roll crusher, a pump and two buddles on the dressing floor. The mine worked, on and off, from 1822 to 1900, kept alive at the last by the demand for arsenic to protect cotton against the boll weevil.

In the woods above lie the abandoned shafts of other mines; and only a short and beautiful walk away, above the Tamar, is Cotehele, a most notable medieval house.

From the logbook
My favourite Landmark!! Excellent building, wonderful surroundings, beautifully kept – all the superlatives. Sleeping in the top bedroom is like being in a tree house.

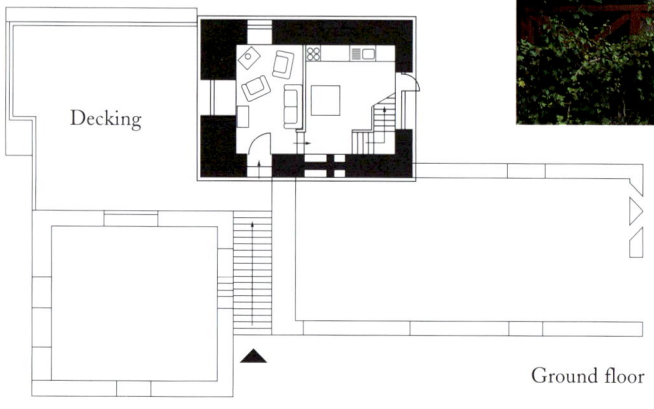

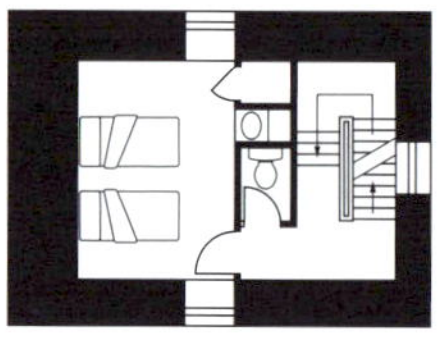

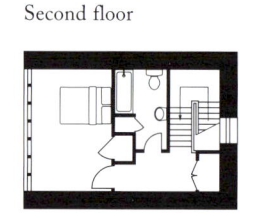

Dolbelydr

Trefnant, Denbighshire [G3]

For up to 6 people
Open fire
Enclosed garden

Adjacent parking
Steep stairs
Dogs allowed

Henry VIII had much to answer for, and for some who live west of the Welsh Marches, not the least of his errors was the imposition of English as the language of government throughout his kingdom. Yet Welsh scholars rose to the challenge of the Tudor regimes, among them humanist and physician Henry Salesbury. Dolbelydr was the family manor and in 1593, Salesbury published his Grammatica Britannica, written in this fine stone house in the pastoral valley of the River Elwy. By imposing a classical discipline on the grammar of this ancient language, his work gives Dolbelydr some claim to be the birthplace of modern Welsh.

The house was built in 1579; when we found it, it had endured a gradual slide from its gentry status, into decades of neglect which had left it finally floorless and roofless. Yet some rare primary features remained, including fine timber mullioned windows. We found the newel post from the original spiral staircase reused in a later one and careful analysis of the building allowed us to reinstate not only this spiral staircase but also the plank-and-muntin screen in their original positions.

On the basis of such survivals, we have taken the house back to its original form, to present a high status sixteenth-century gentry home much as Henry Salesbury would have known it, with first floor solar open to the roof beams and high courtyard walls typical of Denbighshire. Here you may cook and eat communally in the hall, before retiring for civilised conversation to the chamber above, just as the Salesburys would have done. One translation of Dolbelydr is 'Meadow of the Rays of the Sun', an accurate description when the sunlight slants across the valley floor. It is not difficult for the centuries to fall away as you gaze through mullioned windows down this tranquil valley, shared only with the sheep and the deer and the sound of the Elwy.

Open days are held at Dolbelydr annually. Please check our website for details.

From the logbook
Dolbelydr is a sanctuary standing solitary in its timeless valley.

Ground floor

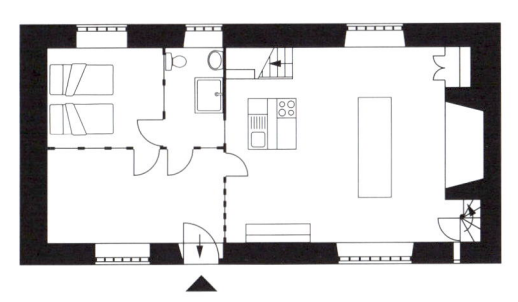

First floor

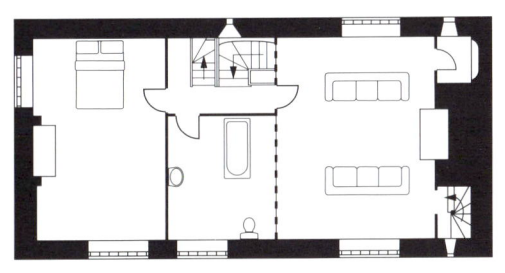

Second floor

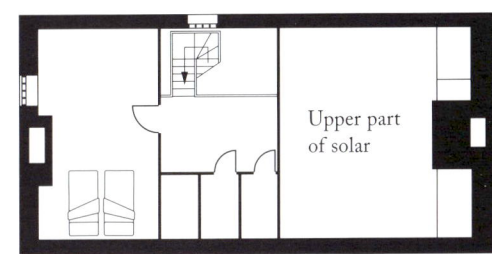

Edale Mill

Edale, Derbyshire [F5]

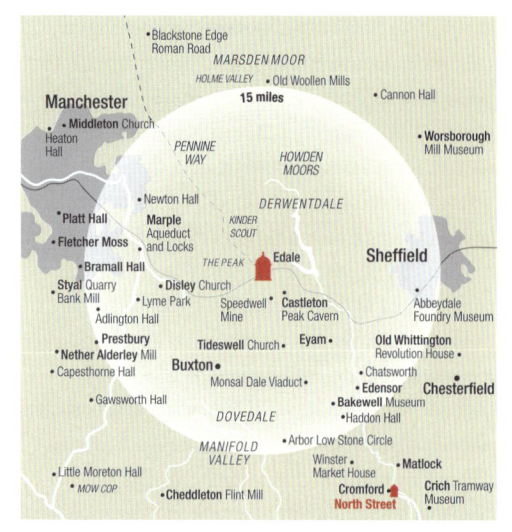

For up to 4 people
Communal grounds

Parking nearby

This cotton mill was built in the late eighteenth century, and during the whole of its long working life survived the hazards of finance and fire, to both of which such mills were prone. After 1800 it was extended at each end, and the stone staircase tower was added. When the Manchester to Sheffield railway was built through the Hope valley in the 1890s it became practicable to use coal; the water wheel was removed and the mill was powered by steam until its then owners, Fine Spinners and Doublers Ltd, closed it in 1934.

We bought it in 1969, restored the slate roof and every single window, and divided the interior into seven dwellings, six of which we sold and one of which, on a middle floor, we kept as a Landmark. Our architect took particular trouble with such details as the downpipes, which were specially made for us square in section, making all the difference to the mill's appearance; we took measures to soundproof between floors, though inevitably some noise remains; and we put cables underground. In spite of these apparent extravagances, the whole project turned out to be economic and the mill, instead of being demolished, now remains an ornament to the dale and a monument to those who laboured in it.

From the logbook
Generally, my husband stayed in and read about the walks while I went out and did them.

The right combination of luxury and puritanism.

Just imagine it with all the looms clattering away.

The Landmark apartment is at the right-hand end of the mill building, on the second floor.

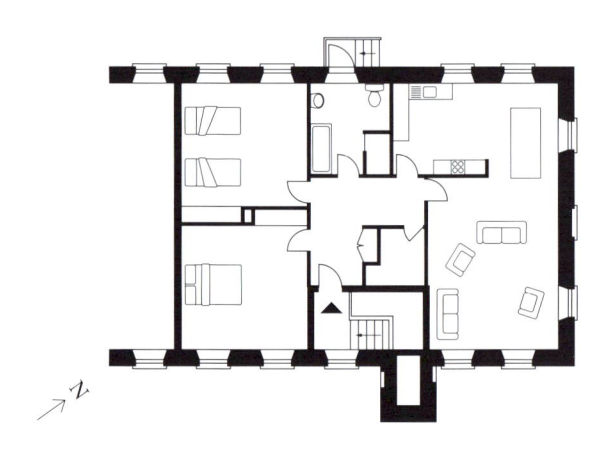

The Egyptian House

Chapel Street, Penzance, Cornwall [L1]

This is a rare and noble survivor of a style that enjoyed a vogue after Napoleon's campaign in Egypt of 1798. It dates from about 1835 and the front elevation is very similar to that of the former Egyptian Hall in Piccadilly, designed in 1812 by P. F. Robinson. Robinson or Foulston of Plymouth are the most likely candidates for its design, though there is no evidence to support the claim of either.

It was built for John Lavin as a museum and geological repository. When we bought it in 1968, its colossal façade, with lotus bud capitals and enrichments of Coade stone, concealed two small granite houses above shops, solid and with a pleasant rear elevation, but very decrepit inside. In the course of our work to the front, we reconstructed these as three compact apartments, the highest of which has a view through a small window of Mounts Bay and St Michael's Mount, over the chimney pots of the town.

Why was there a geological shop here? Although picked over by the Victorians (doubtless including Mr Lavin) the beaches at Penzance still hold every kind of pebble, from quartz to chalcedony. Penzance itself, accessible by train as well as by road, is a handsome town, and you will find yourselves at its bustling heart. Beyond it lies that hard old peninsula in which, at places like Chysauster and the Botallack mine, can be found moving evidence of human labour, over an immense span of time.

From the logbook
No photograph or drawing can depict the astonishing and eccentric elevation of the Egyptian House.

Arriving and departing by train we made extensive use of the coastal bus system to travel wherever we wanted to go.

We've enjoyed our 'Flight into Egypt'.

We much appreciated the furniture and delighted in the witty Egyptian motifs.

One apartment for 3 and two for 4.

First floor
for up to 3 people

Second floor
for up to 4 people

Third floor
for up to 4 people

Gas coal fire
No private parking
Narrow oval staircase

First floor

First floor

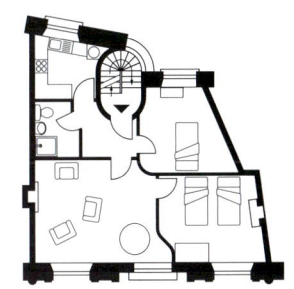

Second floor

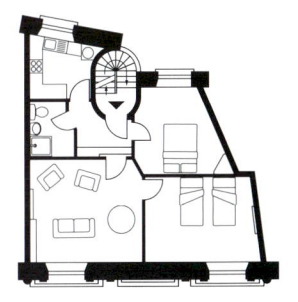

Third floor

Elton House

Abbey Street, Bath [J5]

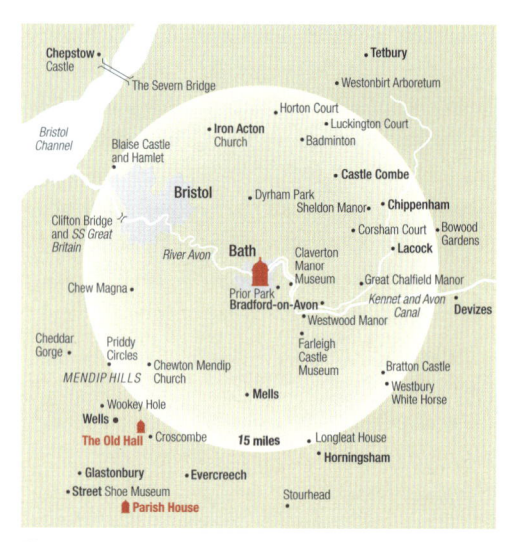

Elton House overlooks Abbey Green, in the centre of Bath. It was given to us, with much desirable furniture, by Miss Philippa Savery, a gallant campaigner for the city's preservation. The earliest part of it dates from just before 1700, but it was subsequently enlarged and re-fronted, becoming by 1750 a handsome robust building on several floors, with a fine staircase and excellent joinery, arranged as sets of lodgings. Thereafter the fashionable world moved up the hill, away from Abbey Green; part of the ground floor became a shop and the rest of the house stayed as it was. It is therefore something of a rarity, even for Bath.

From the logbook

Beautiful house close to everything you need to see in the centre of Bath. Felt as though I belonged to the city for a weekend.

Bath kept us well entertained for the whole week.

Elton House is a large historic house which manages to feel intimate and welcoming.

Walks to Beckford's Tower … the American museum at Claverton …the Sham Castle.

For up to 10 people
Small walled garden
No private parking

Other Landmarks in Bath:
Marshal Wade's House
Beckford's Tower

68 The Landmark Trust Handbook

First floor

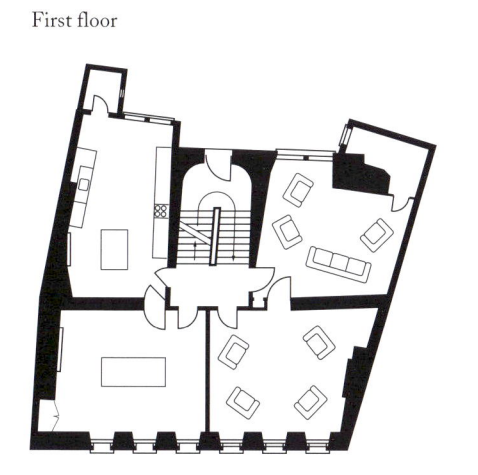

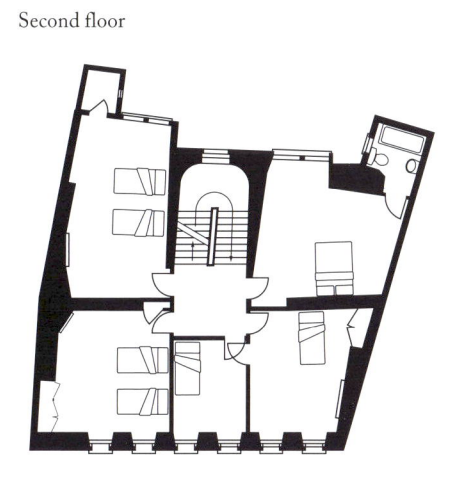

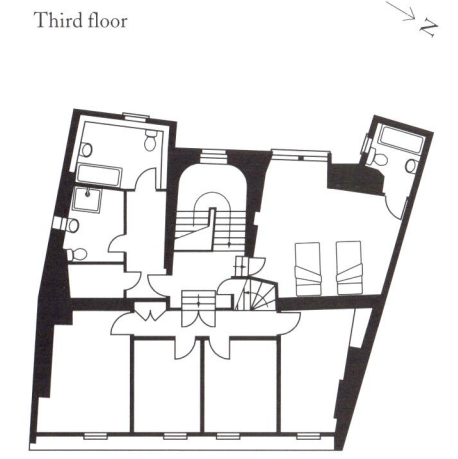

Second floor

Third floor

Endsleigh

Near Tavistock, Devon [L3]

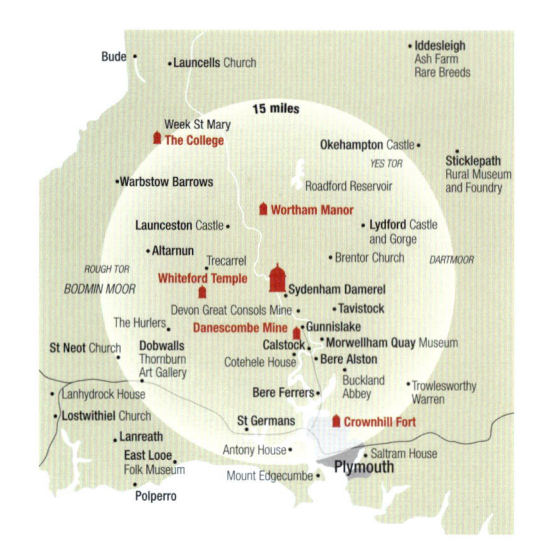

This most naturally beautiful stretch of the River Tamar (Turner, among others, sketched here and called it 'altogether Italian') was chosen by Georgiana, Duchess of Bedford, as the setting for a new house; between 1810 and 1816 both Humphry Repton and Jeffrey Wyatville played a part in shaping it to perfection, and in placing suitable buildings within it.

Endsleigh today is still a very complete example of that most imaginative and English taste, the Picturesque. From the 1950s, most of it was leased and then owned by a fishing syndicate, who used the main house, known as the Cottage, as a fishing lodge-cum-hotel and did much to restore the garden and arboretum. Other parts of the woods were sold separately, and it was inevitable that unfunctional buildings should suffer. It was to save some of them that we became involved. Then, in 2004, the fishing syndicate decided that it was no longer feasible for it to maintain so large an estate and so the Cottage and grounds were sold for use as a discreet private hotel. Our two Landmarks, safe within their freehold tenure, are sufficiently secluded to be unaffected by such changes in ownership and continue their tranquil existence.

Pond Cottage

In 1983 we took on the Dairy, a strongly Picturesque building, and with it Pond Cottage, previously used by visiting fishermen (you too can fly-fish in the pond). Both buildings were designed by Wyatville, but the idea for creating 'Dairy Dell', with its streams and cascades, its still dark pond and overhung ancient well, was Repton's, proposed in his *Red Book* for Endsleigh.

Pond Cottage has a Rustic porch, with tree-trunk columns and honeysuckle, and cosy rooms. The Dairy, which had to be rescued from the undergrowth, is perched on a knoll above, a cool chamber of marble (a local variety) and ivy-leaf tiles. From its verandah, 'embosomed', as Repton put it, 'in all the sublimity of umbrageous majesty', you may open yourself to those keen responses to the surrounding scene that were so carefully planned by its creators – while contemplating the making of a very superior butter.

For up to 5 people
Open fire
Parking a short walk away
Garden with stream and pond
Dogs allowed

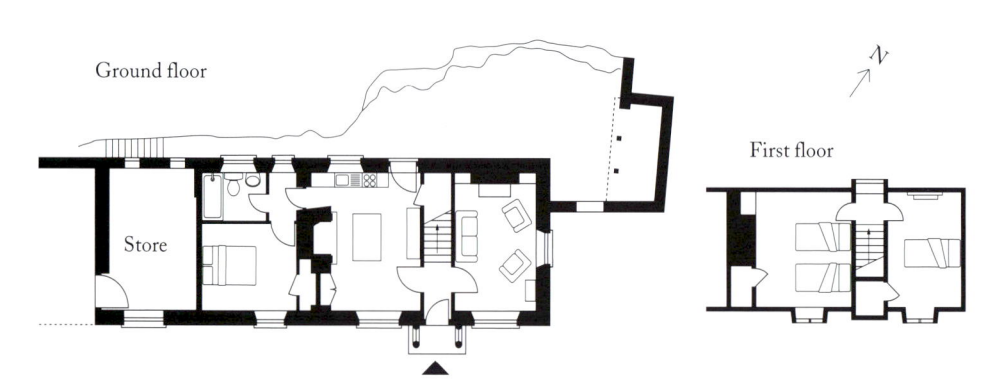

Swiss Cottage

In 1977 we aquired Swiss Cottage, perhaps the most important of Endsleigh's buildings. It is an early, and wonderfully well-made, example of the nineteenth-century passion for the Alps, designed in about 1815 by Wyatville, complete with an Alpine garden, and Swiss furniture and crockery. We repaired it and reversed some later alterations. In 2007, a chance find in an auction room enabled us to reinstate the original corner cupboard in the main room. Opening on to a verandah, this room was used by the Dukes for picnics and shooting lunches and there, perched high above the steep drop to the river, you have a heady feeling of surveying a world apart.

For up to 2+2 people
Steep garden
Low ceiling on top floor
Parking a short walk away
Dogs allowed

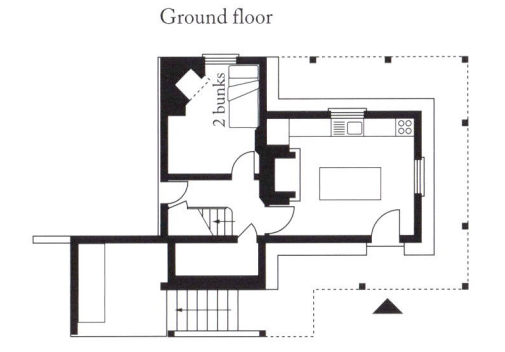

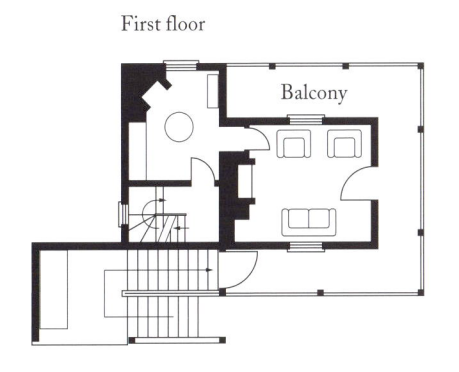

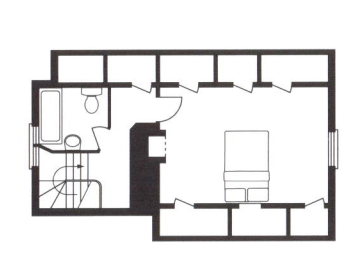

Field House

Minchinhampton, Gloucestershire [I5]

This handsome stone house was left to us with the surrounding land by Miss Eileen Jenkins, who had lived here for the previous 20 years. It is an unusual building, since although it looks like a single house, and indeed has been one for over a century, it was clearly once four separate dwellings round a narrow yard, each with one room up and one down. But by 1884 the yard had been roofed over and filled with a staircase, and the whole building became one farmhouse.

The thick party walls of the old dwellings give Field House a pleasant solid feel inside. It stands in a large and sheltered walled garden high up on the top of the Cotswolds, once a land of sheep but now more given over to the horse.

From the logbook
Our seventh Landmark and the most comfortable and child-friendly.

Enjoyed our stay at Field House thoroughly, especially eating the ripe figs from the tree in the garden for breakfast and blackberries from the hedge.

We really found it difficult sometimes to leave Field House and garden to explore more of the Cotswolds.

For up to 6 people
Open fire
Large enclosed garden
Adjacent parking
Dogs allowed

Ground floor

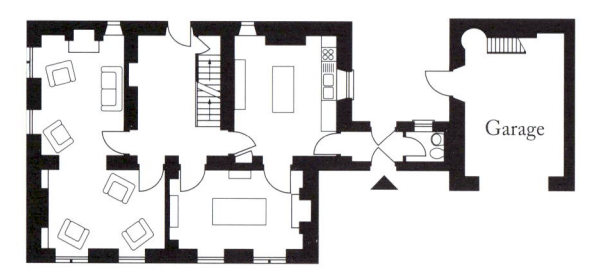

First floor

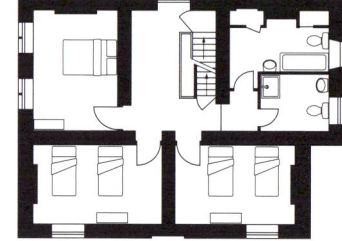

72   The Landmark Trust Handbook

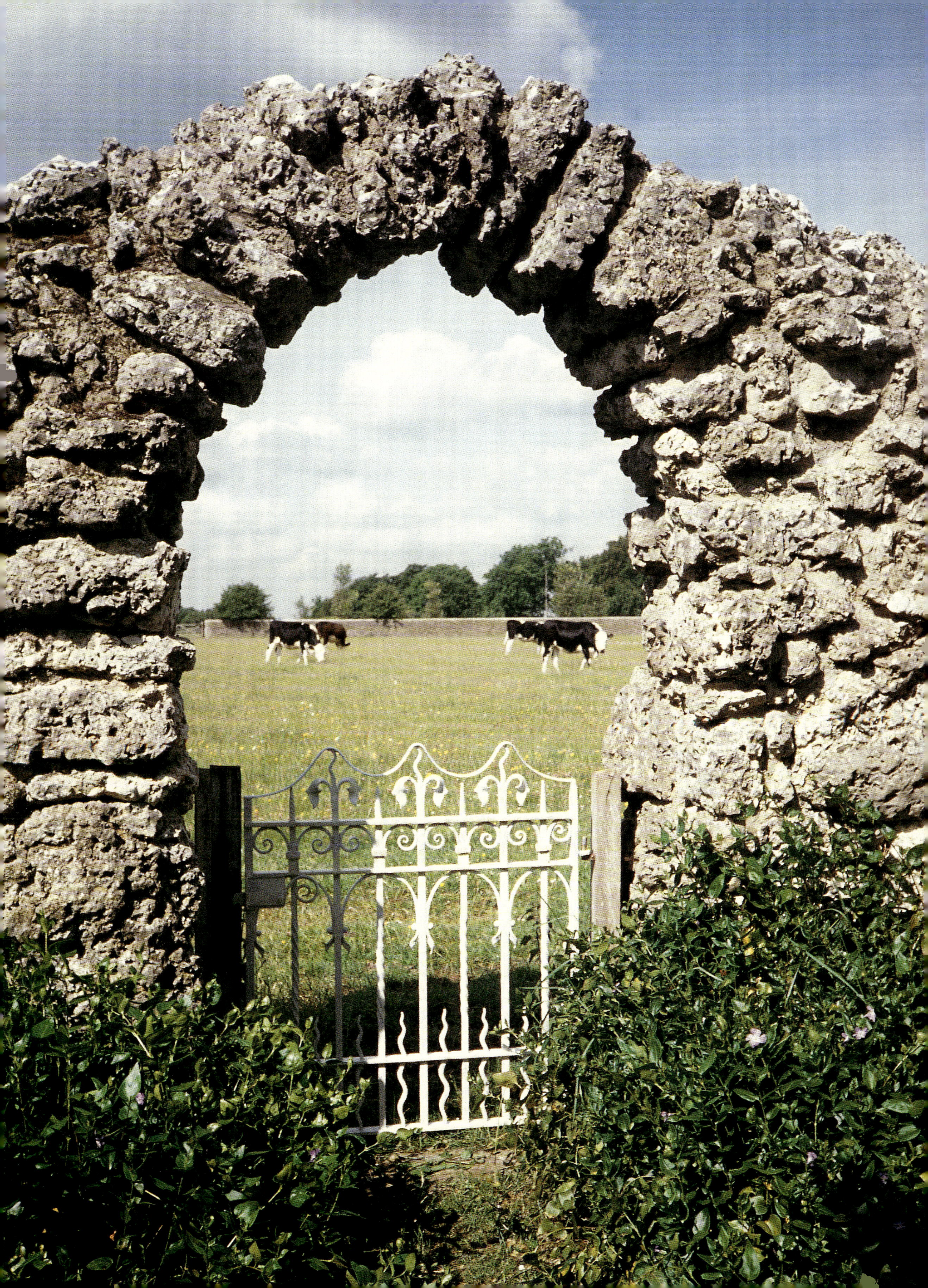

Fort Clonque

Alderney, Channel Islands [M5]

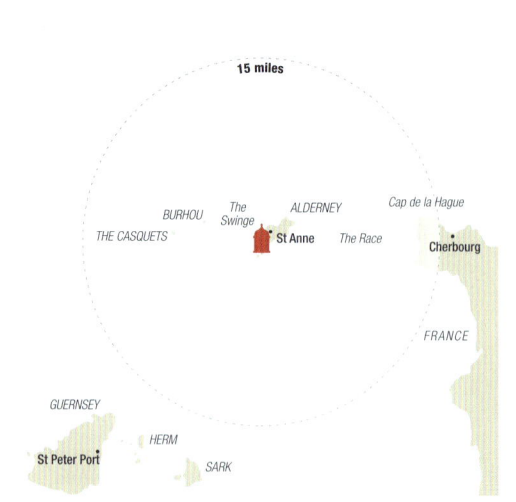

For up to 13 people
Open fire
The island can be cut off at high tide

There are flights to Alderney from Southampton and Bournemouth

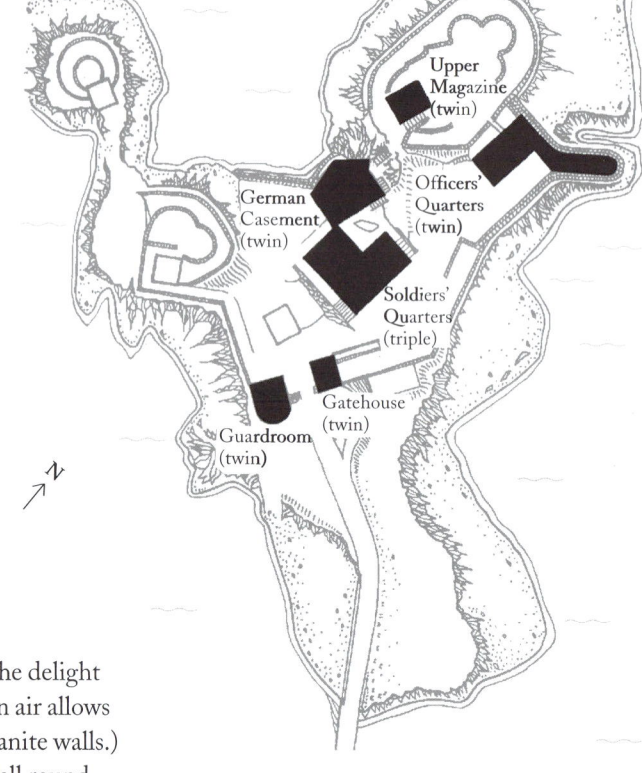

In the 1840s it was thought that the advent of steam would make the Channel Islands more important as an advanced naval base, and also more liable to capture by the French. Accordingly the great harbour works of Alderney were begun in 1847. Fort Clonque, the most remarkable of them, occupies a group of large rocks off the steep south-west tip of the island, commanding the passage between it and Burhou. It is reached by a causeway leading to a drawbridge entrance and was originally designed for ten 64-pounder guns in four open batteries, manned by two officers and 50 men.

Very soon, however, the further development of steam brought the Channel Islands within easy reach of mainland bases, and made another in Alderney unnecessary. In 1886 the Defence Committee recommended that Clonque, and all the other works except Fort Albert, should be disarmed but left standing.

It was thus that Hitler found them in 1940 and, imagining again that the Channel Islands had strategic value, vigorously refortified them. At Fort Clonque part of the Victorian soldiers' quarters was replaced by an enormous casemate, housing a gun so large that its emplacement now makes a handsome bedroom looking towards Guernsey.

Most forts are of necessity large and grim, but Clonque, because it has had to be fitted to the great rocks round which it is built, is small, open and picturesque, ingeniously contrived on many levels, with stretches of grass, samphire and mesembryanthemum here and there. Any cold or damp, characteristic of such a fort, will be more than compensated for by the delight of its spectacular setting. (The clean air allows all sorts of lichen to grow on the granite walls.) On calm days the sea can be heard all round, restlessly searching the rocks; and on rough days it is comforting to reflect that the wall of the East Flank Battery is 19 feet thick. During some high tides the fort is cut off and the sea runs between it and the mainland.

The marine views are second to none: of the other islands, rocks and stacks; of two great colonies of gannets, which fish round the fort; of the lighthouses on the Casquets; and of the formidable race or current called the Swinge, which runs between Clonque and Burhou.

On all counts Fort Clonque is a most worthwhile place to have tackled, not least because when we embarked on it in 1966 military works such as this were disregarded everywhere. The rest of **Alderney** is also extremely pleasant; the island **is just small** enough to be explored entirely on foot or, **very** easily, by bicycle; all the Victorian and German defence works are interesting; the beaches at the north end are exceptional; and in the centre is St Anne, a very pretty little town, English with a hint of France.

From the logbook
The fort is fantastic, especially during a good blow, when the sky rains sea foam!

It was like being in a big granite ocean liner!

The cycling on Alderney is fabulous.

Officers' Quarters

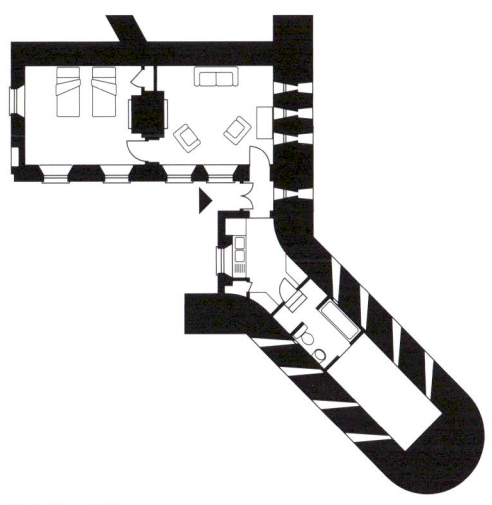

Soldiers' Quarters

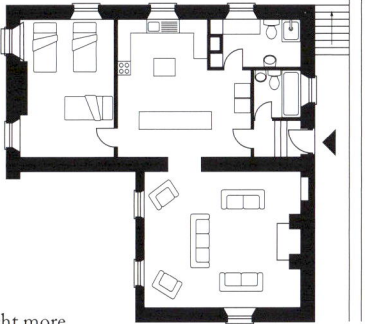

There are eight more beds in other parts of the fort, as shown on the plan opposite.

www.landmarktrust.org.uk 75

Fox Hall

Charlton, West Sussex [K7]

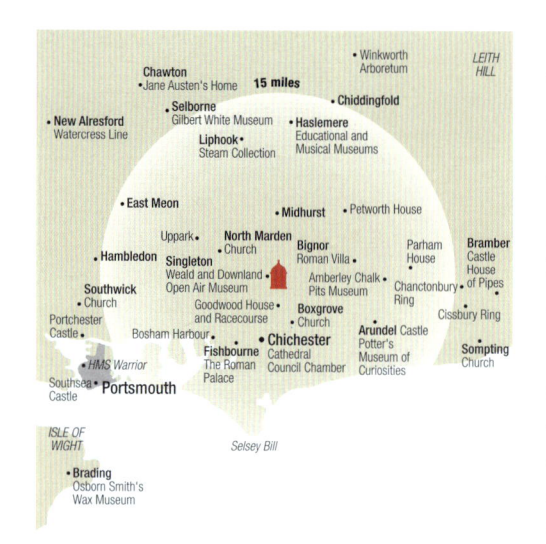

For up to 2+2 people
Open fire
Garden
Adjacent parking

Charlton is just a small village, but at one time, when the Charlton Hunt was famous and fashionable, its name was familiar and dear to every sportsman in England. Even Goodwood was described as 'near Charlton'. The hunt was founded in the 1670s by the Duke of Monmouth and was continued after his death by his son-in-law the Duke of Bolton and then by the Duke of Richmond.

Apart from the sport, what attracted high-spirited noblemen here, surely, was that they could live in lodgings away from the constraints of home. They clubbed together and built a dining-room for themselves, which they christened 'Fox Hall', designed by Lord Burlington, no less, and here 'these votaries of Diana feasted after the chase and recounted the feats of the day'. Not to miss such affairs and to be in good time for the meets, the Duke of Richmond commissioned the small Palladian building that we now possess. The designer of this rich sample of architecture, built in 1730, was most probably Lord Burlington's assistant Roger Morris.

It consists of a plain brick box with a small stylish hall and staircase leading to one magnificent room above, undoubtedly Britain's premier bedsit. There is a gilded alcove for the Duke's bed and in the pediment over the fireplace an indicator shows the direction of the wind, important information for the fox hunter. The front door to all this grandeur leads very sensibly straight to the stable yard.

In the 1750s the Hunt was moved away from Charlton to Goodwood. The old Fox Hall disappeared and somehow its name was transferred to our building a few yards off, which, grievously altered, for a long time housed the manager of the Duke of Richmond's sawmill. So far as possible we have given it back its original form.

Apart from Fox Hall, and a detail or two in some of the houses, no visible trace remains at Charlton of the famous Hunt; but the pub is called The Fox Goes Free, a modest clue to great doings here in former times.

Ground floor

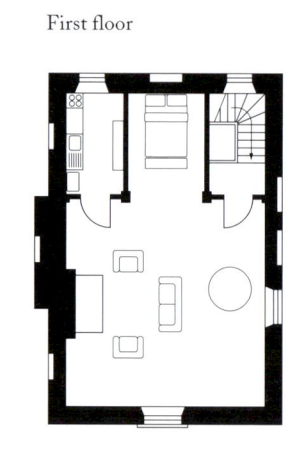

First floor

Frenchman's Creek

Helford, Cornwall [L2]

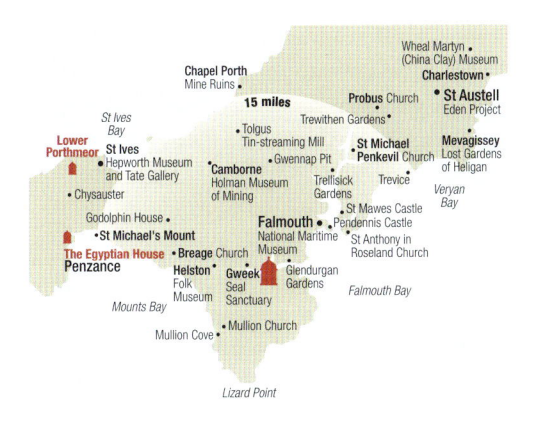

You can see small granite cottages like this in their hundreds in Cornwall, but it would be hard to find one in a more remote, romantic and secluded place than this, tucked down at the head of Frenchman's Creek on the Helford River. It was built in about 1840 for a farm worker or boatman; there were once two more cottages here and a small quay. Between the Wars, it was rented as a retreat by Maria Pendragon and Clara Vyvyan, who describes it in her book *The Helford River*. The last inhabitants moved out a few years ago, and the National Trust, which owns the land around, suggested a joint scheme to us, as the only alternative to letting it fall down.

The Creek, one of many along the shores of the tidal river, runs like a finger, deep into the woods, giving brief sparkling glimpses of water between the trees; at high tide it is passable by boat. The quarter-mile path down to the cottage is steep (and sometimes slippery; you may need to leave your car at the top). In summer you descend into greenness, for the woods are mainly oak, with the light filtered through leaves. It is a place for those who worship the woods and the water and are prepared to be temporarily dominated by them. Should you want to go elsewhere there is the Lizard to explore, and Mounts Bay, or to the east the granite elegance of Falmouth.

For up to 4 people
Solid fuel stove
Garden
Parking nearby
Dogs allowed

Ground floor

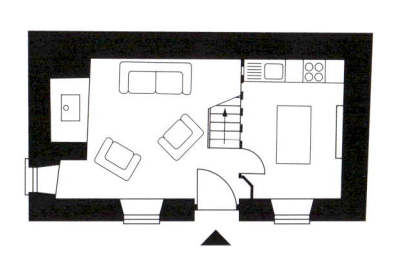

First floor

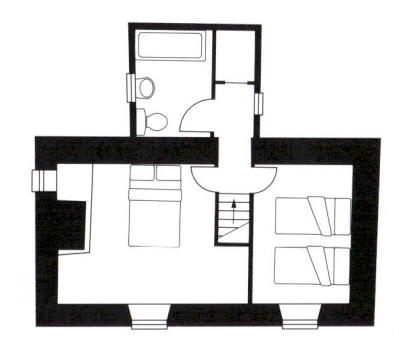

www.landmarktrust.org.uk

Freston Tower

Near Ipswich, Suffolk [I9]

For up to 4 people
Small enclosed garden

Adjacent parking
Steep spiral staircase
Dogs allowed

Freston Tower was given to Landmark through the great generosity of its owner, who wished it to have a secure future and be enjoyed by many. Set in old and undulating parkland of oaks, sweet chestnuts, cedar and beech trees, the tower was built in the mid-1550s overlooking the broad expanse of the River Orwell estuary. We have yet to discover why or by whom it was built, but its most likely builder was a wealthy Ipswich merchant called Thomas Gooding who bought Freston Manor in 1553.

Freston Tower was built both to admire from the outside and to look out from on the inside – there are no fewer than 26 windows dotted over its six storeys, arranged in careful hierarchy. Its crisp brickwork with distinctive blue diapering suggests that it was always intended to perform as an eyecatcher in the landscape. It may also have acted as a lookout tower for Gooding's returning ships, or simply as an extravagant folly (and if so, one of the earliest in the country). It may even have been built to coincide with Queen Elizabeth's progress to Ipswich in 1561, when the citizens were warned in advance of Perambulacion [of] liberty by water with the Queen. There shall be two vessells or botes decently furnished to attend upon the Queen's Majestie so far as the liberty doe extend.'

Just as it did to build, this carefully designed tower demanded the highest standards of craftsmanship to restore. Using early photographs as sources, we re-rendered the brick mullions and window surrounds in imitation of stone, a building material so lacking in East Anglia.

We chose to put the sitting-room on the top floor, to take advantage of unrivalled views of the River Orwell and its handsome modern bridge. Did Sir Thomas Gooding go one stage further, as our visitors may, and sit amid the pinnacles to make a banquet house of the roof? We cannot be sure of this either, but it would certainly be in keeping with the bravura of this fine tower.

From the logbook
We have enjoyed living vertically for a week – sad to be coming back down to earth.

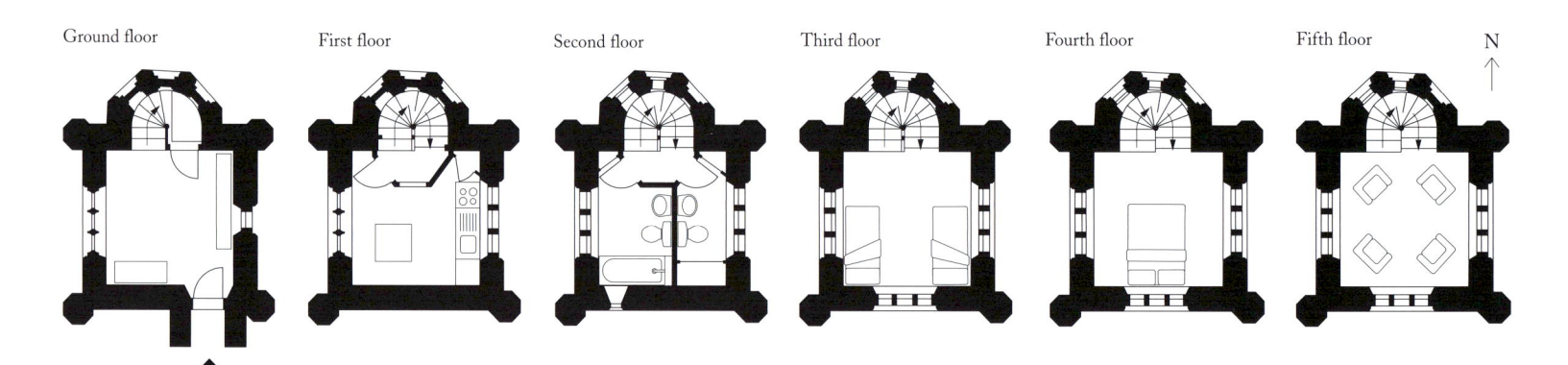

Ground floor　First floor　Second floor　Third floor　Fourth floor　Fifth floor

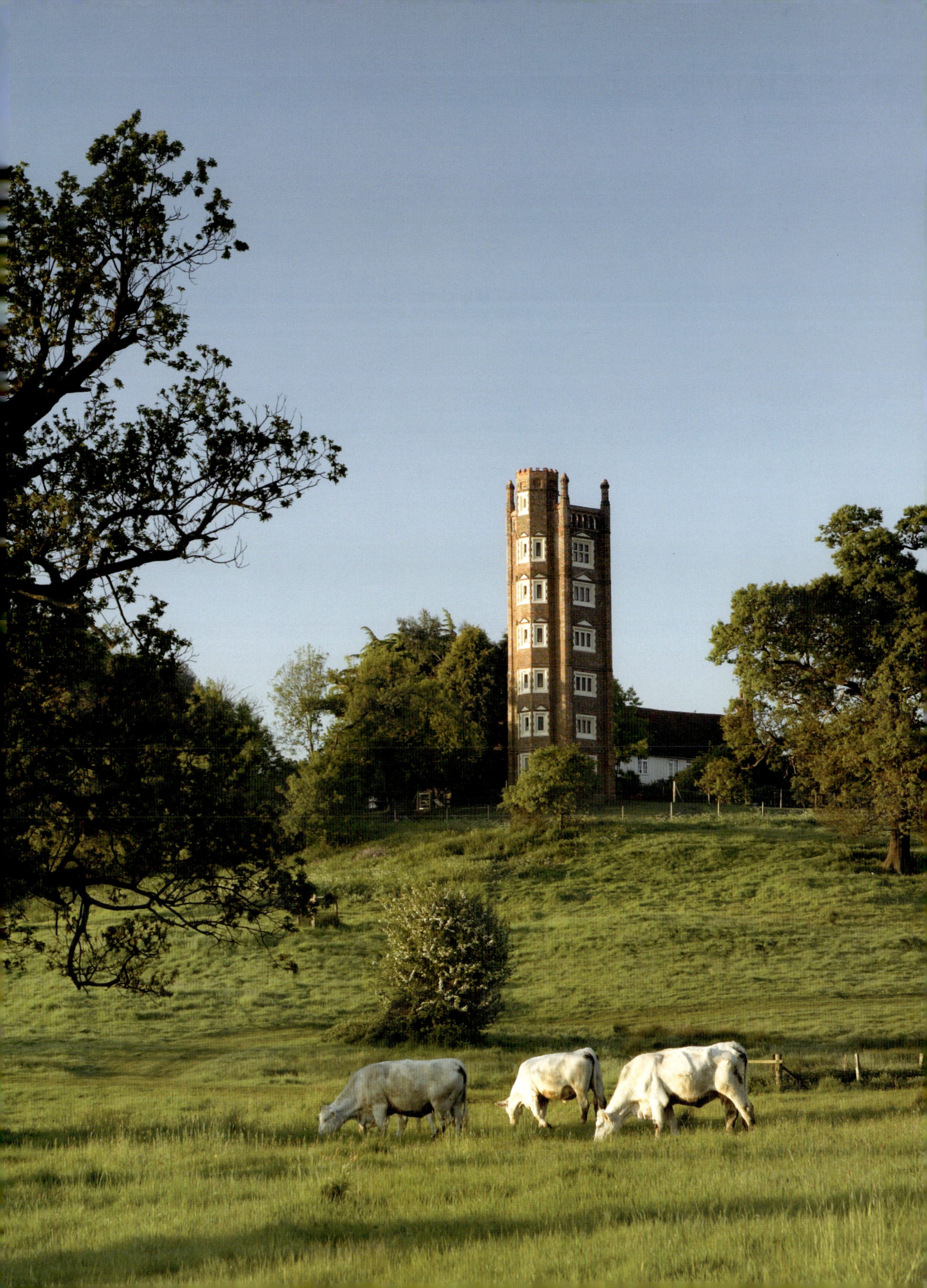

Gargunnock House

Near Stirling, Central Scotland [A3]

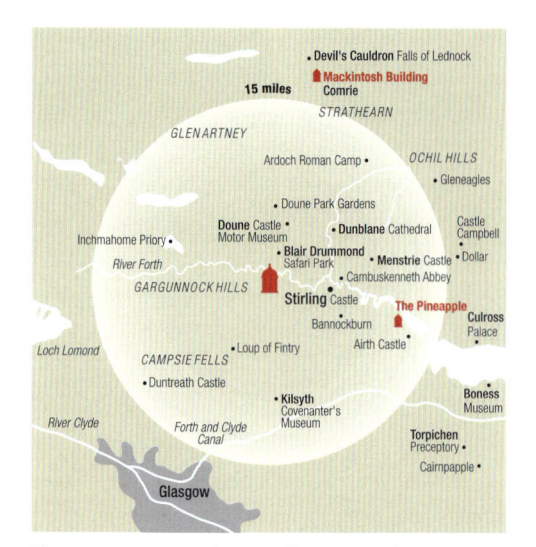

For up to 16 people
Open fire
Large garden
Adjacent parking

The main front of Gargunnock, when approached through the park, looks regular, classical, serenely late Georgian. But this façade of 1794 is only skin deep, imposing order on additions made then and in the previous two centuries to an old tower, which still forms the core of the house.

The old tower also dictates that the main rooms are on the first floor, above the traditional vaulted basement. Of these, unquestionably the finest is the drawing-room; it contains a piano (now ornamental) on which, just possibly, Frédéric Chopin once played. Gargunnock was bought in 1835 by Charles Stirling, a Glasgow merchant and son of an old Perthshire family. His sister, Jane, was Chopin's pupil and friend. She brought him to Scotland in 1848, taking him to stay with her sisters and cousins, and family tradition is firm that he came here too.

The late Miss Viola Stirling was the last of her family. She left Gargunnock to trustees who now let it, with our help, for holidays. Staying here feels rather as if the family has gone away for a while. They have taken their personal things with them, but the furniture remains, the flower garden is cared for, the park is grazed and the estate maintained in orderly fashion.

There is fine country in all directions, and Stirling is nearby, but most of all you can enjoy living briefly in this graceful and pleasantly old-fashioned country house at the foot of the Gargunnock Hills.

The gardens are open to the public on Wednesdays in April, May, September and October.

There is a further double bedroom, twin bedroom and two bathrooms on the third floor.

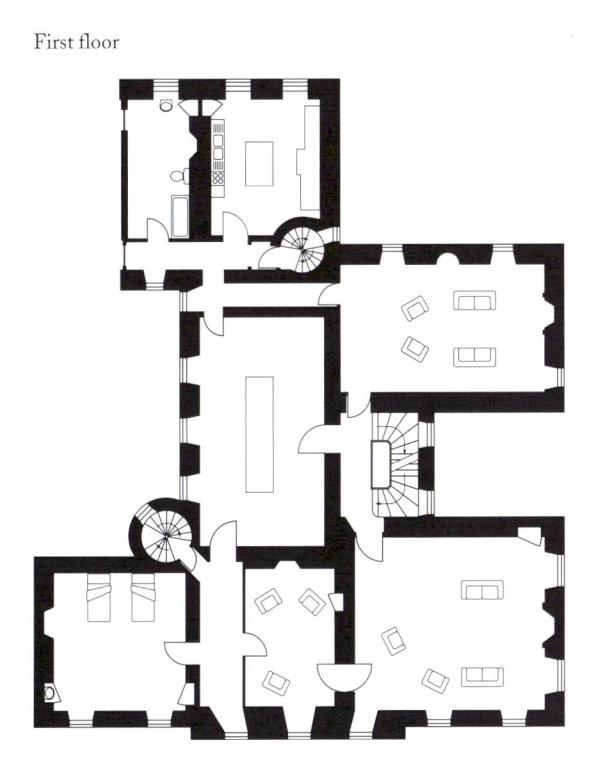

First floor

Second floor

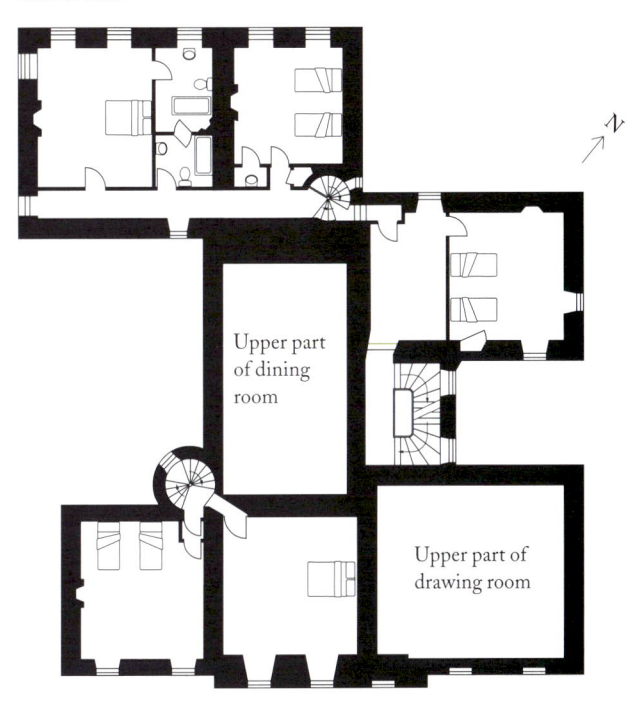

Glenmalloch Lodge

Newton Stewart, Dumfries and Galloway [C2]

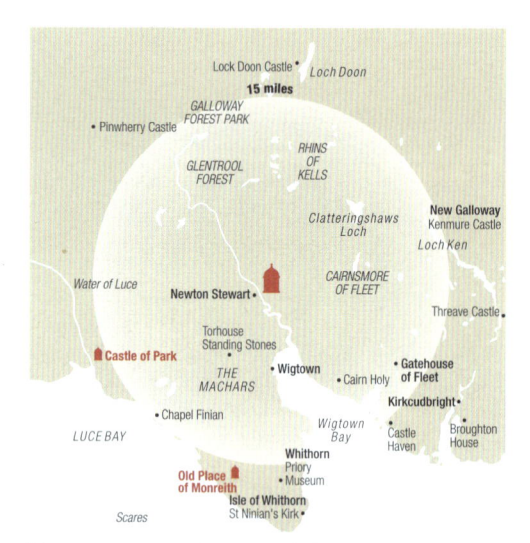

For up to 2 people
Solid fuel stove
Enclosed garden
Adjacent parking
Dogs allowed

Glenmalloch Lodge represents the aristocratic philanthropy that characterised the Victorian Age at its best. It lies in the middle of a wild glen, framed by wide views of the surrounding hills, with the Solway Firth just a mile or so away. The cottage was built originally not as a lodge, but rather as a picturesque schoolhouse through the philanthropy of Harriet, Countess of Galloway, some time before 1842. The Earls of Galloway had been shaping and planning these Galloway parishes for decades and Harriet worked with her husband, the 9th Earl, to orchestrate an impressive programme of educational and social initiatives over some forty years. Once, twenty-five girls were instructed in reading, writing, arithmetic and needlework in this tiny building.

The cottage's pretty overhanging eaves give the impression of a building snuggling down into its setting. A handsome bay window hints at an opulence of detail despite the wildness around and the whole is an endearing mix of Classical, Tudor and Gothic elements. The Countess of Galloway clearly wished to demonstrate that she accorded some importance to education.

We had no hesitation in taking a long lease to enable this delightful remnant of a countess's bounty to be saved. Claiming it as your own for a spell we think you will agree that the Countess of Galloway's generous embellishment of a humble building in the cause of education was not been in vain.

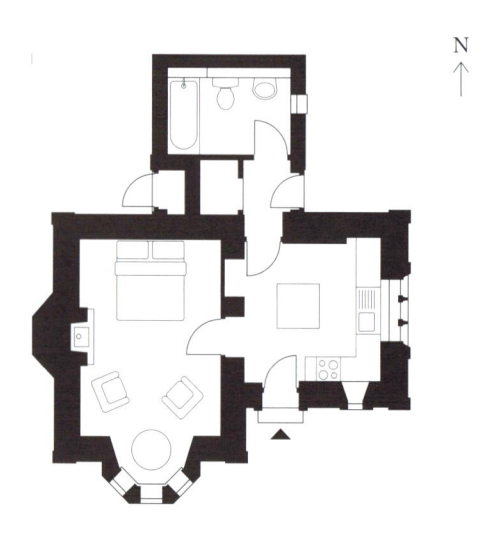

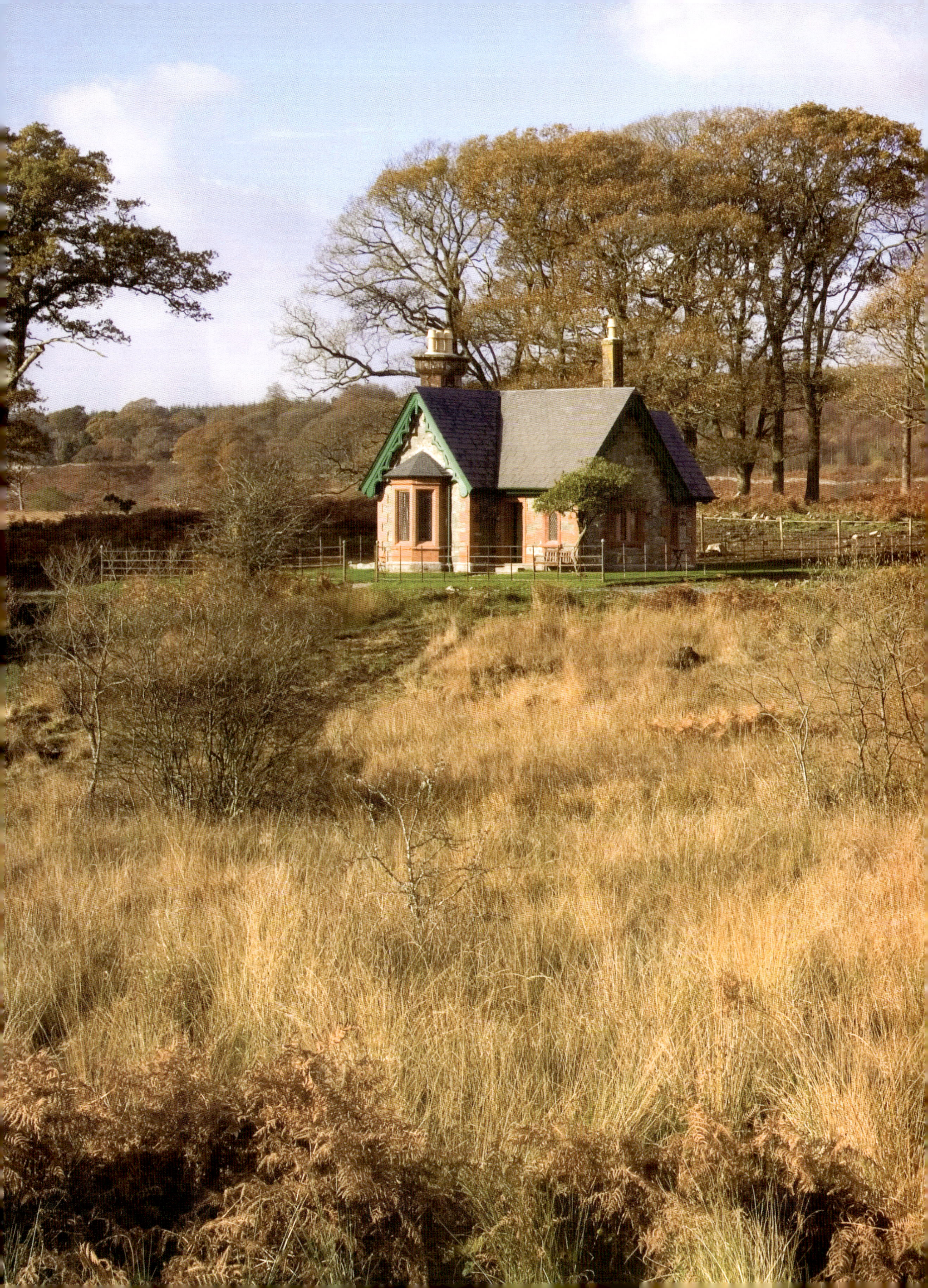

Goddards

Abinger Common, Surrey [J7]

For up to 12 people
Open fire
Adjacent parking

Dogs allowed
Large enclosed garden

Goddards was built by Edwin Lutyens from 1898–1900 and enlarged by him in 1910. It is considered one of his most important early houses, designed in the traditional Surrey style and with a garden laid out in collaboration with Gertrude Jekyll.

The commission was an unusual one. In the words of Lawrence Weaver, writing on Lutyens' houses in 1913, it was built 'as a Home of Rest to which ladies of small means might repair for holiday'. This was the idea of Frederick Mirrielees, a wealthy businessman who had married an heiress of the Union Castle shipping line. A central range with common rooms on both floors divided two cottages, the southern of which also contained a bowling alley. Here Lutyens played a game of skittles in 1901 with the three nurses and two old governesses then staying here. They all loved the house and 'invariably weep when they leave it'.

In 1910 Mirrielees adapted the house for his son to live in. The upper common room was divided and the cottages were extended to provide large bedrooms over a dining-room and library: two diverging wings, which hold the courtyard garden in loose embrace.

It was in a state little changed from this that the house was given to the Lutyens Trust in 1991 by Mr and Mrs M.W. Hall, its owners since 1953. The Trust, having found its care too costly, has now leased it to us, and it is once again a place to repair to for holidays and skittles. The Lutyens Trust retains the use of the Library.

Goddards stands on a little green, approached by lanes so deeply sunk as to be almost tunnels. Large estates (one of them John Evelyn's Wootton) and the National Trust guard the surrounding country, in whose wooded landscape and brick and tile villages are concealed many masterpieces of the Arts and Crafts movement.

Part of the ground floor and the garden are open by appointment only for guided tours on Wednesday afternoons, from the Wednesday after Easter to the last Wednesday in October.

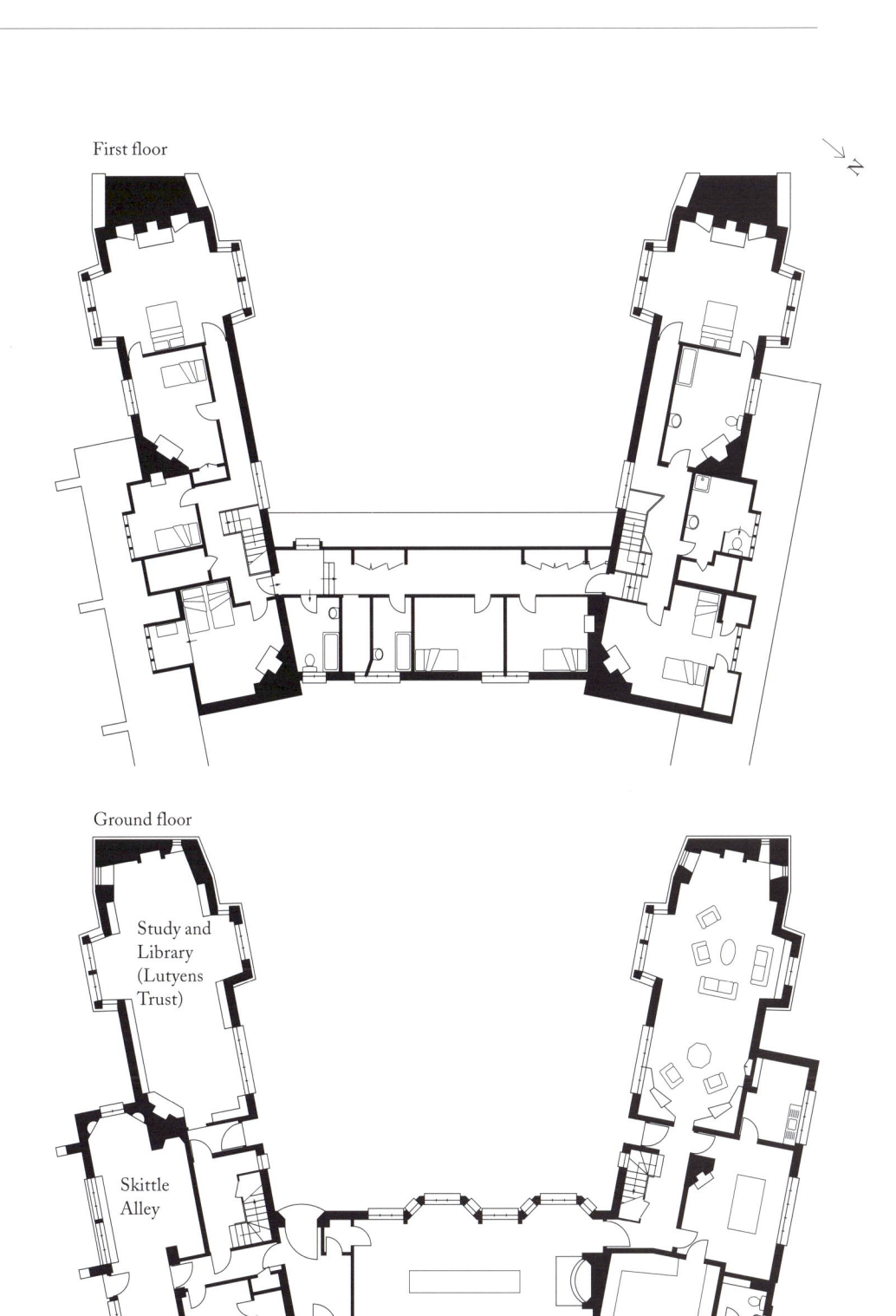

First floor

Ground floor

Study and
Library
(Lutyens
Trust)

Skittle
Alley

www.landmarktrust.org.uk   85

Gothic Temple

Stowe, Buckinghamshire [I6]

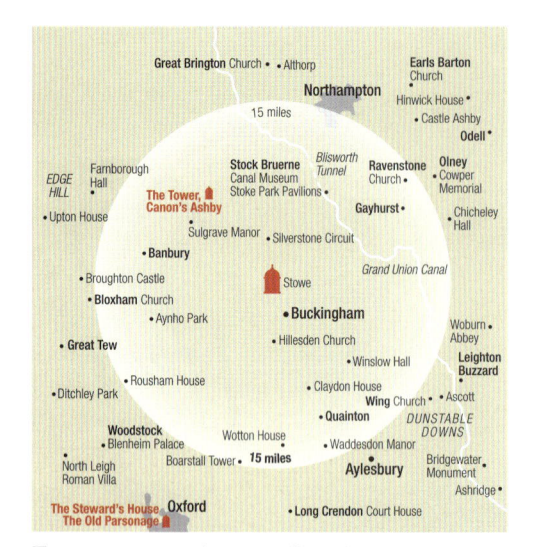

For up to 4 people
Open grounds
Adjacent parking
Spiral staircase
Dogs allowed

This temple, built in 1741, is one of the last additions to the garden at Stowe formed for Lord Cobham by Charles Bridgeman and his successor, William Kent. That same year, 'Capability' Brown arrived as gardener, to begin his own transformation of the landscape.

Lord Cobham dedicated his new temple, designed by James Gibbs, 'to the Liberty of our Ancestors', for which the Gothic style was deemed appropriate. Inside, the rooms are all circular, with moulded stone pilasters and plaster vaults – the main vault of the central space being gorgeously painted with heraldry. To be on the first floor gallery is an important architectural experience; and at the top of the staircase there is a belvedere with stone seats and a fine view over this former demesne of Lord Cobham and his successors, of which the National Trust is now guardian.

Stowe School gave us a long lease of the temple in 1970. It does have modern conveniences, if in rather surprising places, but the heating has to work hard to be noticed. We hope that the splendour of the temple and its surroundings will compensate those who stay here – it is one of the finest landscape gardens in the world.

From the logbook
It has proved to the children that the world does not come to an end when there is no telly.

I'm glad the Gothic Temple exists, so ordinary people can stay in places as extraordinary as this.

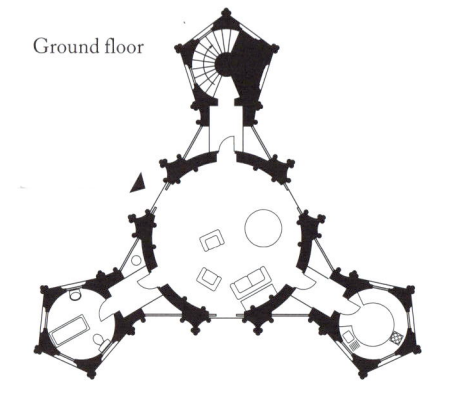

Ground floor   First floor

86   The Landmark Trust Handbook

The Grammar School

Kirby Hill, North Yorkshire [D5]

For up to 4 people
Open fire
Parking nearby
Steep staircase
Dogs allowed

Built in the discouraging reign of Queen Mary, this is one of a group of stone-roofed buildings that surround the large and airy village green of Kirby Hill. The Trust that owns the school was founded by Dr Dakyn on 11 May 1556. After Mass he explained to a numerous congregation how the Wardens of the Trust were to be chosen. On the feast of the Decollation of St John the names of six respectable parishioners were to be written on slips of paper and enclosed in balls of wax. These were to be put into a jar of water. Two names were then to be drawn and the jar of water with the remaining names put away in a cupboard, which he also provided. If a vacancy occurred during the year, a further ball of wax was to be drawn from the jar and opened. This is still done, and the jar is still kept in his cupboard, a very handsome one.

In 1957, after a life of 401 years, his school was closed, and in 1973 the Trustees gave us a long lease of it. We repaired the ground-floor schoolroom for use as a village hall, and the Tudor lodging of the master, upstairs, we turned into a flat. It has one particularly fine bedroom, looking into the churchyard, with views over the surrounding countryside, the village living up to its name. There is a large library of old school books (in the building when we arrived) and a general atmosphere of ancient peace, abetted by the church clock with its tranquillizing strike.

From the logbook
To quote Pevsner, 'a perfect and exceptional village'.

We have now slept in over 30 Landmarks, but the Grammar School remains our most favourite.

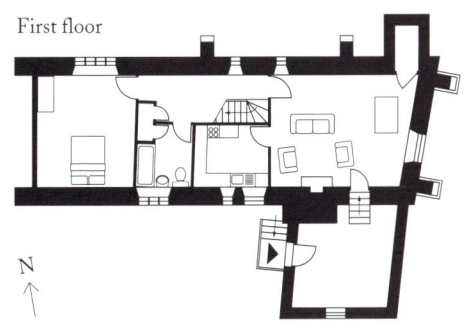

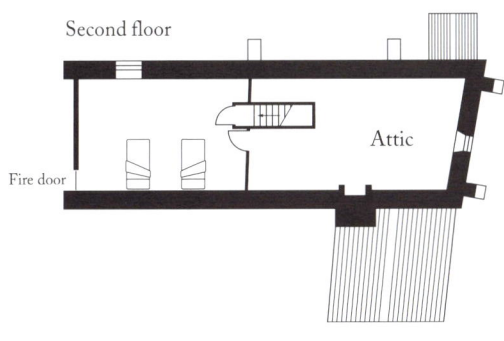

The Grange

Ramsgate, Kent [J9]

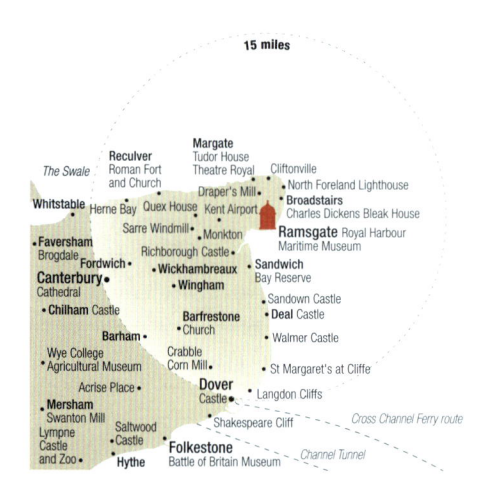

For up to 8 people
Open fire
Garden with small pond

Roof platform
Parking a short walk away

Augustus Pugin came to Ramsgate in 1843, in search of 'the delight of the sea with catholic architecture & a Library'. Here he built St Augustine's Grange, to live out his ideal of life in the Middle Ages in a family home nestling in the shadow of a benevolent monastery next door, completed by his son Edward and still thriving today.

The Grange reflects Pugin's belief in the Gothic style as the only true Christian architecture (he was a fervent convert to Catholicism). Here in his library, surrounded and sometimes interrupted by his large family, Pugin produced much of his finest work, working at prodigious speed as designs for the House of Lords and the Medieval Court at the Great Exhibition flowed effortlessly from his pen. He reserved some of his finest flourishes for his own home: some remain, others we have reinstated. The house has a private chapel and a tower, from whose roof Pugin trained his telescope on ships in distress (today's Landmarkers can also climb out to watch more modern shipping from the freight ferry terminal, visible from the first floor and above).

Ramsgate itself is a thriving town with growing arts and local history activity and plenty of jaunty seaside architecture, much of it dating from the days when the harbour formed a busy embarkation point to defend the country against Napoleon. Ramsgate Sands, beside the harbour, are in the best English seaside tradition, and there is also a small beach, reached by steps, directly below The Grange.

We have returned most of the house to an appearance that Pugin himself would recognise, including the intricate, jewel-bright interiors (the north courtyard and a bedroom are presented as left by Edward Pugin, who lived at The Grange after his father's death).

Today, the house has regained the glowing vitality it enjoyed in the lifetime of its brilliant and mercurial designer. It offers a unique chance to step into the colourful and idiosyncratic world Augustus Pugin created for himself: to share the same merriment in the panelled dining-room; and to sit, as he did, in the library, surrounded by walls painted with the names of his favourite people and places.

Open Days are held at The Grange annually. Please check our website for details. Also parts of the ground floor will be open by appointment only for guided tours on Wednesday afternoons.

From the logbook
The Wednesday afternoon tour is a must, though it's rather strange being shown around your own home!

Ground floor

First floor

Chapel

There is a further bathroom with a WC on the second floor.

www.landmarktrust.org.uk 89

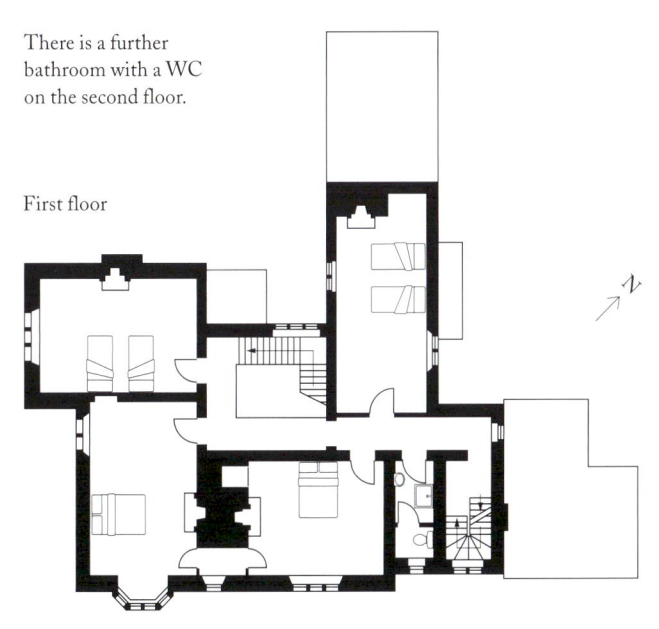

Gurney Manor

Cannington, Somerset [J4]

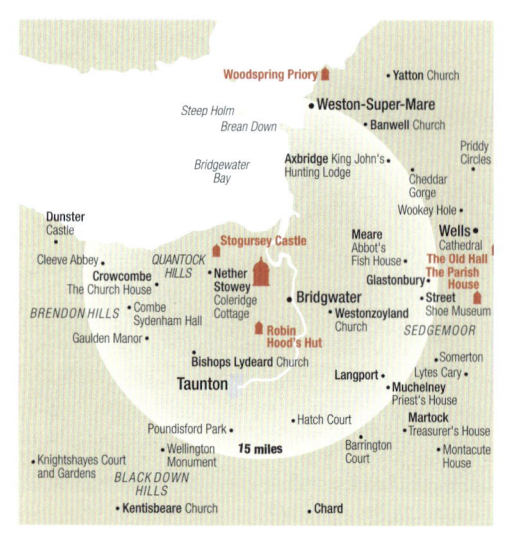

For up to 9 people
Open fire

Enclosed garden
Dogs allowed

When we first saw Gurney Manor it was divided into seven run-down flats. It is mainly late medieval, built, unusually, round a courtyard. Apart from the hall roof, which was renewed in about 1900, and Tudor windows and fireplaces in the adjoining solar block, the best medieval work survives unaltered, including a tiny oratory and a pentice, or covered passage, across the yard.

The man responsible for this was, as often, a lawyer, William Dodisham, son of a Gurney daughter. His heirs, the Mitchells, faded out before the Civil War and life thereafter as a tenant farm kept the house from major rebuilding. In the 1940s it was bought by a local developer, who divided it up into flats.

We have returned the house itself to its original undivided state. Its repair took eight years, carried out under the careful eye of our foreman, Philip Ford. New roof trusses were made in the traditional way, from oak shaped with an adze. The walls are rendered with lime plaster, buttered to a thinness equal to that achieved by medieval craftsmen.

The medieval house in its final and most fully developed form, with its balance of private and communal rooms, was a comfortable and convenient one. There can be few better ways of learning this than by staying here, in this tranquil and enclosed place. Cannington is a pleasant town not far from the Quantocks, with an excellent nursery garden.

Ground floor

First floor

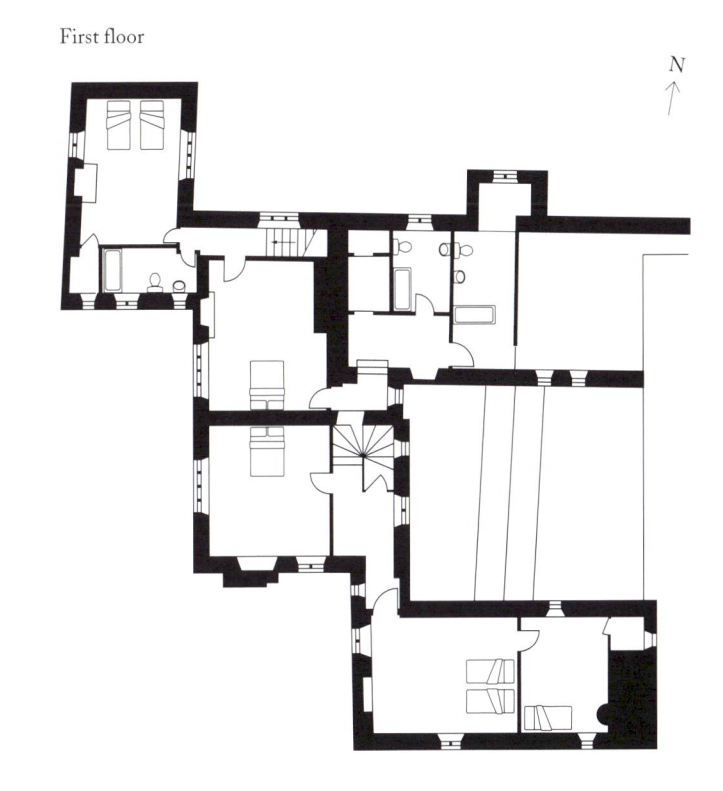

N

Hampton Court Palace

East Molesey, Surrey [J7]

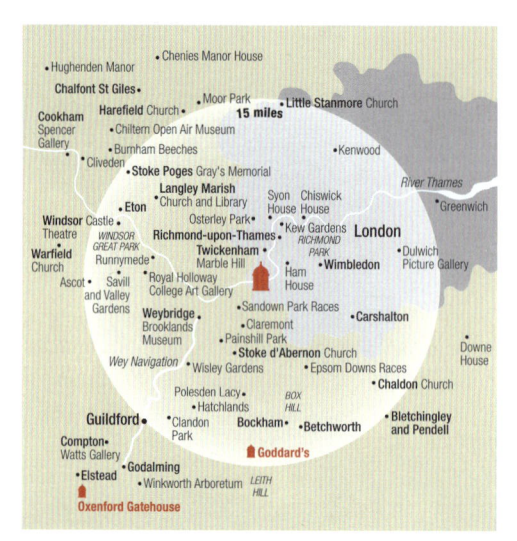

One house for 8 and one flat for 6.

Hampton Court Palace is no empty museum, but a large and thriving community, following a tradition set by George III, who allowed loyal servants to live here by Grace and Favour. Now home mainly to institutions and only a few residents, the sense of a secret life beyond the public eye survives – of doors leading to invisible corridors, of figures disappearing up a staircase with briefcase or shopping basket.

The opportunity we offer our visitors, on behalf of Historic Royal Palaces, is to become part of this life, to go past the security barrier, to make yourself at home in a palace. Hampton Court is so much a part of our history that it needs no new introduction. The details are best learned there, slowly and at first hand: our visitors are free to explore the gardens and most of the courtyards at all times, early and late, and the public rooms of the palace during opening hours.

Hampton Court has always been loved. Ernest Law, its chief historian, wrote, 'There is something so essentially homelike in the old Palace, that very few can dwell within it long, without growing attached to it'. Alexander Pope, visiting in 1718, was entranced: 'No lone house in Wales is more contemplative than Hampton Court. I walked there the other day by the moon, and met no creature of quality but the King, who was giving audience all alone to the birds under the garden wall.'

From the logbook
We are sure that not even Hogwarts could seem more magical.

We never dreamed we would be able to stay in Henry VIII's home. What a gracious host he was.

Fish Court and The Georgian House are in the middle on the left of the photograph. Whichever you choose, central London is only 35 minutes away by train.

Fish Court

This apartment has its front door in Fish Court. It was originally for the Officers of the Pastry and lies in the service wing of the Tudor palace. Begun by Cardinal Wolsey, this was enlarged by Henry VIII, who entertained even more lavishly and added new kitchens, one entirely for the baking of pies. The windows look south over Master Carpenter's Court and north towards Bushey Park.

For up to 6 people
Use of public gardens
Parking nearby

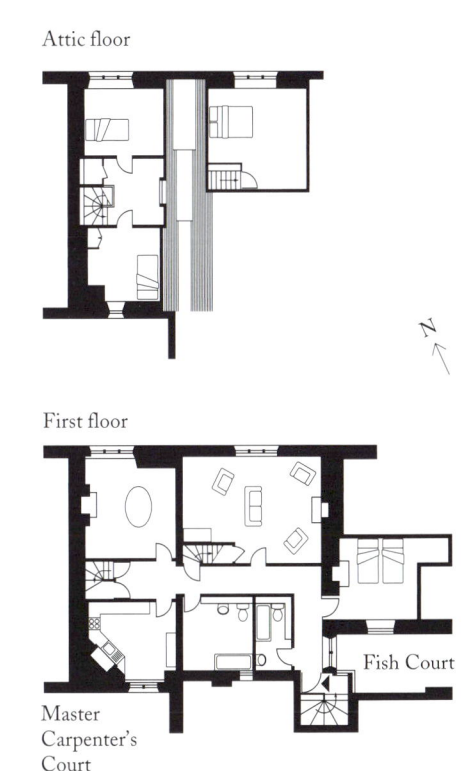

Attic floor

First floor

Fish Court

Master Carpenter's Court

The Georgian House

The alternative is to stay in The Georgian House, an imposing building just north of the palace. It looks like a garrison commander's house, but was in fact a kitchen built in 1719 for George, Prince of Wales. Its near-twin at St James's Palace is thought to be by Vanbrugh. Later it became two houses, for the Clerk of Works and the Gardener. You can stay in the eastern one, with a private walled garden into which the morning sun shines. The main rooms are handsome, the attics have a fine view of the palace roofs, and in the kitchen is a huge blocked arch, once a royal cooking hearth.

For up to 8 people
Enclosed garden
Adjacent parking

There are a twin bedroom, a single bedroom and a bathroom on the second floor.

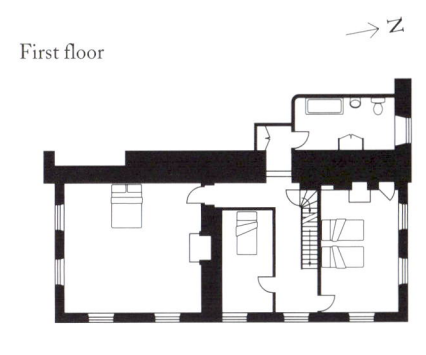

First floor

Ground floor

Door to cloakroom

www.landmarktrust.org.uk

The Hill House

Helensburgh, near Glasgow [A2]

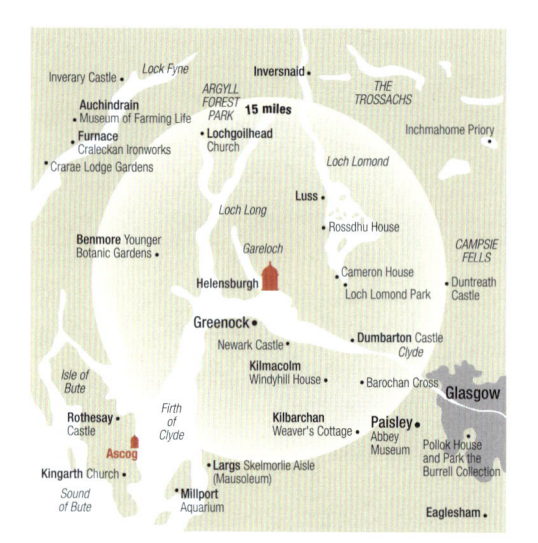

For up to 6 people
Enclosed garden
Parking nearby
Steep spiral staircase

The Hill House is the domestic masterpiece of the great Scottish architect Charles Rennie Mackintosh. Not particularly successful or lucky, he was an undoubted genius, a product of the flowering of art in Glasgow at the end of the nineteenth century. His influence is still discernible in many buildings and artefacts today. In 1902 he was commissioned by Walter Blackie, the publisher, to design this house for him and everything in it, a bold decision indeed.

The house (and the British public) has since been very lucky. With much of its original contents, it is now cared for by the National Trust for Scotland. In 1978 we came to the aid of the previous owner, the Royal Incorporation of Architects in Scotland. Bravely departing from its usual role as a professional body, it had in 1972 raised the money to buy the house when no other preservation body would take it on, but had scarce means to maintain it. As well as helping the RIAS directly, we took a lease of the top floor, which had been turned into a flat, and here we remain as tenants.

The principal room of our flat was the schoolroom of the Blackie family. Like all rooms once the domain of children, it has the feeling of a place where much spirit and energy have been expended. It is large and irregularly shaped, under the roof, with bookcases (now filled by us with Blackie's Annuals) and toy cupboards designed by Mackintosh – and with a large three-sided bay window, flooded with daylight, looking over the Firth of Clyde and beyond.

For those who admire Mackintosh or who wish to find out why others do so, to stay here is a privilege and experience without compare. The NTS usually opens the house between Easter and October.

Helensburgh, on the upper edge of which The Hill House stands, is a pleasant, interesting place. An early and far-sighted example of town-planning, it was laid out on very generous lines in 1775. Big houses in big gardens line its broad tree-planted roads. And over the top of the hill the road leads down to Loch Lomond.

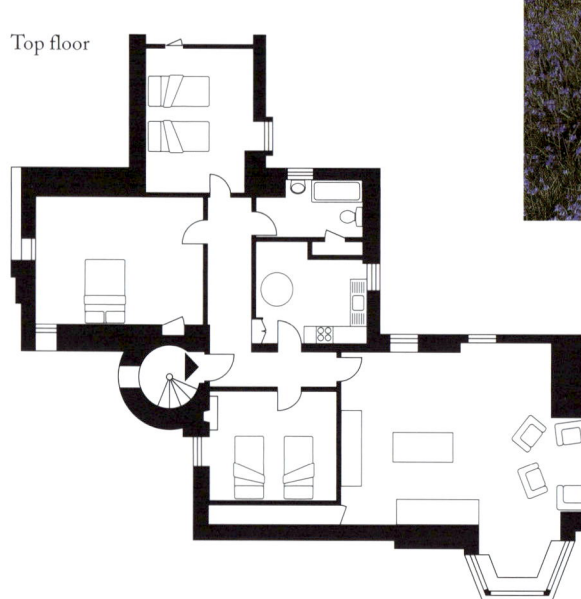

Top floor

The Landmark apartment is on the top floor to the right of the photograph.

94   The Landmark Trust Handbook

Hole Cottage

Cowden, Kent [J8]

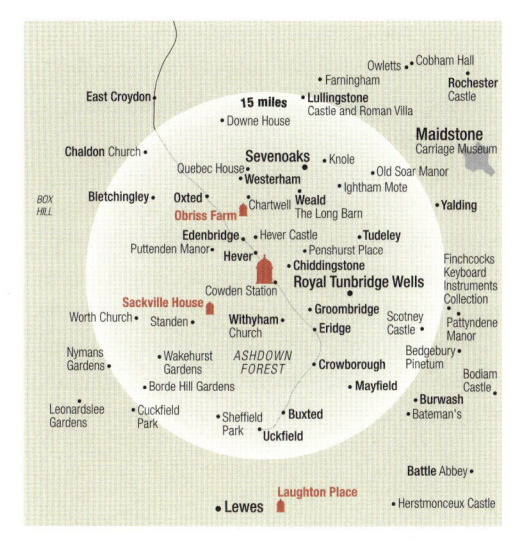

This is the cross-wing of a late medieval timber-framed hall-house, of high quality, the rest of which was pulled down in 1833. It lies by a small stream in a woodland clearing and, curiously enough, is easily accessible by railway, since it is only a 15 minute walk through the wood from Cowden station.

The Hole still has the true feeling of the Weald and of the deep woods in whose drip and shade the forges and furnaces of the Sussex ironmasters were established. This Wealden scene persists despite the great storm of October 1987. The logbook records the events of that night as the wind gathered strength: 'At about 3.30 we decided to go down to the sitting-room. As we sat with our one candle burning we heard a terrific crash in the big room upstairs: a big tree had fallen right on the peak of the roof. As the night went on trees fell one after another all about the house … Mr Dale arrived with a flask of hot water at about 8.30 and a very welcome sight he was.' New trees have grown up fast, to enclose once again this solitary place, where you may enjoy a sleepy fire, the smell of its smoke and the sound of the stream.

From the logbook
It's all green, and suddenly the cottage is standing there as it has been all the time.

To be woken up by birdsong and to be able to sit outside in the sun surrounded by bluebell woods is wonderful.

For up to 2+2 people
Open fire
Garden
Adjacent parking
Uneven track
Dogs allowed

First floor

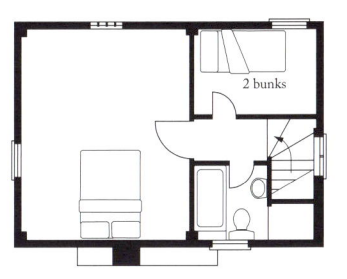

Ground floor

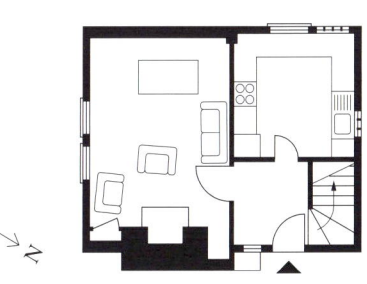

www.landmarktrust.org.uk

Houghton West Lodge

Houghton, Norfolk [G8]

For up to 2 people
Open fire
Garden
Adjacent parking

This is one of four lodges guarding the approaches to Houghton Hall, Sir Robert Walpole's splendid rural palace. However, neither this, nor the similar North and South Lodges, formed part of the architectural and landscape improvements to which our first Prime Minister devoted so much energy and care. The work of Repton or Loudon, rather than Palladio, provided the model for their design, because they were not built until the 1840s. Sensibly, these new lodges made no attempt to rival the great house; they are entirely correct for a secondary entrance to the park, but pretend to be nothing more.

Houghton West Lodge is small and neat, built around a central chimney, with a little yard and wash-house at the back, and large windows looking out into the surrounding woods. It stands by a drive that is now only a grassy track, set back from a country road. The last inhabitant left the lodge some years ago, and the estate, having no further need of it, leased it to us.

This northern part of Norfolk has the character of a peninsula: the bright light, the sense of the sea not far away, the remoteness, the fearless and prolific wildlife. At the same time, the countryside for many miles around bears the stamp of civilised owners over several centuries. The opportunity to stay so agreeably at a nobleman's gate is not one to be missed.

From the logbook
Such a variety of coastal scenery within a short distance, and so many delightful villages to visit.

Do read the logbook – it quickly yields enough to do in three weeks or more.

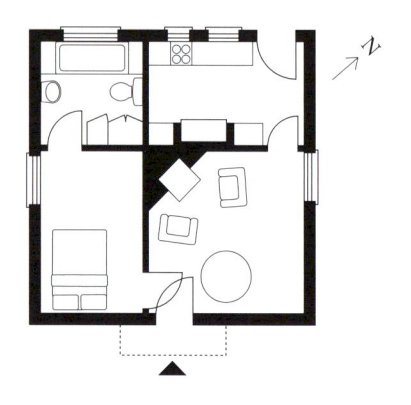

96 The Landmark Trust Handbook

The House of Correction

Folkingham, Lincolnshire [G7]

For up to 4 people
Open fire
Moated garden

Adjacent parking
Steep narrow staircase
Dogs allowed

Folkingham is one of those agreeable places that are less important than they used to be. It has a single very wide street, lined on each side by handsome buildings, with a large eighteenth-century inn across the top end. Behind the houses, to the east, lie the moat and earthworks of a big medieval castle.

The House of Correction occupies the site of this castle. These minor prisons were originally intended for minor offenders – the idle (regarded as subversive) and the disorderly. Folkingham had a house of correction by 1611, replaced in 1808 by a new one built inside the castle moat and intended to serve the whole of Kesteven. This was enlarged in 1825 and given a grand new entrance. In 1878 the prison was closed and the inner buildings converted into ten dwellings, all demolished in 1955.

The grand entrance alone survives. It was designed by Bryan Browning, an original and scholarly Lincolnshire architect also responsible for the Sessions House at Bourne. It is a bold and monumental work, borrowing from the styles of Vanbrugh, Sanmichele and Ledoux. Apart from cowing the malefactor it was intended to house the turnkey, and the Governor's horses and carriage. Now it gives entrance only to a moated expanse of grass – a noble piece of architecture in a beautiful and interesting place.

From the logbook
Anyone who doesn't love their stay here needs to be locked up.

… the children were particularly taken with the handcuffs.

Alas, parole came too early!

What a pleasure to be an inmate!

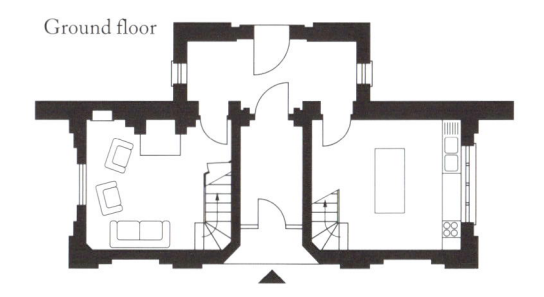

Ground floor

First floor

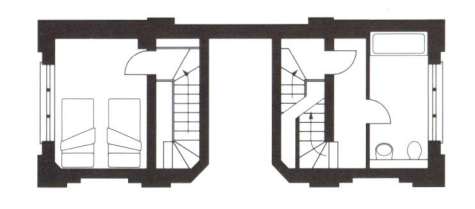

Attic

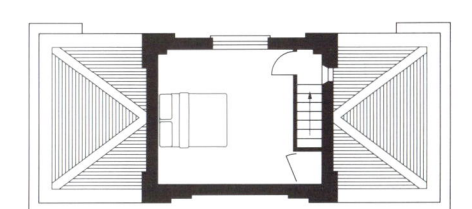

www.landmarktrust.org.uk 97

Howthwaite

Grasmere, Cumbria [D4]

For up to 8 people
Open fire
Large wild garden
Parking nearby

Dogs allowed
Steep steps from parking area

The land on which this house stands is immediately behind and above Dove Cottage. Wordsworth used to walk and sit here composing his poems, as his sister Dorothy records in her diary. For that reason, when it was offered for sale, the Trustees of Dove Cottage were anxious that it should fall into friendly hands and asked if we would join with them in buying it.

The house was built in 1926 by Miss Jessie Macdougall, of the family of millers, who bought the land from the widow of the famous Warden Spooner of New College. It seemed to us a good unaltered example of the solid houses put up by those cultivated, well-to-do people who were attracted to the Lake District; the kind of people who, among other things, had prompted the foundation of the National Trust. Certainly its light airy rooms and fine outlook and surroundings will give pleasure to many, particularly those who enjoy Wordsworth and the landscape that inspired him, whether to walk in or simply to look at.

The steep driveway may not be usable in the wet or winter. Otherwise, cars can be parked at the garage which is only a short walk from the house.

From the logbook
Spectacular views, spectacular house. What more could one (or seven people) ask?

We saw a red squirrel and two young deer. The children thought the garden was wonderful for exploring.

So many places to visit, and the house and garden so spacious, a happy place to which to return at the end of the day.

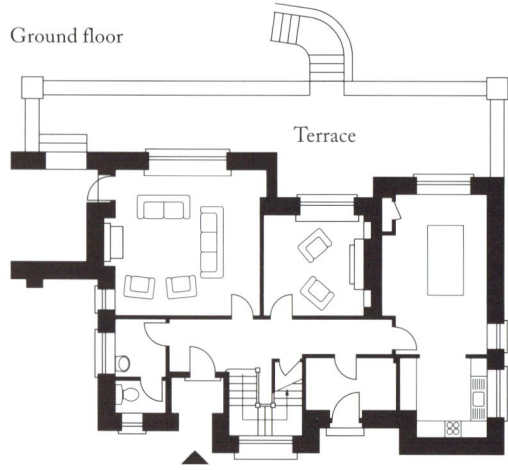

Ground floor

First floor

98   The Landmark Trust Handbook

Ingestre Pavilion

Tixall, Staffordshire [G5]

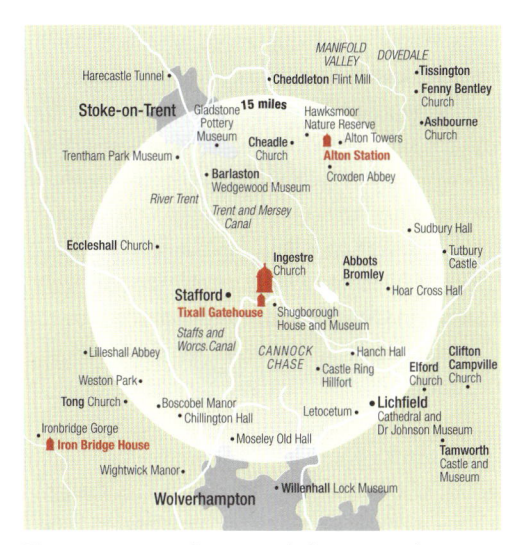

For up to 6 people
Open fire
Garden

Adjacent parking
Dogs allowed

The approach to this building is now from the side along a forest ride, but the long vista from it, between plantations to the Trent, is as it was when 'Capability' Brown drew up a scheme for 'an Intended Lawn' at Ingestre for the 2nd Viscount Chetwynd in 1756. The Pavilion was already there by then, added in about 1752 to an earlier, more formal layout.

The façade is a powerful and distinguished one. Curiously, for nearly two centuries it has been little more than that: by 1802 the building behind it, which the foundations show to have been surprisingly large and grand, had been demolished. In its place there are now new rooms designed by architect Philip Jebb, including a central octagonal saloon.

A local mason-architect named Charles Trubshaw (who trained as a sculptor under Scheemakers) worked at Ingestre around 1750. He probably put up the Pavilion, although it is unlikely that he was also its designer, able though he was. The Chetwynds, and after them the Talbots, were enlightened patrons of architecture – the parish church is by Wren – and undoubtedly this is the work of one of the best architects then available, adapted by one of the least sung but most skilfull architects of our time.

From the logbook
Fabulous walks all within a five-mile drive.

Evenings spent by a roaring fire, with jigsaws.

Our walk to Tixall yielded the biggest bunches of elderberries imaginable, from which we brewed our own cordial.

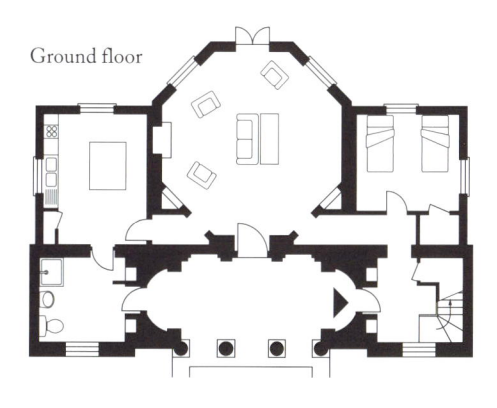

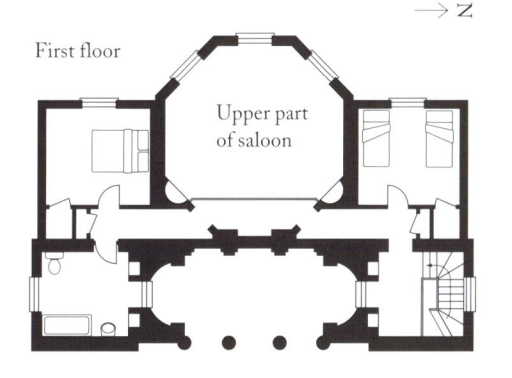

Ground floor

First floor

Upper part of saloon

Iron Bridge House

Ironbridge, Shropshire [G4]

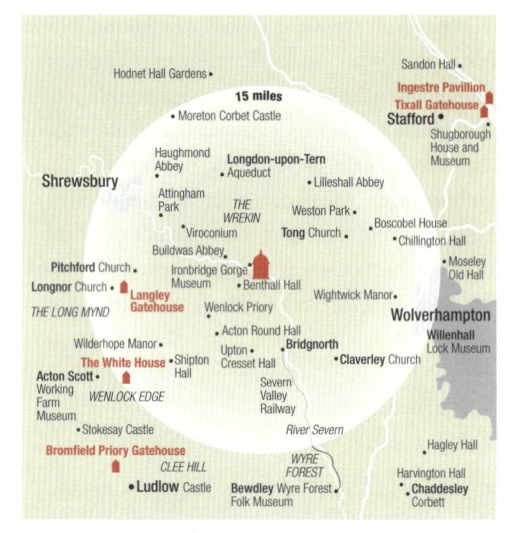

The sale particulars said: 'These premises have been occupied by the Firm of Messrs Egerton Smith & Sons for many years. They were specially built, at a great cost, by the late Mr Smith and occupy a Unique Position in Ironbridge.' They certainly do – unique in the world, overlooking that harbinger of our age, forerunner and survivor, the Iron Bridge.

This building is the complete establishment of a substantial grocer, with a large house over a double-fronted shop, and all the offices behind, from storerooms to stables. From the cellars a tunnel used to run to the bank of the River Severn, up which, until the late nineteenth century, the cargoes were brought by barge.

The shop is let to the Ironbridge Gorge Museum Trust. On the top two floors is where you can stay. The living-room has a fine iron fireplace cast here in Coalbrookdale, and this and every other room face the river, the bridge and the steep woods beyond. It is a wonderful place to be, with coal smoke drifting against the trees, and the sun glittering on the rather muddy Severn as it flows inexhaustibly beneath Abraham Darby's iron arch. All around, in Coalport, Ironbridge and Coalbrookdale, are the remains of industry's beginning.

From the logbook
We knew we were going to be close to the bridge but we were pleasantly surprised to find we were right next door. The views from the house are superb and because you are so far up you can people-watch all day without being seen.

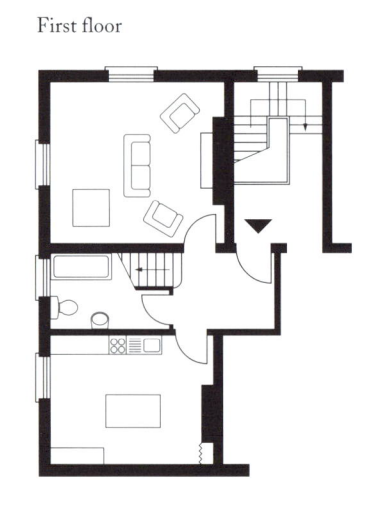

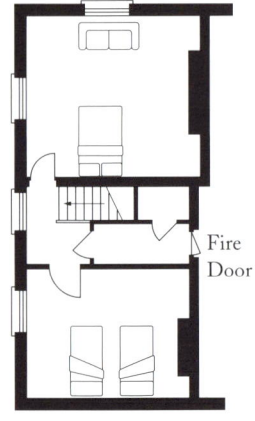

For up to 4 people
Open fire
Parking nearby for 1 car

First floor
Second floor
Fire Door

Kingswear Castle

Near Dartmouth, Devon [L4]

In 1481 a new castle was begun at Dartmouth, to defend the harbour there. To support it from the opposite shore, Kingswear Castle was completed in 1502. Together they represent the most advanced military design of their day. For the first time large guns, such as murderers and serpyntynes, were mounted inside on the ground floor, with rectangular ports through which to fire them.

Within 50 years Kingswear Castle was redundant; for another century it was manned in time of war, but thereafter was left to decay, until rescued and turned into a summer residence in 1855 by a rich young bachelor, Charles Seale Hayne. During the last World War, a concrete Blockhouse was built 50 yards from it.

We have restored the castle's ground floor to look as it did in 1502, with the living quarters above. The rooms have that sense of sturdy habitability in an exposed place, which the Victorians knew so well how to achieve, despite the building's inherent susceptibility to damp and cold (not even twenty-first century devices can fully overcome this). The tower stands almost on the water's edge (those with children beware) and its rooms are filled with shifting reflected light. From the windows you can look across to Dartmouth; or down the rocky coast, with its woods of maritime pine, and out to sea. Above all you can watch the river, busy now with friendly shipping.

From the logbook
In a place where time is meaningless, we didn't have enough.

I would like to spend all night on the battlements watching the stars.

For up to 4 people
Garden
Roof platform
Parking nearby

Steep steps and staircases
Dogs allowed

Ground floor

First floor

Second floor

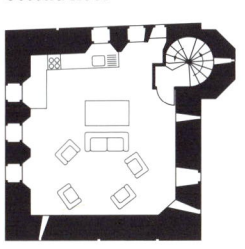

The bathroom is on the third floor.

www.landmarktrust.org.uk   101

Knowle Hill

Near Ticknall, Derbyshire [G6]

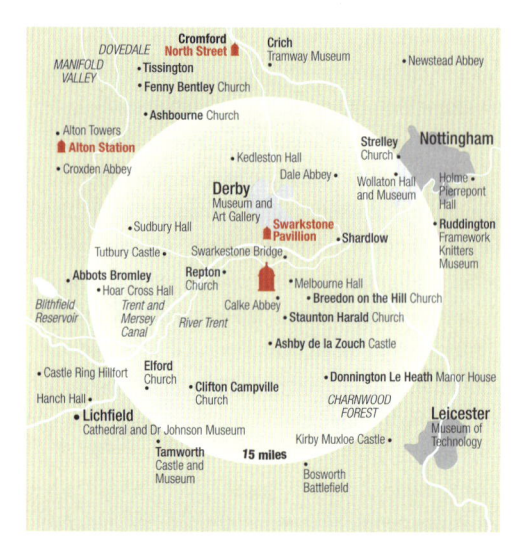

For up to 5 people
Solid fuel stove
Long gated access track
Enclosed garden
Steep steps outside
Dogs allowed

In 1698 Walter Burdett, a younger son born nearby at Foremark, retired from the Middle Temple. On land leased from his friend, Thomas Coke of Melbourne, he built for himself a most curious house on the side of a ravine. Here, being a likeable and sociable person, he entertained his many friends; and around it he formed a garden which, for all its formal structure of terraces and pools, blended evocatively with the natural landscape – remarkably so at that early date.

In the 1760s the house was pulled down by Walter's great-nephew, but the atmosphere of a woodland retreat was preserved – and so was a tunnel leading to a mysterious rock-cut chamber from the cellars. A Gothick summerhouse, which soars like a ruined castle on the valley's edge, was built on an upper terrace, with a cottage for a custodian behind. Until abandoned in the twentieth century, parties came often to walk here amid the picturesque delights of trees and water. Picturesque it still is, but parents will want to keep a close eye on small children because of steep drops and the stream in the ravine below.

By 1989 Knowle Hill was divided between three owners. Its remote position down a long gated farm track deterred most would-be rescuers, but it is now reunited, and the quiet process of revival is under way.

We have repaired the cottage for you to stay in, with the summerhouse as your drawing-room. It opens on to a sunny lawn, with a view into the woods beyond and, if you are lucky, a glimpse of water tumbling over a cascade.

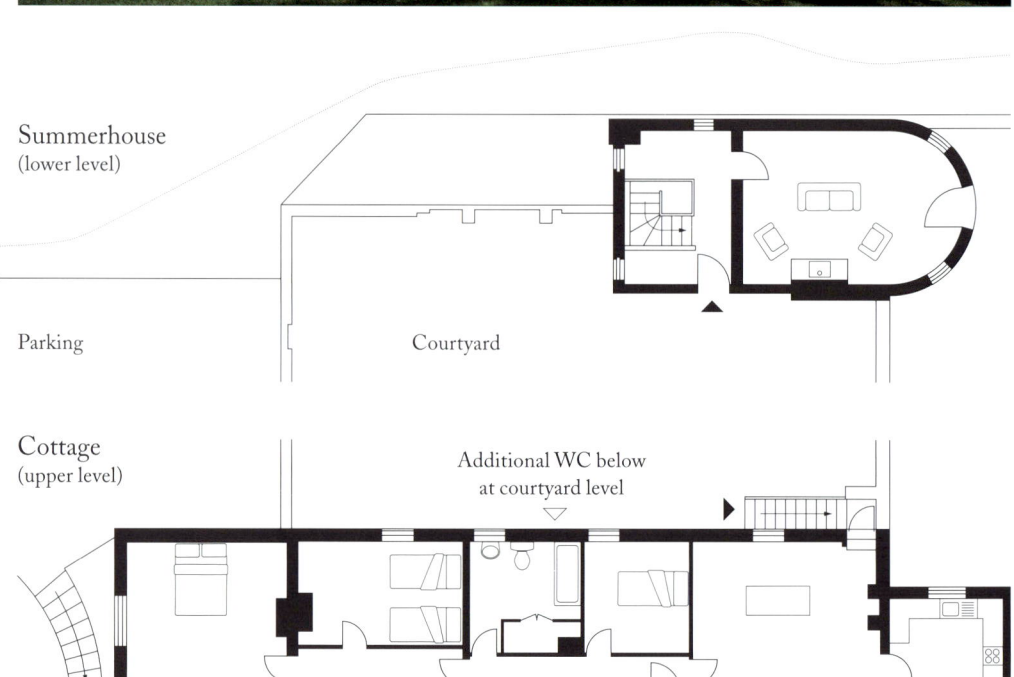

Langley Gatehouse

Near Acton Burnell, Shropshire [H4]

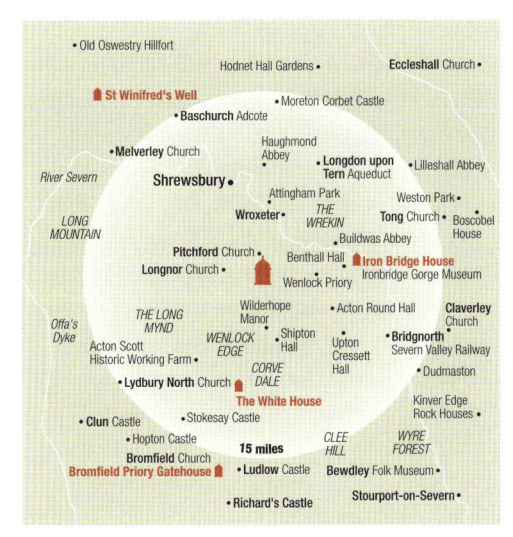

For up to 6 people
Solid fuel stove
Enclosed garden

Parking nearby
Dogs allowed

Like all the best buildings this one is hard to find. To add confusion, its two faces are each quite different: one, formerly presented to the outside world but now looking on to a working farm, is of plain dressed stone. The other, which once looked inwards at Langley Hall (demolished by 1880), is timber-framed in the best local tradition. Both are Jacobean, although the lower part of the outer wall was already ancient when Sir Humphrey Lee added this gatehouse above it in about 1610.

The new building was probably for the Steward, or important guests. The parlour, over the gate passage, was panelled (and is again) with a moulded plaster cornice. On either side are rooms of generous size, and above are attics, squeezed in among the aisled structure of the queen-post roof. The roof slates of moss-covered Harnage stone are thick with fossilised shells.

The gatehouse was near to collapse when, as a joint operation with English Heritage, we began work on it in 1992 – indeed its north-east corner post appeared to be supported solely by a wine bottle wedged beneath its decayed foot. The exemplary quality of the repairs is a pleasure to see; as also is the view from the main windows down a wide valley to the Wrekin.

From the logbook
We loved being so close to the farm – tractors and cattle sounds reminding us we were away from home!

Ground floor

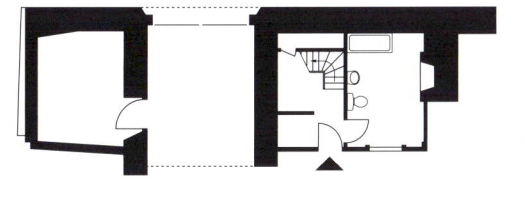

First floor

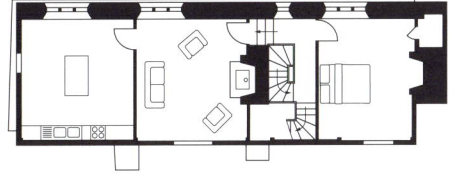

Second floor

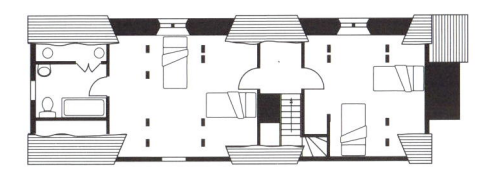

www.landmarktrust.org.uk 103

Laughton Place

Near Lewes, East Sussex [K8]

For up to 4 people
Moated garden
Roof platform

Parking nearby
Steep spiral staircase
Dogs allowed

This building has an illustrious pedigree, which it wears with the lonely and battered dignity of a nobleman fallen on hard times. From about 1400, Laughton was the chief manor of the Pelhams, without whom eastern Sussex would not have been as it is. In 1534 Sir William, who had attended his king at the Field of the Cloth of Gold, remodelled the house on a grand scale, round a moated courtyard and with terracotta decoration in the newest Renaissance fashion. All that has survived is this bold brick tower, which stood close to the main hall, an outlook post and set of secure private rooms combined. By 1600 the family had abandoned Laughton, driven by the damp (a problem still, on which we are working) to build again on higher ground, and slowly the house decayed.

Then, in 1753, Henry Pelham, politician and brother to the splendid Duke of Newcastle, had the idea of surrounding the tower with a new Gothick farmhouse. The result was very charming, with a pediment between crenellated side-wings, and pointed windows. Thus it continued until sold by the Pelhams in 1927. The new owner pulled down the wings, leaving only the tower. It stands, with a couple of other buildings, within the wide circle of the Downs, down a long drive.

When we bought it in 1978, the tower had great cracks in its sides, and the floors had fallen in – much engineering and lime mortar went into its repair. The rooms inside are plain, apart from the delicate arabesque decoration of the terracotta windows, the moulded terracotta doors and the Pelham Buckle, the badge won by prowess in the Middle Ages and used as a family emblem ever since. The building, if long neglected, was obviously once something to be proud of.

From the logbook
The sun shone. The moon shone. The mists rolled in. The best way to watch the world from the battlements is with mugs of mulled wine in your hands.

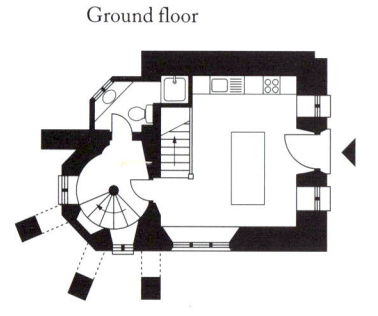

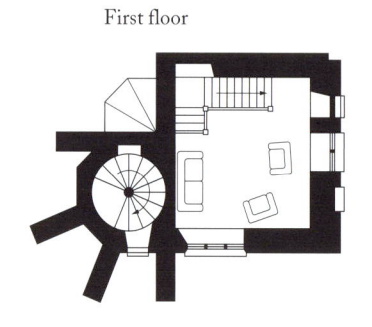

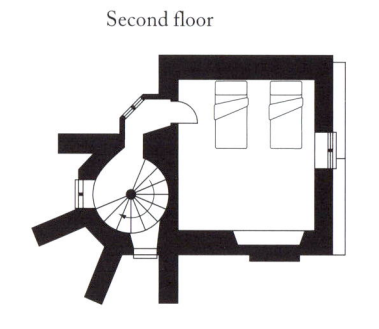

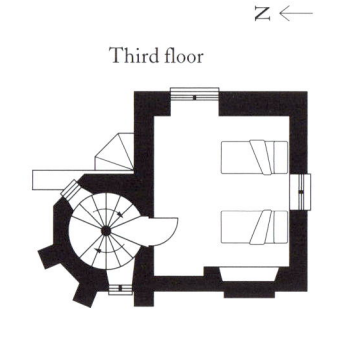

Ground floor First floor Second floor Third floor

104 The Landmark Trust Handbook

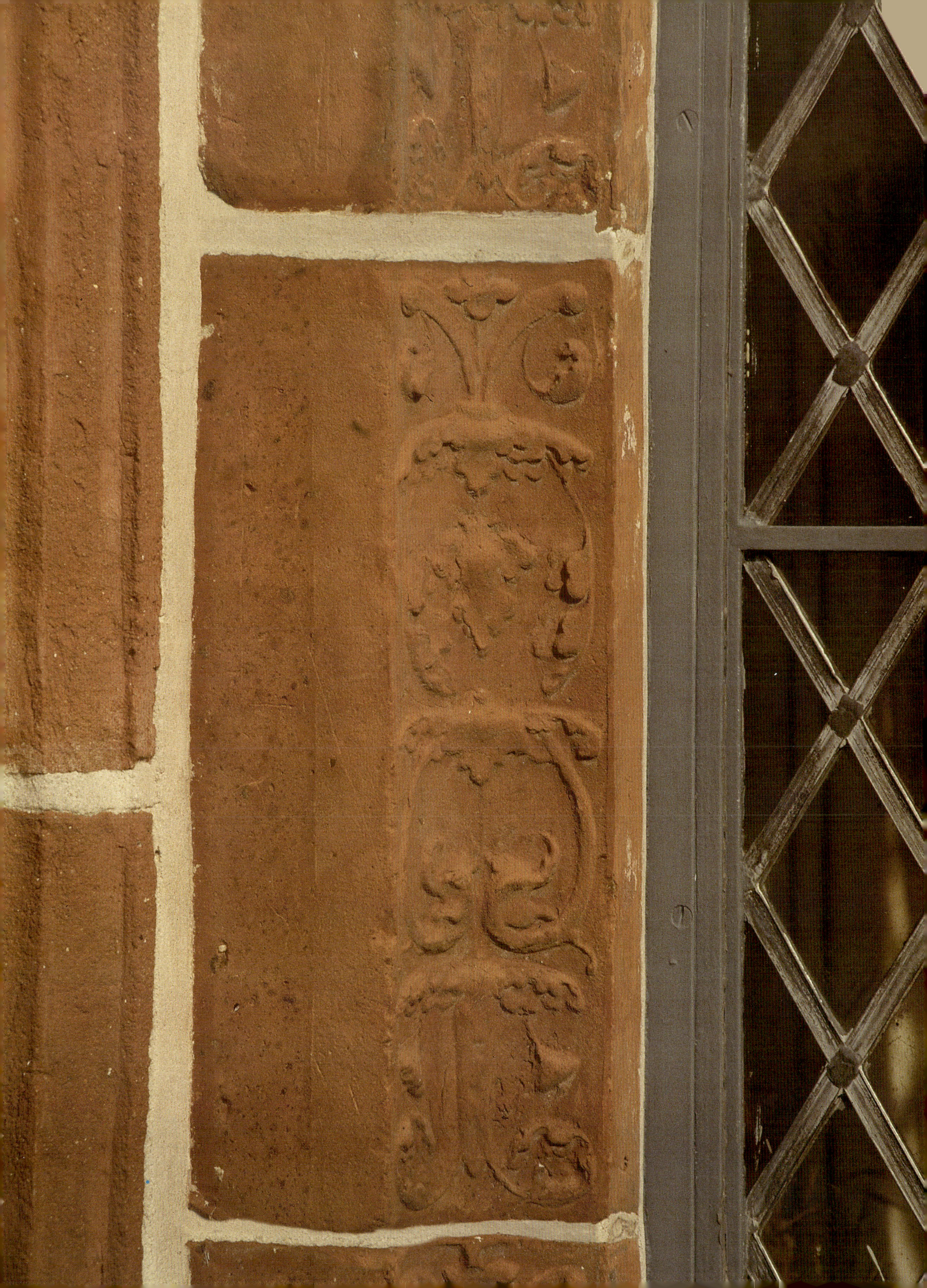

Lengthsman's Cottage

Lowsonford, Warwickshire [H6]

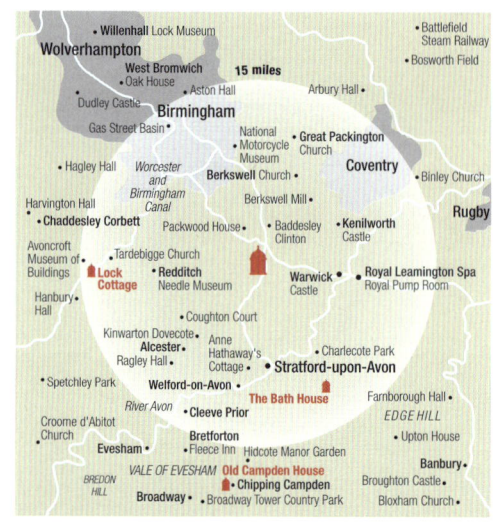

For up to 4 people
Open fire
Enclosed garden

Adjacent parking
Dogs allowed

The construction of the Stratford-upon-Avon canal began in 1793, during the heady days after the French Revolution. Its projecteers did not foresee the credit squeeze that would follow the opening of hostilities against Napoleon, but fortunately, an astute local land agent called William James stepped into the breach to complete the southern stretch of the canal, which includes Lowsonford. Working with engineer William Whitmore, James cut costs dramatically. His engineers, more accustomed to building bridges than houses, simply adapted the techniques they knew best to house the men who worked on the canal, building them snug, barrel-roofed cottages next to the locks they supervised.

Lengthsman's Cottage is one such, its resident's title, properly, a 'lengthsman', since he maintained not just the lock but also the stretch of canal to the next one. The cottage was probably built in 1812–13, its simple, limewashed finish and complete absence of foundations reflecting the uncertain but vigorous days of its construction. Here too are towpath, lock and small road bridge, a complete assemblage of the canal builder's art. We acquired the cottage in 1992 when the National Trust took on this stretch of the canal, which passes on through gentle Warwickshire. The cottage came with a life tenant, Ned Taylor, who had been born in the cottage in 1921 as the second of 11 children and was content to see out his days there.

In 2006, we needed only to refurbish the cottage and it is now preserved as a rare example of the expedients adopted in those years when the Industrial Revolution was changing the face of Britain. Things have perhaps changed even more since, but here is a sociable spot where you can sit and reflect upon the talents of those Regency engineers, watching the narrowboats negotiate the lock.

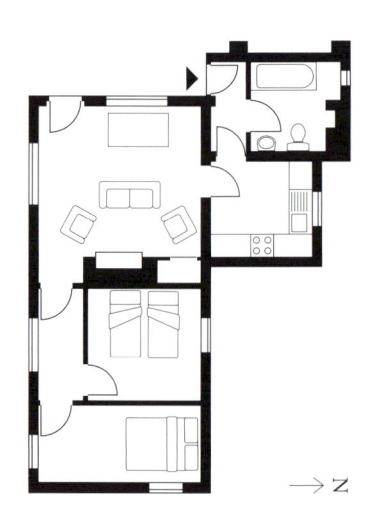

Lettaford

North Bovey, Devon [K3]

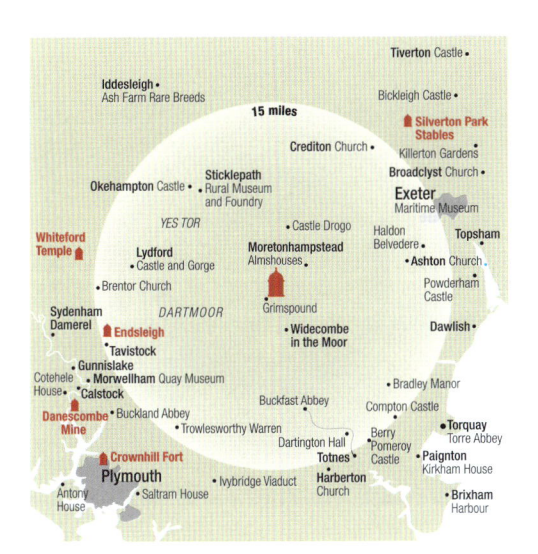

One house for 7, one for 5 and a former chapel for 2.

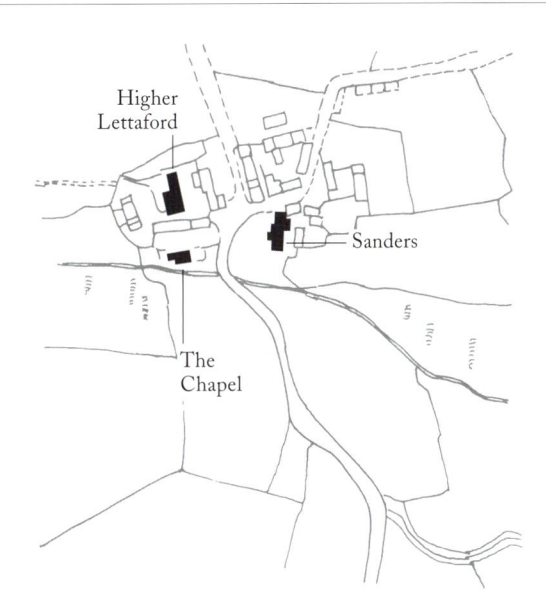

The fringes of Dartmoor gave a surprisingly good living to those who had the tenacity to carry on in its sometimes harsh climate, grazing their cattle on the rough upland pasture, cultivating crops in the tiny fields lower down. Throughout the Middle Ages they maintained their own way of life and their own economy, carefully adapted to suit their surroundings and best seen now in the longhouses in which they chose to live, found nowhere else in such numbers in the comfortable South West of England. It is in the building of these on a grander scale, with fine masonry and even carved ornament, that we see evidence of renewed activity from 1500 onwards, when a growth of population and prosperity in Devon as a whole led to new buildings and new settlements.

Lettaford is an old settlement, men having lived here from before 1300. The public road that leads to it breaks up into tracks, taking you on to the moor itself; and all its three farmhouses are, in origin at least, sixteenth-century longhouses. It is sited in a hollow for shelter, its buildings grouped around a green, including a former Methodist chapel, the only one not related directly to farming. It is like many other, similar hamlets but few remain so secret or complete. The self-contained resourceful life of an upland people goes on around you as it always has; and the world contracts to Dartmoor's limits, beyond which only the adventurous go.

Higher Lettaford is on the far left of the picture and Sanders on the right in the foreground.

Lettaford

The Chapel

The Chapel is a plain granite building typical of rural Nonconformity, built by Miss Pynsent of Higher Lettaford in 1866. Firstly Bible Christian, and later Methodist, it closed in 1978. With little chance of survival on its own, its loss would have been a pity for Lettaford, so we took it on. Here two of you can cook, eat and sleep all in one big room, with an open fire, tucked away at the edge of the green beside a small stream.

For up to 2 people
Open fire
Shared grounds
Adjacent parking
Dogs allowed

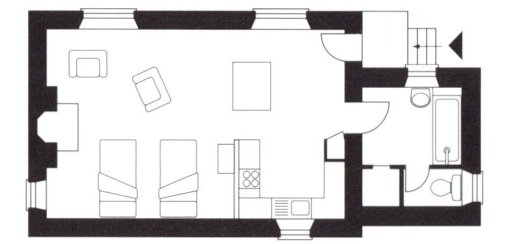

Higher Lettaford

Higher Lettaford had been empty for some years when we bought it in 1987. It was once a longhouse, but in about 1840 its lower end was rebuilt, most comfortably, by two Misses Pynsent, who may have run a small Nonconformist school here.

Their house has large windows, and a verandah, introducing a whiff of Torquay and a life of seaside ease to this hard-working place. The bedrooms are some of the prettiest in any Landmark, and from the front door, the old track leads up to the moor.

For up to 7 people
Open fire
Garden
Adjacent parking
Dogs allowed

Ground floor 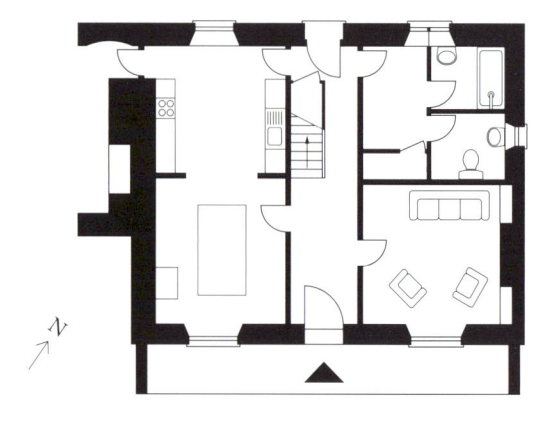   First floor

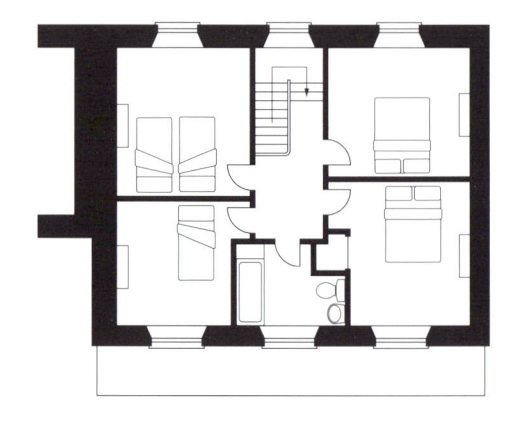

Sanders

Sanders is a near perfect Dartmoor longhouse of about 1500, arranged on the usual plan of inner room, hall, cross-passage and shippon, all under one roof, with a shouldered porch originally the entrance for both cows and people. The walls are made of blocks of granite ashlar, some of them enormous. This was a house of high quality, but it declined into a labourer's cottage long enough ago to avoid damaging improvements.

For up to 5 people
Open fire
Garden
Parking nearby
Steep staircase
Dogs allowed

From logbook
Wonderful house, lovely walks – heard cuckoos, saw tiny new-born foals and a beautiful array of wild flowers.

Ground floor

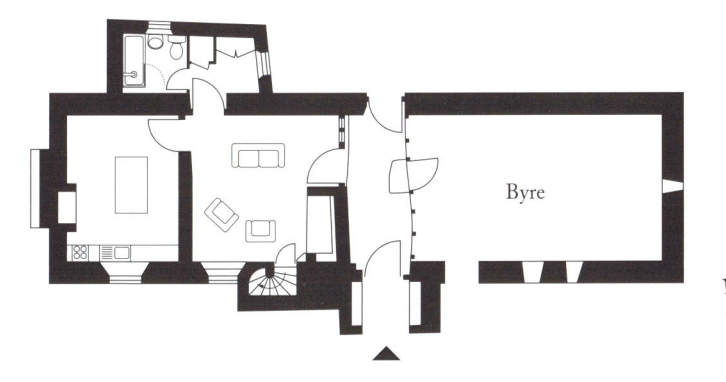

First floor

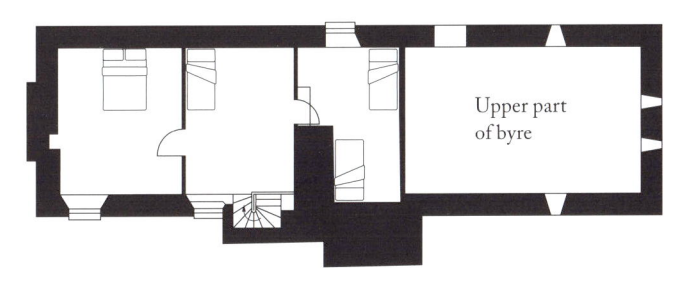

The Library

Stevenstone, near Great Torrington, Devon [K3]

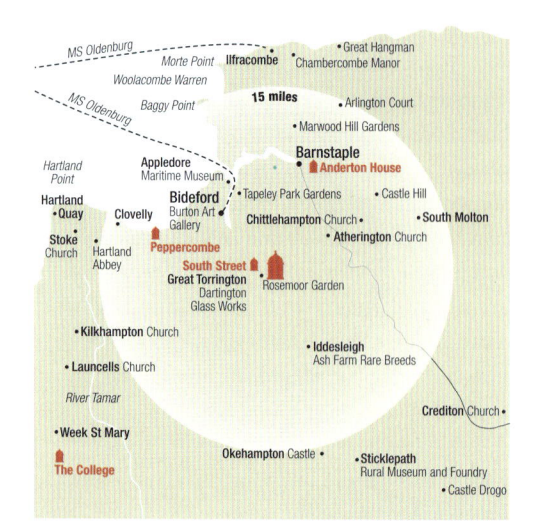

The Library, and its smaller companion the Orangery, stand in well-mannered incongruity beside the ruins of Victorian Stevenstone, with the remains of a grand arboretum around them. Stevenstone was rebuilt by the very last of the Rolles in 1870, but these two pavilions survive from an earlier remodelling of 1710–20. The façade of the Library, with its giant order and modillion cornice, looks like the work of a lively, probably local, mason-architect, familiar with the work of such as Talman and Wren.

Why a library in the garden? It probably started life as a perfectly ordinary banqueting house and only assumed its more learned character later on. Why it should have done so is a mystery, of a pleasantly unimportant kind. By the time we first saw it, when it came up for sale in 1978, the bookshelves had been dispersed and the Library had been a house for many years, the fine upper room divided and the loggia closed in, while the Orangery was about to collapse altogether. We put new roofs on both buildings and, on the Library, a new eaves cornice carved from 170 feet of yellow pine by a local craftsman, Richard Barnett. The loggia is open again, and the main room has returned to its full size. To stay in this particularly handsome building, even without the books, is an enlightening experience.

From the logbook
What an exquisite building – who needs to go anywhere else?

For up to 2+2 people
Open fire
Enclosed garden
Parking nearby
Steep narrow spiral staircase

There are two beds (no bathroom) in the Orangery, *top left*, which stands 100 ft from the main building. It is unheated and therefore we do not recommend it for winter use.

Ground floor

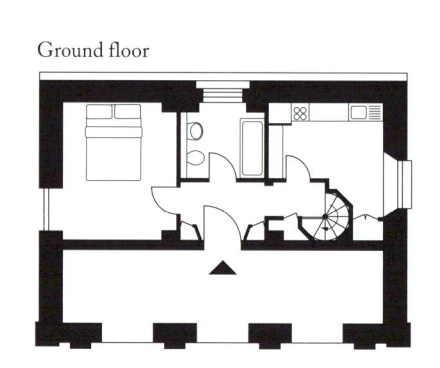

First floor

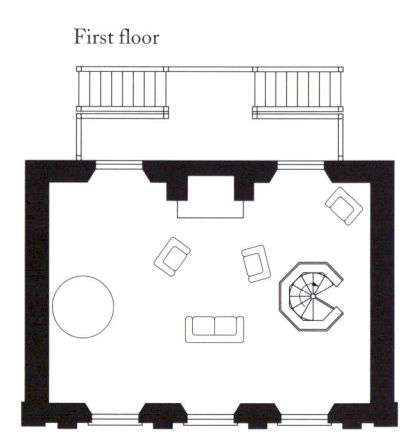

Lock Cottage

Stoke Pound, Worcestershire [H5]

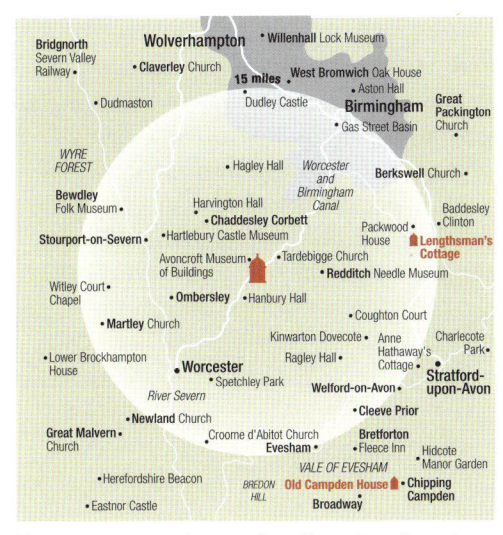

For up to 4 people
Open fire

Small enclosed yard
Parking 75 yards away

We hope that this lock cottage will give you a taste for travel by canal, which is the prime way to see England at walking pace without actually having to walk. Until the 1950s many such handsome unpretentious buildings served and graced our canal system; but they were demolished ruthlessly. Indeed it was, in particular, the destruction of Thomas Telford's Junction House at Hurlestone on the Shropshire Union canal which maddened us into starting the Landmark Trust.

This survivor lies on the Worcester & Birmingham Canal, built between 1790 and 1815, which runs for 30 miles from Diglis Basin in Worcester to Gas Street in Birmingham.

Birmingham, as boaters all discover, is on a hill, and it takes 58 locks in 16 miles to lift this canal from the Severn to the Birmingham level. Of these locks, 30 are here at Tardebigge, the longest flight in Britain.

Our cottage is between locks 31 and 32, by bridge 49, a bridge as beautiful as all the others (which you must cross after leaving your car and walk along the towpath to reach the cottage, with a wheelbarrow thoughtfully provided to assist the transfer of luggage and provisions); canals are a wonderful demonstration that beauty and utility can be combined. Alas today only pleasure boats and towpath walkers will pass in front of your windows, but at the lock, you may well be offered a lift up the flight; and at the top, with its surprising view, you will, if you possess any spirit at all, decide to navigate one day still further, through the tunnel under the green hill beyond.

From the logbook
Sitting in the cottage with a cup of tea and watching the boats go by is infinitely preferable to jumping on and off a boat watching the cottages go by.

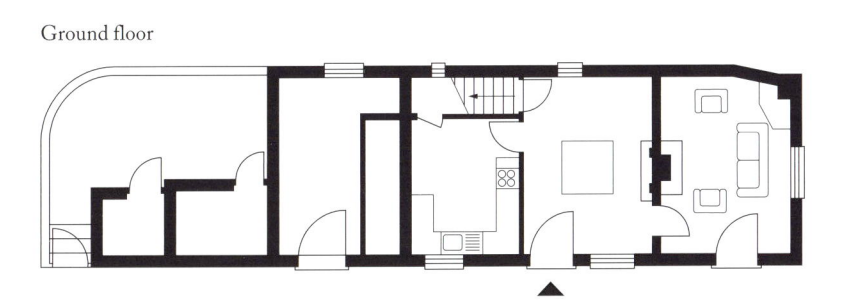

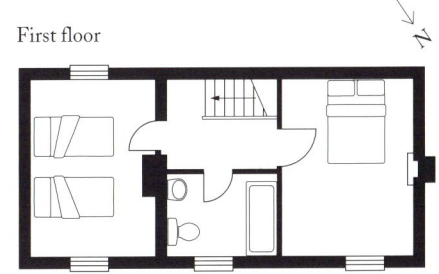

Ground floor

First floor

www.landmarktrust.org.uk

Lower Porthmeor

Near Zennor, Cornwall [L1]

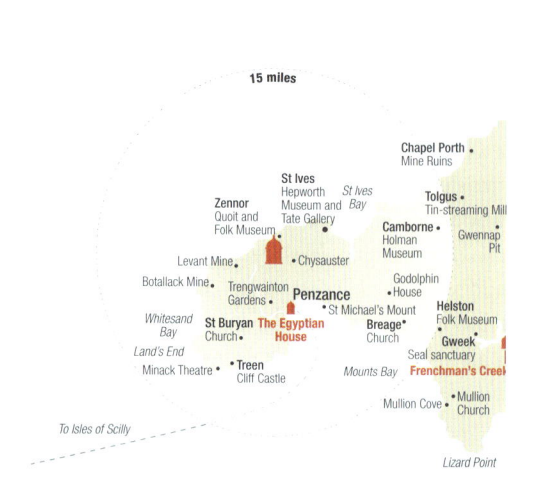

Lower Porthmeor is a township, or farm hamlet, typical of this area of West Penwith, where sometimes as many as four houses are grouped round a single farmyard. The houses are not themselves of great age, but they represent a tradition as old as the tiny stone-hedged fields in which they stand, fields that have scarcely changed since the Iron Age. With their pleasant sturdy buildings, such settlements can be seen dotted all along the green coastal shelf running west from St Ives, bounded on one side by a ridge of high moor, on the other by the Atlantic cliffs.

We bought the farm, which had been derelict for some years, in conjunction with the National Trust. There are two houses, separated by the farmyard, both facing south, and each with its own granite-walled garden. From their back doors, it is a short walk across fields to where a little valley cuts through the cliffs to form a rocky bay.

Two houses for 4 and one for 5.

Arra Venton

Arra Venton, a house of somewhat mixed parentage, came on the market just after we had taken on Lower Porthmeor. There were once two buildings, a chapel and a smithy, on to one end of which a cottage was added early last century. Then, in 1952, the whole was joined together, in an eccentric if imaginative fashion. Altered again since then, and treated and painted in an unsympathetic way, it spoiled the elemental landscape of which it is part, and looked horrible from our other buildings. So we bought it, and de-improved it, to make it simple and unified again; and very pleasant it is.

For up to 5 people
Solid fuel stove
Garden
Adjacent parking
Dogs allowed

First floor

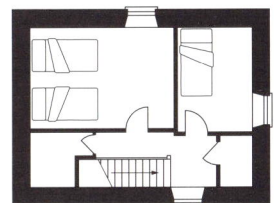

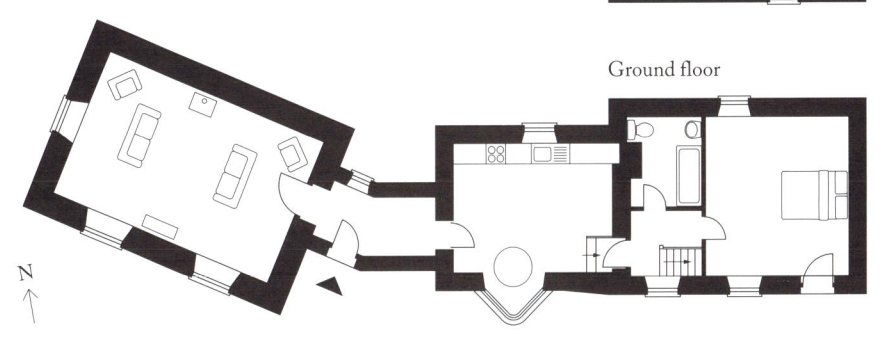

Ground floor

Lower Porthmeor

The Captain's House

The Captain's House is simpler than its companion, The Farmhouse, and dates from the 1840s. It, too, has a massive kitchen fireplace and a snug parlour. There were once two houses, but the lower half was long ago given over to animals. This was the childhood home of Arthur Berryman, the last of the Lower Porthmeor Berrymans, who was both farmer and Captain in a local tin mine. His forebears settled here before 1600, and cousins still farm Higher Porthmeor.

For up to 4 people
Solid fuel stove
Enclosed garden
Adjacent parking
Dogs allowed

Ground floor   First floor

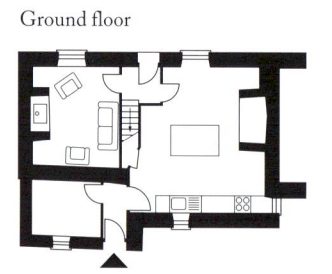

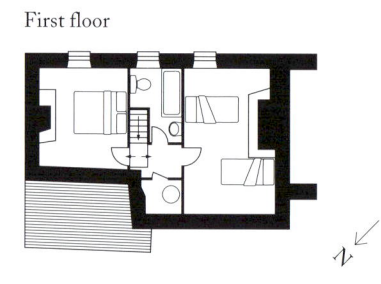

The Farmhouse

The Farmhouse was built in about 1800 and has a handsome front of granite ashlar, paid for perhaps with money from the tin stamps nearby. Inside are further hints of wealth, in a bedroom with a dado and a pretty fireplace. But the great chimney piece in the kitchen has a granite monolith for its lintel, like many older houses in the area.

For up to 4 people
Solid fuel stove
Garden
Adjacent parking
Dogs allowed

Ground floor   First floor

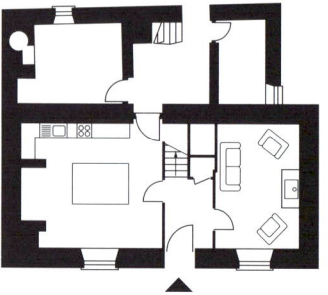

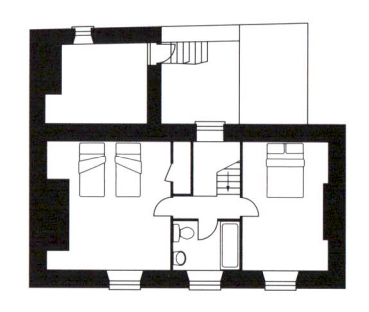

Luttrell's Tower

Eaglehurst, Southampton, Hampshire [K6]

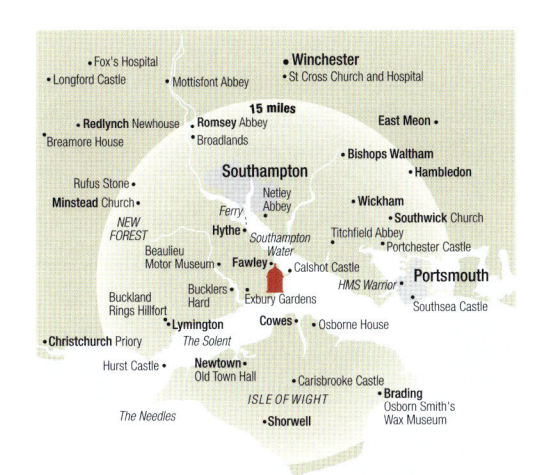

For up to 4 people
Open fire
Roof terrace
Adjacent parking

Spiral staircase
Dogs allowed
Direct access to the beach

This is an exceptionally fine Georgian folly, possibly the only surviving work of Thomas Sandby, first Professor of Architecture at the Royal Academy. It stands on the shore of the Solent looking towards Cowes. The view, particularly of ships entering and leaving Southampton by the deep water channel, is magnificent – as, in another way, is the sight, from its top, of the Fawley refinery and power station. It also has the magic of those places where trees, especially yews and ilexes as here, come right down to the salt sea's edge.

It was built for Temple Luttrell, a Member of Parliament (but reputedly a smuggler here) who died in Paris in 1803. His brother-in-law, Lord Cavan, who commanded our forces in Egypt from 1801, was the next owner and brought with him the two mysterious feet on a plinth of Nubian granite, now at the tower and thought to be the base of a XIXth dynasty statue of Rameses II.

Thereafter the tower passed through various hands; Queen Victoria nearly bought it (with Eaglehurst House) instead of Osborne, and Marconi used it for his wireless experiments of 1912. Sir Clough Williams-Ellis designed the double staircase that gives access to it from the beach, too grand really for anyone but Neptune.

We bought the tower in 1968. Inside, all the rooms have handsome chimney pieces and the top room has fine plaster and shellwork as well. We have arranged this splendid eyrie so that you can cook, eat and sit in it, watching the Solent all the while. There is also a tunnel from the basement to the beach, made perhaps for the smuggling Member.

Ground floor First floor Second floor

There is also a WC with a basin off the staircase on a mezzanine floor.

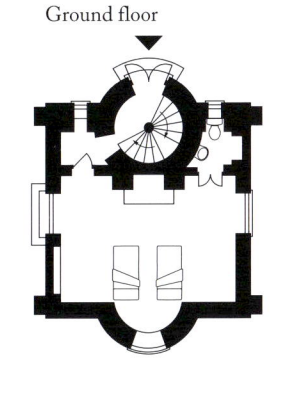

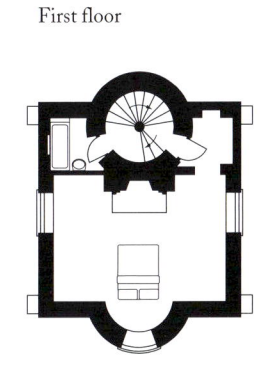

www.landmarktrust.org.uk

Lynch Lodge

Alwalton, near Peterborough, Cambridgeshire [H7]

For up to 2 people
Open fire
Garden

Adjacent parking
Dogs allowed

Alwalton lies in the extreme north of the former county of Huntingdon, on the river Nene a few hundred yards from the Great North Road. Despite its nearness to poor overgrown Peterborough it has a quiet open village street, a cul-de-sac ending in a patch of green, on which stands the Lynch Lodge. This building is the fine, two-storey Jacobean porch from the Drydens' house at Chesterton, where the poet often stayed with his favourite cousin. It was brought here when the house was demolished in 1807 and erected as a lodge to Milton Park by the Fitzwilliam family, who had a dower-house in the village. The Lynch drive having been closed (not surprisingly as it was three miles long), it now presides over a farm entrance and a rough track to the river.

We were told about it by a neighbour and bought it from the Fitzwilliam estate. Never a very convenient dwelling, it had been altered and enlarged over the years to accommodate bigger families. We have restored it to its original form, with one small room up and one more generous room down, joined by a new staircase.

From the logbook
The highlight of my week was seeing a kingfisher for the first time flying low across the river.

I really loved the simplicity and beauty of the furniture and decor, the spiral staircase – castle-like, gorgeous.

What an enchanting way to begin the Landmark experience.

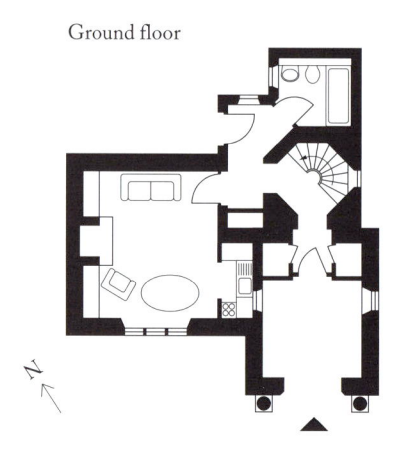

Ground floor   First floor

116   The Landmark Trust Handbook

The Mackintosh Building

Comrie, Perthshire [A3]

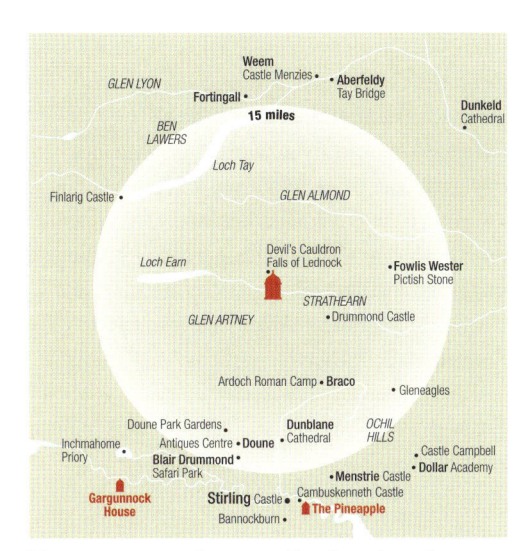

For up to 4 people
Open fire
Enclosed garden
Parking nearby

This building was designed by Charles Rennie Mackintosh and dates from 1903–4, a time when he was doing his very best work (see The Hill House). It was commissioned (at whose suggestion we know not) by a local draper and ironmonger, Peter Macpherson, as a shop with a flat above and workrooms in the attics. The flat passed into separate ownership some years ago, but we were able to reunite the two, by buying the flat in 1985, and then the shop as well, from Mr. Macpherson's granddaughter.

We have redecorated the flat, which has good and characteristic detail. The main room runs into the projecting turret, or tourelle, which Mackintosh added to the outer angle of the building in a nod towards Scottish Baronial architecture. This gives it an airy feel, and a pleasant view of the River Earn and the wooded hills beyond. At the back is a long garden, reached by a passage from the street.

Comrie is an unfussy highland town, with a bridge over a pebbly river, a whitewashed church and a small square, on the corner of which, right at the centre of things, stands this distinguished and surprising building.

From the logbook
Magnificent countryside and enough to do and see to fill a lifetime.

It has made us quite determined to find out more about Charles Rennie Mackintosh.

The marriage of Mackintosh building to Landmark Trust is a truly happy one.

First floor

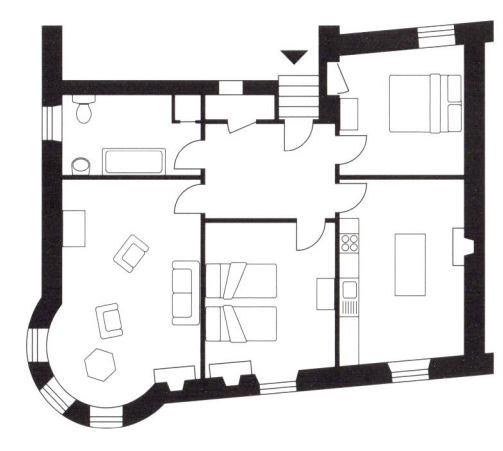

www.landmarktrust.org.uk

Maesyronen Chapel

Near Hay-on-Wye, Powys [I4]

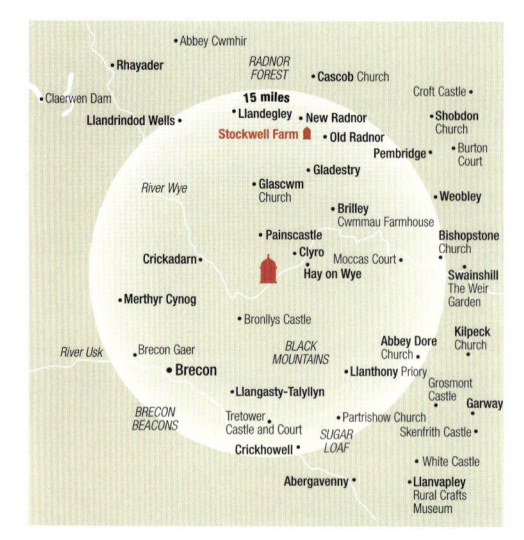

For up to 4 people
Open fire
Enclosed garden

Adjacent parking
Dogs allowed

Here we have taken on the neat and tiny cottage built before 1750 on to the end of one of Wales's shrines of Nonconformity, the Maesyronen chapel. The chapel itself, converted from a barn in 1696, dates from the early vernacular days when any suitable building was made use of for enthusiastic worship. Although officially founded just after the Act of Toleration, it had probably been used for secret meetings before that, which explains its isolated position. Its simple layout and furniture, added as and when the congregation could afford it, follows the basic pattern that prevailed for the next two centuries. It has high box-pews and a higher pulpit, lit from behind by a window, and all of a plainness that fully conveys the essentials of this new and radical rural faith.

The chapel, where services are still held, is cared for by Trustees, who asked for our help. By taking a lease on the cottage we hope we have given both buildings a future. Staying here, perched on a high shelf above the Wye (wrapped up warmly in winter), you can look out across the Black Mountains. Here you can sample a different and earlier kind of life from one that has tended to eclipse it in the public imagination, that which grew up around the chapels of the South Wales valleys in the nineteenth century.

From the logbook
All objectives achieved. 1. good walking; 2. peace and quiet; 3. cosy cottage; 4. escape rat race.

Come to Maesyronen especially to 'do' the Hay bookshops.

We will miss the mountains tomorrow night.

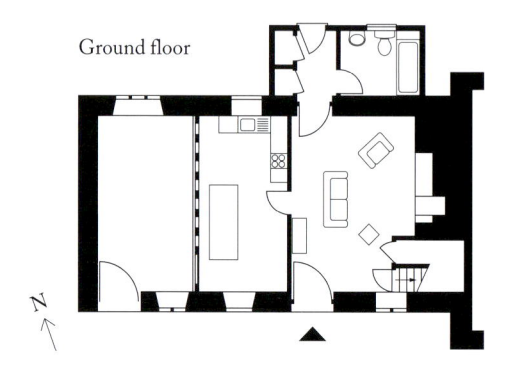

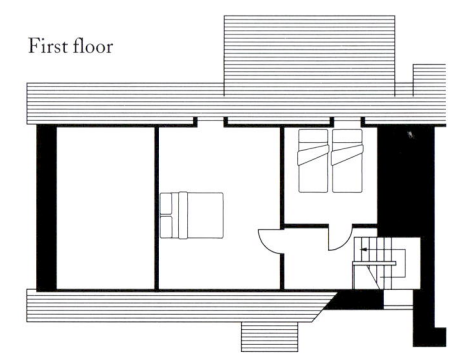

Ground floor   First floor

Manor Farm

Pulham Market, near Diss, Norfolk [H9]

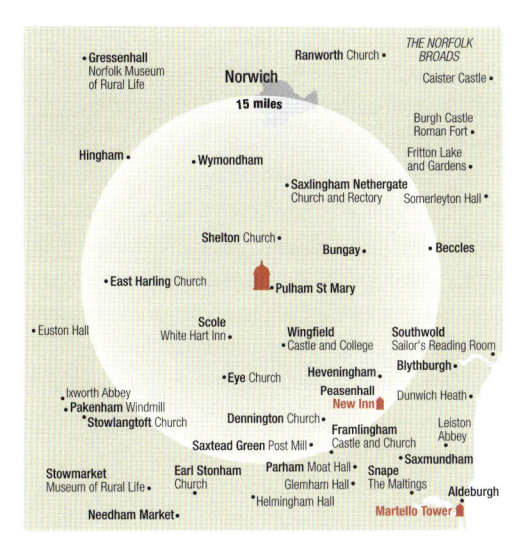

For up to 8 people
Open fire
Garden
Small moat nearby
Adjacent parking
Steep staircases
Dogs allowed

Manor Farm is a vernacular building, put up by men who had done the same job many times before and knew just what they were doing. It is mainly late Elizabethan and, apart from minor additions, has not been altered since. South Norfolk was then more thickly populated, and wooded, than today; Pulham was a thriving market town and there is no sign here that oak was in short supply. The yeoman farmer whose home it was added to his income with a bit of weaving – Pulham work, a furnishing fabric, was well-known. To judge by his house, he was quite comfortably off.

In the first half of the twentieth century a good living was more difficult to come by for a small farmer. Manor Farm decayed, and its vulnerable thatch and plaster disintegrated. The lavish oak partitions and moulded beams were nearly sold as antiques. But in 1948 it was recognised for what it was and rescued in the nick of time by Mr and Mrs Dance of the Society for the Protection of Ancient Buildings, who repaired it to the highest of William Morris's standards, and who later bequeathed Methwold Old Vicarage to the SPAB (now leased to us to be enjoyed as a Landmark).

We continue to maintain the building with a light touch that helps keep traditional craft skills alive: in 2006, much of the roof was rethatched with longstraw, once a material in common use but now rarely used.

From the logbook
Landmark holidays are so enjoyable we have resolved to give up flying and explore the UK. Seven of us here without a car – the perfect break from city life.

Ground floor

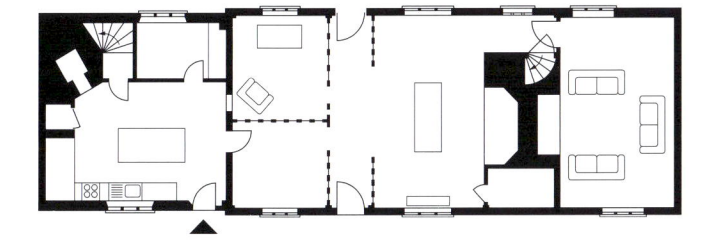

First floor

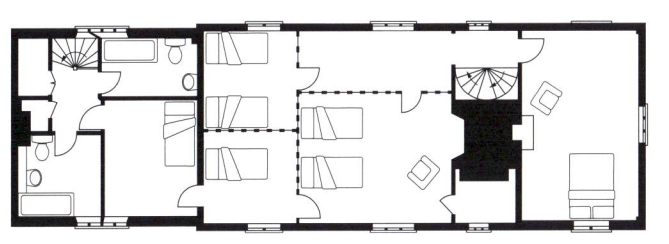

www.landmarktrust.org.uk

Margells

Branscombe, Devon [K4]

For up to 5 people
Open fire
Garden

Parking nearby
Dogs allowed

From outside this is just a plain stone cottage, pleasant enough if unremarkable; but inside it is another matter. The broad passage running across the middle of the house has oak partitions on each side, and both the downstairs rooms have ceilings of heavily moulded oak beams. Upstairs the rooms are open to the roof, and a contemporary wall painting remains in one of them. The staircase has solid oak treads and all the doorways are of well-above-average quality. It is a very strong, interesting and well-preserved interior, dating from the end of the sixteenth century.

What is all this doing in so small a house and where, indeed, was the kitchen? The explanation may be that this was the parlour wing of a larger house, which was later divided into several cottages. Whatever the answer, the result is most satisfying.

Moreover, the surroundings are extremely pleasant. The group of old cottages, of which Margells is one, includes a distinctly agreeable pub. Near the house a stream of water comes out of a spout in the wall and flows away under the road. Opposite, over the roofs, a wood climbs up a hill, and beyond that is the sea.

From the logbook
We have loved the fresh air and exercise and long evenings with the fire lit in a wonderful, warm, welcoming house.

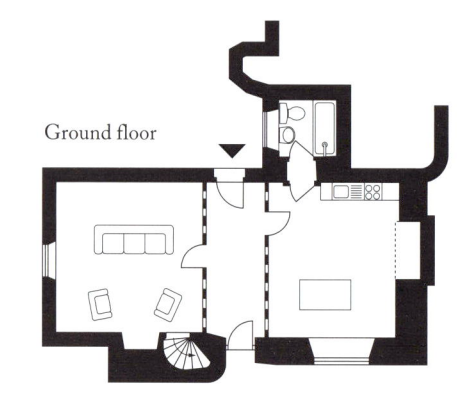

Marshal Wade's House

Abbey Churchyard, Bath [J5]

For up to 4 people
Access by narrow, steep stairs

No private parking
Gas coal fire

Other Landmarks in Bath:
Beckford's Tower
Elton House

This is a sophisticated building of about 1720 in the very centre of the town. Once there were others like it, but they have gone, taking with them the reputation of good architects practising in Bath before the more famous Woods. They must have found a good patron in George Wade (made Field Marshal in 1744) who was the city's MP and whose London house was designed by Lord Burlington.

When we took it on in 1975, we first of all restored the windows and the shop front, and decluttered and restored the interiors. Later, we cleaned the front too, with sprinkled water and lime poultices to dissolve encrusted grime.

The second-floor rooms have good panelling, and all the windows look along the west front of the Abbey. From here, on a level with the angels, you can see the great carving of Jacob's ladder. There is also an exceptional view from the bathroom on the third floor, and from the bath.

All around there are more good things to see within walking distance than almost anywhere in Britain. Leave your car behind, come by train, live over the shop, just be in Bath.

From the logbook
This is such a special Landmark; one of those that you can't believe you're actually allowed to stay in.

Everything within easy reach on foot – essential in Bath!

The Abbey Square was like an Italian piazza.

Living here is like having a box at the theatre.

Martello Tower

Aldeburgh, Suffolk [H9]

For up to 4 people
Solid fuel stove
Roof terrace

Parking nearby
Shower only
Dogs allowed

This is the largest and most northerly of the chain of towers put up by the Board of Ordnance to keep out Napoleon. Built in the shape of a quatrefoil for four heavy guns, nearly a million bricks were used in its construction. It stands at the root of the Orford Ness peninsula, between the River Alde and the sea, a few hundred yards from Aldeburgh. We bought it, sadly damaged, in 1971, with eight acres of saltings. We removed the derelict 1930s superstructure (once rather elegant, by Justin Vulliamy), repaired the outer brickwork and parapet (a tremendous job) and restored the vaulted interior, which has a floor of teak and an intriguing echo. The bedrooms are screened from the central living area but not fully divided, so that, lying in bed, you can still have a sense of being in a larger loftier space – and you can enjoy some conversation with your fellow guests.

Martello Towers were built to deter the French, not the elements, and inevitably, in this exposed position, some of the water finds its way inside. Purpose-made canopies over the main living space now provides significant protection, giving an agreeable nautical resonance of sails and campaign tents. Here you may live with the sea, the wind and rain sometimes, the light at Orford Ness flashing at night, and Aldeburgh at just the right distance. The stone-flagged battery on the roof, with the mountings of guns and a high, thick parapet for shelter, is a very pleasant place to be. Amber and bloodstones, brought by glaciers from Scandinavia, have been found on the beach. Many visitors bring sailing dinghies.

Main floor

Bridge

Methwold Old Vicarage

Methwold, Norfolk [H8]

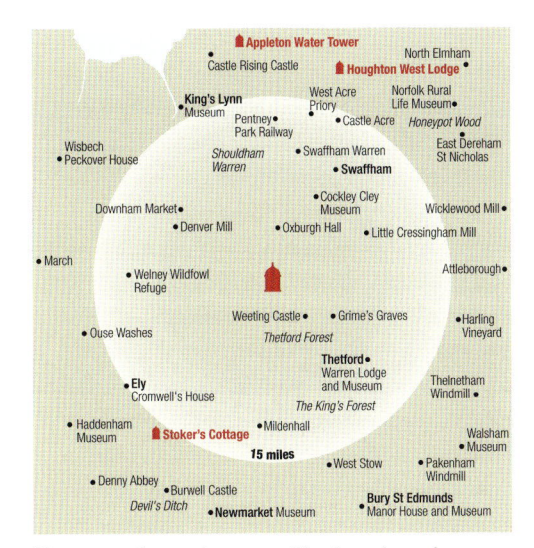

For up to 5 people
Open fire and solid fuel stove
Enclosed garden
Adjacent parking
Dogs allowed

No vicar has lived in the Old Vicarage at Methwold for over two hundred years, but this is the least of the puzzles about this intriguing building. Externally, its chief glory is the late fifteenth-century brick gable-end, whose octagonal stack seems a sampler of early Tudor patterns. This gable-end is unique in Norfolk and possibly beyond, and despite its modest village setting, bears comparison with the greatest early East Anglian brickwork such as that of Oxburgh and Layer Marney.

The jettied, timber-framed range behind the gable is also advanced for its day, the stout cruciform spine beams on both floors telling of a building designed to have two storeys from the start. These beams are beautifully moulded and so too are the fireplace surrounds and bressumer. Upstairs acanthus leaves by the hand of a late sixteenth-century craftsman run rampant across stud and plasterwork.

The greatest puzzle is why such a richly decorated house should have been built for the priest of a village on the edge of the fens, famed only for its rabbits – but this need not trouble unduly those who come to take pleasure in its rarity. The Old Vicarage had been condemned for demolition when Monica and Harry Dance came to its rescue in 1964, and they eventually relinquished Manor Farm to Landmark in order to move to Methwold. The Dances later bequeathed the Old Vicarage to the Society for the Protection of Ancient Buildings, of which Monica was the renowned Secretary for many years and from whom we were happy to accept a long lease.

An engaging nineteenth-century vicar of Methwold, the Reverend Denny Gedge, bemoaned the dilapidated state of the Old Vicarage even in his own day (living himself in a 'neat new vicarage at the other end of the parish') and wailed, 'Oh! if some charitable millionaire even now would buy it … its price would be very small.' We think he would have approved of today's solution.

From the logbook
[I wonder] who was sitting here by the fire to be told of the Armada, or Cromwell's victory?

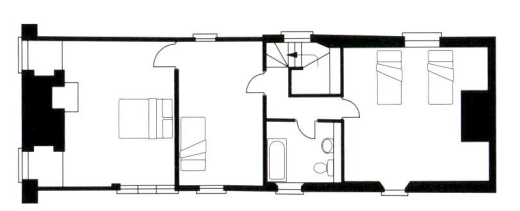

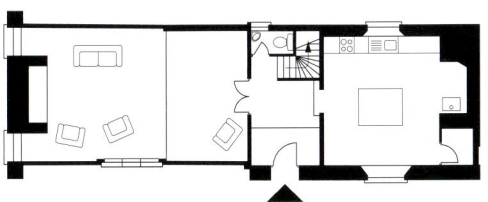

First floor

Ground floor

www.landmarktrust.org.uk

Monkton Old Hall

Monkton, Pembrokeshire [I2]

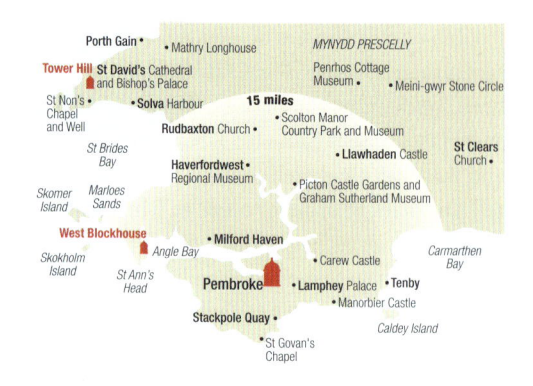

For up to 7 people
Open fire
Enclosed garden

Adjacent parking
Steep spiral staircase
Dogs allowed

Although much altered and rebuilt, the Old Hall has a strongly medieval character, a mixture of spareness and solidity. It dates from before 1400 and was probably the guest house of a small priory outside the walls of Pembroke. Just off the pilgrim route to St David's, and close to a great castle, the monks could expect to put up any number of people at unexpected times. Since then the house has been left to become ruinous at least twice, and then been rescued in the nick of time.

Its Victorian saviour was J. R. Cobb, a scholar and romantic who restored several castles in South Wales. In the 1930s it was discovered again, by Miss Muriel Thompson, another romantic. She repaired the house, with help from Clough Williams-Ellis, and created a garden, on a long and possibly ancient terrace cut out of the hillside. She wanted to share her home with others, to revive a monastic sense of hospitality: many people came to stay and her Christmas parties were famous. It was the memory of this and the appeal the Old Hall has, especially for children, that made Mrs Campbell, to whom it was left, think of passing it on to us.

We made the house slightly smaller by removing a decaying nineteenth-century wing, and moved a massive stone chimney piece from a bedroom to the hall. To improve this lofty and noble room further we painted its roof timbers a deep Pugin red. With this and the long vaulted undercroft beneath, an empty space for children to let off steam, and the large and interesting garden, with its old walls and grandstand view of Pembroke Castle, you may feel little temptation to stray into the lively town just beyond its walls. But should you wish to make your own pilgrimage to St David's, or explore the cliffs and castles of Pembrokeshire, or just go to the beach, the house will welcome you back, to warm yourself by the fire.

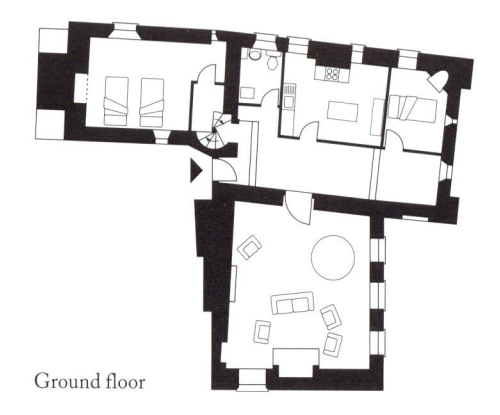

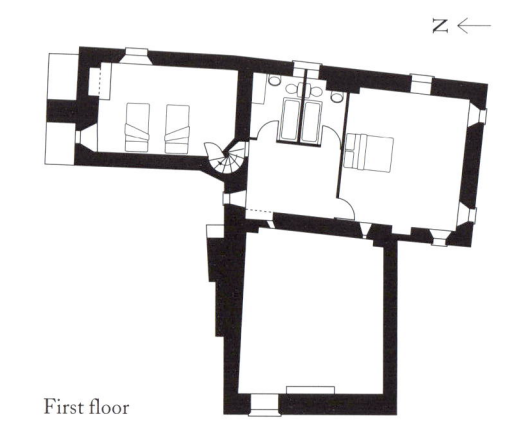

Please note there are stairs to the twin bedroom shown on the ground floor and further stairs between the double and the twin on the first floor.

Ground floor

First floor

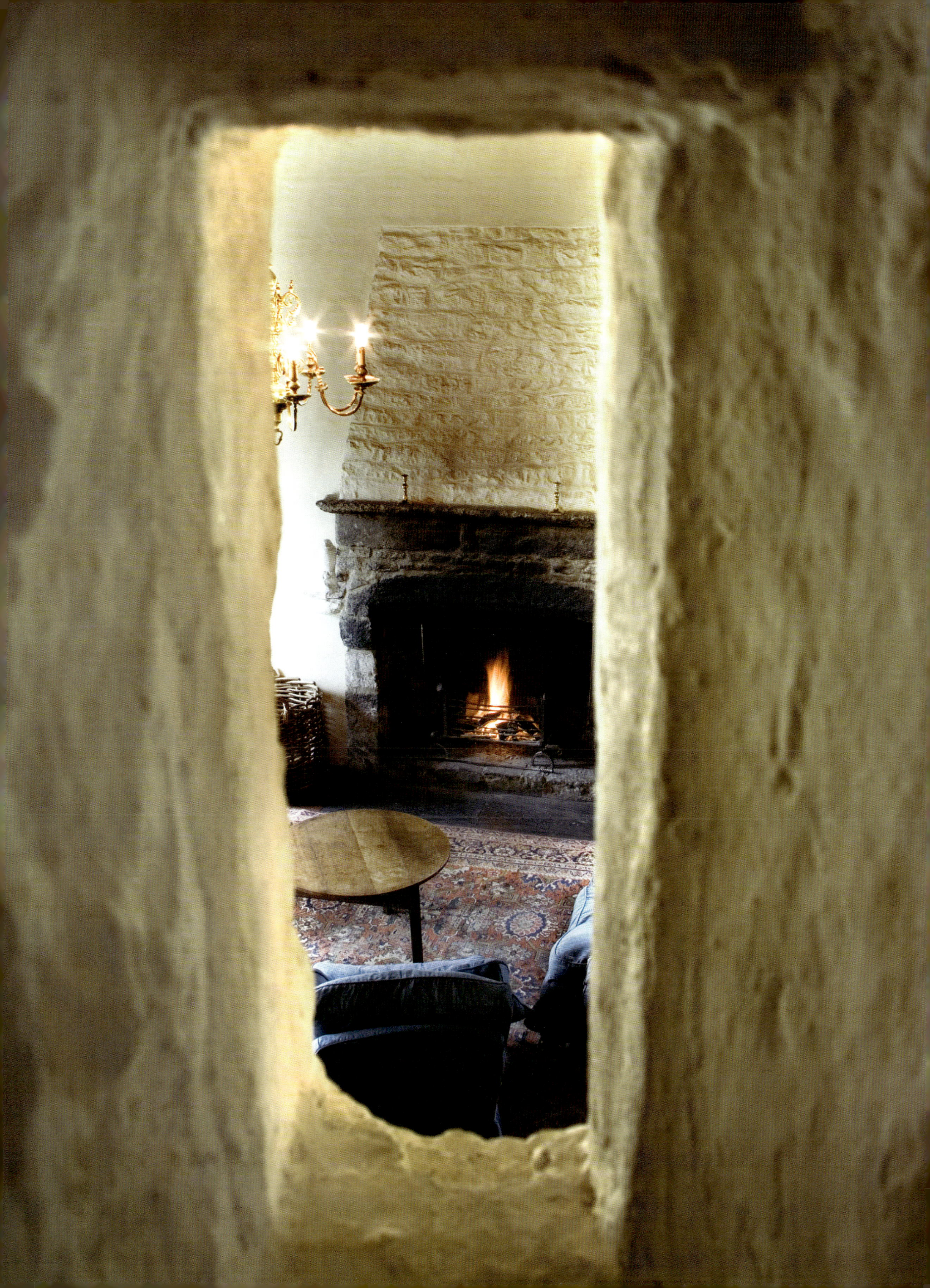

Morpeth Castle

Morpeth, Northumberland [C5]

For up to 7 people
Solid fuel stove
Enclosed garden

Adjacent parking
Steep spiral staircase
Dogs allowed

The walls of a new castle in Morpeth were built soon after 1200, on a hill overlooking the River Wansbeck. Our gatehouse was added a century later, more for show than defence. Its builder, Lord Greystoke, wanted its presence felt, because this was to be a court-house, in which manorial justice was dispensed – an important function in the unruly Borders. The court was held in the large room on the first floor.

This room was divided by a screen, behind which the plaintiffs waited (its replacement hides nothing more dangerous than the kitchen). Between sittings the gatehouse served as a lodging, probably for the bailiff. These arrangements disappeared in later alterations, however, just before 1700 and again in 1860. Each time, a new house was formed inside the walls. We have tried to keep something of each but to make sense of the medieval layout as well.

In 1516 Margaret, sister of Henry VIII and widow of James IV of Scotland, stayed for four months in Morpeth Castle as she fled from her enemies in Scotland and sought refuge with her brother. The one great military event in the castle's history was in 1644 when a garrison of 500 Lowland Scots held it for Parliament for 20 days against 2,700 Royalists.

The castle stands on a small plateau, above Morpeth and with fine views of it, but completely removed from the bustle. Once inside the curtain wall, whose circuit is battered but still complete, you could be inside the most remote Border stronghold.

From the logbook
The castle is warm and welcoming – a home from home, except we don't live in castles.

Marvellous acoustics in the great hall – we brought our own minstrels.

Attic floor

Second floor

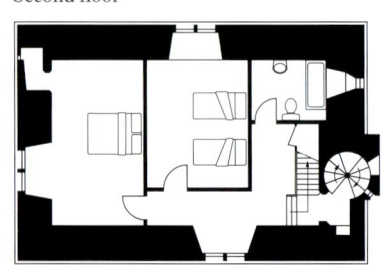

First floor

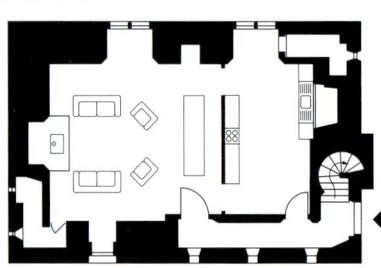

The Music Room

Sun Street, Lancaster [E4]

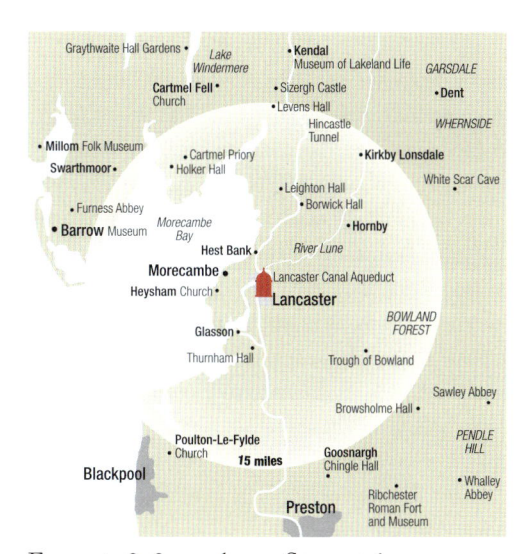

For up to 2+2 people
Roof terrace
Steep staircase
Parking for 1 car

Second floor

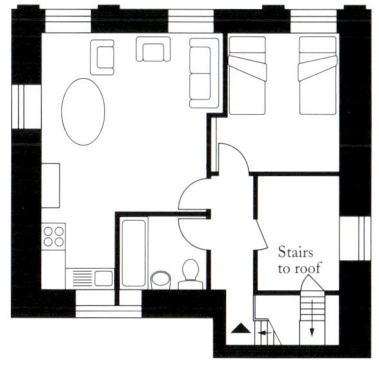

First floor

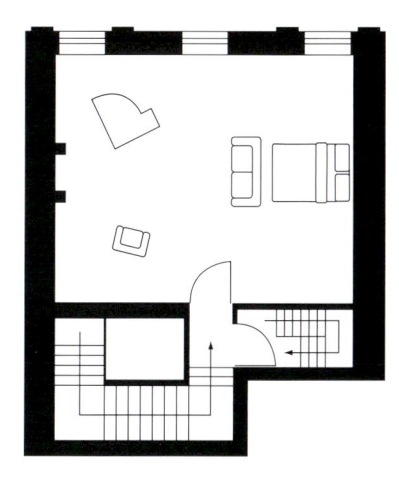

The Music Room had been well known for years as a building in distress, but nothing could be done because it had other buildings hard up against it on all four sides. On our first visit we had to reach it by walking through the toy warehouse of which it formed a part. We had to buy all these buildings and demolish them (a long job) to give the builders access.

It seems to have been built in about 1730 as a garden pavilion, but its surroundings have long been overlaid with streets. In the nineteenth century it became part of a stained-glass factory. When we arrived it had a temporary roof and many broken windows. Most of the plasterwork had fallen, but luckily almost all of it was in the building.

We turned the loggia into a shop by glazing the central Ionic arch and removing an inserted floor; it did not seem sensible to leave this large space lifeless and empty in the middle of a town. In front, a lively pedestrian square had sprung up.

The plasterwork of the music room itself took 6,000 hours of work to repair. It is an exceptional Baroque interior, where you may now sleep as well as play the piano. On the walls are the muses: eloquence, history, music, astronomy, tragedy, rhetoric, dancing, comedy and amorous poetry; with Apollo over the fireplace. A fruitful goddess with a torch presides over the ceiling. One muse had vanished entirely and was recreated by the plasterers from Sutton Coldfield as a modern girl, big and busty, with a cheerful eye; she makes an excellent muse of dancing.

In the attic above, reached by a narrow stair, we made a flat. From it and from the small terrace on its roof there are distant views over Lancaster (including a fine view of the Castle from the sink); and at all times, waiting for you to enter it, there is the stillness of the music room below, both full and empty at the same time, as is the way with rich interiors. Lancaster is a fine town, with many things worthy of attention, not least Rennie's monumental aqueduct on the Lancaster Canal, bridging the River Lune like a vestige of imperial Rome.

www.landmarktrust.org.uk

New Inn

Peasenhall, Suffolk [H9]

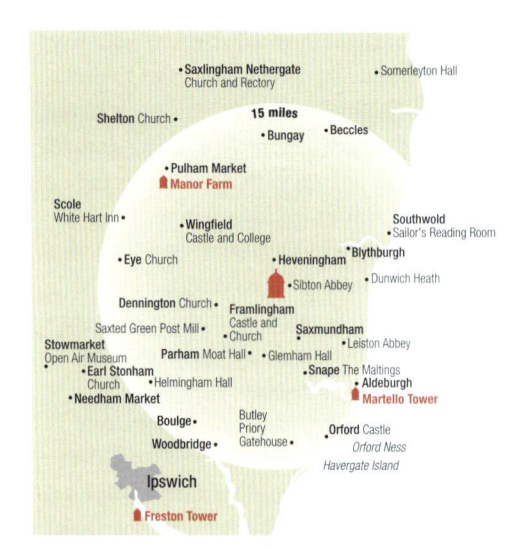

High End
For up to 2+2 people
Shared garden
Adjacent parking

Low End
For up to 4 people
Open fire
Shared garden
Adjacent parking

The Cottage
For up to 5 people
Solid fuel stove
Shared garden
Parking nearby
Steep staircase
Low ceiling on upper floors

All have shared use of the hall

The centre of this handsome range of buildings is a late medieval hall-house, in use as an inn by 1478, and almost certainly built as such. Inns were then a fairly new invention, which had arrived in response to an increase in trade and therefore of travellers. It was some time before they evolved into a distinct building type, however; until then most kept to the basic form that everyone knew, of a hall with chambers off it – and this is just what there is at the New Inn.

We repaired the hall and all the other cottages in the row as well. The three oldest we kept as Landmarks. Two of them, at each end of the impressive hall, are entered from it, as they would have been originally. (The hall is open to the public and is sometimes visited.) The high end is the grander, with one particularly fine bedroom – a solar or great chamber with a crown-post roof.

At the backs of the cottages we removed some decayed sheds to make a garden and a place to hide cars. We also bought the land in front, closed the road that ran across it, and turned it into a village green. Peasenhall is a long, open village, with a stream running beside the road. It is much-visited by connoisseurs of sausages and ham, sold in more than one of its excellent shops. Add oysters from Orford, fish from Aldeburgh, wines from Framlingham vineyards, and sit down to your own feast in the lofty hall, as might those medieval travellers over 500 years ago.

From the logbook
Spent hours studying the beautiful carpentry of the building's oak frame.

The Landmark Trust library here is too good. Too much interest and no time to read.

High End

Low End

Ground floor   First floor   Second floor

High End

Hall

Low End

The Cottage

N ↑

www.landmarktrust.org.uk   129

Nicolle Tower

St Clement, Jersey [N5]

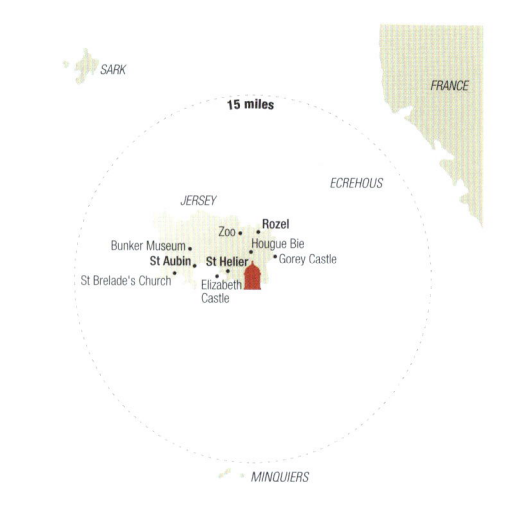

For up to 2 people
Garden
Adjacent parking
Steep staircase

We were reluctant to take on this building until we actually went to see it. As often, there proved to be much more to it, and to the place, than a description or a snapshot could convey. Therefore we bought it, and its owner also sold us the field of five vergees in which the tower stands.

The field is called *Le Clos de Hercanty*. Hercanty means 'tilted menhir', and one corner of the tower, tantalisingly, is built on a large half-buried slab of diorite. Moreover, on this boulder is carved a compass rose and a date, 1644, so something has been going on here for a long time. It seems that the menhir was once a navigation mark, next to which a small rectangular lookout was built. In 1821 Philippe Nicolle, who had just bought the field, added a light-hearted Gothick octagon with the present very pretty sitting-room on the first floor.

In 1943 the Germans, to make an observation or control position here, astutely raised the roof of the octagon by one more storey, so that no change would be noticed from the air. As this latest addition is part of the history of the tower, we have left it there, with its slit eyes and German ranging marks on its thick concrete ceiling. The tower stands 160 feet up, well back from the coast, with, it need hardly be said, views over the sea and island in every direction.

From the logbook
Peace, lovely walks, our own tower to live in – what more could you want?

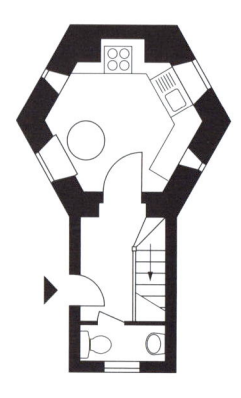

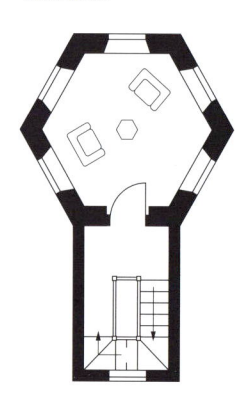

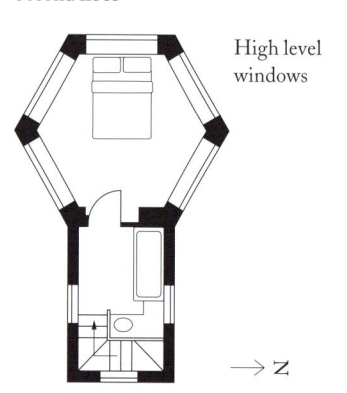

Ground floor First floor Second floor

High level windows

North Street

Cromford, Derbyshire [G6]

For up to 4 people
Open fire
Small rear yard

Parking nearby
Steep staircase
Dogs allowed

North Street is one of Landmark's quiet gems. To stay here is to stay in an important piece of history, because North Street is the earliest planned industrial housing in the world and the finest of its type ever built – vastly superior to that of the next century, and now lying at the heart of a designated World Heritage Site. It was built in 1771 by Richard Arkwright to house his mill workers, and named after the Prime Minister. The three-storey gritstone houses have one room on each floor, with a room for framework-knitting in the attic. Each has a small garden and an allotment at a distance. No. 10 has a croft, or paddock, as well, at the back of the houses, which our visitors (and their children) can use.

In 1974, the Ancient Monuments Society, with then unfashionable foresight, bought six of the houses to save them from demolition. We took them on from the Society, then bought a further three houses on the same side of the street and re-roofed and improved all nine, restoring the long windows of the attic workrooms. One house with a particularly well-preserved interior (No.10) we repaired as a Landmark so that people can experience and reflect upon the living quarters of these earliest of factory workers. Their lot was perhaps a gentler one than that of later workers, but you may still find yourself touched and inspired.

Cromford is an excellent little town, with a fascinating and ongoing local project to restore Arkwright's mills. The area is full of interest for those absorbed by industrial archaeology, while nearby Bolsover, Hardwick Hall and Chatsworth cater for those with a taste for the more polite. The Derby Dales and Cromford Canal offer good walking, and then there is Matlock, a genuine inland resort, at whose petrifying wells you can have your bowler hat turned into stone.

From the logbook
We love the house, we have been immersed in the world of Richard Arkwright, cotton mills, canals and buildings.

No. 10 is the second house from the right.

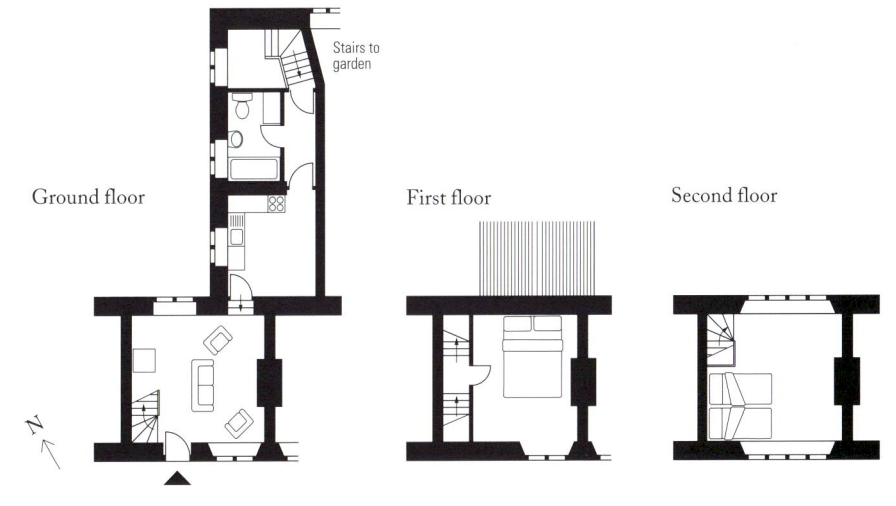

Ground floor   First floor   Second floor

www.landmarktrust.org.uk   131

Obriss Farm

Near Westerham, Kent [J8]

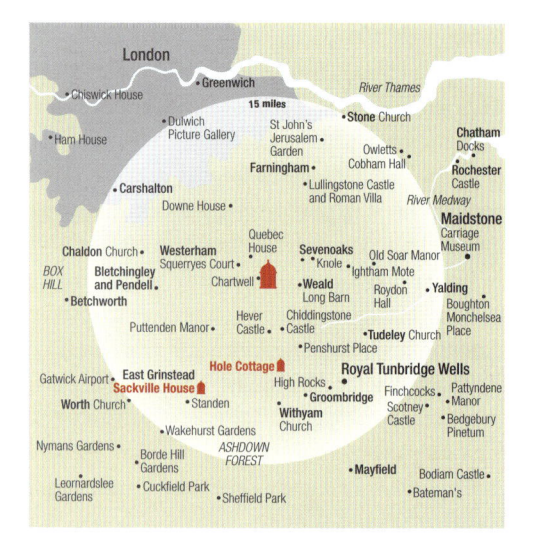

Obriss Farm sits on the lower slopes of Toys Hill, looking south over the Weald. It was given to us by the executors of Mrs Helena Cooper – 160 acres, mainly of pasture, with some woods, and at the centre, well away from any roads, a compact group of buildings which, with their mixture of brick, timber and tile, fit comfortably into the landscape. The field pattern here has not changed since 1840, probably even before that. Besides the farmhouse in which you stay and a smoke house behind it with a tall chimney, all the traditional buildings are here: byres, stable and sheds round the yard in front of the house, and off to one side the great threshing barn. Our farmer continues to farm the land around and uses some of the outbuildings for lambing. The gentle activity which goes on around you will be part of the pleasure and interest of staying here, yet surrounded by ancient woodland, Obriss is unexpectedly peaceful, an island out of time in this busy part of the country.

From the logbook
Difficult to believe we are so close to London when the view from the windows convinces us we are alone in Eden.

We didn't need to count the sheep to fall asleep.

We felt generations of people having lived with us.

For up to 5 people
Open fire
Garden and access to farmland
Adjacent parking

First floor

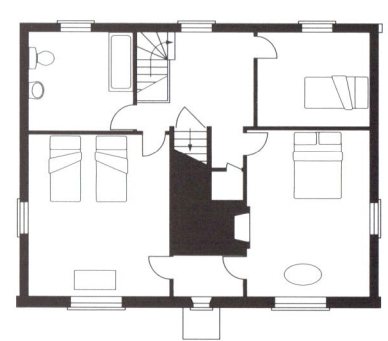

Ground floor

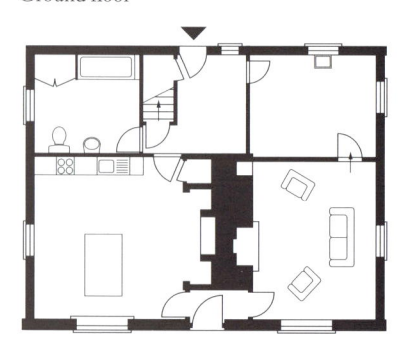

132   The Landmark Trust Handbook

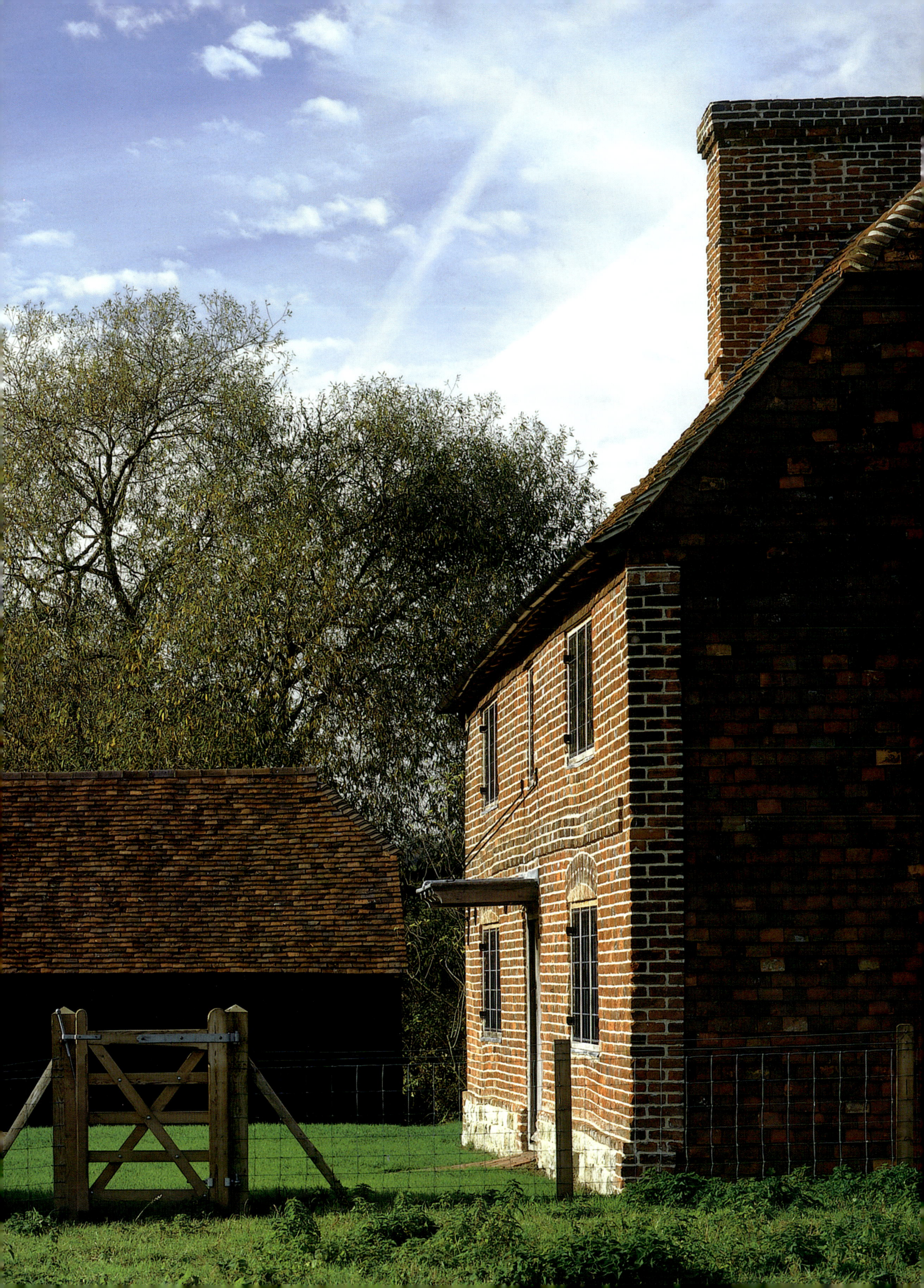

Old Campden House

Chipping Campden, Gloucestershire [I6]

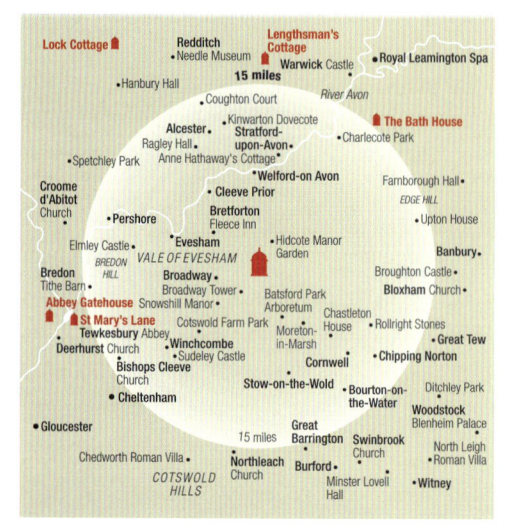

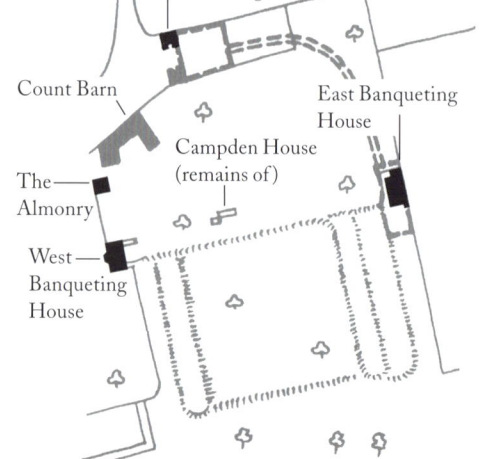

Two banqueting houses, one for 4+2 and one for 2+2.

In 1613 the newly enriched Sir Baptist Hicks began work on a house in Chipping Campden. It was a noble work in the latest fashion, with intricate gardens. 30 years later it was destroyed, wantonly, by the Royalists, when in 1645 they withdrew from the town. 'The house (which was so faire) burnt,' noted one, sadly.

Only a shell was left, now shrunk to a single fragment. But other, lesser, buildings escaped the fire, and are still there, together with the raised walks of the garden.

The ogee domes of the lodges are well known, but in the field beyond are two banqueting houses with ebullient strapwork parapets which have been given to us by a descendant of Sir Baptist, together with the lodges, the small building known as the Almonry and the historic site.

The banqueting houses stand at either end of the broad terrace that ran along the garden front of the house. Sir Baptist would bring his guests to them at the end of dinner, to drink rare wines, eat dried fruit and sweetmeats, and admire his domain. After the razing of the main house, the passing years have given each banqueting house its separate history and character, which we have acknowledged adjusting them for use as Landmarks.

To get to either, you must walk along a grassy path, leaving your car just outside in the former henyard. Both banqueting houses have their annexes, the North Lodge or the Almonry. Whether you choose to sip Tokay and nibble the crystallised petals of a flower, or make do with fish and chips and beer, in this place it cannot fail to taste sublime.

Open Days are held at Old Campden House annually. Please check our website for details. The grounds will also be open to the public on certain days during the year but this is most unlikely to happen while the buildings are occupied.

From the logbook
The view out of the bathroom window at sunrise is spectacular.

Couldn't recommend many places of interest as we didn't feel the urge to leave this beautiful house…

East Banqueting House

Deceptively diminutive from the terrace, this banqueting house has two further floors below, hidden by the lie of the land, once holding a self-contained apartment and executed with crisp Jacobean élan. It overlooks the Coneygree, an ancient ground now owned by the National Trust and no doubt the scene of many a hare course for the entertainment of Sir Baptist's guests after dinner. More recently, in the nineteenth century, the Earl of Gainsborough used the loggia to review his militia as they ran through their drill on the Coneygree. A further twin bedroom and bathroom are provided in one of the pepperpot lodges – this time as diminutive as it looks.

For up to 4+2 people
Solid fuel stove
Open grounds
Parking nearby
Steep staircases

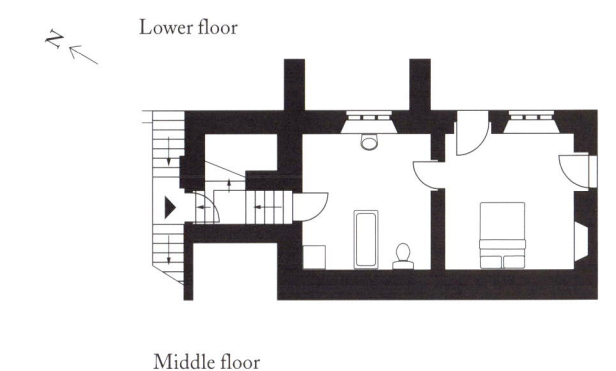

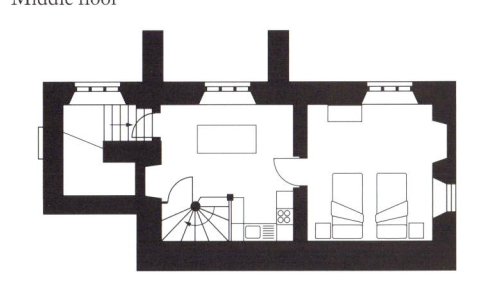

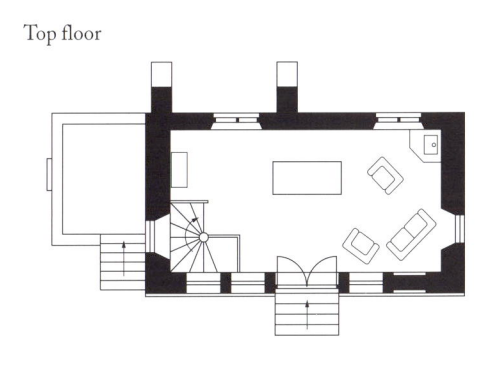

Lower floor

Middle floor

Top floor

There is a twin bedroom and a bathroom in the North Lodge (not shown), a short walk away.

www.landmarktrust.org.uk

Old Campden House

West Banqueting House and Almonry

The West Banqueting House is also more spacious than it looks, with a large, barrel vaulted chamber on the ground floor and a hearth at either end – perhaps once a kitchen, as it now is again. The first floor chamber yields the only fragments of Jacobean frieze of the rich and elegant plasterwork and panelling that must once have adorned all the buildings on this site. Yet this banqueting house was converted at an early stage for humbler domestic accommodation and it may well have been the house of William Harrison, steward to Lady Juliana Hicks and a key player in the mystery known as The Campden Wonder. We have allowed this era to continue to speak in the building, by keeping a rough studwork partition and leaving the loggia windows blocked, as we found them. There is a further sitting-room and twin bedroom (with cunningly concealed bathroom) in the little building across the former bleach garden, known as the Almonry for its proximity to Sir Baptist's fine almshouses. It was previously rescued from decay in the 1920s by F. L. Griggs, providing a happy link with the Arts & Crafts movement that continues to flourish in Chipping Campden to this day.

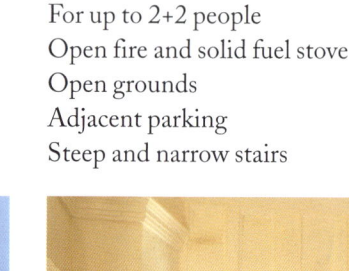

For up to 2+2 people
Open fire and solid fuel stove
Open grounds
Adjacent parking
Steep and narrow stairs

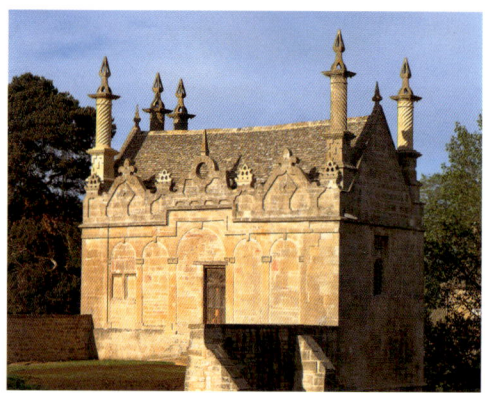

The West Banqueting House, *above*, *right* and *far right*.

West Banqueting House

The Almonry

Ground floor

First floor

Lower floor

Loggia floor

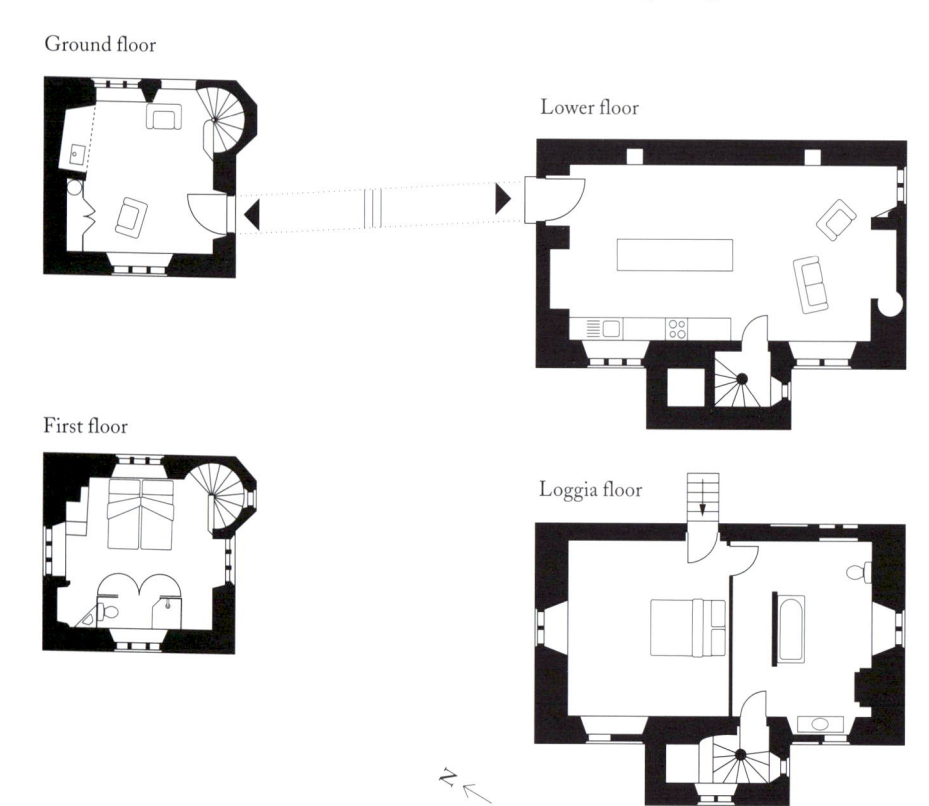

The Almonry

136   The Landmark Trust Handbook

The Old Hall

Croscombe, Somerset [J5]

Originally the great hall of a manor house built by Sir William Palton in about 1420, this building was for 250 years a Baptist chapel. It lies just north of the handsome parish church and looks into a small tranquil enclosure, part garden and part graveyard.

The Baptists, but for whom the building would certainly have disappeared, made a number of harmless alterations. Removal of these – and the repair and consolidation of the tottering structure, with its wavy roof of pantiles, like a shaken rug – revealed quite a grand hall with a particularly fine arch-braced open roof.

In its south wall we found the great blocked arch of an oriel chamber, which once linked the hall to a vanished wing to the east. Beside it a rare medieval light-bracket appeared, decorated with the arms of Sir William and his wife. The service end of the hall we turned into bedrooms and kitchen, simple rooms of wood and stone.

When working on this building, we were offered a fully operational Gurney's Patent Stove from Romsey Abbey, which we installed here to give extra heat in the hall, a challenge in view of its size. Keeping it stoked up provides much entertainment, and some strenuous exercise.

From the logbook
Though we sought out two other 15th century hall houses we saw nothing as fine as this great hall.

Years spent as an archaeologist working on ruins cannot equal the pleasure of living in the real thing.

For up to 5 people
Solid fuel stove
Enclosed garden

Parking nearby
Dogs allowed

Ground floor

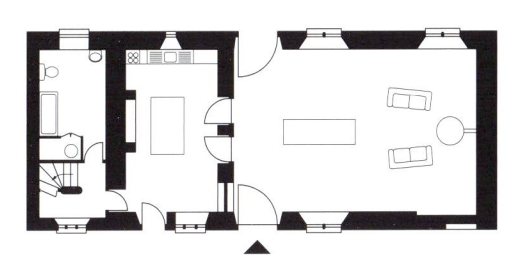

First floor

Upper part of hall

N

www.landmarktrust.org.uk   137

The Old Parsonage

Iffley, Oxford [I6]

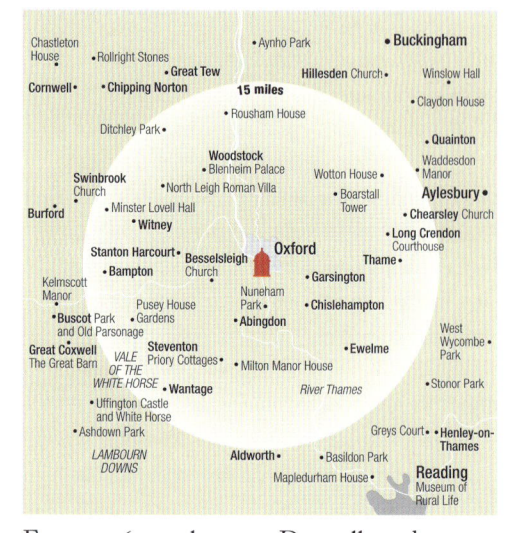

For up to 6 people
Open fire
Garden parking area

Dogs allowed
Riverside garden

Other Landmarks in Oxford:
The Steward's House

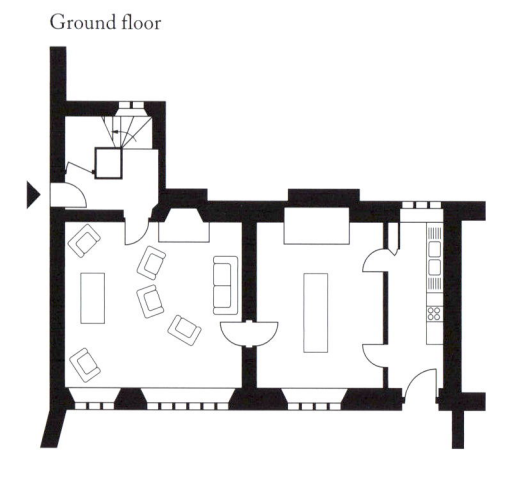

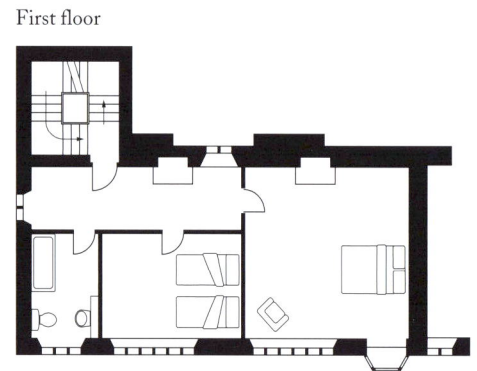

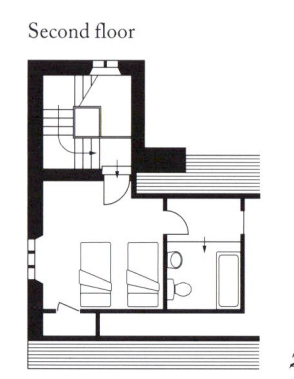

Not only an important building in its own right, this house also conveys a strong impression of a parson's life in former days. A rectory was first built here at the same time as the elaborate Norman church a few yards away (and the earlier half of the house still is a rectory, modernised by us). In about 1500, a smart new wing was added, and in it are the handsome rooms that you can occupy. Some of them were later panelled and given new fireplaces. In the parlour, probably added when J. C. Buckler worked on the house in 1857, is a tremendous Latin inscription running round the room. It says, in tall Gothic letters, 'For we know that, if our earthly house were destroyed, we have a building of God, a house not made with hands, eternal in the heavens'. Here, within its dark temporal panels, you may sit looking down the garden, as did many a scholarly leisured parson, pondering his sermon as he watched the Thames slide by.

The staircase, in a square tower of its own, is strong and plain, and reminiscent of staircases in Oxford colleges nearby. The house is entered straight off the pavement of Mill Lane, giving no hint of the long garden on the other side running down to the river at the tail of Iffley lock. The contrast is very agreeable.

From the logbook
In Oxford we walked in the footsteps of Inspector Morse and enjoyed it thoroughly.

Seriously considering never going home…

Ground floor

First floor

Second floor

Old Place of Monreith

Portwilliam, Dumfries and Galloway [D2]

For up to 8 people
Open fire and solid fuel stove
Enclosed garden
Adjacent parking
Spiral staircase
Dogs allowed

The Old Place, also known as Dowies, is a house that was left behind by the family that built it when they prospered and went to live in a castle they bought nearby in 1683. It then became a farmhouse on their estate.

Before that, however, it was the home of the Maxwells, forebears of both Sir Herbert, historian and gardener, and the author Gavin Maxwell and his brother, Sir Aymer Maxwell, who arranged its transfer to us. Built in about 1600, it is a typical, plain, lowland laird's house, still nominally fortified, at the end of a long uneven track.

When we bought it, it had been empty for 20 years. The roof and floors had fallen in, but two good fireplaces survived inside. We opened up the turnpike stair, which had been bricked up, and unblocked the main door with its stone panel for a coat of arms above.

The sea is only two miles away – the same coastline on which the Maxwell brothers grew up, at Elrig, seven miles away. Whithorn, across the peninsula, was a centre of early Christian culture around the Irish Sea, which produced such saints as Ninian, Patrick and Columba. A cross once stood near the Old Place but was moved in the nineteenth century and is now in Whithorn museum. There remains behind a strong sense of a continuous civilised life, lived here over two millennia, in a place that, even for a Landmark, is exceptionally quiet and remote.

From the logbook
Powerful sense of an ancient culture and sense of peace which has cast a spell on us all.

Wigtown, the Scottish book town, now has 23 bookshops.

Sunset over the Torhousie stone circle!

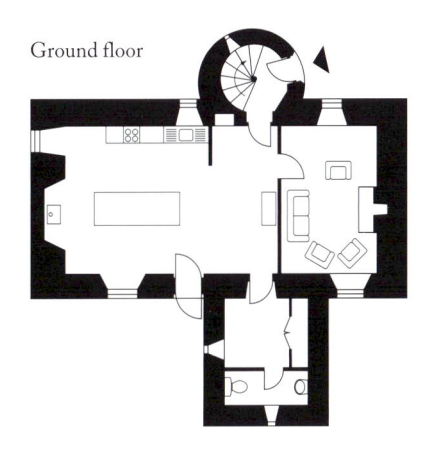

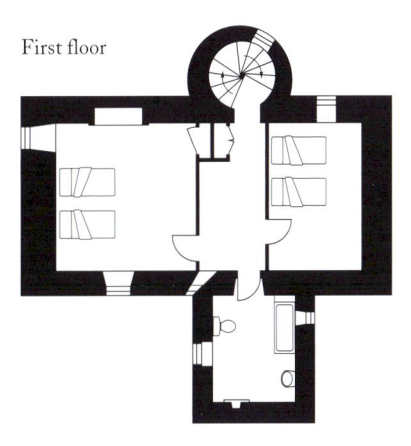

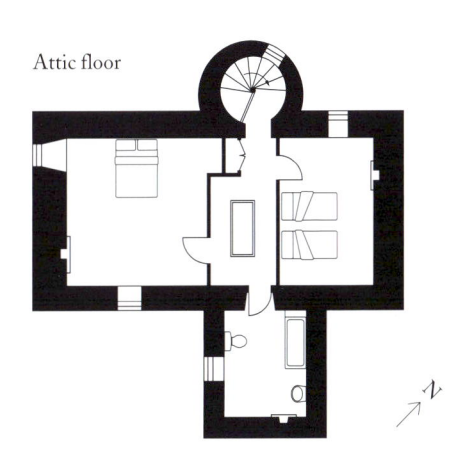

Ground floor First floor Attic floor

www.landmarktrust.org.uk 139

Oxenford Gatehouse

Elstead, Surrey [J7]

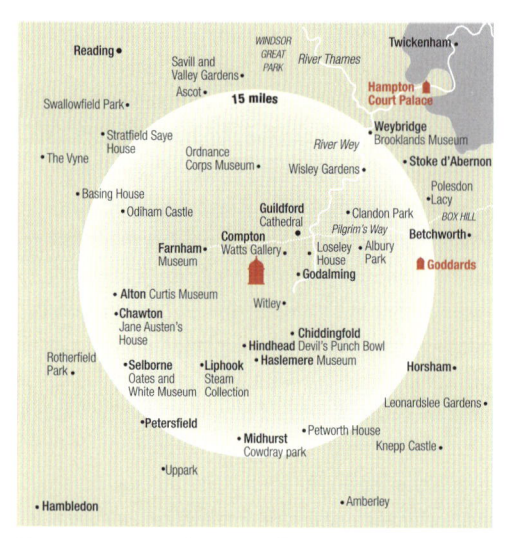

For up to 4 people
Open fire
Enclosed garden

Adjacent parking
Steep spiral staircase

Deep in the Surrey countryside stands a cluster of buildings that might, at first glance, be taken for the remnants of some ancient abbey: a great tithe barn, perhaps, next to a medieval fishpond, and a handsome, asymmetric gatehouse such as might offer hospitality at the entrance to a great estate. An ancient abbey, Waverley, did once stand near this site, but these buildings belong to more recent times.

In 1843, Lord Midleton, a young Anglican aristocrat, commissioned Augustus Pugin to dress the landscape at Oxenford with farm outbuildings and a gatehouse, to guard an entrance to his adjacent Peper Harow estate.

It was a chance to recreate the sort of honest, utilitarian buildings that Pugin so admired from the Middle Ages, a time when he felt that 'in matters of ordinary use, a man must go out of his way to produce a bad thing'.

With ample funds, for once, and at the height of his powers, Pugin produced a group of buildings generally agreed to be among his finest work, using good local materials in a Picturesque style that adapted that of the Middle Ages for his own time.

Peper Harow House, to which this gatehouse once formed an entrance, was divided into flats some years ago, and the gatehouse reverted to serve, in a residual way, Oxenford Farm, on whose lands it stands.

Today, this handsome group still fulfills its original farming purpose, with the exception of the gatehouse, for which the owner has turned to us for a use to ensure its future.

Oxenford Gatehouse will open in 2009 following restoration.

First floor

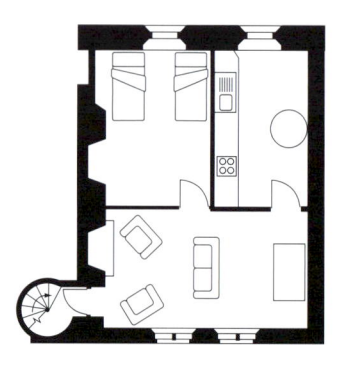

Ground floor

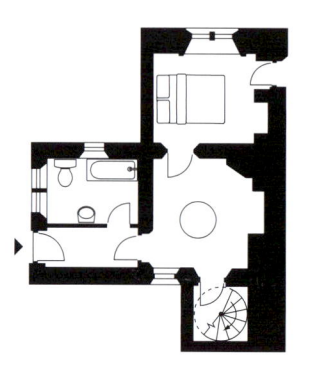

140 The Landmark Trust Handbook

Parish House

Baltonsborough, Somerset [J5]

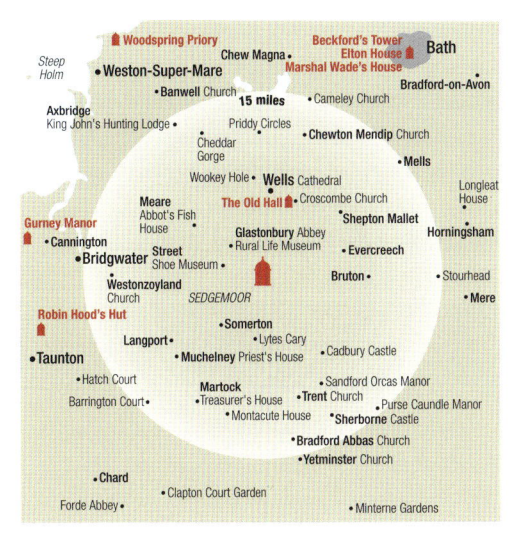

For up to 4 people
Solid fuel stove
Garden

Parking nearby
Dogs allowed

This is a rare example of a church house that has remained in the ownership and use of the parish. We have been brought in to preserve the link and to take on its care. Built in about 1500, on the edge of the churchyard, it has long served the village of Baltonsborough for meetings and festivals, both formal and convivial.

We have improved the parish meeting room on the ground floor, which still has its great hearth across one end. Above, in the part you can stay in, was a long room with an open arch-braced roof. The Tudor churchwardens exercised great economy in their building works: no timber is heavier than it need be. When this floor was later fitted out for a tenant, similar frugality ensured that the alterations were minimal and undamaging.

The long room was divided by an oak partition, which we have kept, but the graceful arched trusses still rise over your head on each side of it. From the windows of the main rooms there is a fine view of the church itself. This is entirely fifteenth-century and is dedicated to St Dunstan, Abbot of Glastonbury and Archbishop of Canterbury in the reign of Edgar the Peaceable. Under Dunstan's patronage, art and learning flourished, and after his death he was chosen as England's first patron saint.

From the logbook
Blissful, enchanting and deeply peaceful. Will never forget lying in that great bed on a sunlit morning with blossom and church song blowing in through the window.

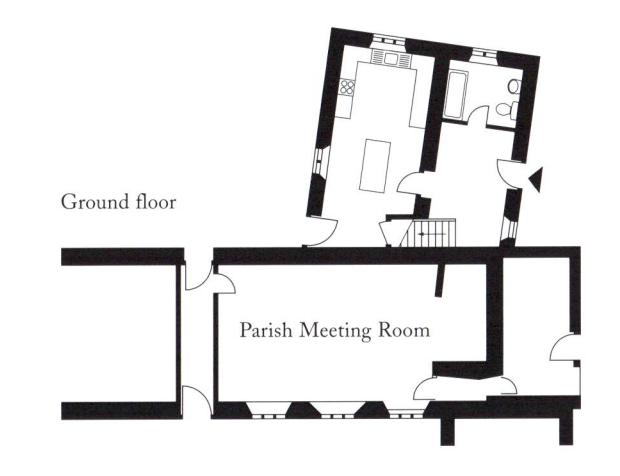

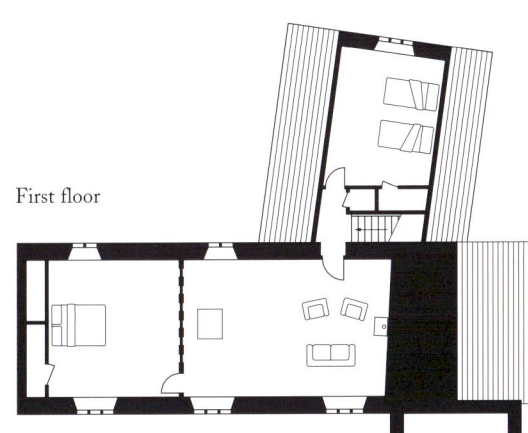

Paxton's Tower Lodge

Llanarthney, Carmarthenshire [I3]

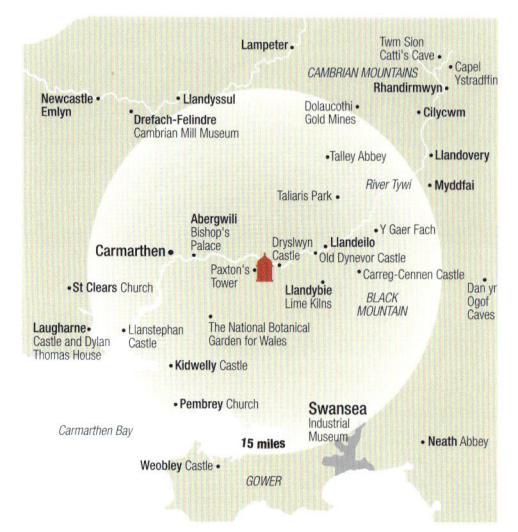

For up to 5 people
Open fire
Enclosed garden

Parking nearby
Dogs allowed

We acquired this building as part of a joint scheme with the National Trust to preserve Paxton's Tower and its surroundings. It is an early nineteenth-century cottage of well above average quality, built for the Tower's caretaker, looking south over an immense expanse of country. It is difficult to imagine a finer view. If, however, you walk a hundred yards or so up the small green hill behind, to the foot of the Tower, there, in the opposite direction, is the finer view – surely one of the best in Britain, a prospect extensive and rich, embracing the whole vale of the Tywi, whose green windings your eye can follow for 30 miles or more.

Paxton's Tower itself, which attracts its share of summertime visitors, was built in about 1811, to designs by S. P. Cockerell, ostensibly as a memorial to Nelson but also as an eye-catcher for Middleton Hall, long since demolished but whose footprint is now preserved at the heart of the National Botanic Gardens of Wales. Our cottage has an interesting arrangement inside, partly due to remodelling by us, and a handsome, very low-beamed attic.

From the logbook
On Wednesday morning nine deer were in the wood next to the cottage.

… the farmer rounding up his sheep on stout mountain pony with aid of whistle and those highly intelligent dogs, fascinating to watch.

We love the way the dome of the National Botanic Garden keeps a steady eye on Paxton's Tower.

Ground floor

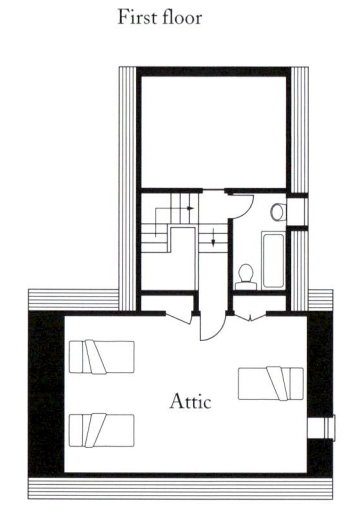

First floor

The attic bedroom has very low beams.

142 The Landmark Trust Handbook

Peake's House

Colchester, Essex [I9]

Peake's House stands in the Dutch Quarter, north of the High Street, which has retained its old street plan and many of its old houses. Here Flemish weavers settled in the 1570s, driven into exile by religious persecution. Colchester had astutely applied to the Privy Council for permission to receive a colony. Trade revived as a result and Colchester baize became a lucrative export for over a century.

Colchester deals in superlatives – the oldest recorded town, the earliest Roman colony, the largest Norman castle, the finest oysters. It offers much else besides, a thriving market town (on some evenings, even a little too lively) with a long and visible history, on the southern edge of East Anglia.

The building has been leased to us by the Borough Council, to which it was given in 1946, by Mr W. O. Peake, who owned a factory and much other property nearby. For many years let to the Red Cross, the house was in need of a new use, which we now provide.

From the logbook
Marvellous creaky old galleon of a house.

Such a snug house.

Great to leave the car in one place and for everything to be on the doorstep.

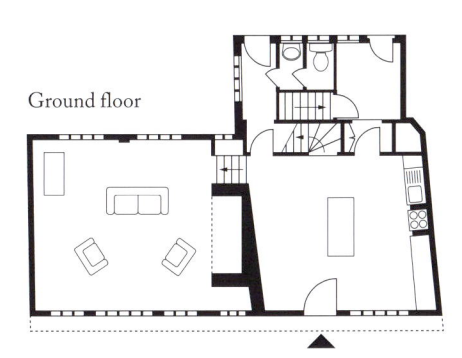

For up to 4 people
Open fire
Enclosed garden
Adjacent parking for 1 car
Steep staircase

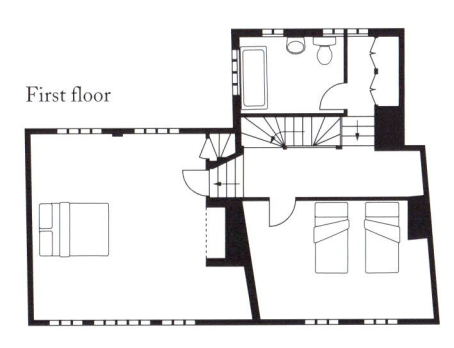

Peppercombe

Horns Cross, North Devon [K3]

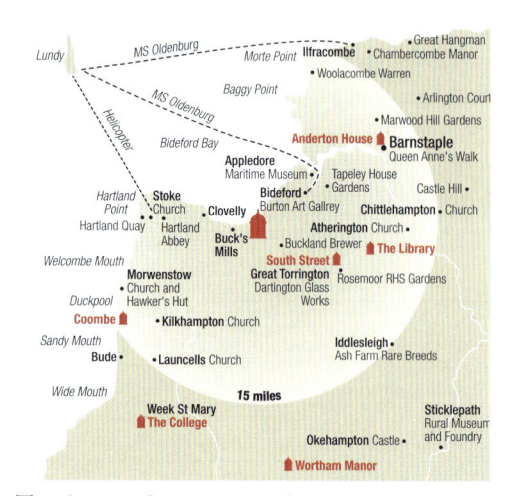

Two houses for up to 3 and 2+2 people.

The cliffs of the North Devon coast around Bideford Bay are broken by deep valleys that run almost down to the sea, but not quite. At the mouth there is usually a drop of some feet to the shore, down which tumbles a stream. Peppercombe is just such a valley, steep and wooded, and then opening out into a meadow, suspended 40 feet or more above the beach. The stream goes straight down the final stretch in a fine waterfall, but there is no need for you to do the same, thanks to a gently sloping path. The cliffs themselves are particularly dramatic here, formed from an outcrop of red Triassic stone. The whole magnificent coastline curves away in both directions, with Lundy on the horizon.

For centuries the combe belonged to the Portledge estate, and the Coffin family (latterly Pine-Coffins). In 1988 it was acquired by the National Trust, and we took on two of the buildings.

From the logbook
Landmarks are not simply places to stay, but places in which it is a pleasure to stay.

Bridge Cottage

Bridge Cottage, built in about 1830, stands in woods at the top of the combe. It had been empty for years, with a tarpaulin over its roof, but the walls of cob and stone were sound. The kitchen and parlour have stone-flagged floors and fireplaces, while the bedrooms follow the line of the roof and seem slightly too small for furniture, as cottage bedrooms should.

For up to 3 people
Open fire
Sloping garden
Parking nearby
Uneven sloping approach path
Dogs allowed

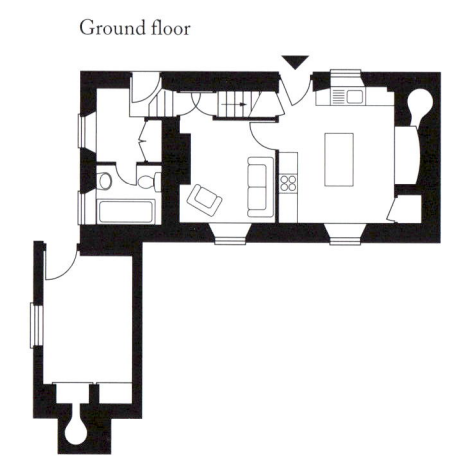

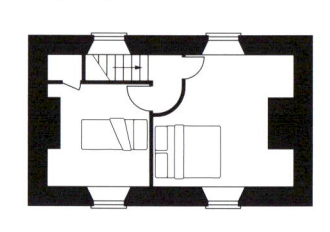

Ground floor   First floor

Castle Bungalow

At the mouth of the combe is Castle Bungalow, which is just that, a 1920s Boulton and Paul bungalow. The company's archivist (it is still going strong in Norwich) found one catalogue of this period for us; it had survived the bombing of the factory in 1940. It has tempting illustrations of 'Residences, Bungalows and Cottages', ranging from a substantial six-bedroom house on two storeys (at £4,000) to Bungalow B49, with just a bedroom, a living-room and a verandah (in case you should live in the tropics). This, with brick foundations and carriage paid to the nearest goods station, cost just £280.

Sadly, although a number of its brothers and sisters are there, our bungalow does not feature in the catalogue, but it is still just as tempting. Its weather-boarded walls are painted in railway colours, cream and brown (like the old Great Western Railway carriages), its windows are latticed, and inside the rooms are snug as only wood-lined rooms can be. Beside it are the remains of Peppercombe Castle, a castellated seaside residence.

For up to 2+2 people
Solid fuel stove
Wild meadow garden
Adjacent parking
Dogs allowed
Direct access to the beach

From the logbook
Our little girl (three and a half) loved this place and thought she was staying in the wooden house that belonged to one of the three pigs.

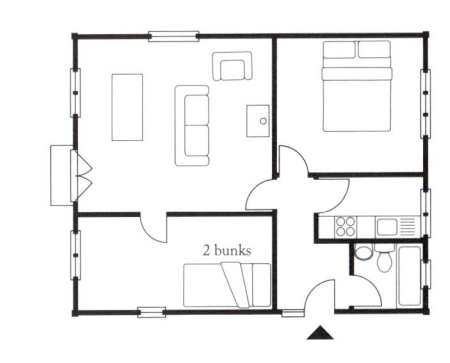

Peters Tower

Lympstone, Devon [K4]

For up to 2 people
No private parking

Steep spiral staircase

The Peters family were successful Liverpool merchants who, in the nineteenth century, served their country as soldiers, sailors and landowners. William Peters, who built this clock tower in 1885 as a memorial to his wife Mary Jane, was in the 7th Dragoons and lived in a sizable classical house nearby. His son was a General and his grandson an Admiral. On the latter's death in 1979 the Trustees of his estate offered us the Tower as a gift.

It is no great work of architecture – a very distant and poor relation of St Mark's in Venice – but it is part of the history of Lympstone, and it does stand, at the end of an alley, actually on the water's edge in this large and pleasant village, looking across the broad estuary of the Exe to the green fields beyond. Moreover, it is only a short walk from a railway station, so there is no need for those who stay here to have a car.

Accordingly we took it on, repaired the polychrome brick, restored the clock with its daytime chimes, and made the tower habitable again – it had been a refuge for fishermen stranded here by the weather. Every inch of space inside its tiny rooms is valuable, so our architect, having spent some time at a boatyard, fitted it out with teak and brass and varnish. The views from all the windows are interesting and some spectacular, and you will find yourself surveying and participating in the daily bustle of life on the foreshore.

From the logbook
Three pubs, a restaurant, and a station within two minutes' walk.

The sanctuary of the Tower seemed like a sleek racing yacht turned through 90 degrees and planted by its stern in the beach.

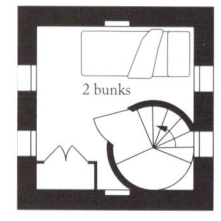

Third floor

Second floor

First floor

Ground floor

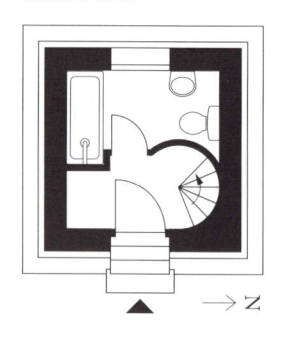

146   The Landmark Trust Handbook

The Pigsty

Robin Hood's Bay, North Yorkshire [D7]

Two pigs were the excuse for this exercise in primitive classicism, supposedly inspired by buildings seen by Squire Barry of Fyling Hall on his travels around the Mediterranean in the 1880s. By his use of timber columns, and his choice of inhabitants, he was perhaps trying to make a point about the roots of Classical architecture; or it may just have been that, as in the song, 'there was a lady loved a swine'. In Walter Crane's illustration for this song (from *The Baby's Opera*, published in 1877), the sty is given a Classical front, which might have been the starting point for Barry's eclectic inspiration.

The pigs' keepers lived in a pair of nearby cottages built close enough to keep an eye on their porcine charges and also architecturally embellished, but this time in more traditional Estate Gothick. It is several decades since they went in for pig-breeding, and alternative uses were hard to think of, until its owner heard of our activities and later gave us a long lease. By the minimum of addition, and the insertion of glass here and there, we hope that we have made it acceptable (if not entirely draught-free) to a higher breed of inhabitant; and although the living quarters will never be palatial, the view over hills and towards Robin Hood's Bay from under the pediment is undoubtedly fit for an Empress.

From the logbook
This is only our 7th Landmark but the stays in them represent the 7 best times I've had in my life.

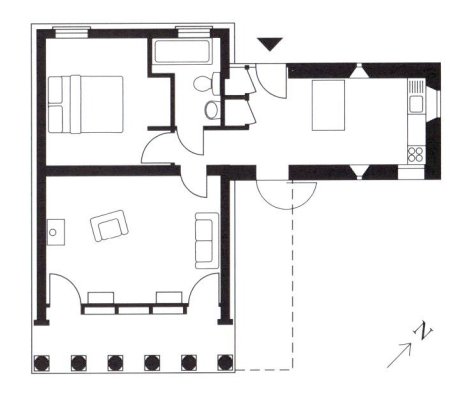

For up to 2 people
Solid fuel stove
Enclosed sloping garden
Parking nearby
Steep steps from parking place

The Pineapple

Dunmore, Central Scotland [A3]

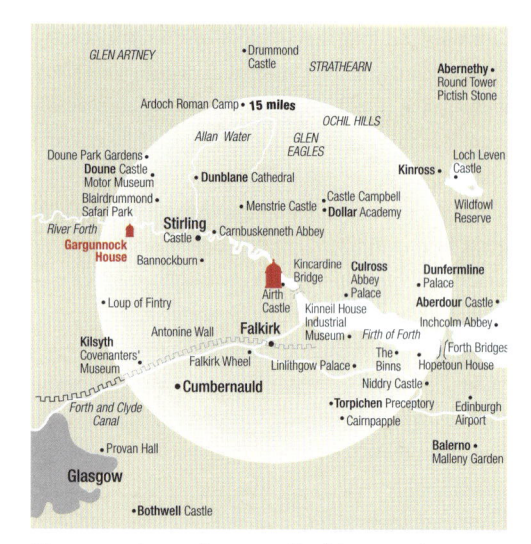

For up to 4 people
Open fire
Garden

Parking nearby
Dogs allowed

The Pineapple is an elaborate summerhouse of two storeys, built for the 4th Earl of Dunmore. Though classical and orthodox at ground level, it grows slowly into something entirely vegetable; conventional architraves put out shoots and end as prickly leaves of stone. It is an eccentric work, of undoubted genius, built of the very finest masonry.

It probably began as a pavilion of one storey, dated 1761, and only grew its fruity dome after 1777, when Lord Dunmore was brought back, forcibly, from serving as Governor of Virginia. There, sailors would put a pineapple on the gatepost to announce their return home. Lord Dunmore, who was fond of a joke, announced his return more prominently.

The Pineapple presides over an immense walled garden. This, in the Scottish tradition, was built some distance from the house, to take advantage of a south-facing slope. To house the gardeners, stone bothies were built on either side of the Pineapple. These make plain, unassuming rooms to stay in, though you have to go out of doors to get from one part to the other.

The Pineapple and its surroundings are owned by the National Trust for Scotland; we took a long lease in 1973 and restored all the buildings and the walled garden, which is now open to the public through the NTS. At the back, where the ground level is higher, is a private garden for our visitors, with steps leading into the elegant room inside the Pineapple itself.

From the logbook
The experience of actually living in such a building is so much more rewarding than merely visiting.

Hooray for the Pineapple, prickly and proud.

Farewell, old fruit.

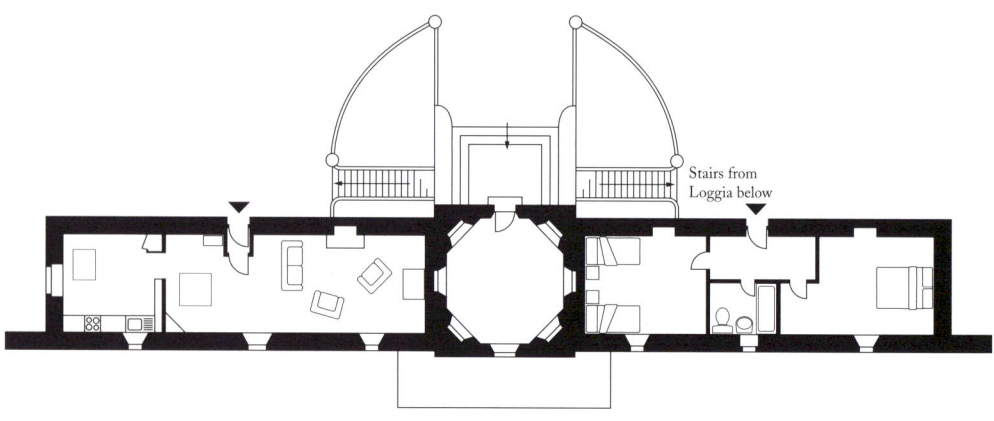

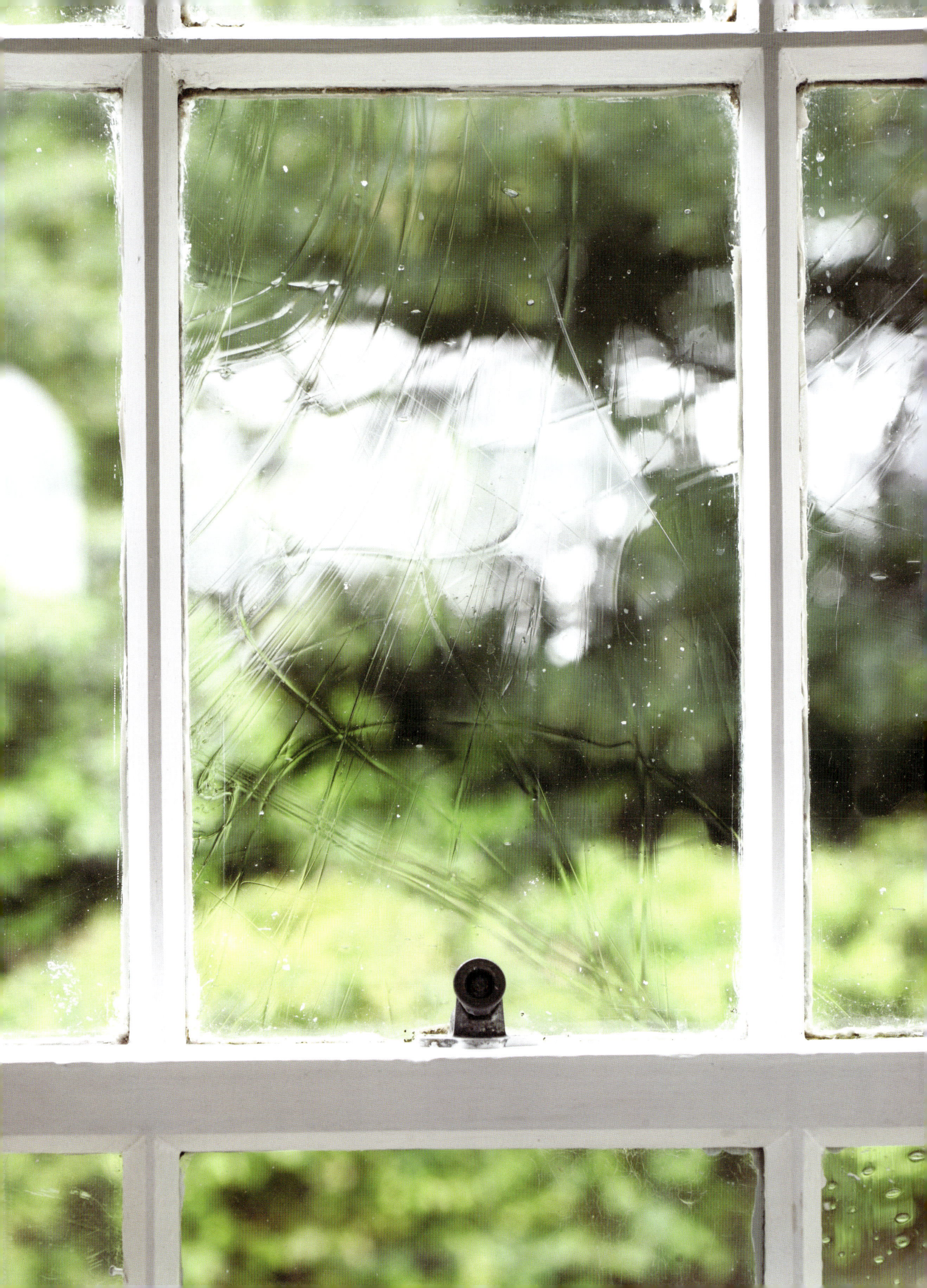

Plas Uchaf

Near Corwen, Powys [G4]

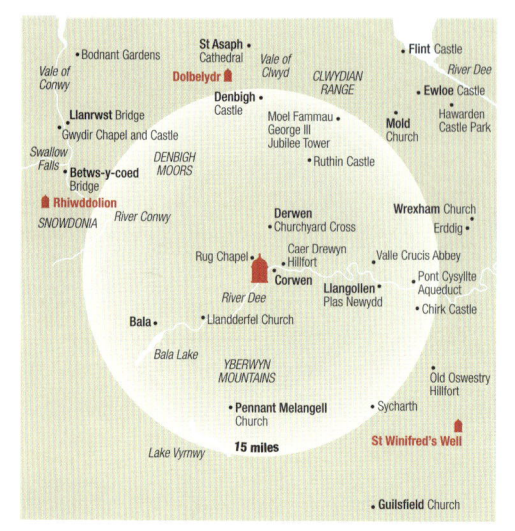

For up to 4 people
Open fire
Garden

Adjacent parking
Dogs allowed

This substantial hall-house was built in about 1400, or perhaps before, on the side of a low hill in the Dee valley. Few houses of this age and type survive in Wales, and the quality of the work at Plas Uchaf is exceptional.

It was in the last stages of dereliction when we arrived here, but the oak frames of medieval houses are remarkably tough, particularly where they have been smoked for generations by the open hearth. Its repair was still possible, and well worthwhile.

The hall is surprisingly grand, with a spere truss, two other moulded trusses, traces of a louvre, and wind and ridge braces – a roof of sophisticated carpentry. In the sixteenth century an immense fireplace was added, which, to a degree, heats this grand space. The alterations necessary to achieve modern standards of heating seemed too intrusive here, and we guessed that true Landmarkers would agree that extra jumpers were a better answer. The fire and the hall are the twin spirits of Plas Uchaf, and at night, with the wooden ribs of the hall moving a little in the firelight, you can imagine that you are Jonah inside the whale.

From the logbook
Thank you Plas Uchaf, Landmark, Mrs Jones, the chap for the logs, Mr Evans the singing butcher, our farmer friend up the road who supplied fresh milk and eggs and many a chat, and farmer Tudor.

You can't really appreciate the hall without the smell and light of the fire.

Ground floor

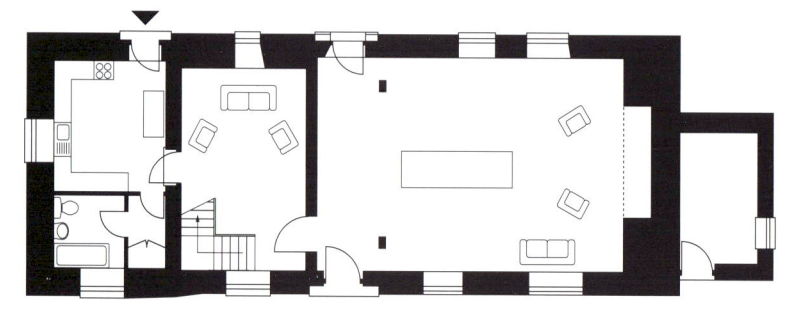

First floor

Upper part of hall

150   The Landmark Trust Handbook

Poultry Cottage

Leighton, Welshpool, Powys [H4]

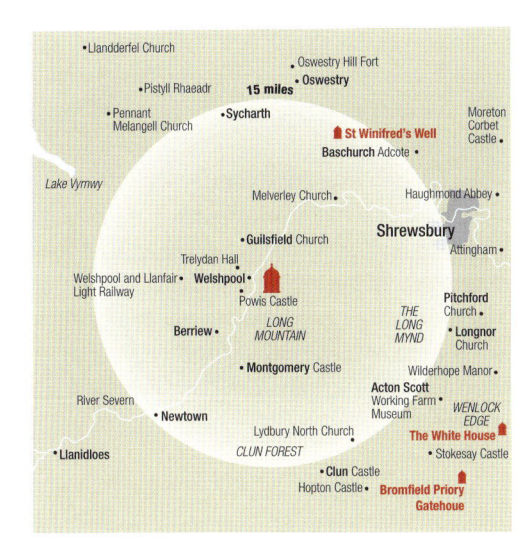

For up to 4 people
Open fire and solid fuel stove
Garden
Parking nearby
Dogs allowed

Leighton is a model estate on a stupendous scale, laid out in the 1850s by John Naylor, a Liverpool banker with a great deal of money to spend. Besides magnificent housing for all kinds of livestock, the estate had its own aqueduct and cable railway to take water, manure and feed to outlying farms.

The Poultry Yard was added in 1861, complete with fowl house, storm shed, pond and scratching yard, and the poultry-keeper's cottage in which you can stay, set in the large and secluded grounds from which the chickens have long gone. The architect was probably W. H. Gee of Liverpool, who was also responsible for Leighton Hall and Church. The designs may have been inspired by Her Majesty's Poultry Houses at Windsor, much praised in Dickson's *Poultry of 1853*. Each species, whether large or small, ornamental, water or humble hen, had its own meticulously designed quarters in the Fowl House: a thorough attention to detail, which is typical of the whole estate.

Another of Mr Naylor's interests was forestry (the Leyland Cypress was first propagated here). Near the Poultry Yard is a grove of giant redwoods, which now belongs to the Royal Forestry Society. Across the Severn Valley are the green hills of Montgomeryshire. There, too, is Powis Castle with its hanging garden, the nearest thing that Wales has to a royal palace.

From the logbook
This was an ideal refuge from life. The silence is really startling for those of us used to cars, trains and planes.

Landmarks never fail to impress. Poultry Cottage is no exception being a magnificent restoration in a remarkable setting.

It was glorious sitting outside the house watching a glorious sunset.

Poultry Cottage is on the right and the now unused Fowl House on the left.

Ground floor

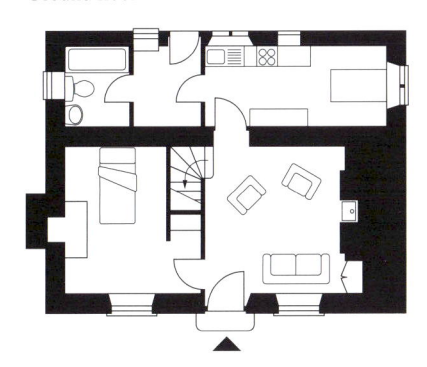

First floor

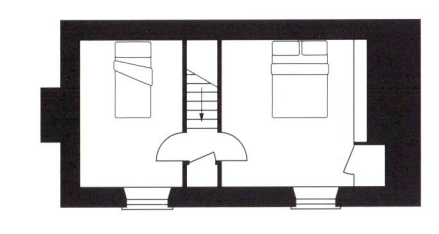

www.landmarktrust.org.uk

The Priest's House

Holcombe Rogus, Devon [K4]

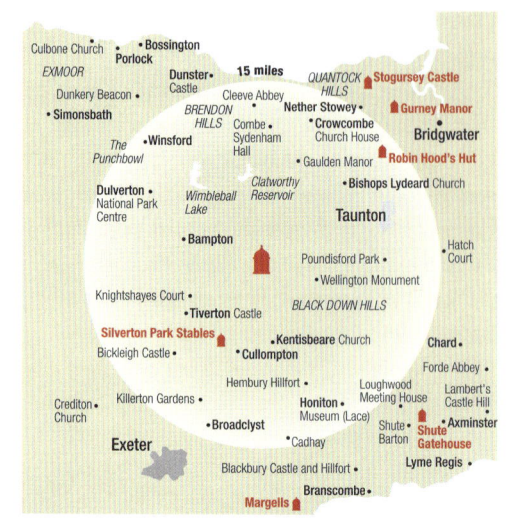

For up to 5 people
Open fire
Parking nearby
Dogs allowed

The Priest's House should really be called the Church House, because that is what it was, acting as half village hall and half inn. Parish feasts were held here on saints' days and other festivals, and hospitality was offered to guests. It had a kitchen and probably a brewery. Many church houses later became pubs, and survive as such to this day.

This one was probably built around 1500; it has fine moulded beams and a cooking hearth across one end, with another fireplace to warm the main room. By some lucky chance it was never converted to another use, but dwindled instead into a parish store. The reason probably lies in its position, squeezed between the garden of Holcombe Court (a fine Tudor house), the stony church lane and the churchyard.

Several old windows survived and inside, where there was evidence to show they had existed, we put back oak partitions and laid a stone floor so that the main rooms have much the same character as they did when used for village gatherings.

Holcombe Rogus is a comfortable village in a beautiful part of Devon, close to the Somerset border, where ancient lanes take you to unexpected but always rewarding places. The church has a good tower, a chiming clock and the memorable pew of the Bluett family who lived at Holcombe Court until the last century.

From the logbook
The pull of the night sky just outside the door, the gentle swoop of a passing bat or hoot of a nearby owl – bliss.

Fascinating house and good country.

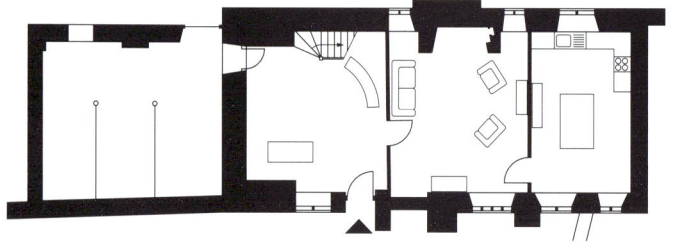

Ground floor

First floor

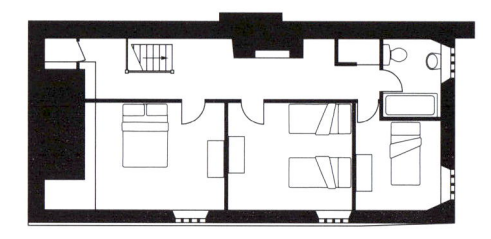

Princelet Street

Spitalfields, London E1 [J8]

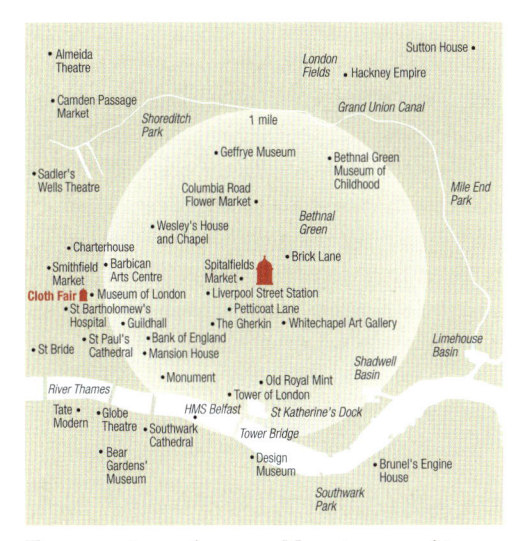

For up to 6 people
Gas coal fire
No private parking
Enclosed terrace

Spitalfields has always been a place where worlds meet. Named after St Marie Spittle, a hospital for the needy founded in the twelfth century, the area sheltered friendly and adventurous foreigners from that time on, living just outside the City walls but originally not admitted to the community of London.

In the late seventeenth and early eighteenth centuries, it was the turn of French Protestants, known as Huguenots, to be washed here by the tide of events, bringing with them their skill and ingenuity. Some were silk weavers, who found an existing incorporation of similar craftsmen already established in Spitalfields. Begun in 1718, Princelet Street contains some of the earliest speculative housing in the area, built to accommodate this new influx.

These are not grand buildings but they are dignified and well-proportioned. They provided their early inhabitants with room both to live and work. (Although this house no longer has its workrooms, others on the street have either attic rooms with the long windows characteristic of the weaver or long, mansarded outbuildings serving the same purpose.)

The house came to us as a generous bequest from its last owner, Peter Lerwill, who had lovingly restored it. The building retains much of its original floor plan and fabric, most notably its simple panelling, partitions and other joinery.

Today Princelet Street is a quiet street with many of its original buildings. The City of London is but a background hum and yet Liverpool Street Station is only a few minutes walk away. Hawksmoor's Christ Church, built in the same years as Princelet Street and now magnificently restored, stands on the corner, and Norman Foster's 30 St Mary Axe (better known as the Gherkin) is not much farther away. The sleek cliffs of modernist glass along Bishopsgate stand in lieu of the city walls to contrast and complement the more intimate scale of the Spitalfields streets. At the end of Princelet Street is the colour and bustle of Brick Lane. It is an area of festivals and markets, cafes and alleyways, where you will bridge continents and centuries with ease.

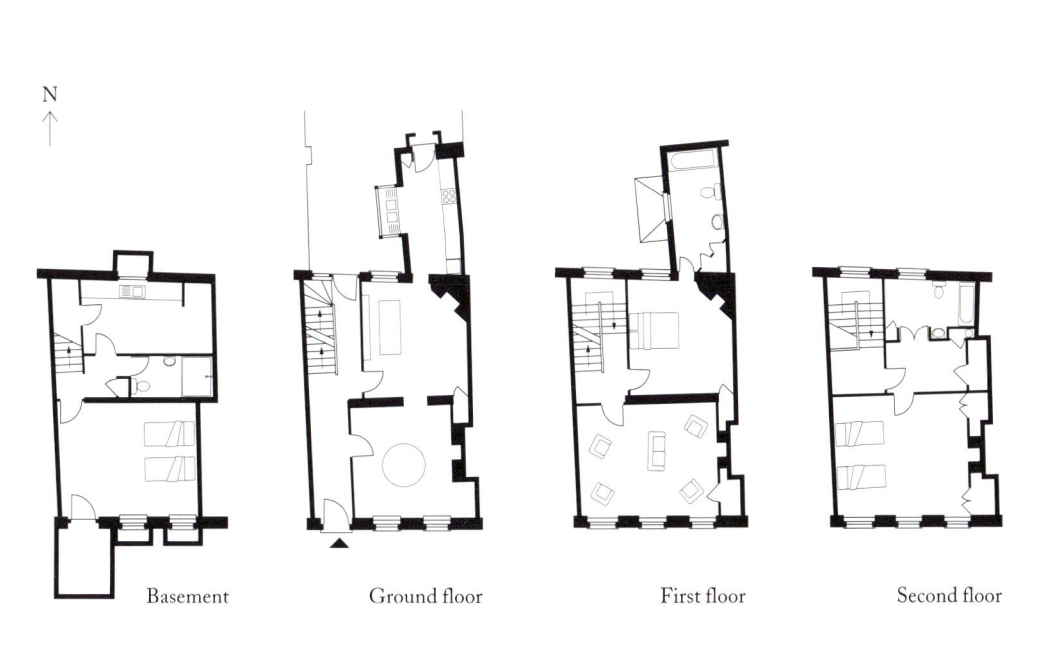

Basement   Ground floor   First floor   Second floor

www.landmarktrust.org.uk   153

The Prospect Tower

Belmont Park, Faversham, Kent [J9]

For 2 people
Open fire
Garden
Parking nearby
Narrow spiral staircase

This small flint tower stands on the very edge of the garden of Belmont Park (the house was remodelled by Samuel Wyatt in 1792), approached by an avenue of walnut trees. On its other side is a mature park and a now ragged cricket pitch. It was built in about 1808 for General, later Lord, Harris of Seringapatam. He called it his 'Whim', and one suspects that the pleasant upper room, at least, was his own den, into which the family were sometimes allowed for tea.

The General bought Belmont, which owed its name to its 'high situation and extensive prospect', in 1801, with prize money won in India. Farming and gardening were his chief enthusiasms and he soon doubled the size of the pleasure grounds to include the land in which the tower still stands.

The enthusiasm of the 4th Lord Harris was of a different kind. He was one of the fathers of cricket, and it was he who created a pitch in about 1870 and commandeered this tower as a changing room: hooks for the gear still decorate the walls. There are only two rooms in the tower for living and sleeping, but the prospect from its windows is still extensive; and you can dream of all those centuries, hoped for and, sometimes, achieved.

From the logbook
The best 'prospect' is from the kitchen window.

On Sunday morning a balloon went over about 8am – quite unusual to say good morning to its occupants from the top of the tower. They landed on the old cricket pitch.

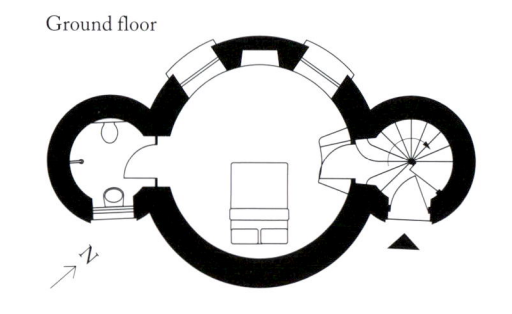

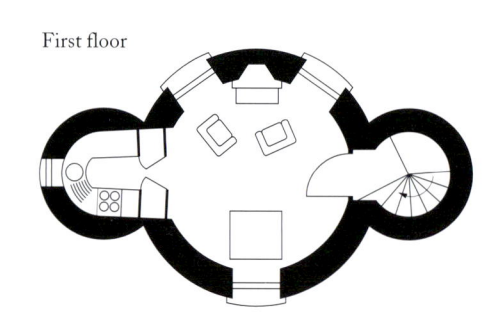

Ground floor

First floor

Purton Green

Stansfield, Suffolk [H8]

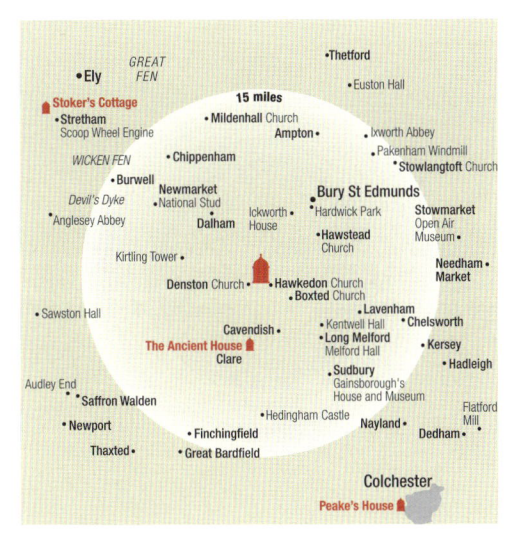

Purton Green is one of the many lost villages of Suffolk, where generations spent their lives, but which are now just patches of lime and fragments in the plough. It lies on an old road running south from Bury St Edmunds, today hardly a path. All that remains is this house. Inside its late medieval walls survives a hall of 1250 – a great rarity. Aisled on both sides, with scissor-braced trusses and a highly ornamental arcade at the low end, it must once have been an important place.

When we bought it in 1969 it was little more than a ruin. As with almost all medieval houses, a floor and central chimney stack had later been inserted, but these additions were so derelict that we felt justified in removing them, to return the hall to its original open state. Part of the house – the high end – was rebuilt in about 1600. Our conversion of this end into living quarters in the 1970s has now also become a part of the building's history.

These can only be reached through the hall, which you must cross and recross if you stay here, as your predecessors have done for 700 years. The house now stands surrounded by fields, with unchanging Suffolk countryside in all directions. After crossing a ford, you leave your car 400 yards from the house; but we provide a wheelbarrow for the rest of the journey.

From the logbook
Purton Green provided a fine time machine back to the 13th century for Landmarkers.

We spent most of our time there admiring the skill displayed by those who created this enduring structure.

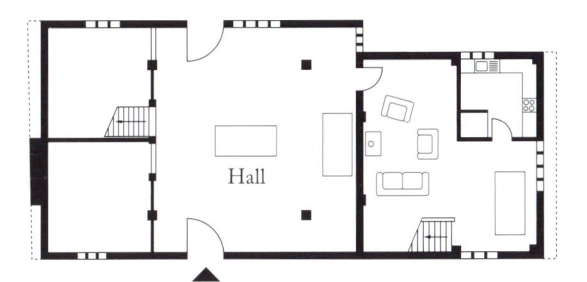

For up to 4 people
Electric stove
Access by footpath
Open grounds
Parking 400 yards away
Dogs allowed

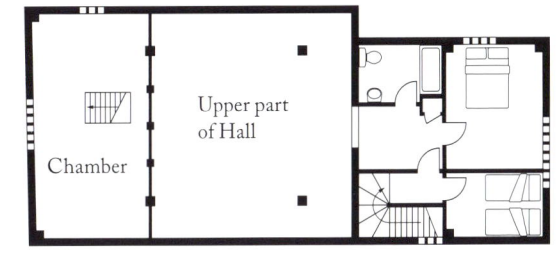

The staircase to the Chamber in the empty part of the building is unenclosed.

www.landmarktrust.org.uk 155

Rhiwddolion

Near Betws-y-coed, Gwynedd [G3]

Houses for up to 2, 2+1 and 4 people.

Rhiwddolion (pronounced Rutholeon) is a remote upland at the head of a valley above Betws-y-coed. For a time there was a slate quarry and community here. Long before that Rhiwddolion was on the Roman road that runs from Merioneth to the Conway valley. It was called Sarn Helen after the mother of the Emperor Constantine, whose father campaigned and died in Britain; Edward I, mindful of this, built Caernarvon Castle with bands of coloured stone, in imitation of Constantinople.

Now, however, Rhiwddolion, with only three houses left besides ours, is given over to the sheep. It is somewhat hemmed in by forestry, but where it remains open, the small-scale landscape of oak trees and rocks emerging from close-cropped pasture is second to none. It is also tranquil and silent except for the sheep and the water; and there is a view far down the valley towards Betws.

It is not possible to get a car to any of our houses; instead, leaving your car by the forestry track, you can walk up (ten minutes, some say longer) on a path of enormous half-buried flagstones, as your predecessors did.

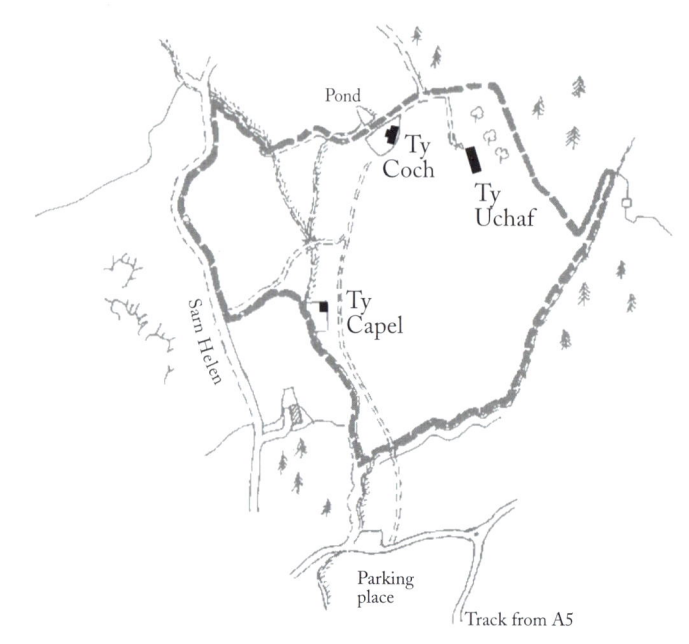

Ty Uchaf

Ty Capel

Ty Capel, beside the stream that flows down the valley, was a school-cum-chapel in the days of the slate quarry. At the end of the nineteenth century the chapel served a community of 150 people.

Essentially a large single space, with a steep staircase up to the sleeping gallery, this robust stone building is lined with varnished pine, which, to an extent, helps to combat winter cold.

For up to 2+1 people
Open fire
Access by footpath only
Open grounds
Parking 400 yards away
Dogs allowed

From the logbook
To my surprise I discovered that I actually quite enjoyed walking.

The pair of elderly ladies in the Oxfam shop, Portmadog, sang for us the Welsh hymn written by the schoolmaster of Rhiwddolion.

Ground floor

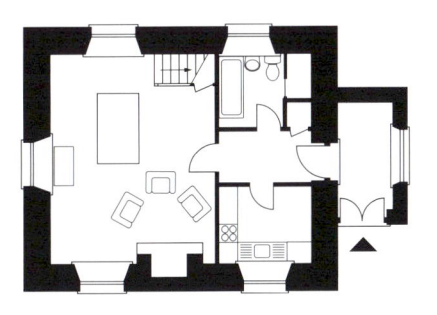

First floor

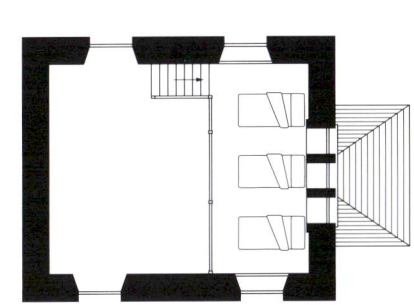

Rhiwddolion

Ty Coch

Ty Coch, which means red house, is a few hundred yards higher up from Ty Capel, looking across the head of the valley, by a small waterfall. In origin much older than Ty Capel, it has a stone-flagged living-room with a large fireplace. The beam that spans this fireplace is a cruck, re-used no doubt from an earlier house that stood here.

For up to 4 people
Woodburning stove
Access by footpath only
Open grounds
Parking 600 yards away
Dogs allowed

From the logbook
Idyllic setting, have not seen the like. Children wonderfully content to be around the waterfall and stream.

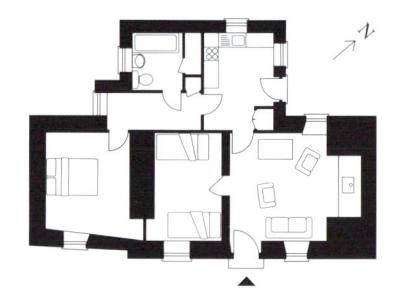

Ty Uchaf

Ty Uchaf stands at the head of the valley, in the lee of woods rich in mosses and lichens, and looking across the sheep pastures. A datestone for 1685 was found in the tumbledown pigsty. We have respected the original division between the barn and domestic end, and kept part of the crog loft to make a bedroom beneath it. The living-room is open to the roof timbers with a large fireplace under its original bressumer. The tie beam had been cruelly cut some time earlier; we did not repair it, thus keeping an airy space for two. Timbers and walls are all limewashed to enhance the sense of light and space in this modest dwelling. The barn is once again utilitarian, a separate entrance leads into a lobby large enough for all the walking gear you will bring to explore this remote and peaceful place.

For up to 2 people
Solid fuel stove
Access by footpath only
Open grounds
Parking 800 yards away
Dogs allowed

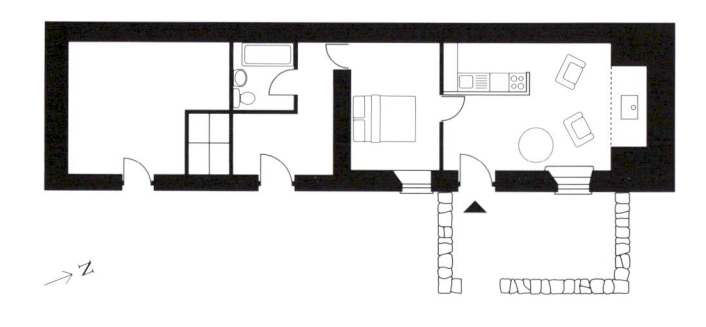

Robin Hood's Hut

Halswell, Goathurst, Somerset [K4]

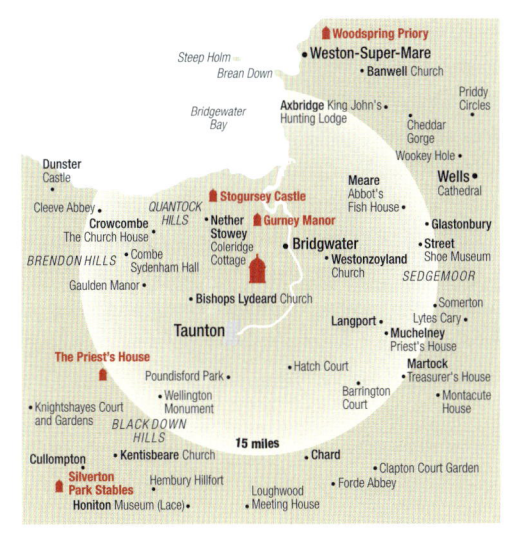

For up to 2 people
Solid fuel stove
Open grounds
Adjacent parking
Dogs allowed

It is sometimes surprising to find how far Robin Hood strayed from Sherwood Forest. In fact, the name of this beautiful little pavilion has less to do with our eponymous hero than with Whiggish ideas of liberty and medieval romance in the eighteenth century. In the 1740s Charles Kemeys Tynte began to transform the landscape around Halswell House into one of the finest Georgian gardens in the south west of England. He built several follies within it; by 1767 he was writing to his steward about 'the Building on the Hill of the Park', instructing that 'the first room, which I call the hermit's room, must have an earthen floor'.

By the time the Somerset Building Preservation Trust came upon Robin Hood's Hut in 1997, it had no roof or windows and had lost much of its plasterwork. Its umbrello was almost gone. After an exemplary restoration of the exterior, the Trust asked Landmark if we would provide a secure future use for the building. We were delighted to help.

Much like The Ruin at Hackfall (page 151), Robin Hood's Hut has two distinct faces and commands a breathtaking panorama. Approaching through a dark wood, you come upon an apparently rustic cottage, with thatched roof and bark-clad door. Once inside, the elegant interior provides a fitting antechamber to the umbrello, from where the view encompasses the Somerset Levels and Mendip Hills and on across the Bristol Channel to the mountains of South Wales. Like earlier visitors, you too may choose to dine al fresco beneath this elegant canopy, whose graceful ogee detailing has more than a hint of the early days of the Raj.

In order not to compromise the views and elegance of a building not designed to hold modern services, we decided to build an equally carefully designed hut of our own to house the bathroom, thus indulging both epochs' notions of civilised existence. Would Robin Hood have approved? We feel sure our present day hermits will, perched above one of the finest views in southern England.

From the logbook
We've made the most of the umbrello, eating nearly all of our meals out there, and looking out over the views.

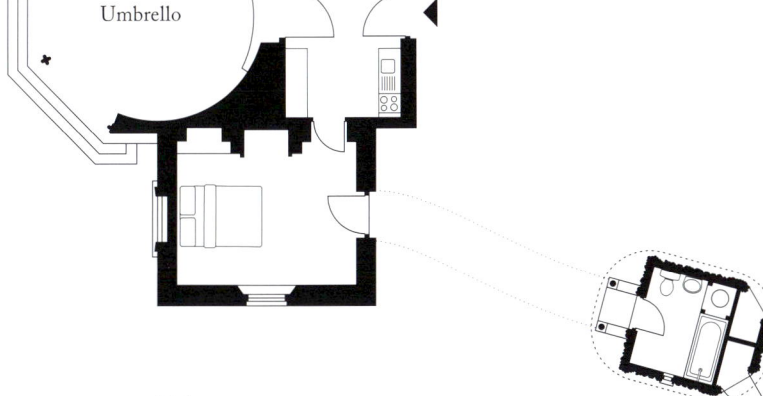

Roslin

Near Edinburgh [B4]

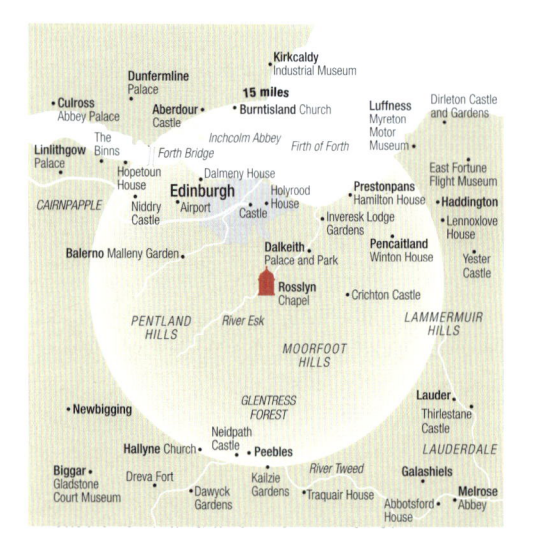

The St. Clairs, an ancient Scottish family, have held the Rosslyn estate at Roslin since the early fourteenth century. Rosslyn has long been famous for its picturesque valley, enhanced by generations of St. Clairs with two extraordinary buildings – its ancient castle and a breathtakingly beautiful chapel. The chapel, just outside the village of Roslin, represents the pinnacle of the fifteenth-century stonemason's craft, embellished on every surface with sinuous and intricate carving, full of imagery that made the chapel a place of mysticism and pilgrimage even through centuries of dereliction. More recently the present Earl and Countess of Rosslyn have been instrumental in the ongoing restoration of the chapel, (as popular a tourist attraction today as it always has been), and in the care of the castle and former inn. To support the Earl in his effort to keep this ancient family's inheritance together, we let both castle and house on his behalf. You can stay in the castle itself or, half a mile away look over the garden wall at the chapel from Collegehill House. As Sir Walter Scott once wrote, 'A morning of leisure can scarcely be anywhere more delightfully spent than in the woods of Rosslyn'.

From the logbook
… a marvellous base for the Edinburgh Festival.

A wild and spectacular setting – it's easy to see why Turner wanted to paint it.

Rosslyn Castle

Collegehill House

Many famous travellers have found rest at Collegehill House, former inn and *de facto* gatehouse to Rosslyn Chapel, a Renaissance jewel lying just over the garden wall and inspiration for many an artist and also the occaisional novelist. Boswell and Dr Johnson, Robbie Burns and Francis Grose, J.M.W. Turner and the Wordsworths – even Queen Victoria found hospitality here. Ben Jonson visited the chapel on foot in 1618, to find William Drummond of Hawthornden resting under a tree: 'Welcome, welcome, ye royal Ben,' said Drummond, to which Jonson replied with quicker wit than style, 'Thank ye, thank ye, Hawthornden.'

Built in the eighteenth century, Roslin became a popular destination for amateur lady painters on day trips from Edinburgh (and Rosslyn Chapel is once again a magnet for visitors today). On the first floor of the house is a grand drawing-room; it is easy enough to conjure up all these many and varied visitors to Roslin as you loll in your armchair with one of the finest expositions of the mason's craft framed in your window.

For up to 6 people
Open fire
Enclosed garden
Adjacent parking
Dogs allowed

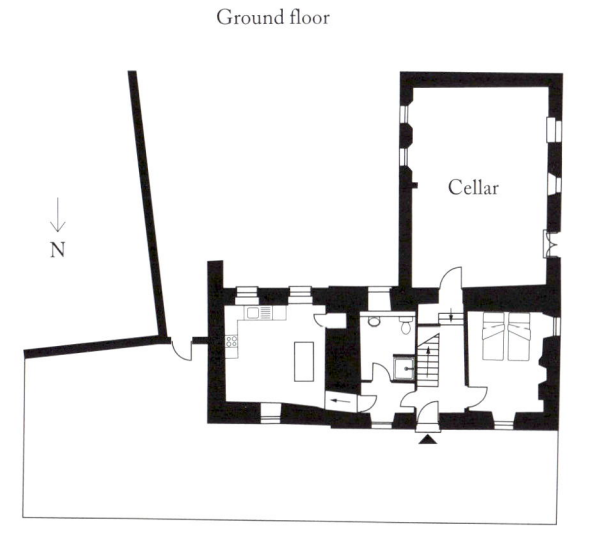

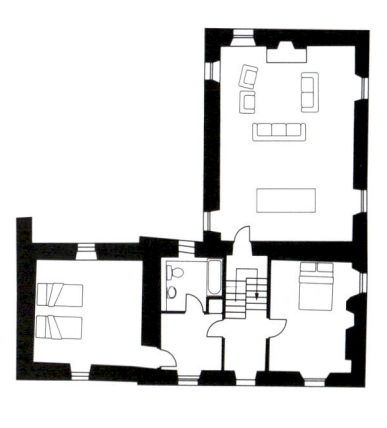

Ground floor

First floor

Roslin

Rosslyn Castle

Most of the castle was built around 1450 by the great William, Prince of Orkney, who lived at Rosslyn in regal state, dining off gold and silver. It was he who built the extraordinary ornament-encrusted chapel of St Matthew at Roslin, one of the wonders of Scotland.

The older fortifications survive only as ruins, but shortly before 1600 Sir William Sinclair replaced the east curtain wall with a more comfortable dwelling, but one which still contains an element of drama. On one side a modest two storey building, on the other it drops five storeys down the side of the rock to reach the ground 60 feet below. Decorated with panelling and moulded plaster ceilings, but later left empty for long periods, the habitable rooms have been restored and furnished by the present Earl of Rosslyn.

For up to 7 people
Open fire
Garden
Adjacent parking
Dogs allowed

First floor

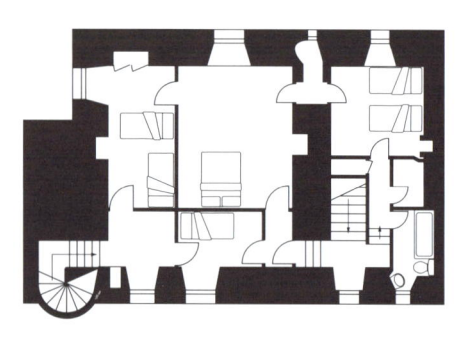

Ground floor

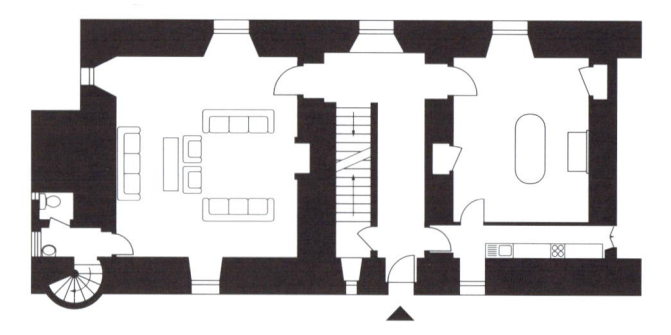

The Ruin

Hackfall, Grewelthorpe, North Yorkshire [E6]

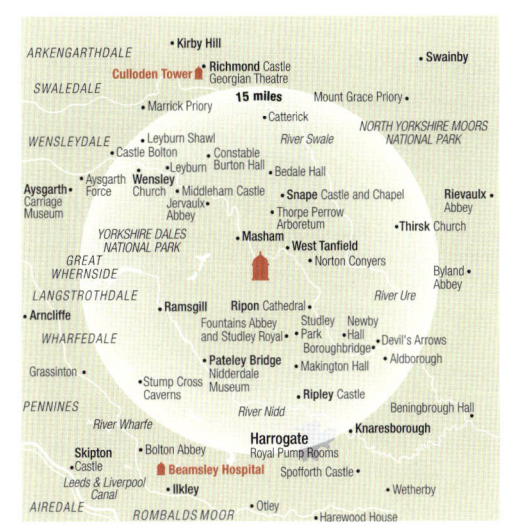

For up to 2 people
Solid fuel stove
Small garden
Parking nearby

However well we get to know our buildings, they can still surprise us. It took Landmark some 15 years to acquire this little pavilion, dramatically perched above a steep wooded gorge in the remnants of an outstanding mid-eighteenth-century picturesque garden at Hackfall. The garden was conceived and created by the Aislabies, who also made the gardens at nearby Studley Royal. Hackfall was Studley's antithesis: a 'natural' Gothic landscape with follies, waterfalls and built structures. The Ruin is one of these, a tiny banqueting house which we have allowed to keep its eighteenth-century name, trusting our visitors to share the Aislabies' sense of irony.

The Ruin is a typically Janus-faced Georgian folly: smoothly Gothic on its public elevation, which leads through to a rugged, Romanesque, triple-domed 'ruin' redolent of ancient Rome and Piranesi, and framing a terrace set before one of the finest views in North Yorkshire. It had indeed become a ruin when we set our stonemasons to work to sift, stitch and point it back together. Work was well underway when we had our surprise – a discovery that was, in fact, entirely consistent with Hackfall's pedigree. Our building archaeologist noticed a striking similarity between The Ruin's Romanesque elevation and a watercolour, *Design for a Roman Ruin,* by Robert Adam. It offers an unusual example of the work of this greatest of eighteenth-century British architects, better known for his more formally Classical houses and interiors.

The three rooms enclosed by this unique exterior never communicated with each other, and we have kept them so. A richly decorated sitting-room is flanked by a bedroom and bathroom; flitting between the two wings across a moonlit terrace is a truly Gothic experience.

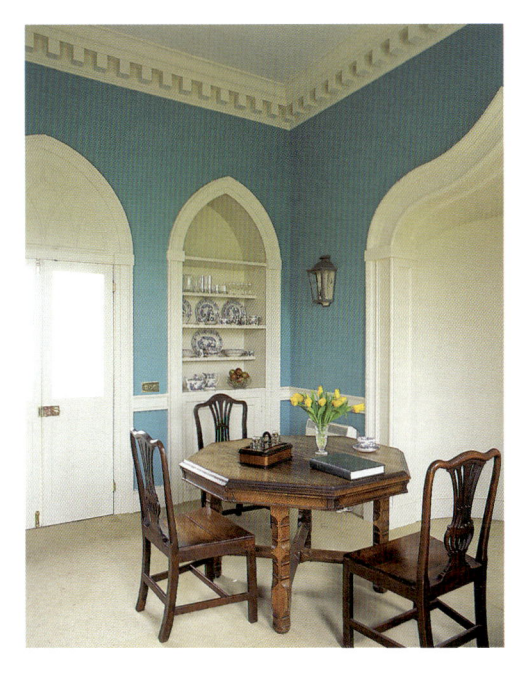

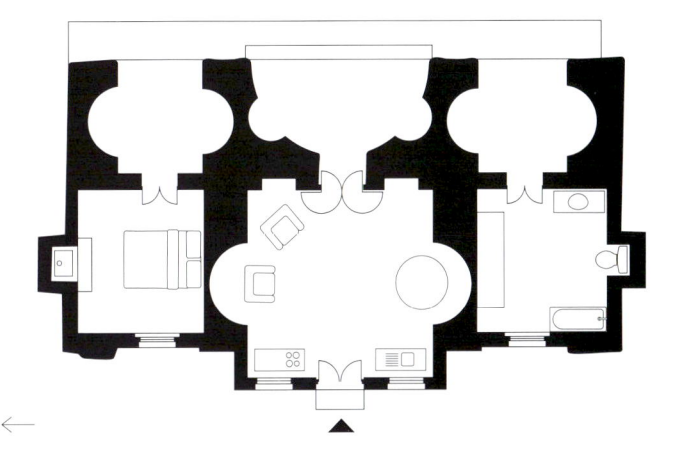

www.landmarktrust.org.uk

Sackville House

East Grinstead, West Sussex [J8]

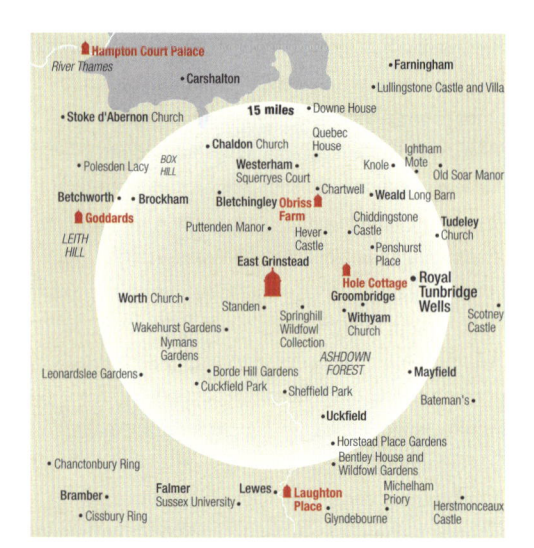

Sackville House was rescued from decay in 1919 by Geoffrey Webb, a stained-glass artist and uncle of Sir Aston Webb, the architect. His daughter left it to us, with the wish that it be kept as a dwelling.

It stands on the south side of East Grinstead's broad High Street. Timber-framed, like most of the older houses here, and roofed in thick Horsham stone, it was built in about 1520 as a hall with chambers at one end, but remodelled 50 years later to form a substantial house running back from the street with a yard at the side.

What is really exceptional about Sackville House lies beyond. East Grinstead was laid out in the thirteenth century, a street of houses each with a long plot of land behind, called a portland. Most of these have since been divided and built on. Only in one small area, opposite the church, do they survive in anything like their original form. The garden here, some 630 feet long, slopes to the south, passing through several stages from formal terrace to wild nuttery. On leaving the sometimes lively High Street and entering the yard, you find yourself with a view of several miles across a wide valley to Ashdown Forest. The contrast, and combination, are delightful.

From the logbook
A bustling town with nice shops and restaurants and all the essentials outside the front door, and the countryside in the form of the fantastic garden out of the back door.

What a wonderful house; we never tired of looking around.

For up to 8 people
Open fire
Enclosed garden

Parking for 3 cars
Dogs allowed

Ground floor

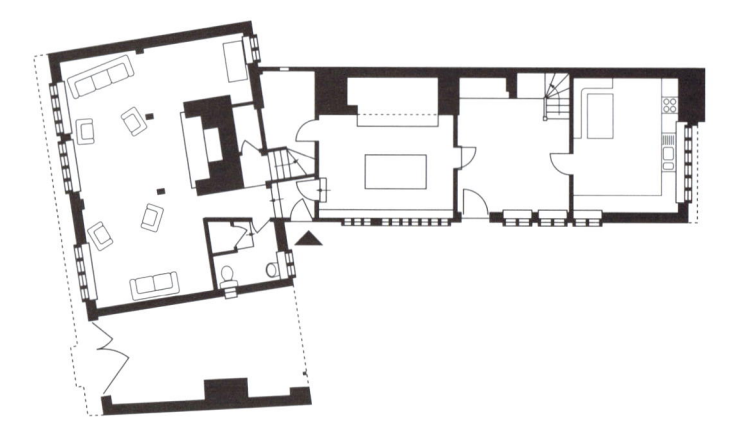

First floor

There is another bathroom in the attic.

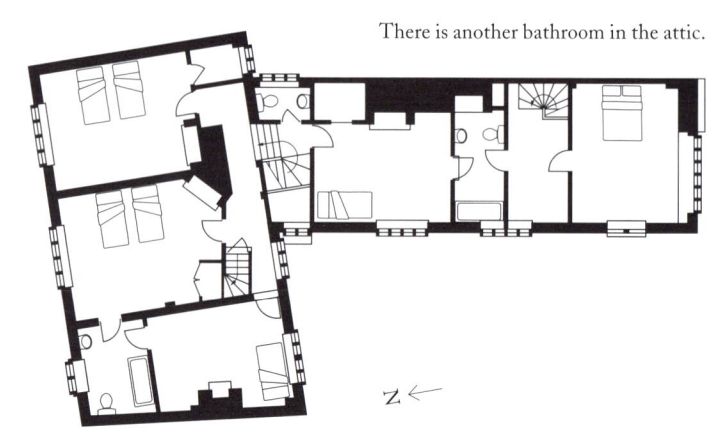

164 The Landmark Trust Handbook

Saddell

Kintyre, Argyll and Bute [B1]

A castle for 8, two houses for 4, one for 5, one for 6 and one for 13.

The fortunate qualities of Saddell have long been recognised. There was an abbey here, sited safely inland. Later it was chosen by the Bishop of Argyll for a new castle, which stands boldly near the shore, by the mouth of a small river looking across to Arran. This castle we now own, together with five houses, the steep old beechwood behind and the whole of Saddell Bay, with its long white strand and rocky point. Those who stay here have the freedom of it all.

Here and there are moulded or carved stones from the ruins of Saddell Abbey, half a mile up the valley. Under the trees in that peaceful place lie many grave slabs of the unruly Scots, gripping their long swords or standing in their ships of war, waiting impatiently for the last trumpet.

From the logbook
Hire the pipers from Kintyre Motors, Campbeltown, to add to the authenticity of a Scottish evening's reeling on the front lawn.

The sea otter is here (if very elusive!) – try the rocks beyond Cul na Shee. Have also spotted heron, kingfisher, swans, adders and basking sharks in the bay.

You will always see seals in Torrisdale Bay 10 minutes away.

Port na Gael is a stone cottage, which can be used for picnics by those staying at Saddell.

Saddell

Cul na Shee

Cul na Shee (or Cul na Sythe) means 'nook of peace' in Gaelic, which in this case refers to a minute bay, backed by steep woods, a few hundred yards beyond the castle. Here in the 1920s a schoolteacher, the daughter of a local minister, built herself a simple home for her retirement, on the grass behind a rocky beach. It would be hard to find a more tranquil place, reached by a path along the beach, overlooked by no other building and with just the sea and Arran to look at. It has, moreover, been a pleasure to preserve a building of a kind so very unfashionable now, to show how suitable it can look and how snug and cheerful its pine-boarded rooms can be.

For up to 4 people
Open fire
Open grounds
Parking a short walk away
Dogs allowed

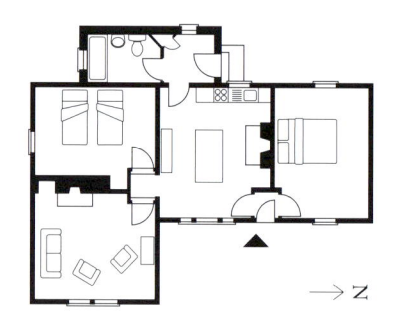

Ferryman's Cottage

Ferryman's Cottage has the same uninterrupted view as Cul na Shee. It was built in about 1930 on the site of a humbler predecessor, the freehold property of an important local figure, the ferryman. Owner of a boat and a house, it was his job to offload provisions from the coastal steamer, or puffer. Before the building of good roads much of Western Scotland was dependent on such deliveries, and Glensaddell was no exception. The house, with light-filled rooms, stands in its own garden, with the remains of the jetty in the rocky bay in front.

For up to 5 people
Open fire
Garden
Adjacent parking
Dogs allowed

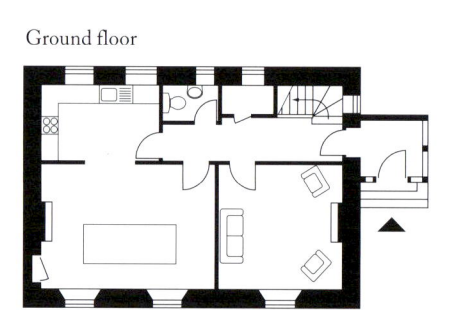

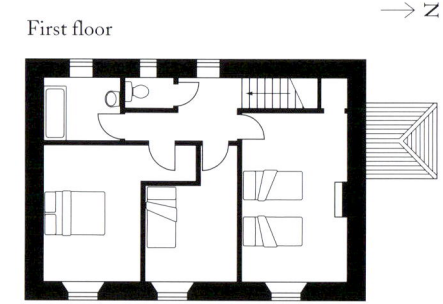

Saddell Castle

Saddell Castle was described as 'a fayre pyle, and a stronge' when it was built in 1508. By 1600 it was firmly in the hands of the Campbells, who thereafter held it for nearly 400 years. It is a fine and complete tower house with a battlemented wall-walk round the roof. When we took it on, there were substantial trees growing from the parapets and all the windows had gone.

Inside, each room is quite different from all the others, and each holds something unexpected and agreeable: panelling or a decorated ceiling, deep window embrasures, or closets in the thickness of the wall. The floor inside the front door is removable so that unwelcome visitors can fall straight into a pit below.

Round a narrow cobbled yard outside, the walls of the attendant outbuildings survive, including part of the old barmkin wall. Built hard up against the castle for protection, they were left because the laird never had any money to spare. Indeed all the later structural repairs seem to have been a struggle, done with whatever lay to hand, even old cart axles.

For up to 8 people
Solid fuel stove
Open grounds
Adjacent parking
Wide spiral staircase
Dogs allowed

First floor

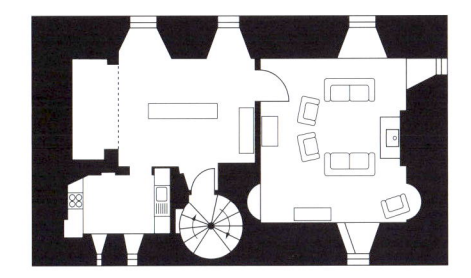

Third floor

Ground floor

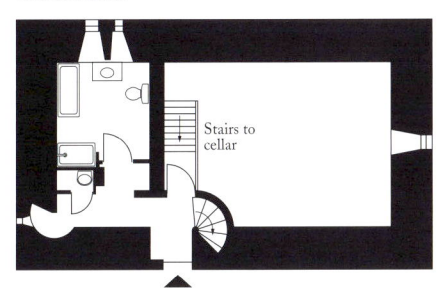

Second floor

www.landmarktrust.org.uk 167

Saddell

Saddell House

Saddell House presides at the centre of the bay, a handsome seat built in 1774 by Colonel Donald Campbell (the Saddell estate had been owned by Campbells since 1600). The Colonel had fought gallantly in India, earning promotion to become Commandant of Madras. He returned to Scotland in 1771, wounded but with rich recompense from the Nawab of Arcot. It was no doubt this that enabled him, even before he entered his inheritance, to build Saddell House, which he positioned on the edge of the beach to take advantage of views across both the Kilbrannan Sound towards Arran and the fertile plain inland. It was a typical Scottish laird's house of its period, with generously proportioned rooms and large light windows.

The house also proved a good base for hunting and fishing and it was while an eventual tenant, a Reverend Bramwell, was out shooting in September 1899 that disaster struck. A chimney fire spread to the attic, destroying the roof and gutting the house. Only the walls and a fine set of service rooms in the basement survived. Fortunately for us, Saddell House was judged worthy of repair and was rebuilt almost at once. It became what it remains today: an eminently sensible Edwardian house for a generation or three to spend a holiday together, close enough to an outdoors life but offering a comfortable haven from the elements when needed. The Moreton family lived here until 1998, after which gentle refurbishment was all that was needed to thread this, the last pearl, onto our Saddell string.

For up to 13 people
Open fire
Open grounds
Adjacent parking
Dogs allowed

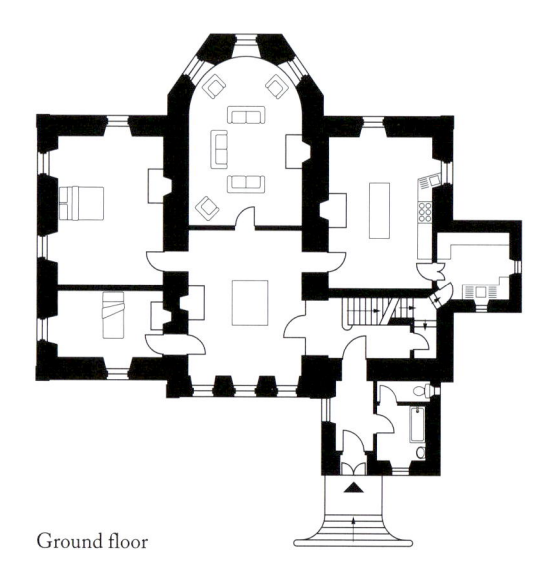

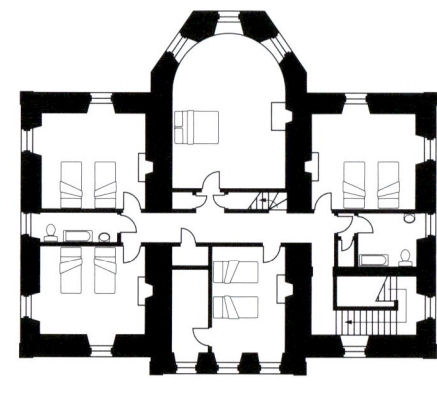

There is a further bathroom on the attic floor.

Ground floor

First floor

Saddell Lodge

Guarding the entrance and wooded drive to the Saddell estate is Saddell Lodge, a handsome granite gate lodge. We do not know exactly when it was built – perhaps when Colonel McLeod was refurbishing the castle in the 1890s, or after the serious fire at Saddell House in 1899. Either way, the lodge avoided any such ravages itself, a simple but considered building to which we added a bedroom. For many years the home of our Regional Property Manager, the lodge now adds its own architectural character to the Landmarks at Saddell, lying snugly at the edge of the estate just across the road from the ruins of Saddell Abbey.

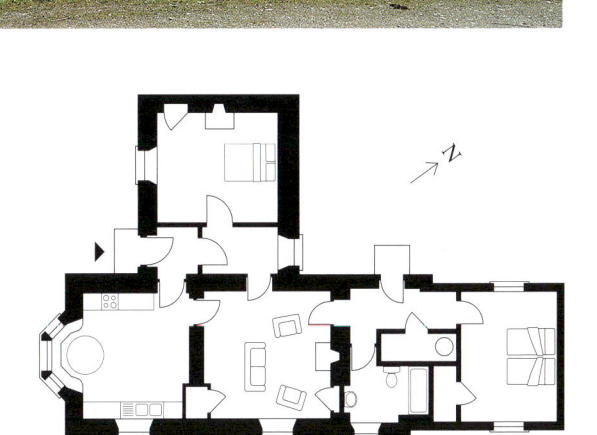

For up to 4 people
Open fire
Open grounds
Adjacent parking
Dogs allowed

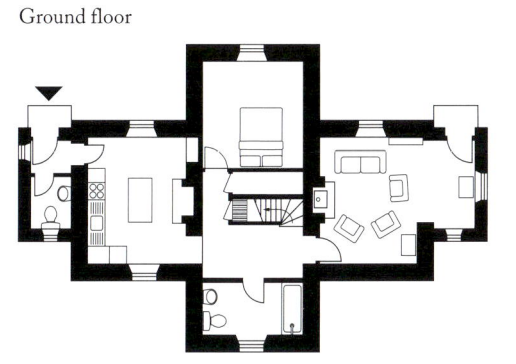

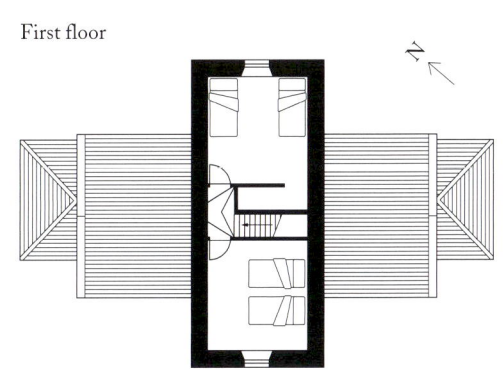

Shore Cottage

Shore Cottage looks at the castle across a little bay. It stands on a rocky point, among trees that grow right down to the sea, and is a plain but stylish Victorian building, imaginative in design as well as situation. From the sitting-room a door leads directly on to the foreshore, where the rock pools at low tide are second to none.

For up to 6 people   Adjacent parking
Solid fuel stove   Dogs allowed
Open grounds

Ground floor   *First floor*

St Mary's Lane

Tewkesbury, Gloucestershire [I5]

For up to 4 people
Small rear yard

Steep twisting staircase
No private parking

Other Landmarks in Tewkesbury:
Abbey Gatehouse

This honest house on St Mary's Lane is a relic of Tewkesbury's eighteenth-century prosperity. It is a rare survival of a house designed for framework knitters or stocking makers, recognisable by its long, first floor window to light the knitting frame (and now the sitting-room). Weaving was an organised but domestic trade – each stocking maker had his own knitting frame, kept in his home, on which he did piecework while his wife and children carded and span the yarn. Stocking making provided the main employment in the town through the eighteenth century, until the quantities of cotton thread provided by Richard Arkwright's factory experiment at Cromford gave the Nottingham stocking knitters the edge over those using Cotswold wool.

This is one of several tall and well-made houses that suggest the living was a decent one. Above and below the weaver's workroom were rooms for the family and there is a small yard at the back. When we took on the row in 1969, their roofs were falling in. We repaired the row and gave one to the local preservation society to further its cause.

St Mary's Lane is a quiet side street, a short walk from Tewkesbury Abbey and another Landmark, Abbey Gatehouse. The cottage is light and cheerful, its steep, winding corner stair still in place and leading up to a fine view across Tewkesbury's marvellous roofscape to the abbey. The town lies in the vale bounded on one side by the Cotswolds and on the other by the Malvern Hills – both are in easy reach, as are the Regency and equine delights of Cheltenham. Tewkesbury itself has much to offer in that quiet, grounded way of our historic towns: an ancient battle site; the watery activity of the Avon and Evensong; if you wish, in the lovely abbey.

From the logbook
We found ourselves so enchanted with Tewkesbury itself that we only ventured out on two days of the whole week.

Evensong every night.

Ground floor 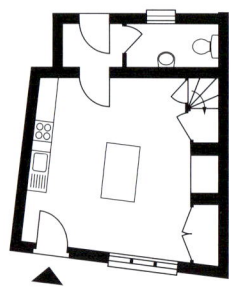   First floor 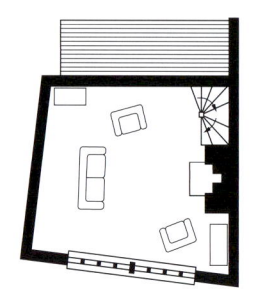   Second floor 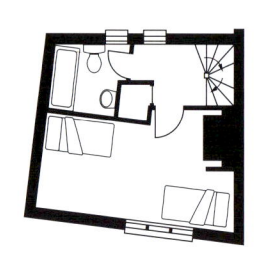   Third floor

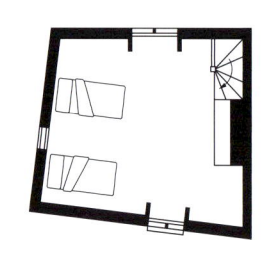

St Winifred's Well

Woolston, near Oswestry, Shropshire [G4]

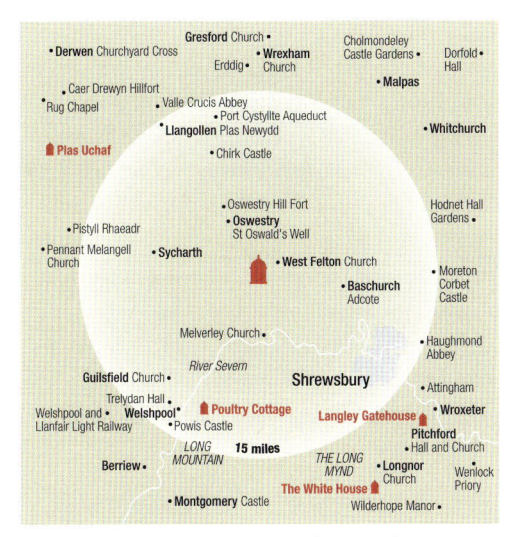

For up to 2 people
Solid fuel stove
Garden

Parking a short walk away
Dogs allowed

St Winifred was a seventh-century Welsh princess, sworn to a life of chastity, who was brought back to life by her uncle, St Beuno, after being decapitated by an angry suitor as she fled from him to take refuge in church. In the twelfth century her body was taken to Shrewsbury Abbey, where many pilgrims came to benefit from her healing miracles.

St Winifred was much loved in this area, so there is good reason to believe the tradition that this well at Woolston was dedicated to her; a lesser sister to the older and more famous St Winifred's Well at Holywell in Flintshire.

Whether it is true or not, the well here has been venerated for centuries, and is still visited by pilgrims. The innermost of the three pools is the medieval well chamber. The little building above is the medieval well chapel, itself a miraculous survival, preserved since the Reformation as a Court House and then as a cottage. Meanwhile, the well itself was enlarged to form a cold bath (your own hot, more private bath is a stone's throw from the cottage), first for a local squire, and later for the general public, whose conduct became so riotous that it was closed to them in 1755.

Thereafter it returned to nature, whose spirit was probably worshipped here long before Christianity. It is on the edge of a hamlet and hard to find (and rather harder to heat), approachable only by public footpath, which runs on, eventually, to a fragment of the old Shropshire Union Canal. Once here, acceptance of the miraculous is easy.

From the logbook

Staying in a building that was built seven years before our country was discovered (Columbus 1492) is a unique experience.

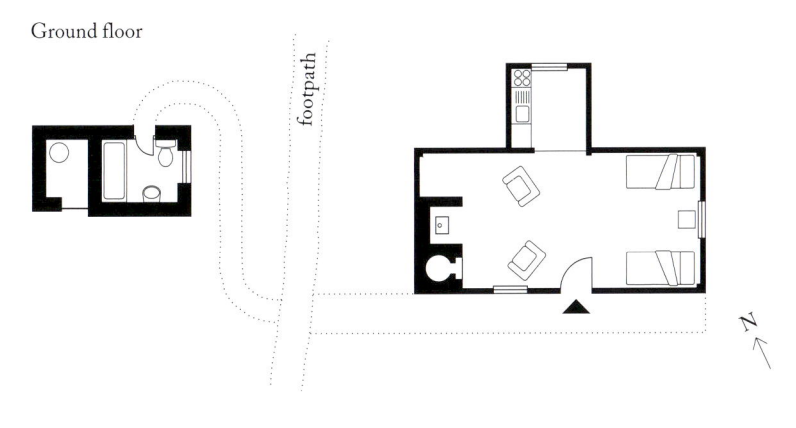

Ground floor

Shelwick Court

Near Hereford, Herefordshire [I4]

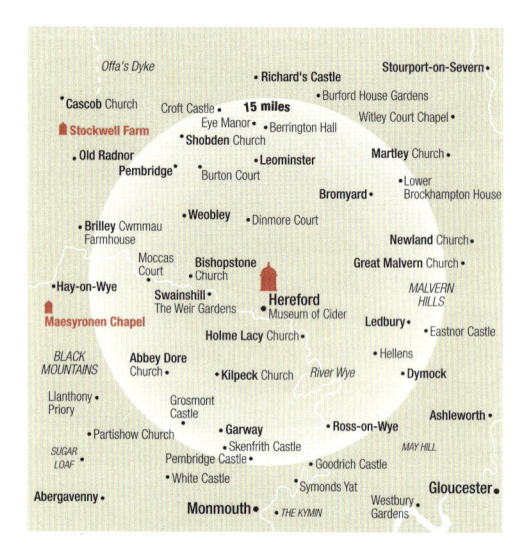

For up to 8 people
Solid fuel stove
Garden
Small pond in grounds
Adjacent parking
Dogs allowed

For many years this house had been falling down about the ears of an old farmer. It lies on the edge of a hamlet near Hereford, beside the long filled-in Gloucester & Hereford canal – made redundant, as so often, by the (still-active) railway and road built next to it.

Although it has a respectable stone front of about 1700, which with some difficulty we restrained from falling outwards, and a staircase of the same date, this alone would not have justified our intervention. But concealed within the house on the first floor, and indeed made almost invisible by later alterations, lies a medieval great chamber, with a six-bay open roof of massive timbers, cusped and chamfered in the Herefordshire manner.

What is more surprising still, this roof of about 1400 and the timber framing which holds it up has clearly been moved here from somewhere else. It looks important enough to have been a hall, but there is no trace of smoke-blackening, and it must have formed, it seems, the solar cross-wing to a really grand hall, perhaps on a nearby site. Whatever its origins, it is a rare interior, which has, very strongly, a life of its own. This is a pleasure to share, even for a short time.

From the logbook
We so enjoyed the house with its wonderfully comforting great hall.

We have spent a lot of time lying on the sofas, gazing up at the roof.

What a lovely space and what a pleasure to have so much of it.

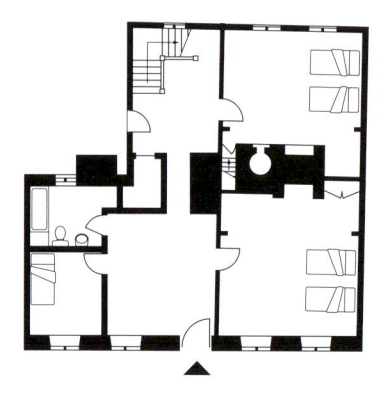

Ground floor

First floor

There is a single bedroom in the attic.

Shute Gatehouse

Near Axminster, Devon [K4]

This gatehouse, which we lease from the National Trust, was probably built by William Pole when he bought Shute in about 1560. Then it led to a large medieval and Tudor house immediately behind, now much reduced in size and known as Shute Barton. When we first saw it, the gatehouse had mouldered picturesquely for some long time, its flues and fireplaces filled with sticks by jackdaws living in the immense elms around it. Much structural work was needed, but the weather has already begun to make what we did invisible.

While the repairs were being carried out North Devon District Council offered us a remarkable Jacobean plaster ceiling, from a house in Barnstaple demolished in the 1930s. The Council had been storing it in pieces ever since, but could do so no longer. Close in date to much of the gatehouse (which is not of a single date in any case), it fitted the upper room perfectly. So, although we would not usually do such a thing, we put it up and it looks wonderful.

The elms in front of the gatehouse, which were some of the best ever seen, succumbed to Dutch elm disease; but we took advantage of this calamity to restore the ground to its original level and lay it out as a green. As a result the gatehouse looks well from the village, and those who stay in it gain a fine view of the old deer-park, particularly from the kitchen sink.

From the logbook
The best part of the week? Seeing the gatehouse coming into view as we approached through the village, waking up to the cockerel crowing his head off in the mornings, feeling superior as people drive up to the gatehouse and get out looking impressed, hearing owls in Shute woods, and watching the bats.

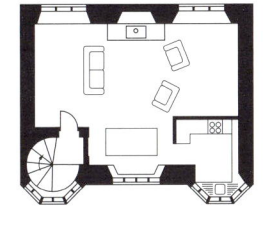

For up to 3+2 people
Solid fuel stove
Open grounds

Parking nearby
Dogs allowed

The turret bedroom is spartan in character, with limited heating.

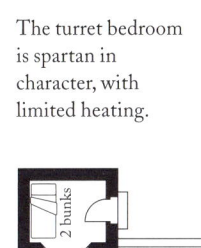

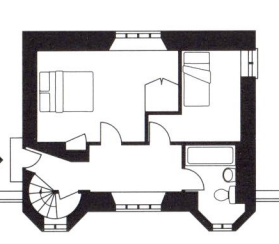

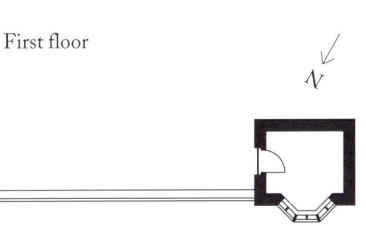

Second floor

First floor

www.landmarktrust.org.uk

Shuttleworth Estate

Old Warden, Bedfordshire [I7]

Other Landmarks in Old Warden:
Warden Abbey

Today the Shuttleworth Estate in Bedfordshire is perhaps best known for its collection of vintage aeroplanes, but its history stretches back far earlier. In the Middle Ages, Warden Abbey ran the area (the remnants of this is another Landmark, on the other side of the village). Then in the 1690s, a wealthy linen draper bought most of what is today's Shuttleworth estate. He fashioned the landscape according to the time, and built the folly, Queen Anne's Summerhouse. His descendants, who became the Barons Ongley, would live on the estate until the mid-nineteenth century, creating in the 1820s the famous Swiss Garden and the model village of Old Warden around it.

The Shuttleworths, rich industrialists who made their fortune from early steam engines, bought the estate in 1872 and commissioned Henry Clutton to rebuild its outdated mansion into today's Jacobethan pile. Golden years followed, when the estate became renowned for its shoot and country house parties, but tragedy struck in 1940, when the young heir Richard Shuttleworth died in a flying accident. His mother Dorothy set up an educational trust, and the former mansion became a college specialising in land-based courses.

We became involved when the Shuttleworth Trust approached us for help with two buildings on the estate's former warren. They personify different periods of this ancient estate's history, an eighteenth-century folly and a model gamekeeper's cottage. Add in the medieval and late Tudor pleasures of Warden Abbey on the other side of the village, and Old Warden has a Landmark to suit everyone's tastes.

Queen Anne's Summerhouse

This satisfyingly foursquare folly bears a date stone for 1878 and the clasped gauntlet of the Shuttleworth family – but this is misleading. Its exceptionally fine rubbed brickwork is far too good for the 1870s and its name gives the clue to its origins. In 1712, Queen Anne knighted the rich draper, Samuel Ongley, who owned the estate at Old Warden, an event that provides the most likely explanation for the building of the folly.

On the crest of the warren, it stood at the hub of radiating avenues of trees that Sir Samuel was planting on the estate, many still alive today. One of these avenues provided views of the mansion, and we are working with the estate to re-open most of them.

The summerhouse earned its date stone when it was renovated in 1878 by Joseph Shuttleworth, who added the pale terracotta balustrade. It then seems to have served as a pavilion and summerhouse through the estate's golden years, but was left without purpose in reluctant dereliction after the Second World War.

Its restoration beyond the remit and means of the Shuttleworth Trust, we were happy to take on this piece of the rich jigsaw of the Shuttleworth Estate. Surrounded by the flora and fauna of beautiful woodland, this is a magical spot.

For up to 2 people
Open fire
Steep spiral staircase
Open grounds
Adjacent parking
Dogs allowed

Before restoration

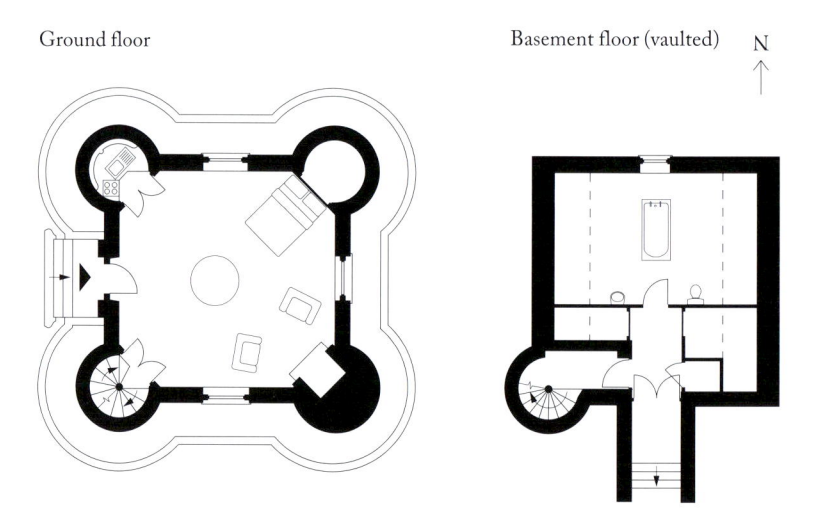

Ground floor

Basement floor (vaulted)   N

Queen Anne's Summerhouse will open in 2009 following restoration.

Keeper's Cottage

Keeper's Cottage is tucked away in the pinewoods and ferns a couple of hundred yards below the summerhouse at the foot of the warren. It is a model gamekeeper's establishment as might have been found in a nineteenth-century pattern book, in the tradition of the *orné* but in a sturdily handsome way.

It was built in 1878 for Joseph Shuttleworth, who wanted to bring the shooting on the estate up to the fashionable standards of the day, orchestrated by the gamekeeper for whom this cottage was built. For a few years we can imagine this cottage at the heart of prodigious Edwardian shooting parties, the pheasants hatched in the sitting house out back and reared in pens on the warren by the keeper.

After Richard Shuttleworth's death, when the estate was turned to different purposes, Keeper's Cottage was left deserted. The sitting house and yard outbuildings collapsed, and the detached kennel block became almost as ruinous. Luckily, the original plans of its local architect builder, John Usher, survived and so we were able not just to restore the cottage, but also to rebuild the outbuildings. You may not have to feed the hounds at dusk or fend off poachers, but you can still appreciate the sensible accommodation wealthy Victorians built for their employees – especially those who could raise a pheasant or two.

For up to 4 people
Open fire and solid fuel stove
Open grounds
Adjacent parking
Dogs allowed

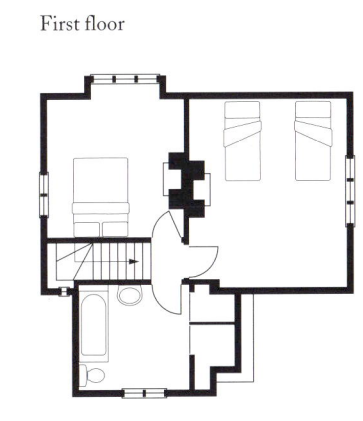

Ground floor

First floor

Silverton Park Stables

Silverton, Devon [K4]

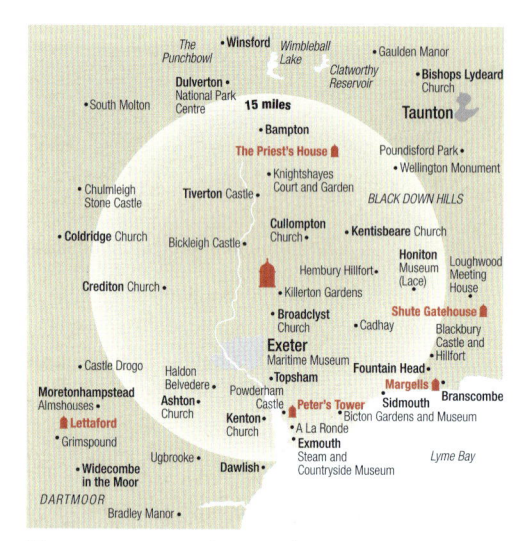

For up to 14 people
Solid fuel stove
Enclosed courtyard
and open grounds

Adjacent parking
Dogs allowed

In 1837 Captain the Hon. George Francis Wyndham, RN unexpectedly found himself 4th Earl of Egremont. His uncle, the 3rd Earl, had failed to legitimise his natural heir by omitting to marry his son's mother. Wyndham also inherited an estate at Silverton and set out to create a vast classical mansion on a scale to rival his cousin's pile at Petworth. He planned a stable block to match.

The 4th Earl's architect was J.T. Knowles (senior), a self-taught Reigate man and a believer in a patented metallic cement render. The mansion that sprang up at Silverton Park exploited this versatile material, using it to clothe double-height colonnades.

On a rise to the rear of the mansion, Wyndham charged Knowles with erecting an imposing block to house and display his carriages and provide stabling for his teams of horses and their grooms.

In 1845, with the stables in use but before the brick cadre could receive its coat of the famous patented cement, Wyndham died. The estate never regained its momentum. The contents of the mansion were auctioned off in 1892 and a few years later the house was demolished. The unfinished stable block was left as an imposing and romantic monument to the 4th Earl's grandiose ambitions and was used in a desultory way for agricultural purposes. It turned out to be one of our most intractable projects, finally unlocked by the enthusiasm of one particularly loyal supporter.

You will stay mainly in the south range, with views of the rolling Devon countryside from a common room behind the giant portico. Bedrooms opening off staircases around the courtyard give a sense of collegiate life, yet we hope too that you still catch a sense of the equestrian as you enter through monumental gates.

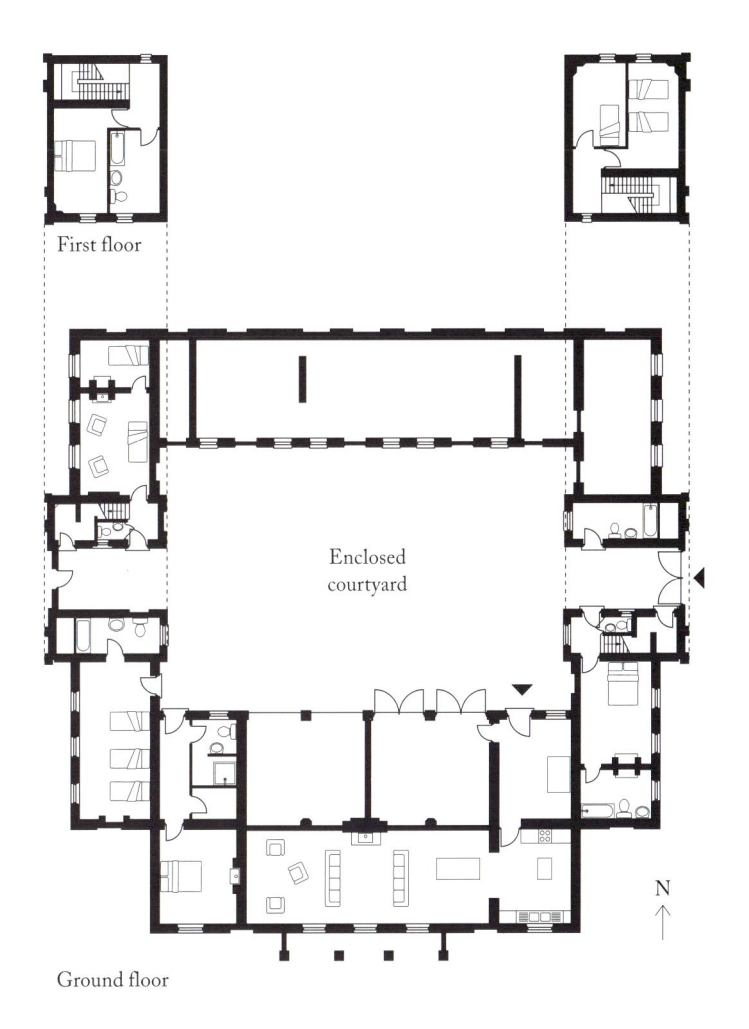

First floor

Ground floor

Enclosed courtyard

N

www.landmarktrust.org.uk 177

South Street

Great Torrington, Devon [K3]

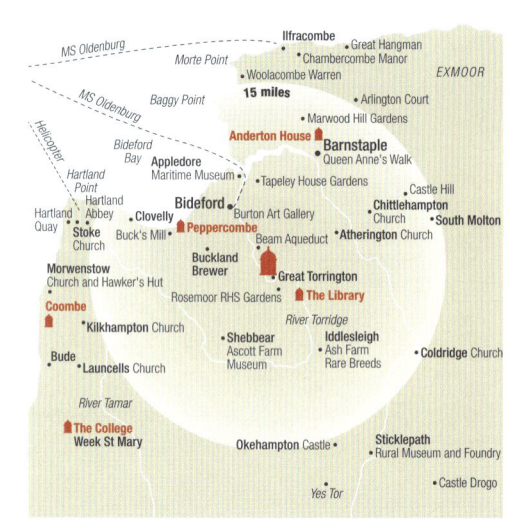

Giles Cawsey, merchant and Town Clerk, built this house in 1701. For nearly the first time in Devon, the main ground-floor rooms were designed for the family, instead of for trade. The panelled dining-room and the drawing-room are on either side of the front door, with a hall between leading to a fine staircase. The charm of the house lies not in its aspiration towards metropolitan high fashion, nor even in the long walled garden behind, but in the ceiling under which you can dine and the shell hood over the front door. One of Devon's most accomplished plasterers was employed to model crisp trophies of arms and musical instruments, amid foliage and stout mouldings.

Although long lived in by leading citizens, 28 South Street belonged to an ancient Town Lands charity. Recently used for offices, but deserving better, it was suggested to us by its Trustees. It offers the rare experience of living in a grand house in the busy and active street of an agreeable country town. Torrington, indeed, is very agreeable, settled on the top of one of North Devon's steep green hills. It has a weekly market, a good museum and enjoyable shops, whether you want fresh bread in the morning or locally made glass.

From the logbook
The house is beautiful – we spent the first hour wandering from room to room, marvelling at the quality of workmanship and attention to detail.

Left Birmingham an ordinary family and arrived at No. 28 South Street feeling like Gentry!

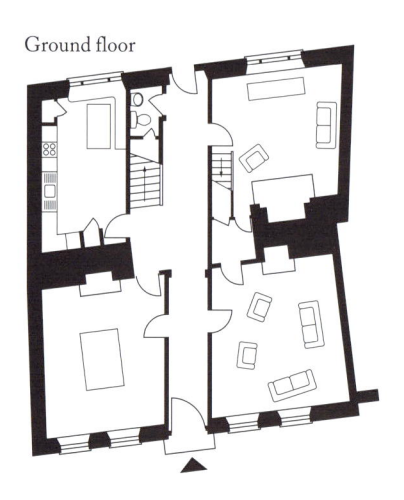

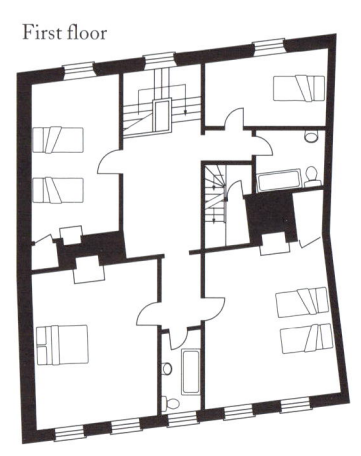

For up to 7 people
Open fire
Gas coal fire
Enclosed garden
Parking nearby
Dogs allowed

The Steward's House

St Michael's Street, Oxford [I6]

For up to 2 people
Gas coal fire

No private parking

Other Landmarks in Oxford:
The Old Parsonage

Oxford has more architectural pleasures and surprises than anywhere else in Britain, and nowhere else has so much spirit and energy been expended, often in marvellously silly ways. When, therefore, the Oxford Union Society needed money to repair their first debating chamber (now the library) we asked if, in return for a contribution, a place could be found where our visitors could stay.

The Union, formed as a debating society in 1823 to encourage free speech and speculation, acquired a site at No. 7 St Michael's Street in 1852. In 1856 their first debating chamber, which was to be a library as well, was built to the design of Benjamin Woodward, a disciple of Ruskin. While he was finishing the building he showed it to D. G. Rossetti and to William Morris, 'a rather rough and unpolished youth', and they offered to paint 'figures of some kind' in the gallery window bays – which they did in the Long Vacation, assisted by their friends, including Edward Burne-Jones. William Morris finished his bay first and began painting the roof. These long-faded scenes from the Arthurian legend by famous painters in their youth, a wonderful possession for the Union, have been brought back to life, and the building restored.

In return for helping them we have a self-contained floor and a half in the former official residence of the Steward of the Union. He was an important, permanent figure who kept the show on the road, and kept order, while generations of undergraduates came and went. His spacious house was added, with a new library, in 1910 to the design of W. E. Mills of Oxford. It is a thoroughgoing Edwardian affair, of a kind and quality that we are pleased to look after; and our generously proportioned rooms, particularly the sitting-room, will give you a true impression of the Oxford of that day, while the vigorous and sometimes rather noisy activities of modern Oxford, and of the modern Union, take place around you.

First floor

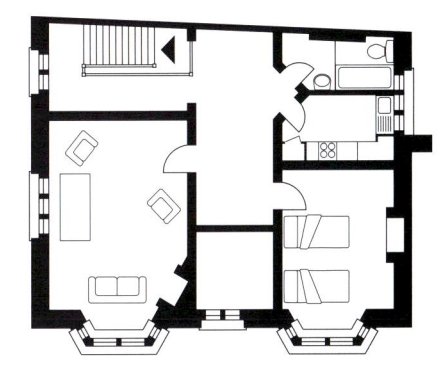

Stockwell Farm

Old Radnor, Powys [H4]

For up to 6 people
Open fire
Enclosed garden

Parking nearby
Steep staircase

Behind an unassuming farmhouse front, there is something rather earlier here, to which one old roof truss in a bedroom is the clue. This belongs to a house of about 1600, which had a sleeping loft above the main living-room and a door from the house to a cow byre (later a barn) under the same roof. At the other end a parlour wing was added in about 1700.

One of our visitors had been here long before, as a child evacuated from wartime London, and has left a moving account in the logbook: 'Missing are the neighbours who came to stare at the new children … Missing too the central fire, the cake hissing on the girdle … the hideous steamy Mondays … and the grisly boiled pig and tapioca.'

The house has a beautiful view; and behind are our own fields, into which you can turn your children, and across which you can walk up to Old Radnor. It is a particularly attractive hillside of rough pasture, full of mysterious hollows, green hummocks, anthills, thorn bushes and other unfunctional things. When the wind gets up, as it can in this exposed position, you can wrap up warm, gather round the fire and plan the next walk.

Old Radnor consists of a few scattered cottages, a fine fifteenth-century church, containing the oldest organ case in Britain, and the Harp Inn, which we once owned and restored. Charles I is known to have been here since he complained about the food.

From the logbook
We would love to return here: the lack of clutter is a pleasure to experience.

For botanists; there is a very good bog at Tregaron.

We have enjoyed the farm and the insight it gives one into the lives of our ancestors.

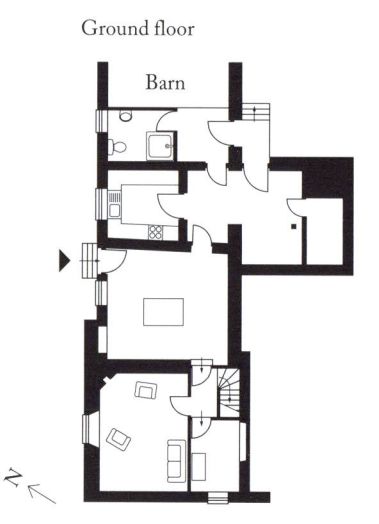

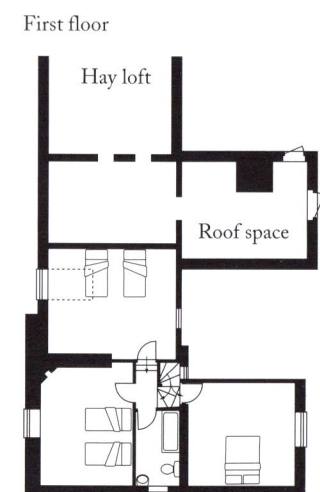

Ground floor — Barn

First floor — Hay loft, Roof space

180   The Landmark Trust Handbook

Stogursey Castle

Stogursey, near Bridgwater, Somerset [J4]

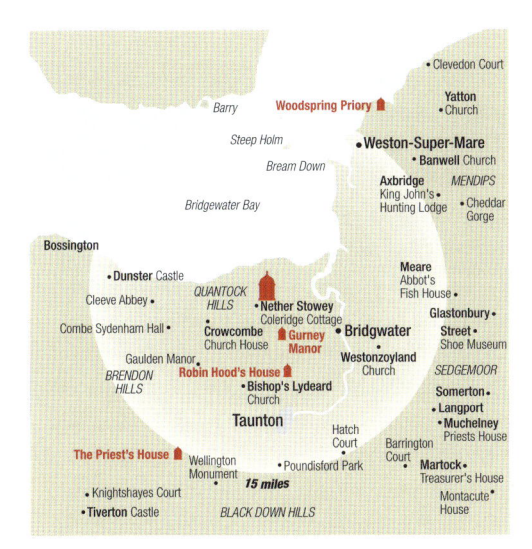

For up to 4 people
Open fire
Moated garden

Parking nearby
Dogs allowed

Stogursey, an old village to the east of the Quantocks, was chosen as his principal base by William de Courcy, Steward to Henry I. Both his son and his grandson married heiresses and the de Courcys became even more important. So, too, did their castle. Then the male line failed, and the castle was inherited by Alice de Courcy. She entertained King John here in 1210, when her husband won 20 shillings from him 'at play'.

Later on the Percys from Northumberland inherited it but, after a minor part in the Wars of the Roses, they could find no useful purpose for it as it stood and they did not think it worth rebuilding as a less fortified seat. So time and neglect, and adaptation to more humble uses, reduced it to ruins, in which it has lain ever since.

The small dwelling formed inside the gate towers of the castle has seventeenth-century roof timbers and was repaired in the 1870s; but when we found it, the entire castle had vanished beneath a mantle of vegetation. Clearing this and dredging the moat revealed an unsuspected thirteenth-century bridge. We also recovered some chain mail and other warlike fragments from the mud. The cottage makes a strange dwelling but a pleasant one, still commanding the only entrance to the castle's grassy inner ward, scene of all those doings long ago.

From the logbook
Our daughters 7 and 6 lived a magical week in their moated castle.

Lots of local walks to do – no need to go further afield.

A public footpath runs past the eastern end of the bridge.

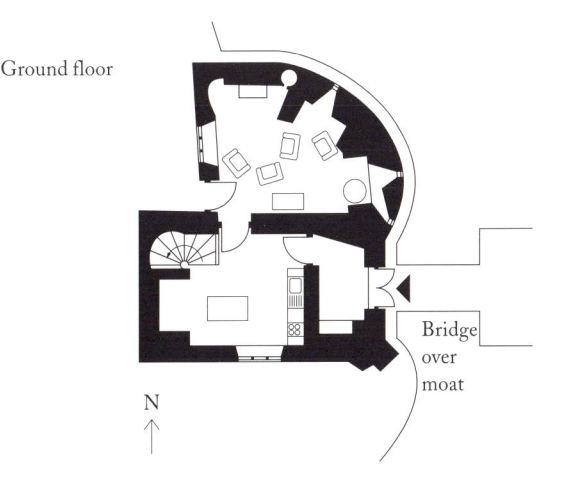

Ground floor

First floor

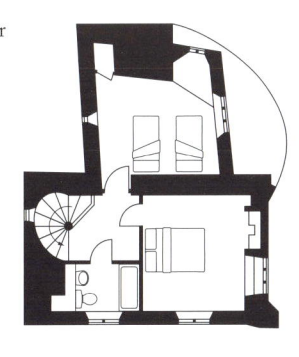

Bridge over moat

N

www.landmarktrust.org.uk

Stoker's Cottage

Stretham, Cambridgeshire [H8]

For up to 2 people
Open fire
Enclosed garden

Adjacent parking
Dogs allowed

The engineers of the seventeenth century did an impressive job of draining the fens of their standing water, perhaps too good a job. By the nineteenth century the exposed peat had shrunk so much that the new river courses were left stranded above the lie of the land. At first, windmills drove large wheels in time of flood to scoop excess water from the fields and into the rivers. Soon even they could no longer cope with the lifts required and steam arrived in the nick of time.

Built in 1831, Stretham Old Engine is a gleaming beast with a scoop wheel 37 feet in diameter, replacing four local windmills. The building the Victorian engineers erected to house their creation calls to mind a Nonconformist chapel in its respectful scale, and from it on a clear day you can glimpse the spire of Ely Cathedral. When called into service, the beam engine got through a ton of coal an hour, brought by barge but shovelled into three hungry boilers by the inhabitant of Stoker's Cottage.

The Old Engine operated as a standby until 1941, and since 1959 has been kept in immaculate condition by the Stretham Engine Trust, its role taken over by electrical pumping stations elsewhere. The Trust found they no longer had a use for Stoker's Cottage and so approached us for help.

Today, the Stretham engine is considered the finest surviving example of its type, and the entire site is designated a Scheduled Ancient Monument. The cottage, meanwhile, finds a place in Simon Jenkins' *Thousand Best Houses in England*. Stoker's Cottage is a simple and evocative retreat for two. It is within easy reach of Cambridge, Ely and Peterborough, with good waterways to discover on foot under the wide fenland skies.

Stretham Old Engine is open to the public (from 1.30-5pm) on the second Sunday of each month from April to September and on Bank Holidays over the same period. Landmarkers may be able to gain access at other times by appointment (charges apply).

Stoker's Cottage, in the left foreground, is next to the Old Engine House.

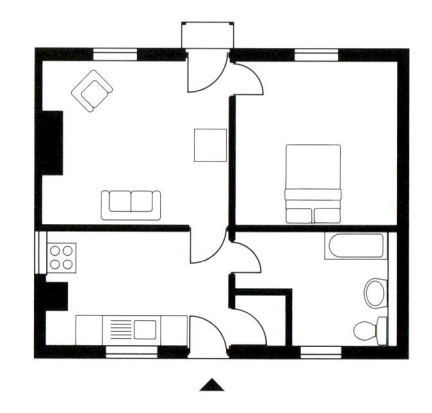

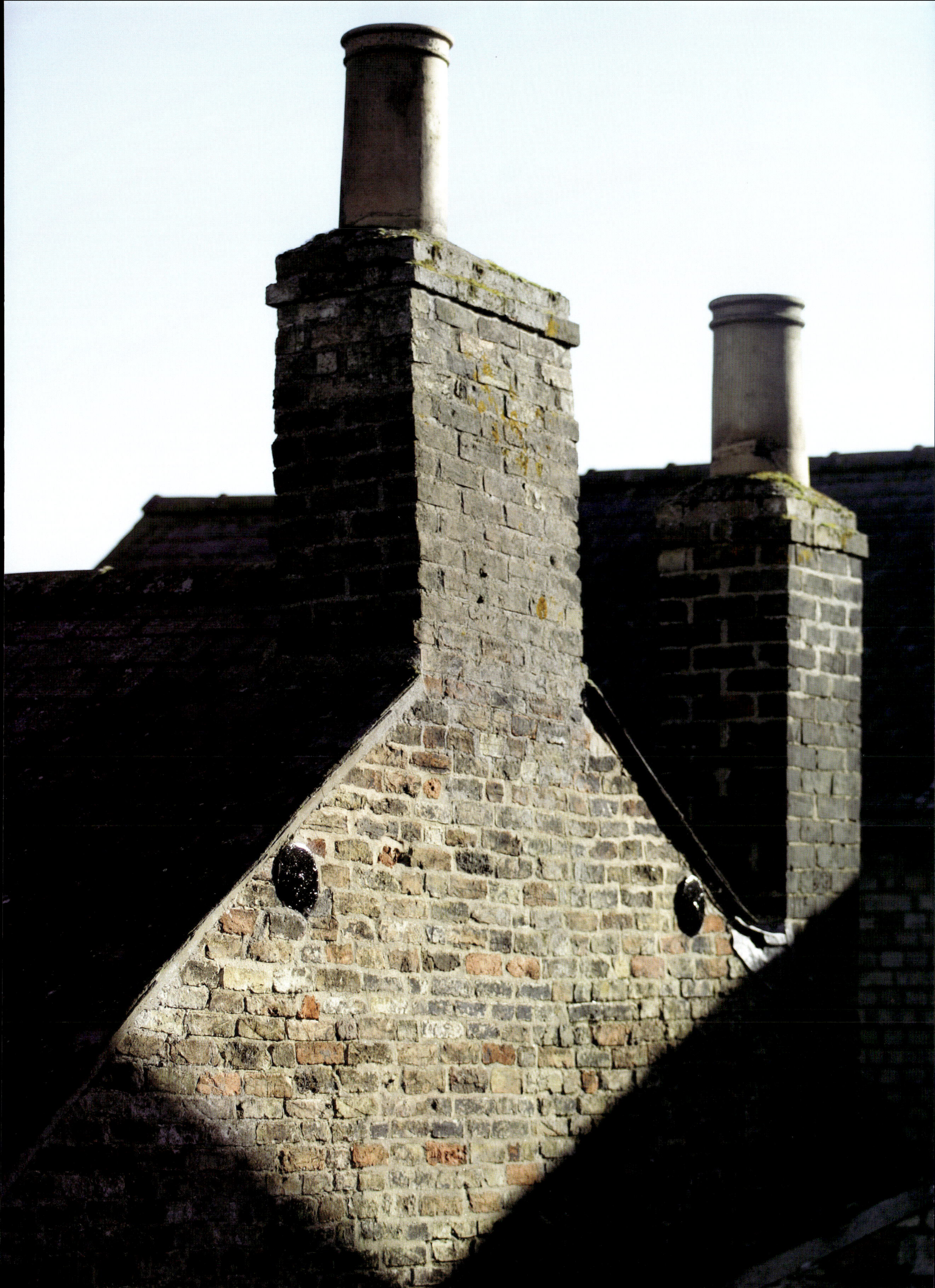

Swarkestone Pavilion

Near Ticknall, Derbyshire [G6]

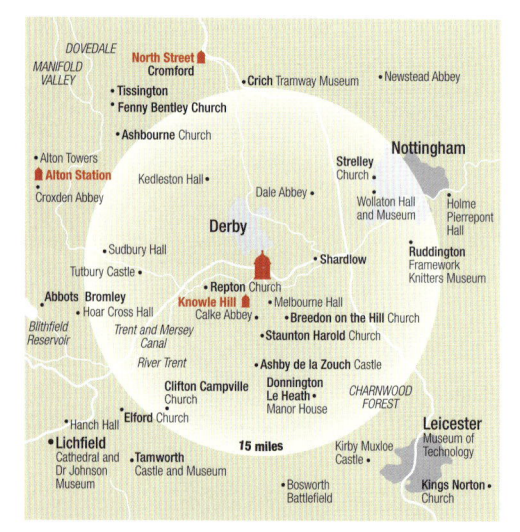

For up to 2 people
Enclosed garden
Roof terrace
Steep staircase
Parking nearby

The excuse for building this majestic little pavilion was to give a grandstand view of whatever went on in the enclosure in front of it. Suggestions range from the romantic (jousting) and the rough (bear-baiting) to the more prosaic (bowls). Evidence supports the latter, with a payment in 1632 for a 'bowle alley house'. It was built by a mason, Richard Shepperd, but its design has been attributed to John Smythson, one of our first true architects and son of the great Robert. So, whatever its purpose, it is a building well worth preserving.

Swarkestone Hall was demolished by 1750. The pavilion survived, thanks to that most conserving of families, the Harpur Crewes of Calke, but it had long been a shell when we bought it. We re-roofed it and put back floors and windows, to recreate the room in which you live and sleep. The bathroom is in the top of one of the turrets, above the kitchen, and to reach it you must cross the open roof – an unlooked-for opportunity to study the sky at night.

Swarkestone, with its important bridge across the Trent, has seen great events: a battle for its control in the Civil War did great damage to the Hall; and in 1745 it was the point at which Bonnie Prince Charlie recognised the futility of his attempt on the English throne and turned his troops back towards Scotland, to meet their fate at Culloden. Today, it stands as a romantic vestige as the modern world goes on around it.

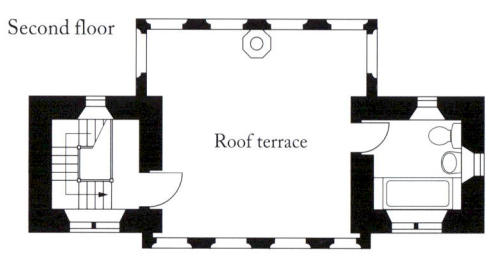

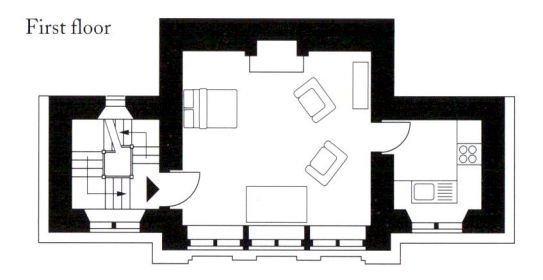

Second floor

First floor

Tangy Mill

Kintyre, Argyll and Bute [B1]

For up to 6 people
Open fire
Open grounds

Adjacent parking
Steep staircase
Dogs allowed

Towards the southern end of Kintyre, on the western side, the landscape changes and there is a broad, open sweep of fertile land. Tangy Mill was built in about 1820, probably on the site of an earlier mill, to serve the big arable farms here. It stands in beautiful remote surroundings on the north bank of the Tangy Burn, near the point where it enters the sea, and is made of harled whinstone with sandstone dressings. For our repairs we obtained more of this sandstone from the original quarry.

Because of the climate (which often merits extra layers of clothing) the grain, mostly oats, had to be dried before grinding, and there is a two-storey kiln with a big revolving ventilator, known as a 'granny', on its roof. Here the oats were spread six inches deep on the perforated iron floor of what is now one of the bedrooms. When we bought the mill, the dressing, drying, hoisting and grinding machinery, the stones and shutes and the backshot wheel, were still there; we have kept all this in position and amongst it you live and sleep. The atmosphere of old places of work is almost impossible to preserve, because one cannot preserve old workmen and old ways of life; but this mill was so complete and in such an unexpected place that here for once, changing as little as possible, we have attempted it.

From the logbook
Delicious lobsters can be bought from fishermen near the Tourist Office in Campbeltown.

We saw dolphins off the beach. There was a whole group of them going quite fast, leaping through the water – it was magical.

We can hardly believe we've seen the Irish Sea, Atlantic Ocean, Ireland, seals, swans in the sea, a golden eagle, jellyfish, peacocks, palm trees, etc etc.

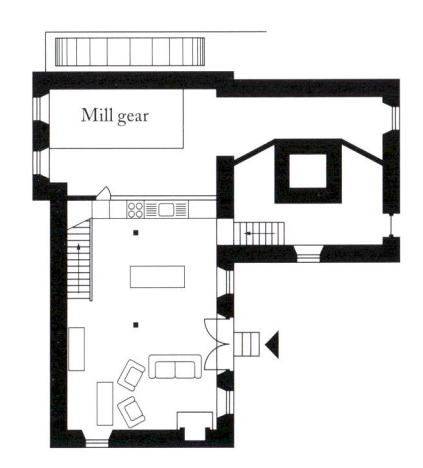

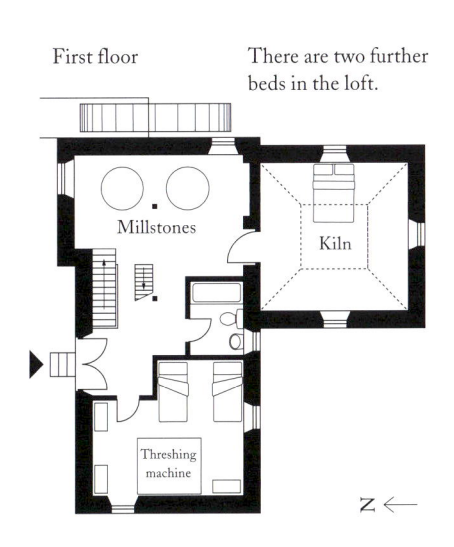

Ground floor

First floor

There are two further beds in the loft.

www.landmarktrust.org.uk

Tixall Gatehouse

Near Stafford, Staffordshire [G5]

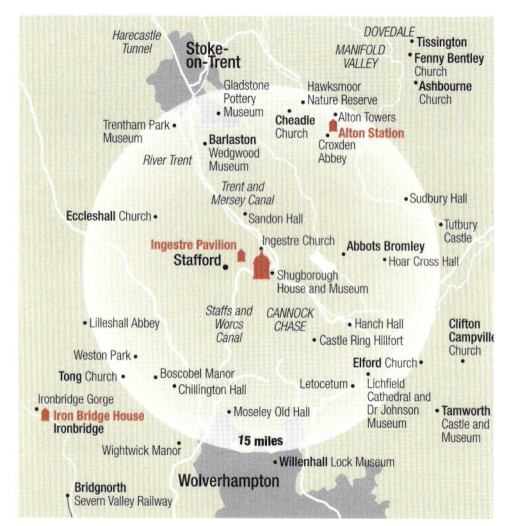

For up to 6 people
Roof terrace
Small fenced garden
Steep spiral staircase

Adjacent parking for 2 cars
Dogs allowed

Tixall Gatehouse was built in about 1580 by Sir Walter Aston to stand in front of an older house. This house and a successor, built in 1780, have disappeared, and the gatehouse today is surrounded by grass. It was described in 1598 as 'one of the fairest pieces of work made of late times in all these counties' and, more recently, as 'an Elizabethan ruin, without roof, floors or windows, used as a shelter for cattle'.

Mary, Queen of Scots, was imprisoned at Tixall for two weeks in 1586. Her son James I came here once for two days. In 1678 the Aston of the day was sent briefly to the Tower, accused of a part in the Titus Oates conspiracy. A century later, his descendant Thomas Clifford, guided by 'the celebrated Brown' and his pupil Eames, ingeniously made use of a new canal to form a lake in his park – known to boaters as Tixall Wide.

We bought the gatehouse for £300 in 1968. On its first floor we made five large rooms, one of them a gallery with an oriel window at each end above the two archways. In the spandrels of these archways are, facing the outside world, armed warriors; and on the inside, voluptuous ladies thinly disguised as angels.

The roof is paved with stone, and to be high up here among the balustrades and turret tops, with Arcadian landscape on every side, is an important Landmark Trust experience. The gatehouse clock lives in one of the turrets (as do two bracing cabin-like bedrooms and the bathrooms); this strikes the hour, and perhaps the half hour, but has no hands or face to show the actual time, which seems unimportant here, even vulgar.

From the logbook
I went up onto the roof to watch the stars coming out.

First floor

There are two small single bedrooms and a bathroom in the turrets on the second floor.

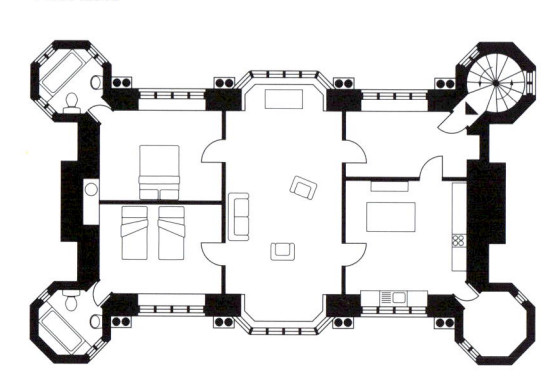

186 The Landmark Trust Handbook

The Tower, Canons Ashby

Northamptonshire [16]

For up to 2+1 people
Garden
Roof terrace

Parking nearby
Steep spiral staircase

There can be few houses in which every detail, inside and out, is pleasing to look at, but this can truly be claimed of Canons Ashby. The last time it was altered in any major way was in 1710. Thereafter, its intelligent and sensitive owners, the Drydens, matched their tastes and needs to those of their house. Early decoration lives happily with later furniture, all of the greatest charm and interest.

In 1980 the house was transferred to the National Trust, after a public appeal. We contributed to the restoration fund and offered to pay for the creation and repair of one flat. Accordingly we were given the top of the sixteenth-century tower, where there were formerly two bedrooms, reached by a newel stair with solid oak treads. We tidied up these light and pleasant rooms, which look down the axis of the slowly reviving garden, and put a bathroom and kitchen in two adjoining attics. A new dormer window was made to light the kitchen, which is invisible from below but provides an agreeable roofscape to look at from the sink.

Meanwhile, the quiet building below has come back to life, and is opened to the public by the National Trust, normally from April to October – and to you, free of charge, within opening times when you stay here. On the top of the tower you have your own hidden refuge, and at the end of the day, when the last visitor has gone, you can enjoy the privilege of an owner and walk in the garden undisturbed.

Second floor

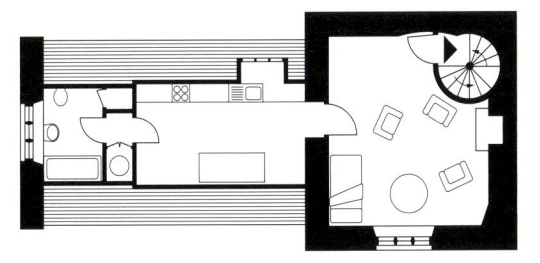

Tower room

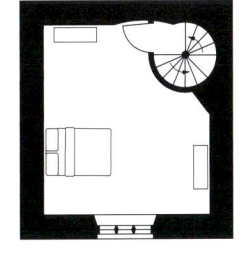

www.landmarktrust.org.uk

Tower Hill

St David's, Pembrokeshire [I2]

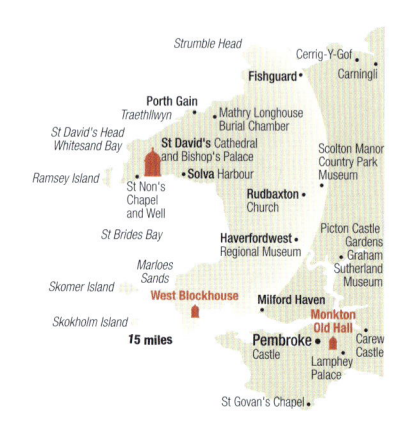

This house occupies a most important site. It is built just above the close wall at St David's and has an astonishing view of the cathedral, facing it squarely at tower level. To arrive here is to feel that you have completed a pilgrimage, drawn down the long Pembrokeshire peninsula towards a place of worship that was already ancient when the Normans built their cathedral beside it. There is still much of the monastery here, in the actual buildings that survive, in their sense of enclosure within the valley and in the warmth of their welcome when finally you top the last hill, and pass between the last houses, to obtain your first full view of them.

The living-room, too, has great serenity, with the sun on one side and the sunlit cathedral on the other. At your door is the reassurance of cathedral life, its services, the bells and the building itself, and also a lively town. The sea is about a mile away in most directions; the coastal path, with stunning views, encircles St David's – 'a long way, but very good for you'.

From the logbook
Tower Hill has its own elevating appeal.

We arrived in the dark and were absolutely knocked out the following morning when we opened the curtains to the view of the Cathedral.

Where better to spend St David's Day!

For up to 4+2 people
Open fire
Enclosed garden
Parking nearby
Dogs allowed

Ground floor

188   The Landmark Trust Handbook

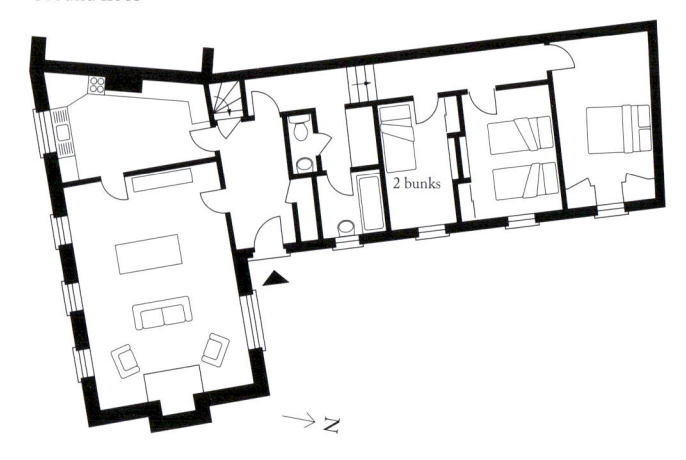

Warden Abbey

Old Warden, Bedfordshire [I7]

Warden Abbey was Cistercian, founded in 1135. Its seal bore three Warden pears, to which it gave its name. The abbey was dissolved in 1537 and a large house was built on the site by the Gostwick family.

Nothing remains of house or abbey above ground except this puzzling fragment, of which we have a long lease. It stands near a big farm, in a meadow made uneven by what lies underneath, and is an extremely perplexing building of very high quality. Clearly it formed part of the Gostwicks' house, but it also incorporates part of the abbey; in the course of our repairs a fourteenth-century tile pavement emerged, one of the finest ever discovered, which you can see for yourselves in Bedford Museum.

The principal room downstairs seems to have been part of a gallery or broad corridor, with a large open fireplace added to one end. Occupying the entire first floor is a single room with a Tudor fireplace, an oriel window and a heavily moulded oak ceiling. It is a pleasure to lie here in bed and wonder for whom such a splendid room can have been constructed: for one of the last abbots, for his guests, or for the Gostwicks? Above is a superb attic, in which one visitor put her three aunts, uproariously sharing a room for the first time since childhood.

The surrounding country has had the advantage of belonging to large estates, and is some of the best in Bedfordshire.

From the logbook
A most wonderful half-term – we always dreamt of a place in the middle of a field in beautiful countryside, and here it is.

After 19 years and 66 Landmarks we have made it to Warden. Well worth the wait!

For up to 5 people
Soild fuel stove
Small fenced garden
Parking a short walk away across a field
Steep spiral staircase
Dogs allowed

Other Landmarks in Old Warden:
Shuttleworth – Keeper's Cottage and Queen Anne's Summerhouse

Ground floor 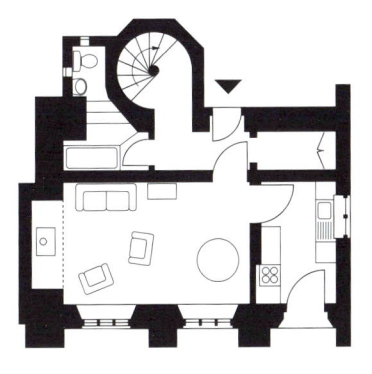   First floor 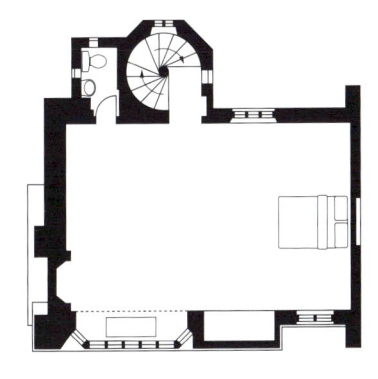   Attic floor

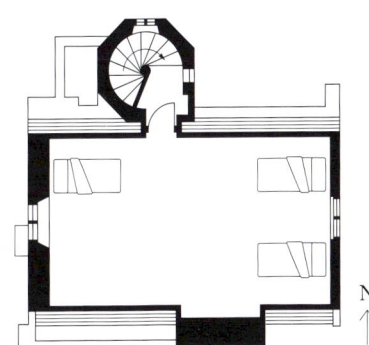

The Wardrobe

The Cathedral Close, Salisbury, Wiltshire [J6]

In return for our help with rehousing their museum in the Wardrobe (which had been empty for some time and needed expensive repairs), the (now disbanded) Berkshire and Wiltshire Regiment allowed us to form a flat high up in the attics. Here, approached by a seventeenth-century staircase, are three lofty rooms, each with a different outlook. The Landmark prides itself on the views from its many windows, but the view from the sitting-room here of the cathedral is one of the best of all, whether by day or by night, when it seems to be floodlit expressly for one's benefit.

The Wardrobe, which contains traces of a substantial medieval hall, was once the Bishop's storehouse, and so got its name. It has been a house since before 1600, mostly let by the Dean and Chapter to laymen, who formed in it some very handsome rooms, now part of the museum. One family, the Husseys, must have used our attics as a nursery, since during our building work we discovered toys, and even a manuscript novel by a 13-year-old Victorian daughter.

All cathedral closes have a special quality, but this is one of the very best, a succession of beautiful houses ranged round the only English cathedral built at one go. Those who stay at the Wardrobe share, with the museum, the use of a long walled garden, which runs down to the swift and silent Avon.

From the logbook
We climbed the stairs and the Cathedral became ours for a week – choirs rehearsing Evensong, the doves, the laughter of children on the green, the sound of cricket bats, bells ringing the changes … just listen.

A must is to read Golding's The Spire, then go on the roof tour of the Cathedral.

Even on the short journey from bedroom to bathroom I could not resist a detour to make sure the view was still there.

For up to 4 people
Gas coal fire
Garden
Parking nearby
Access by steep staircase

The Landmark is at the top of the building in the centre of the photograph to the left, which was taken from the cathedral spire.

Second floor

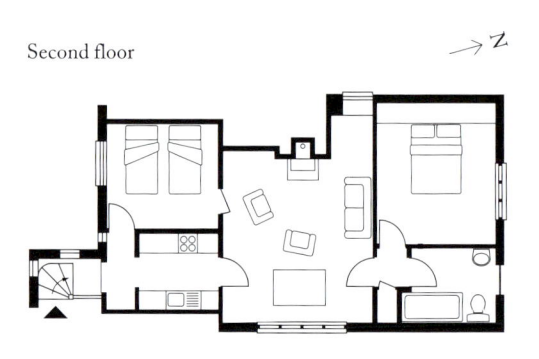

West Blockhouse

Dale, Pembrokeshire [I2]

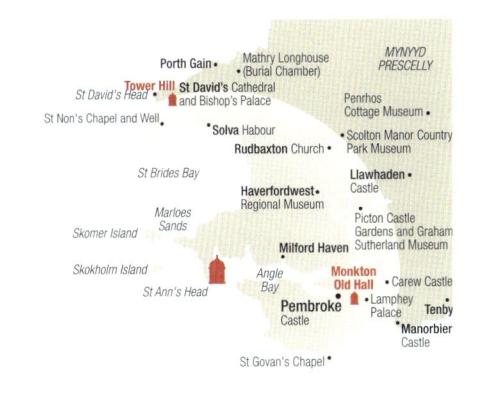

This is the outermost work of the mid-nineteenth-century fortification of Milford Haven. It had a single battery of six heavy guns commanding the entrance to the harbour, with defensible barracks behind to give protection from attack on the landward side. The fort was completed in 1857 and contained accommodation for a garrison of 34 men and one officer. It continued in use until after the Second World War, updated from time to time with new guns and new emplacements.

The walls of finely dressed limestone are of exceptional quality (as too were the repairs to them). The size of the granite coping stones on the parapet of the battery itself will astonish even those familiar with Victorian ideas of how a job should be done. The Victorians also knew how to make themselves comfortable: inside, the rooms on the first floor are lined with thick pine boards so that, with the coal fire burning, you are cosily remote from the elements.

It is a vertiginous spot, but the view down the coast of Pembrokeshire is one to savour. Victorian fortification and more recent industry alike are dwarfed and absorbed. There is still, occasionally, the spectacle of a big ship feeling her way into the mouth of the haven at one's feet. In contrast, there is a sheltered, south-facing beach within a few hundred yards.

From the logbook
What a building, what a history and what a weekend.

Where else would you get such a view? Ships going into the haven, gannets diving for fish, ravens overhead and wild flowers down the path.

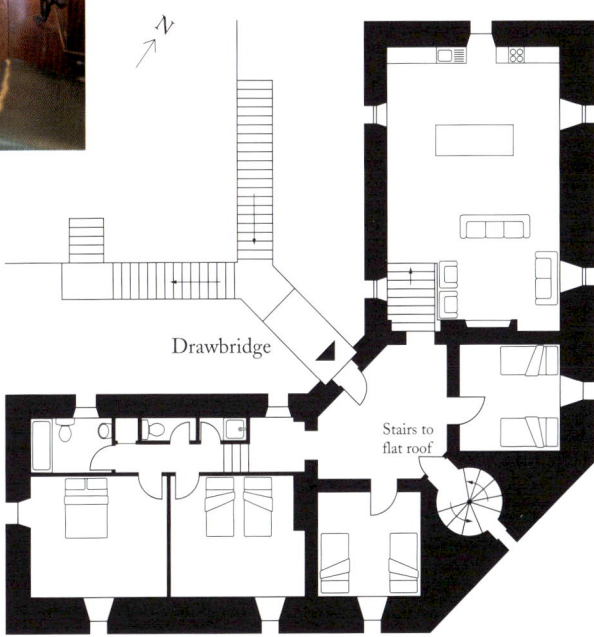

For up to 8 people
Open fire
Roof platform
Dogs allowed

Parking a short walk by steep footpath
External staircases and drawbridge

First floor

Whiteford Temple

Near Callington, Cornwall [L2]

For up to 2 people
Open fire
Small garden
Adjacent parking

The Duchy of Cornwall generously gave us this handsome granite building. It was put up in 1799 for Sir John Call, a military engineer who had made a fortune in India. By 1770, at the age of 38, he was able to retire, marry and build himself a substantial mansion. This, with the estate, was sold to the Duchy in 1879. The house was largely demolished in 1913, and today all that remains are traces of its garden, part of the stables, and this temple, on its own, high above.

It is not clear how it was reached from the house, how its surroundings were laid out, nor how it was used – though its three arches were certainly glazed at one time. Accounts of a party held in it in 1847 make one suppose that it must then have been larger; and also that it was nearer to the house, so perhaps it has been moved. It had become a shelter for cattle when we first saw it, with a roof of corrugated iron and a floor of earth.

It has a fine open view, looking towards the estuary of the Tamar in the distance; and it is well designed, an ornament in the landscape which it would be sad to lose. Accordingly, we restored it, as a single large room with two small wings, which is our best guess at what its unknown architect intended.

From the logbook
What a room with a view.

The temple is a pleasure worth waiting for.

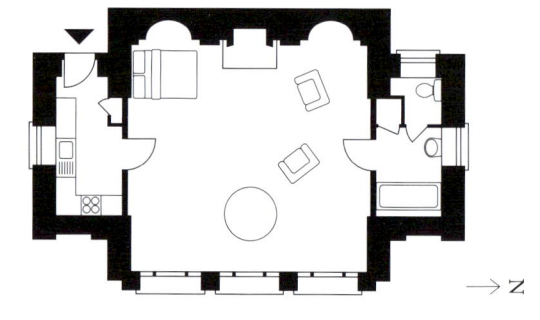

192 The Landmark Trust Handbook

The White House

Aston Munslow, Shropshire [H4]

This was long the home of Miss Constance Purser, who nurtured it and uncovered its past, building up a collection of household and agricultural implements, and opened it to the public in a small way. In 1990 she passed the house and its contents on to us.

Until 1945 the White House belonged to the Stedmans, who had lived here from soon after 1300 in a nearly unbroken line. The tops of the great cruck trusses of their hall can be seen in the roof space. Below are rooms of Tudor and Jacobean date, with wide uneven oak floorboards and a pleasing jumble of different windows. After a fire in 1780, a polite new drawing-room was added at one end, with a bedroom above.

The house stands on the south side of Wenlock Edge, and the garden runs down the hill in front, with long views of Corvedale towards Ludlow, capital of the Marches. Just below is the village of Aston Munslow. Behind the house are outbuildings of all shapes and dates and sizes, many containing equipment appropriate to their original use.

From the logbook
The sheep grazing on the hill, the smell of the farm crops, the silent and restful ambience of this wonderful old house.

We took a tarpaulin on to the lawn and lay on our backs to watch the shooting stars.

For up to 8 people
Open fire
Large garden
Adjacent parking
Dogs allowed

Ground floor

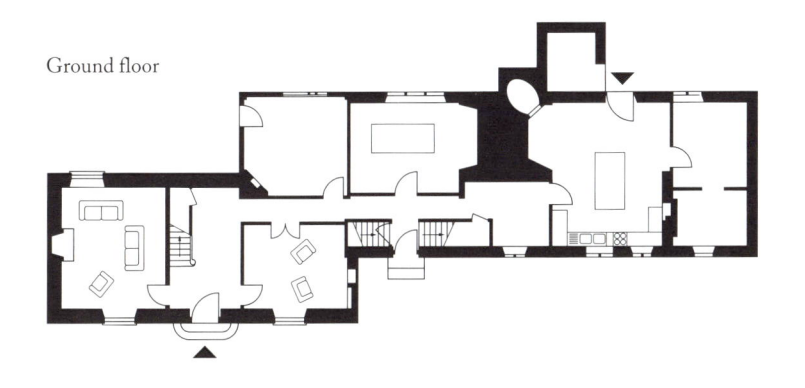

First floor

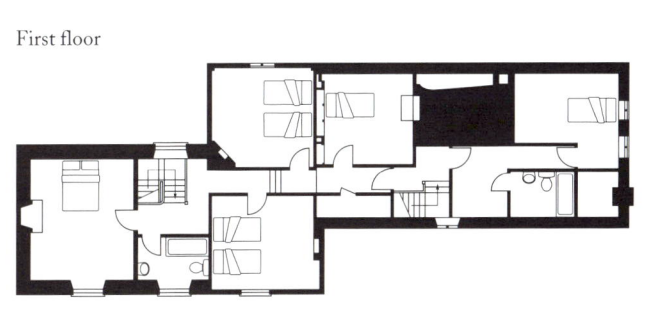

www.landmarktrust.org.uk

Wilmington Priory

Wilmington, near Eastbourne, East Sussex [K8]

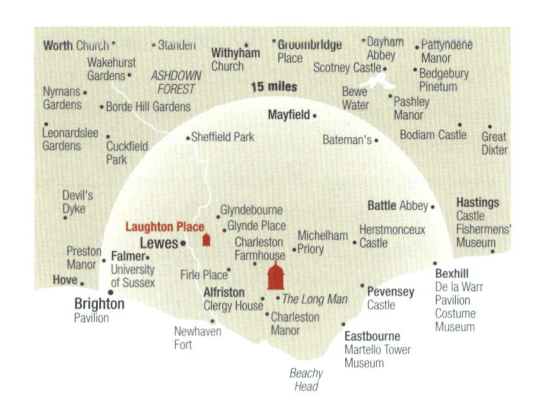

Wilmington Priory was a cell of the Benedictine Abbey at Grestain in Normandy. Never a conventional priory with cloister and chapter, the monks prayed in the adjoining parish church, where the thousand-year-old yews are testimony to the age of the site. The Priory has been added to and altered in every age, some of it has been lost to ruin and decay, but what is left shows how highly it was once regarded.

Staying here you will have the benefit of enjoying the medieval site with its fine vaulted entrance porch, mullioned window in the wall of the ruined Great Chamber, and stair turrets, combined with the comfort of living in rooms improved by the Georgians. Add to that the sense of adventure as you make your way to bed in the first floor medieval porch bedroom, through the unconverted chamber above the kitchen with its open cathedral-like roof and tracery. Once there, look out at the Long Man in this peaceful, unchanged landscape.

From this ancient place you can go to the opera at Glyndebourne, admire the work of the Bloomsbury group or perhaps go bucket and spading in Eastbourne. Whatever you choose, Wilmington itself with its agreeable village street, pub, and downland walks, all overlooked by the famous Long Man, has much to offer.

Open Days are held at Wilmington Priory annually. Please check our website for details.

From the logbook
It's nice having a kitchen big enough to waltz in and no doubt polka if we only knew how.

For up to 6 people
Open fire
Enclosed garden
Parking nearby
Dogs allowed

Ground floor

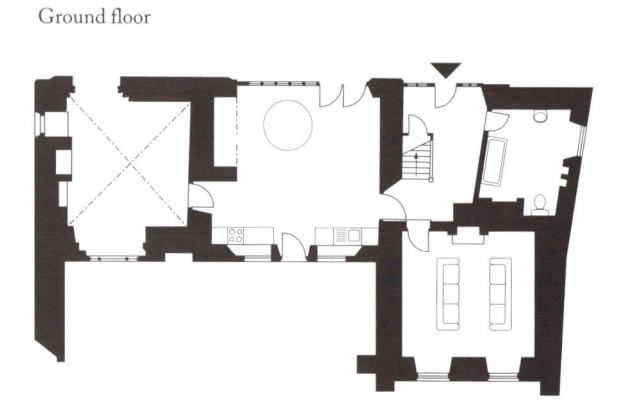

First floor

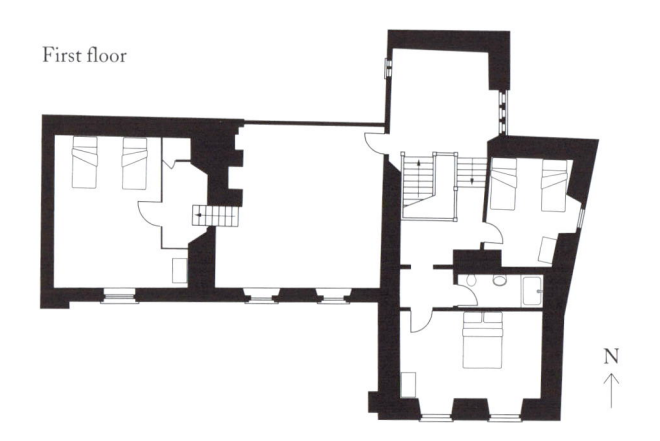

194   The Landmark Trust Handbook

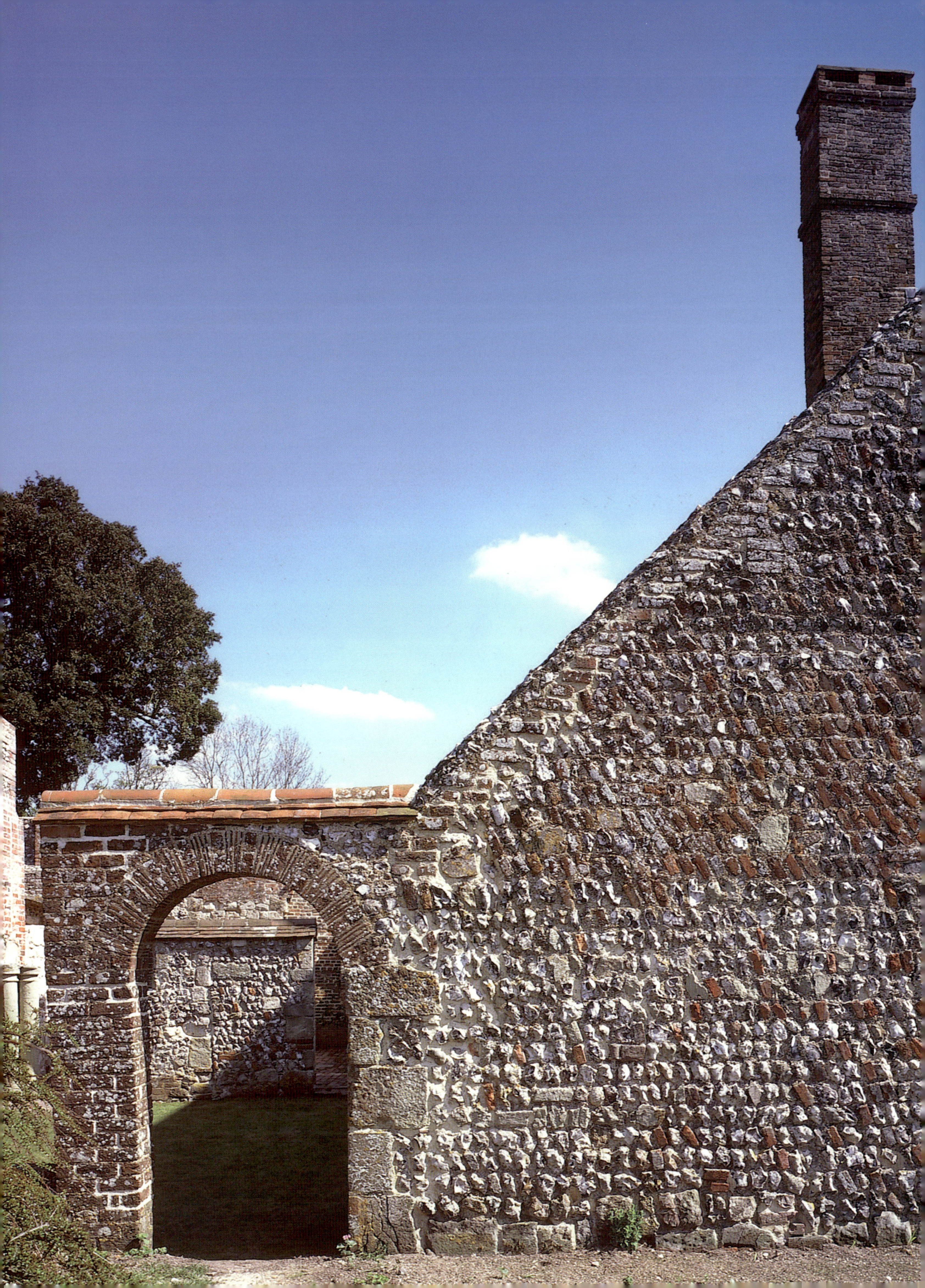

Wolveton Gatehouse

Near Dorchester, Dorset [K5]

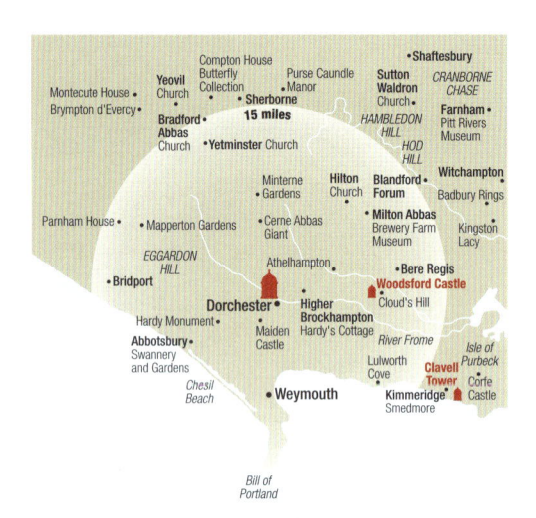

For up to 6 people
Open fire
Garden

Parking nearby
Spiral staircase
Uneven drive

Dorset families did well under the Tudors, and many passed their good fortune on to us in the houses they built. The Trenchards of Wolveton, in the water-meadows west of Dorchester, put up one of the finest. John Trenchard inherited Wolveton through his mother, Christian Mohun, in 1480 and began work on the house. Sir Thomas Trenchard completed the Gatehouse in the reign of Henry VIII. Most of Sir Thomas's house was demolished in the 1820s, leaving the lavish Elizabethan wing, erected by Sir George Trenchard. What remains is exceptional: windows with the delicate decoration of the Tudor Renaissance, an Elizabethan display of glass and much moulded oak and plaster.

The present owner opens his home to the public and has also repaired and furnished the Gatehouse, which we now let on his behalf. On two of its corners are twin towers from an earlier fortified gatehouse. Thought to be fourteenth century, each has a dovecot in its top. The two rooms on the first floor were, and still are, fitted out for guests. They are reached by a wide and ancient spiral stair in which newel post and tread are carved of single blocks, not of stone but of oak. Both have Jacobean fireplaces, and turret rooms leading off them. A garret above and the guardroom below provide extra bedrooms. In winter, stoke up the fire and wear an extra layer, as the Dorset nobility would have done hundreds of years ago.

The Gatehouse once framed the approach to a grand forecourt and the great of many kinds have passed through it. Today it reminds us of the noble house that Wolveton once was. Thomas Hardy came to tea at Wolveton in 1900 and the tragic tale of Lady Penelope D'Arcy, the second wife of George Trenchard, appears in his book of short stories, *A Group of Noble Dames*.

Wolveton House (not the Gatehouse) is open to the public during the summer.

Ground floor

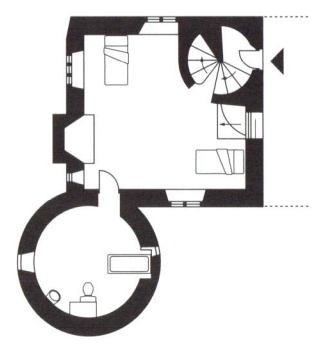

First floor

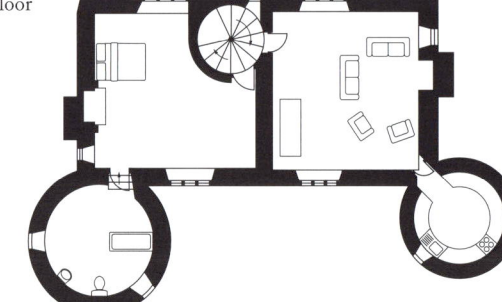

Second floor

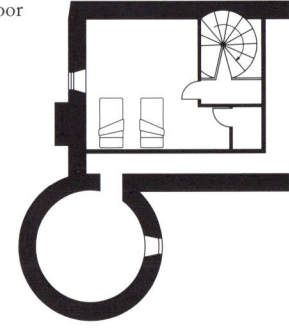

196   The Landmark Trust Handbook

Woodsford Castle

Near Dorchester, Dorset [K5]

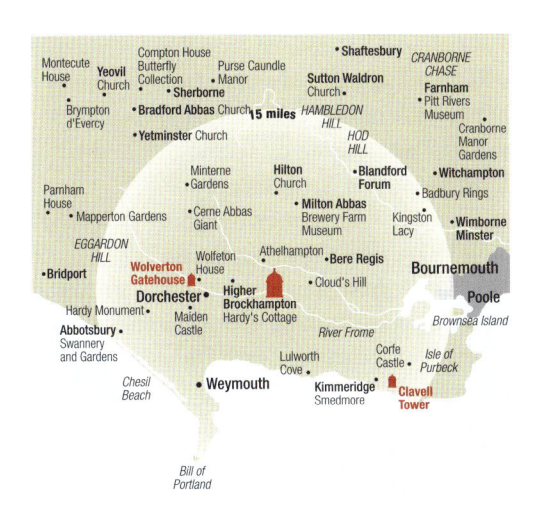

For up to 8 people
Open fire
Garden
Parking nearby

Dogs allowed
Steep staircases
Outside steps
without railings

All that remains here is one side of a quadrangular castle, licensed in 1335 and completed in about 1370. The grand apartment and lesser lodgings that make up the existing building were almost certainly the work of Sir Guy de Bryan KG, a close friend and servant of King Edward III, who bought the castle in 1367. Defence is just beginning to give way to a more domestic way of life; but although the hall and the chapel next to it have large windows in the outer walls, they are still up on the first floor, over vaulted kitchens and store rooms.

When we acquired the castle it had passed by inheritance for over 600 years. Two of its owners, the Earls of Ormonde and Devon, were executed in succession during the Wars of the Roses. It then went by marriage to the Strangways, fell into decay and became a farmhouse – an enormous roof of thatch (largely renewed in 2008) replacing the original turrets and crenellations. Meanwhile, the other three sides of the castle gradually disappeared, their stone put to more useful purpose elsewhere.

Inside, among much other work, we have restored the King's Room, or hall, and given it a new oak ceiling. This, with the chapel and the adjoining Queen's Room, form the main rooms in which you will stay; their size could justify bringing an extra jersey in the winter. The kitchen, and more bedrooms, are in a warmer eighteenth-century wing on the north-west corner.

An earlier restoration in 1850 was carried out by the builder father of Thomas Hardy, and Hardy himself came here often. It is indeed a prime spot for those who like his books. The castle stands on the south bank of the Frome, three miles below Dorchester, and the north window of the hall looks out across the river and water-meadows to the high ground of Egdon Heath. All this is Hardy's; here his characters act out their narrow parts, against a backdrop of the Universe.

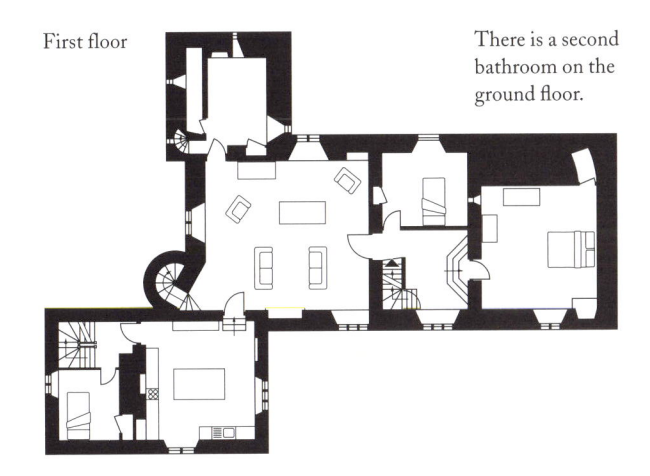

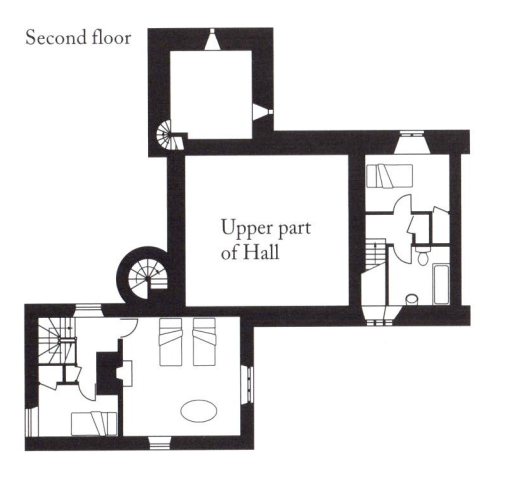

First floor

There is a second bathroom on the ground floor.

Second floor

Upper part of Hall

Woodspring Priory

Near Weston-super-Mare, Somerset [J4]

For up to 8 people
Open fire
Large garden

Parking for 3 cars
Spiral staircase
Dogs allowed

Woodspring Priory was founded in 1210, perhaps as an expiatory gesture, by William de Courtenay, grandson of Reginald FitzUrse who, with other West Countrymen, murdered Thomas à Becket. It was an Augustinian house of the rare Victorine rule, and had St Thomas the Martyr as a patron saint.

The priory was a small one but, as elsewhere in Somerset, flourished in the fifteenth century, when the tower and nave of the church, the infirmary and a great barn were built of a beautiful golden stone. The north aisle was unfinished when, in 1536, the priory was suppressed and the church, most unusually, turned into a house, a chimney-stack built up through the roof of the nave.

We found Woodspring in 1969 as it had been since the Dissolution, the church still inhabited as the farmhouse of a picturesque and rather old-fashioned farm. However, the buildings had suffered greatly from the ravages of time. We repaired the church tower (one man and a boy, using ladders) and reinstated the crossing and north aisle inside it.

The rest of the priory, including the range built in 1701 on the site of the prior's lodging, we have repaired for you to stay in. Two bedrooms and the sitting-room occupy the nave of the church, each containing some token of its ecclesiastical past. Their windows look south on to walled gardens, once the cloister and outer court.

Other monastic remains are grander, others more complete than Woodspring, but few have kept so well the serene atmosphere of an isolated religious community, surrounded by a working farm, and lying by the sea.

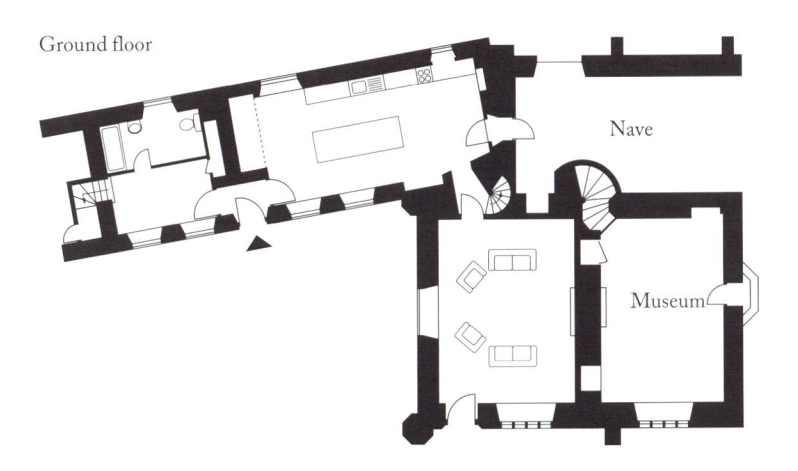

Ground floor

Nave

Museum

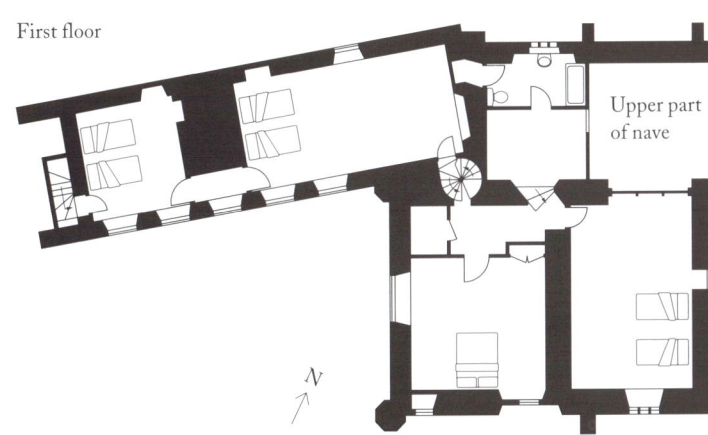

First floor

Upper part of nave

N

www.landmarktrust.org.uk 199

Wortham Manor

Lifton, Devon [K3]

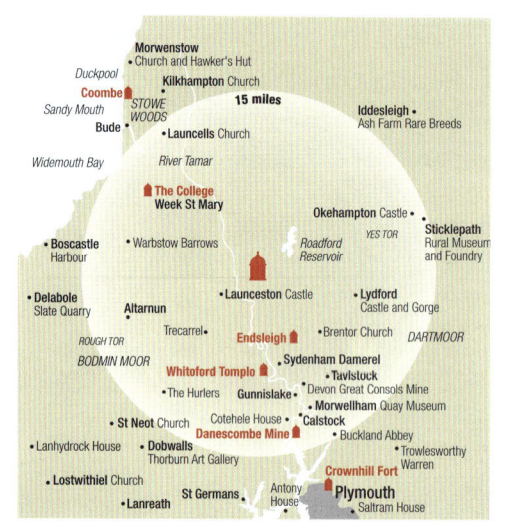

This is a medieval and Tudor house of the highest quality, built and then remodelled by a junior branch of the great Devon family of Dinham, but little altered since. Doors and windows are of finely dressed granite, a noble if intractable material seen to great advantage here.

The chamber over the hall has an open arch-braced roof, less massive but otherwise very like that in the great hall at Cotehele, further down the Tamar valley. The hall itself has a ceiling of heavily moulded oak beams and rich late Gothic carving. Both are close in date, and may even have been put up together soon after 1500. Together with the carved surround of the front door, they are probably the work of John Dinham, cousin of Dame Thomasine of Week St Mary, whose building work at The College he oversaw. Like her, he had lived, and prospered, in London. In 1533, when an old man, he was pressed to take a knighthood, but declined.

Along with much other work, the house had to be entirely re-roofed, which gave us the opportunity to recover its original plan. We also bought some of the farm buildings on two sides of the house so that its setting could be preserved as well. Those who stay here have an unrivalled opportunity to experience the life of a prosperous, and quite sophisticated, Tudor gentleman, in that distant part of Devon once known as Cornwall in England.

From the logbook
Ran around like children choosing rooms. Still can't believe this is our home for a few days.

For up to 15 people
Open fire
Enclosed garden
Parking nearby
Some steep staircases
Large millpond nearby
Dogs allowed

Ground floor

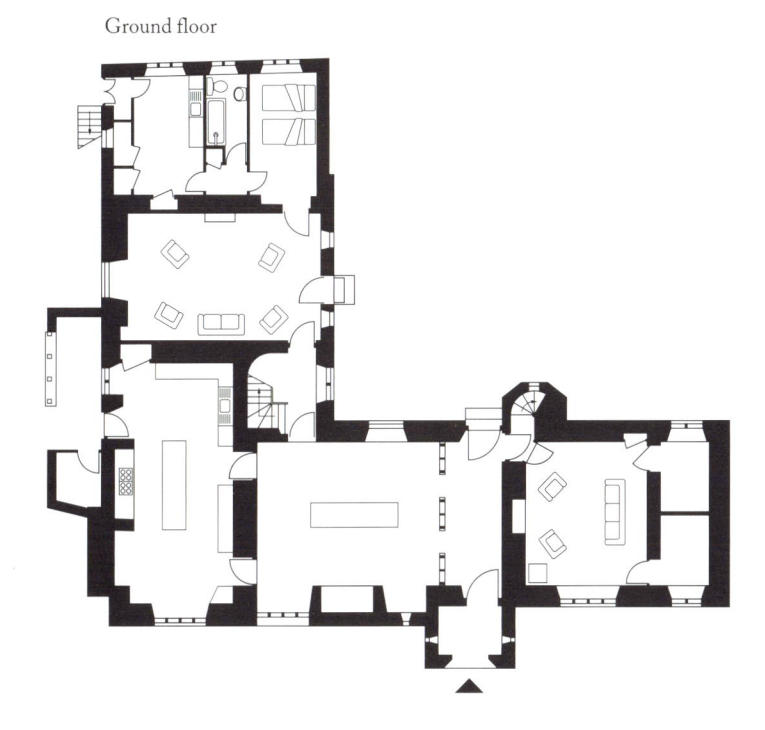

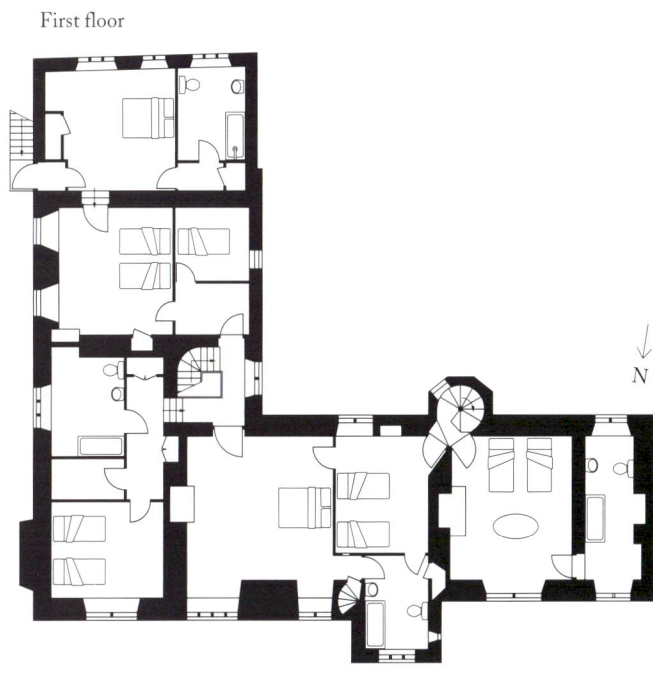

First floor

Lundy

Jenny's Cove, Lundy

Lundy

Bristol Channel, Devon [J2]

23 houses and cottages, including a castle and a lighthouse.

Lundy ('Puffin Island'), in the approaches to the Bristol Channel, is three miles long and rises over 400 feet out of the sea, commanding a tremendous view of England, Wales and the Atlantic. It has tall cliffs towards the south and west, with grass and heather on top, and steep side lands with trees, shrubs and bracken in small hanging valleys, rich in wildflowers, on the east coast facing the mainland. There are three lighthouses (two in use), a castle, a church, an active farm, a pub, several handsome houses and cottages, and a population of about 25. Most of the buildings and all the field walls are made of the island's beautiful light-coloured granite.

When Lundy was taken on by the National Trust in 1969 (thanks mainly to the generosity of Sir Jack Hayward), we undertook to restore and run the island. The formidable task of tidying up and restoring the buildings and services for both visitors and residents took us over 20 years. Much of this work remains invisible, but without it, ordinary people would soon have been unable to live on or visit the island.

Lundy offers the public a very rare experience. It is large enough to have a genuine life of its own, which visitors can share and enjoy, but small and far enough away to be a world apart and undefaced. It offers both the pleasures of escape and the pleasures of participation: walks or wanderings high up, in the silence, looking east across the blue floor of the sea to the coast of Devon, or westward over the limitless Atlantic; or sociable visits to the tavern and shop.

www.landmarktrust.org.uk

Lundy

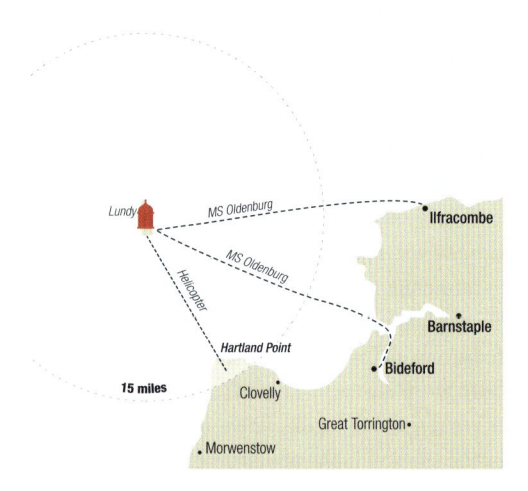

Opportunities abound for field studies of all kinds; and for the energetic there is rock climbing, or diving and snorkelling in the Marine Nature Reserve. Everybody has the free run of the whole island, and it is surprising how much out of the ordinary there is to do and see at all times of the year.

Our handsome supply ship, the *MS Oldenburg*, runs between March and November from Bideford or Ilfracombe, carrying day and staying visitors, weather permitting. Between November and March a helicopter transfers visitors between the mainland and the island from Hartland Point. On the island we have made it possible to stay at various levels of price and comfort – in cottages, in a hostel, or by camping – so that almost anyone can afford to be here. Your arrival on the island is an event. To come here, even for the day, is a small adventure. All those who experience the space and light, the life of the island, and the natural beauty on every hand, have thereafter something in common which they treasure.

If you would like to know more, we can send you our free, full-colour guide to staying on Lundy.

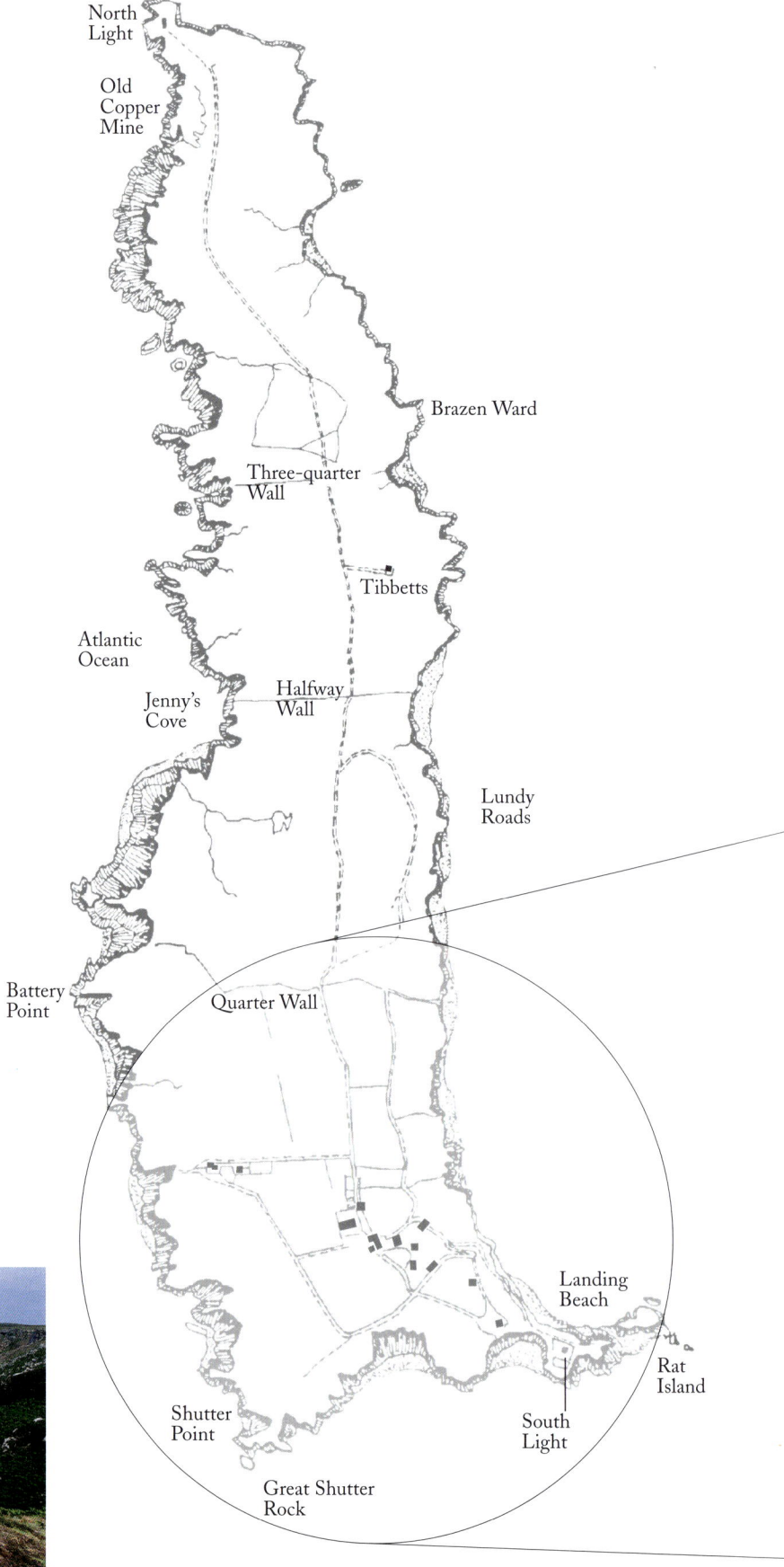

204 The Landmark Trust Handbook

Old
Light
Stoneycroft
Campsite
The Barn
Shop
and
Tavern
Millcombe House
The Quarters
Old House
Government House
Radio Room
Old School
Bramble Villa
Square Cottage
Hanmers
St Johns
Castle

Lundy

The Barn

The Barn, which was roofless when we arrived, is now a hostel, at the centre of island life. The dormitory rooms are lined with varnished wood; it has a large living-room with a big open fire and, from the sleeping gallery, one of the best views on the island.

For up to 14 people
Open fire
Steep stairs

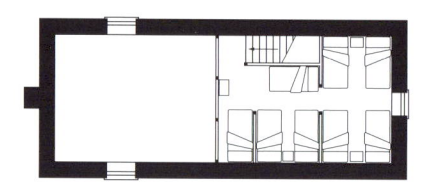

First floor

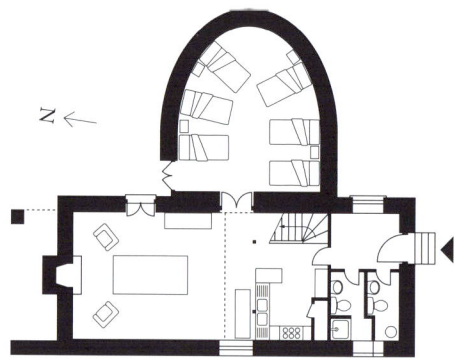

Ground floor

Bramble Villa

Bramble Villa is in the St John's Valley, on the site of a ruinous corrugated iron building of the same name, and the same rather colonial appearance. It was shipped, ready-made, from the mainland, and put up to house those who were to carry out the restoration work for us on Lundy. Now divided in two, East looks over the sea towards Devon and has the light off the sea in its rooms. West also has a glimpse of the sea, but is more sheltered.

Bramble Villa East
For up to 4 people
Solid fuel stove

Bramble Villa West
For up to 4 people
Solid fuel stove

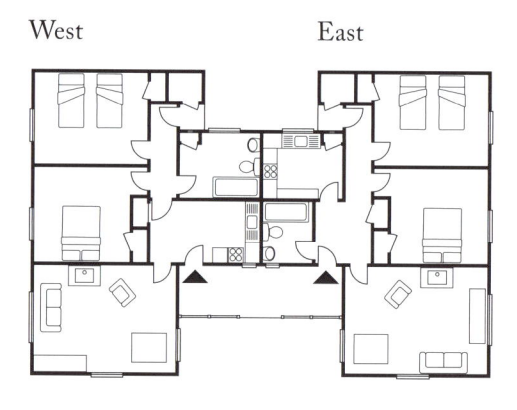

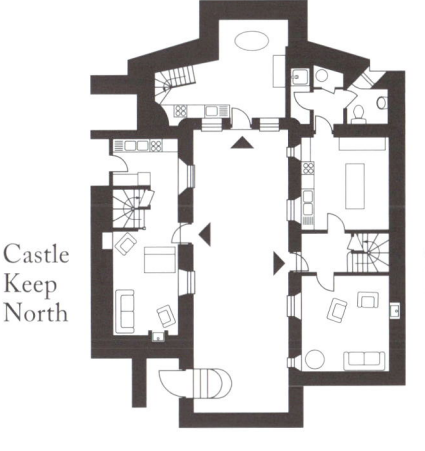

The Castle

The Castle was built by Henry III in about 1250, and paid for by the sale of rabbits. High up on the south-east point of the island, it replaced the earlier castle of the unruly Mariscos, which stood in Bull's Paradise behind the farm. In the Civil War Lundy was held for the Royalists to the very end by Thomas Bushell, who rebuilt the castle. He owned a silver mine and tradition says he minted coins here.

By 1787 cottages had been built round the small courtyard inside the Keep. These have decayed and been rebuilt several times, most recently by us, as three Castle Keep Cottages. They are snug and sociable, inward-looking except for one or two windows in the outer walls which have spectacular marine views.

Castle Keep East
For up to 2 people
Solid fuel stove

Castle Keep South
For up to 4 people
Solid fuel stove

Castle Keep North
For up to 2 people
Solid fuel stove

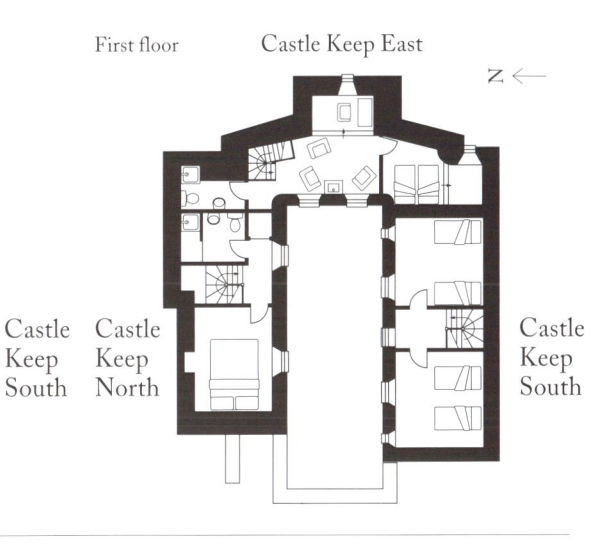

Castle Cottage

Castle Cottage is a granite structure built against the Castle Keep by the Post Office in 1887 as a cable station. When first extended and converted, it was the second holiday cottage on the island. Its living-room is dominated by the spectacular view overlooking the Landing Bay.

For up to 2 people
Small outside adjoining WC

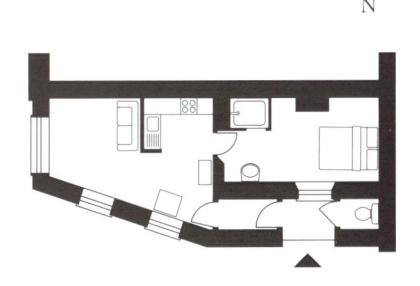

www.landmarktrust.org.uk

Lundy

Government House

Government House was designed by Philip Jebb to house whoever runs the island, and to make use of and preserve the fine granite dressings left when additions to Old House were removed. However, our agents since have unselfishly preferred to remain in humbler quarters, and so it is available for you to stay in. It is one of the best houses we possess, and so well sited that it seems always to have been there, sheltered on three sides and looking down the Millcombe valley towards the sea.

For up to 5 people
Open fire

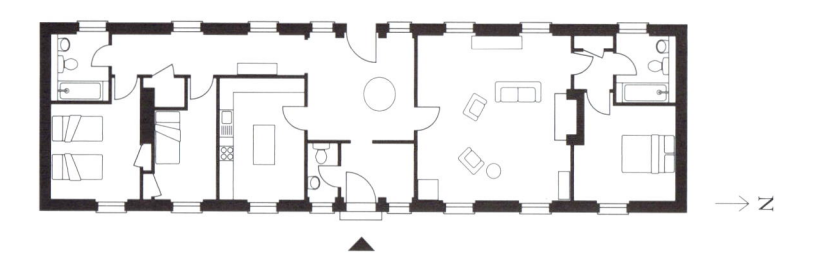

Hanmers

Hanmers was built by a fisherman in 1902. He chose a good site, a dip in the hill, on the path from the beach to the castle, so the place is sheltered but has the usual wonderful view out to sea towards Devon. It is weather-boarded outside and its interior is also of wood, painted white in the front rooms, which gives it a warm and solid feel.

For up to 2+2 people
Solid fuel stove

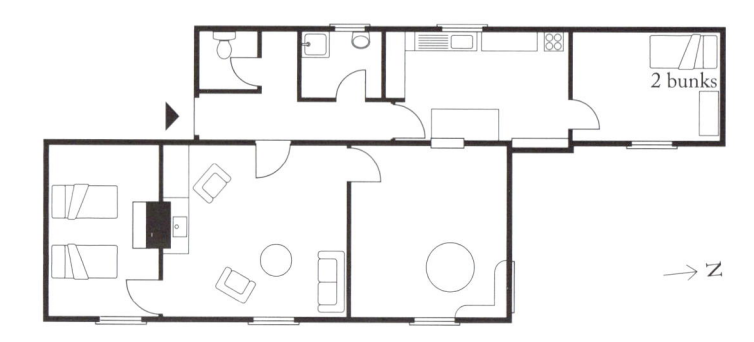

Millcombe House

Millcombe House was built in 1836 for the Heaven family, looking down a wooded valley and out to sea. Most of the furniture in its well-proportioned rooms is also nineteenth-century, and some of the pictures are very interesting. The curious inward-sloping roof, which we have restored to its original form, was designed to catch rainwater.

For up to 12 people
Solid fuel stove

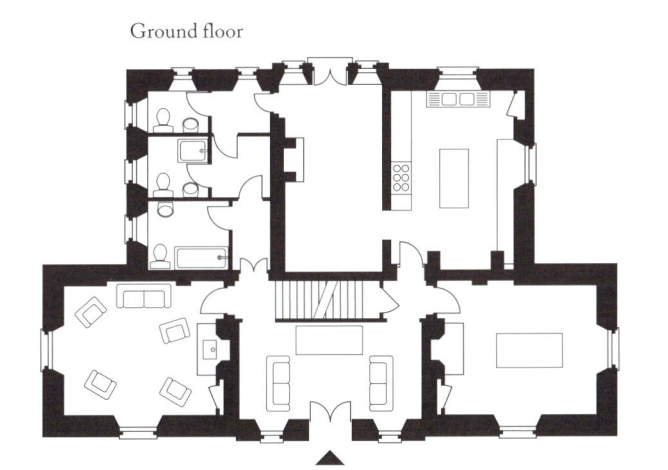

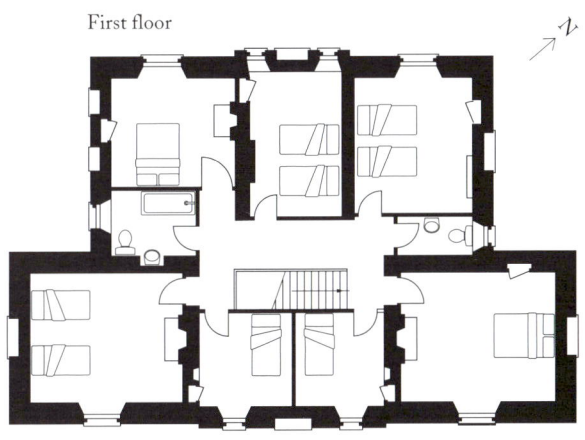

Lundy

Old House

Old House, North and South, is the most handsome building on the island, in perhaps the best position, and made of the best-looking granite. It began life in about 1775, built for Sir John Borlase Warren, a young MP who owned Lundy briefly. Until replaced by Millcombe it was indeed the island's chief residence. William Heaven gave it its present form, to which it has now returned after the removal, by us, of haphazard additions on three sides. We also made a garden in the courtyard behind and divided the house, invisibly, in two.

Old House North
For up to 2 people
Solid fuel stove

Old House South
For up to 5 people
Open fire

The interior of Old House South, *right*.

Old House, *below*.

Old House North   Old House South

Ground floor

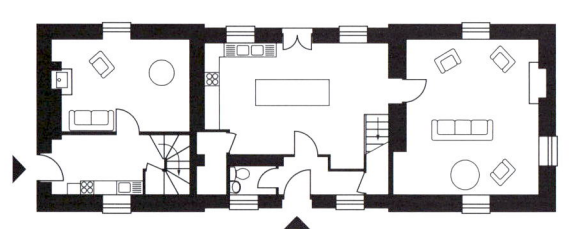

Old House North   Old House South

First floor

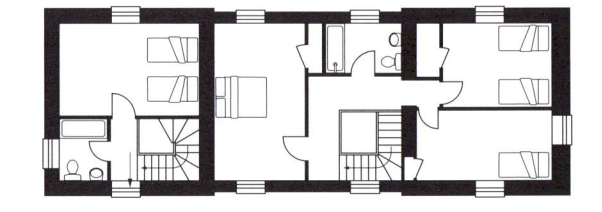

Old Light

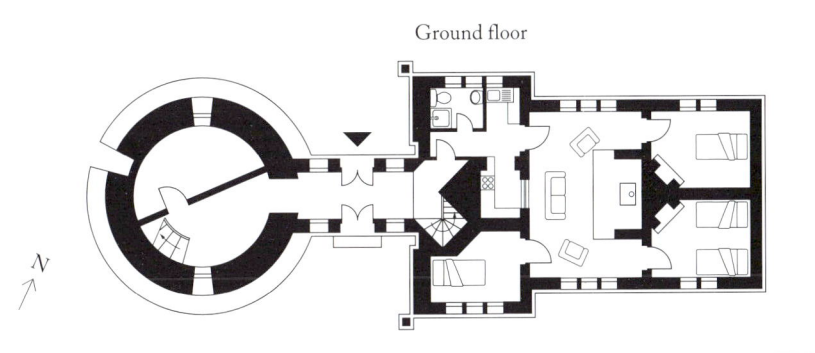

Old Light, completed in 1820, was designed by Daniel Asher Alexander. Built of Cyclopean blocks of granite, it stands on the highest point of the island. The keepers' quarters are still divided into the two original flats, Lower and Upper, very satisfying in design and detail. Unusually for Lundy, they look out over the northern part of the island.

Old Light Lower
For up to 4 people
Solid fuel stove

Old Light Upper
For up to 5 people
Solid fuel stove

Old Light Lower

Old Light Lower
Ground floor

Old Light Upper
First floor

Old Light Cottage

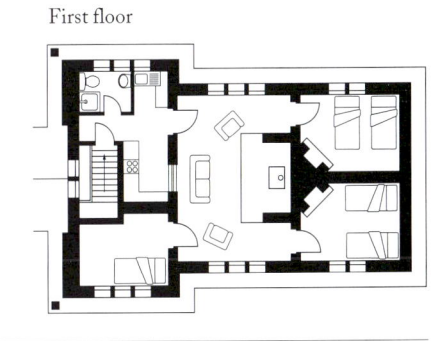

Old Light Cottage was the lighthouse keepers' store, solidly built of granite to the usual Trinity House standard. We have equipped it, and the Radio Room near the Tavern, for those who come to Lundy on their own. It stands in the same compound as the Old Light, and has in it just about everything that one person can want.

For 1 person

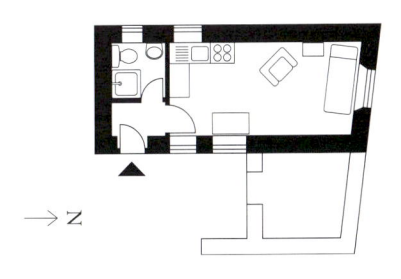

www.landmarktrust.org.uk

Lundy

Old School

Old School, long known as 'the Blue Bung', lies near St John's Cottages and shares much the same outlook. It is a small building of corrugated iron, with a snug interior lined with match boarding. Designed and made with care, it has, like many such buildings, considerable point and charm.

For up to 2 people
Steep stairs

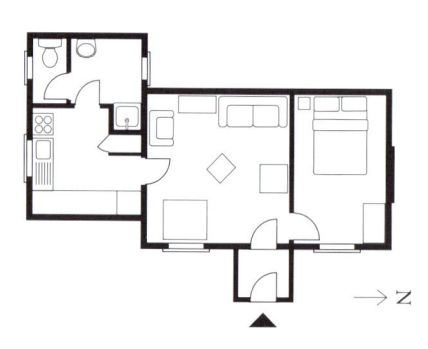

The Quarters

The Quarters is the name traditionally given to the long wooden buildings, one behind the other, which were originally put up to house teams of builders on the island. The Landmark within the Quarters has recently been improved: moved to the end of the block and refurbished to a higher standard than the previous accommodation. Sleeping fewer than before, the Quarters has the feel of a cottage: you can now have a bath here and sit in your own enclosed garden, while still enjoying that fine view of the church and beyond to Hartland Point.

For up to 5 people
Solid fuel stove

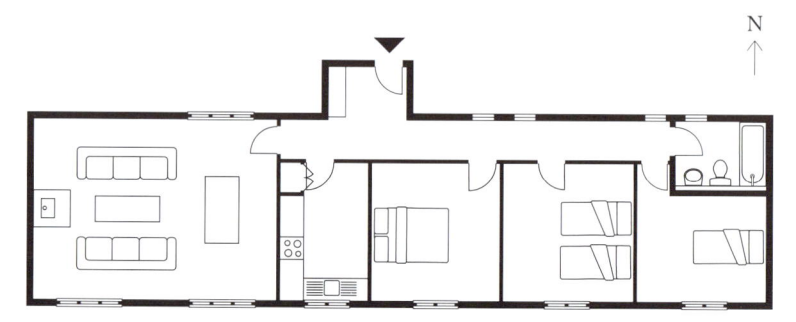

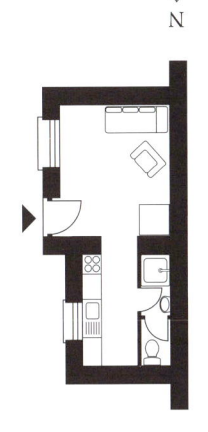

Radio Room

The Radio Room is a small solid building in the walled garden behind Old House. It used to house the ancient wireless transmitter with which for many years the island kept in touch with the mainland. It is cosy and self-contained, with an east-facing terrace.

For 1 person

St John's

Big and Little St John's are a pair of single storey cottages, added by the Harman family to an existing granite barn in the St John's valley. Although they are not the most handsome buildings on the island, they are two of the best loved. They occupy a fine position, sheltered and secluded, with a beautiful view towards Devon.

Big St John's
For up to 2+1 people

Little St John's
For up to 2 people

St John's is shown in the foreground.

Big St John's

Ground floor

Little St John's

Little St John's

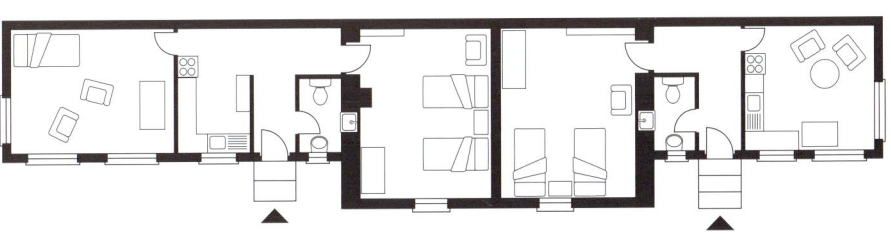

Lundy

Square Cottage

Square Cottage was formed by us from the remains of the nineteenth-century quarry manager's house. Its front door opens on to the garden behind Old House, but to south and east it has spectacular views, especially from the upstairs sitting-room, which has a good Victorian fireplace. It also has central heating, using up surplus energy from the island's generator, and is very comfortable in winter.

For up to 3 people
Solid fuel stove

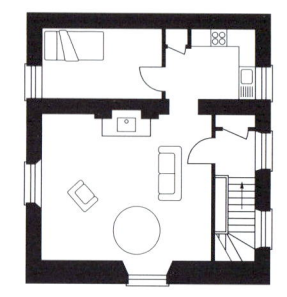

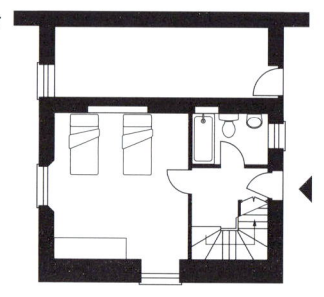

Square Cottage is shown on the *left* of the photograph.

Stoneycroft

Stoneycroft was where the lighthouse inspectors stayed when they visited Lundy. It stands in its own walled enclosure, near the Old Light, facing south.

For up to 4 people
Enclosed garden
Solid fuel stove

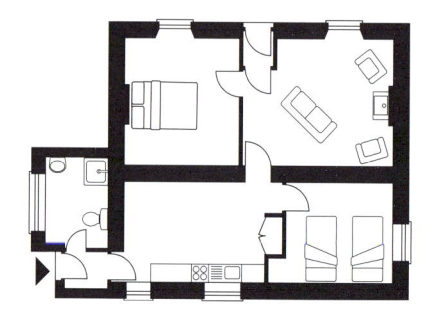

Tibbetts

Tibbetts was built of pale granite to a functional and satisfying design, in 1909, on the second highest point of the island. It is about 1¾ miles from the village along the main track to the north, and is as remote and simple as anyone could wish. It is said that 14 lighthouses can be seen from it on a clear night. The interior is lined with varnished matchboarding and keeps its original purposeful atmosphere because of its distance from the village. Tibbetts is the only property that has no electricity; however it has a pumped water supply and a shower. It also retains the original four built-in bunks and is the sort of place where you can wander around in your pyjamas collecting mushrooms for breakfast.

For up to 4 people
Solid fuel stove
Gas lighting
No electricity

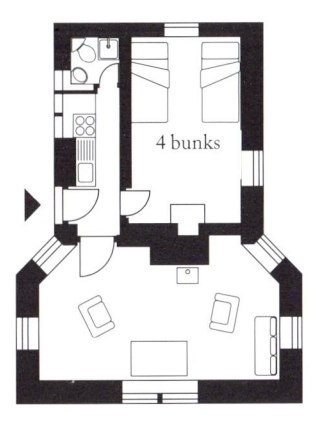

Landmarks in Italy

Villa Saraceno, Vicenza

Landmarks in Italy

Italian culture has had a profound effect on the British, from the days of the Roman Empire, through the Renaissance and that institution for young aristocratic tourists known as the Grand Tour, to the Romantic poets of the nineteenth century. The revival of Classical architecture, so prevalent in the country seats of our own eighteenth-century gentry, found initial inspiration in Andrea Palladio's *Quattro Libri dell'Architettura*, based on close study of the ruins of antiquity that lay everywhere around, and the most important architectural treatise of the Renaissance.

On this basis then, it becomes less surprising to encounter the following handful of carefully selected Italian Landmarks in this Handbook, all of which have some connection with British culture, which has always been a guiding principle in our selection of Landmarks abroad. If you have stayed in other Landmarks, you will find much that is familiar in our Italian buildings, and here the beauty of both the Italian landscape and its climate lie just outside your door.

Sant'Antonio *left*, Piazza di Spagna *top* and Casa Guidi *above*.

Casa Guidi

Piazza S. Felice, Florence

For up to 4+2 people   No private parking

Pen Browning, son of the poets Elizabeth and Robert, wished his parents' Florentine home, in which they had spent nearly all the happy and productive years of their marriage, to be recreated in their memory. He did not live to see his wish fulfilled, but it was remembered.

In 1971 the suite of rooms on the first floor of the Palazzo Guidi was acquired by the Browning Institute. Restoration began, with the eventual aim of refurnishing the drawing-room, a romantic literary sanctum recorded by the painter Mignaty after Elizabeth's death in 1861. The familiar writer's clutter of books and paper-burdened tables was here given a grand setting, of richly carved furniture and Renaissance paintings, mingled with comfortable sofas and armchairs, all bought by the Brownings with the excitement of a young married couple.

Casa Guidi is now owned by Eton College and leased to us. Parties of boys undergo its civilising influence at intervals but at all other times it is available for our visitors. The tall main rooms, with graceful eighteenth-century decoration, are furnished much as they were by the two poets. Like them, you can savour the agreeable and busy streets of Florence through Casa Guidi's windows.

Part of the apartment is open to the public on Monday, Wednesday and Friday afternoons, between April and November. It has some double glazing and partial air conditioning.

From the logbook
Having come to Florence before as a mere tourist it was wonderful to come to Casa Guidi and really feel part of the place.

It has been a week of sheer cultural enrichment; surrounded by Browning anthologies we were able to continue indulging long after the museums and palazzos had closed for the night.

Gallery   First floor

There are two bunks in the room above the shower room behind the double bedroom. This is reached by narrow spiral stairs.

Piazza di Spagna

Rome

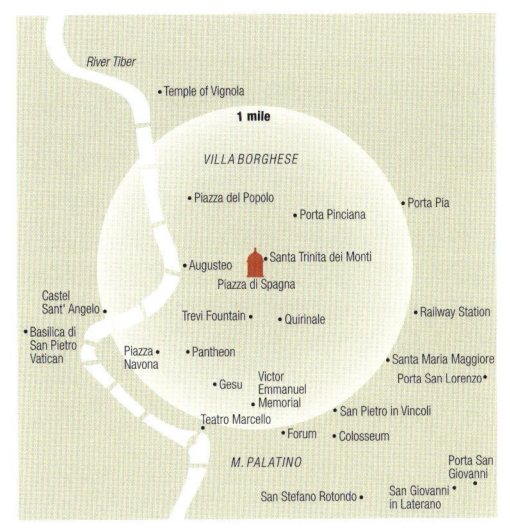

For up to 3+1 people   No private parking

All architects, and many artists, owe a debt to Rome, and we had long wanted a foothold there. So when the Keats-Shelley Memorial Association launched an appeal for funds to maintain 26 Piazza di Spagna, we asked whether there was a part of it that we could occupy in return for helping them. Happily there was, a flat on the third floor, now restored by us to its condition in about 1800 – spacious rooms with tiled floors and high, beamed ceilings painted in soft colours. The house itself was built around 1600, but owes its external appearance today to changes made by Francesco de Sanctis in 1724–5.

Our apartment is not the rooms in which Keats died in 1821 – those are on the floor below – but they are identical in form and layout, and are more in a condition he would recognise. Every tall shuttered window has a view unchanged almost since the days of the Grand Tour, and the sitting-room looks up the Spanish Steps – certainly the world's grandest and most sophisticated outdoor staircase – to the church of S. Trinita dei Monti at the top. At the front door is Bernini's fountain in the form of a stone boat sinking into the Piazza di Spagna. There is hardly any motor traffic, but instead all the noises of humanity, some of them very unusual – for example when the steps are cleared by water-cannon, or when the horsedrawn cabs, which form a rank at the far end of the Piazza, arrive over the cobbles, seemingly at dawn and at a gallop.

The Steps were designed in 1721 by Francesco de Sanctis, who also designed this house to fit in with his plan. It was probably apartments from the first, in a part of the city long frequented by foreign and particularly English visitors. There can be few places in Rome available to their successors so central, so handsome, so famous or so unaltered as this.

Third floor

The apartment has double glazing and partial air conditioning. It does not have a lift.

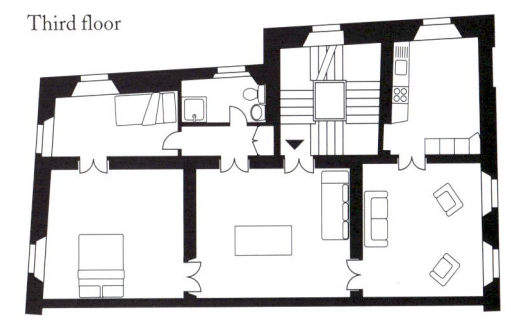

Sant'Antonio

Tivoli, near Rome

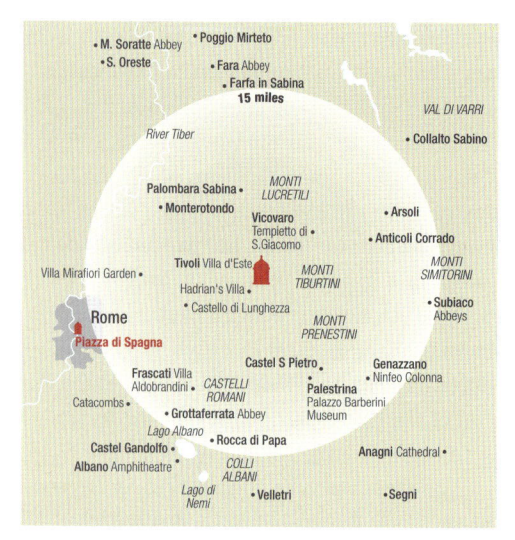

For up to 12 people
Open fire
Enclosed garden
Adjacent parking

Frederick Searle, who bought the old monastery of Sant'Antonio near Tivoli in 1878, first saw and fell in love with it when looking for a place from which to paint the great waterfall, across the ravine from the town. A visit today is equally one of enchantment: the little church at the top dedicated to the kindly Sant'Antonio of Padua; the simple rooms, each with a shuttered window opening on to the valley, the waterfall and Tivoli itself; the upper belvedere, giving a first full taste of what, with a few battered edges, can still be recognised as the 'loveliest view in the world'. Hints of a distant past appear in cells with mosaic floors, and in the kitchen, where on the inner wall is some 'opus reticulatum', a sign of Romans at work; but no moment is more thrilling than when, having passed through an arcaded loggia and down to the level of the fruitful, scented and beautiful terraced garden, an old door is opened in the house wall – a moment it would be unfair to spoil by describing in advance.

The truth is that the walls of a Roman villa, dated to about 60 BC and believed to have belonged to the poet Horace, survive up to the middle floor of the present house, itself begun in about 850 AD. Franciscan monks have lived here, and Popes. The final additions were made 'as late as the 17th century'. It was abandoned around 1870 and rescued by the Searles, who spent many years gently repairing it.

Sant'Antonio has descended to their great-great-grandson, who sought to give it a safe future. Knowing of our involvement with Keats' House in Rome, he asked us for help. With the greatest of pleasure, we are letting his house for him.

As if Sant'Antonio itself were not enough, at Tivoli you can visit the Villa d'Este, with its incomparable fountains, and Hadrian's Villa, the inspiration for many British garden buildings. Lazio, with its hills and lakes, its castles, gardens and wines, its relics of Rome and Etrusca, is one of the most beautiful and least-known regions of Italy.

From the logbook
A room with a view is all very well – but a bathroom with a view; bliss.

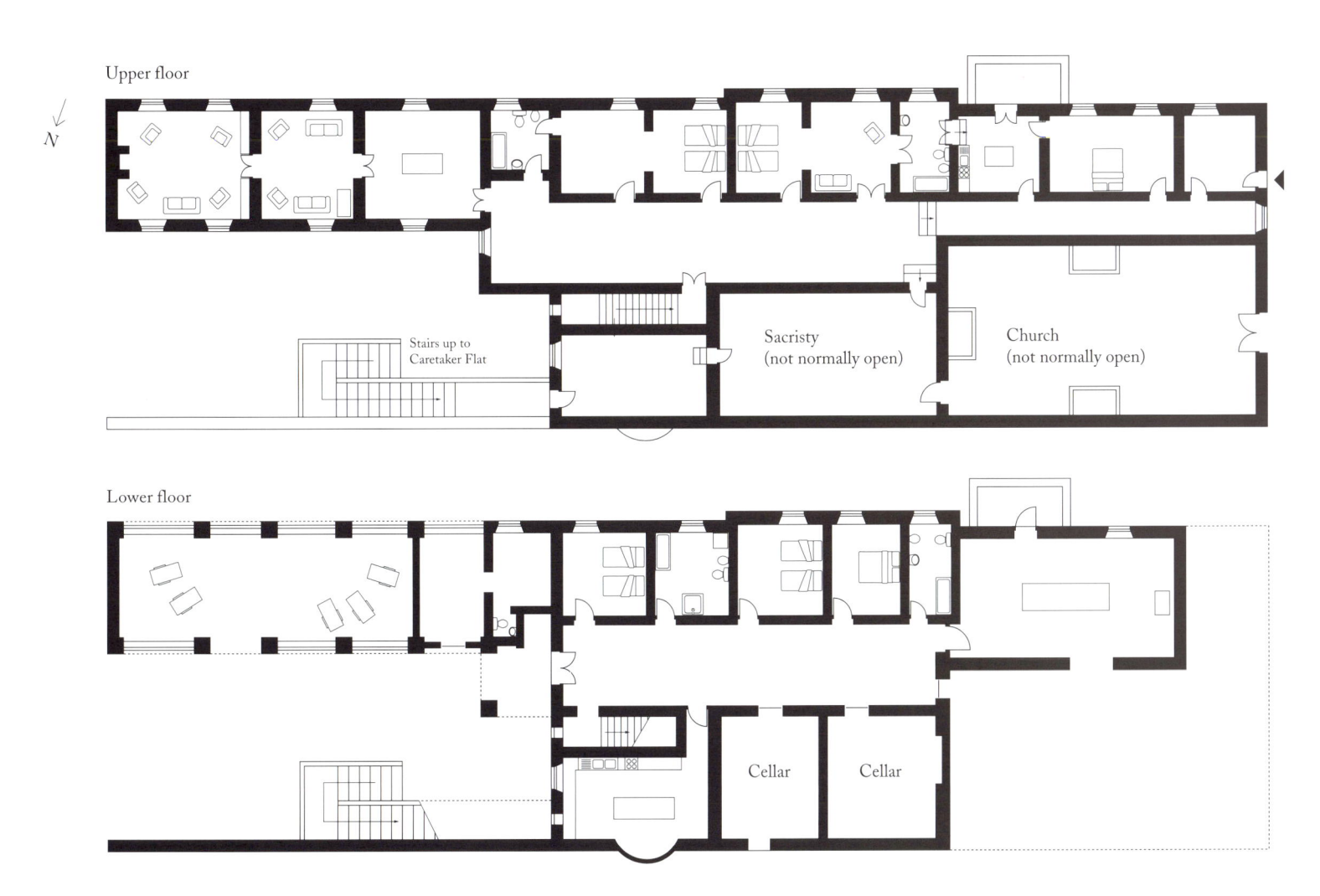

Upper floor

Stairs up to Caretaker Flat

Sacristy (not normally open)

Church (not normally open)

Lower floor

Cellar

Cellar

Villa Saraceno

Finale, Vicenza

For up to 16 people
Open fire
Enclosed garden

Parking nearby
Dogs allowed

During the peaceful years in the middle of the sixteenth century, Italian culture displayed a desire to escape the bustle of the city that is strangely familiar to us today. The manner in which Andrea Palladio realised this ideal of a peaceful but cultured existence is one that had particular influence upon British architects. The fertile plain of the Veneto is sprinkled with archetypal Palladian villas like our own Villa Saraceno; some of these you can visit, but no other can you have to yourselves to taste this life of fulfilled recreation.

The Villa was built c.1550 for Biagio Saraceno, a minor nobleman from Vicenza, to be both country retreat and working farm. Palladio's designs for the villa show a courtyard of colonnaded barns, although in the event only the main house was built. The adjoining buildings are mostly earlier in date, including the early Renaissance house in which most of you will sleep. The walled grounds provide a sense of seclusion, perfect for a quiet evening stroll in search of a ripe fig (and, if younger members of your party are so inclined, they make a splendid playing field).

After decades of neglect, we found all the buildings in a state of serious decay and their restoration was a lengthy and exciting process. Inside the main house, the original arrangement of entering through a grand sala has been recreated. The sala has huge granaries to explore above and is once again flanked by apartments of spacious rooms in which you will dine and sit. To our delight, beneath later layers of limewash we found lively frescoed friezes running around the sala's lofty cornices. There are more frescoes in the loggia and sitting-room, which also has an open hearth for log fires on cooler evenings.

Just like the Renaissance noblemen for whom these villas were built, you can easily dip into urban sophistication if you wish. Our villa is little more than an hour from Venice and the towns of Padua and Vicenza are even closer, all full of architectural and modern day delights to discover. The plain rolls away on all sides of the villa, a country of poplars and canals and still mainly agricultural. How you choose to spend your days at the villa is up to you, but the chances are that you too like Palladio's clients, will appreciate the benefits of villa life.

Parts of the villa are open to the public on Wednesday afternoons between April and October.

From the logbook
Late night walks by the cornfields with miniature fireflies lighting your way.

Magic evenings dining al fresco in the loggia.

Have felt no wish to leave the bounds of the Villa all week.

Upper floor
Villa

Upper floor
Barchessa

Granary

Upper floor
Casa Vecchia

Lower floor
Piano Nobile
Villa

Lower floor
Barchessa

Garden Room

Loggia (at Ground Level)

First floor
Casa Vecchia

Entrance floor
Casa Vecchia

N

www.landmarktrust.org.uk   223

The Landmark Trust USA

Naulakha, Vermont

The Landmark Trust USA

The Landmark Trust USA is a tax-exempt non profit corporation established in 1991 in order to carry on preservation work in America according to the model established by the Landmark Trust. We are fully independent and responsible for our own projects and funding. Naulakha, Rudyard Kipling's Vermont home, was our first project.

The Landmark Trust USA considers education to be an essential part of our mission. We therefore make the process of conservative, traditional repair of our buildings an opportunity for fostering the building crafts through on-site training and workshops. At the Amos Brown House, our second project, we offered training sessions on the use of lime mortars.

The Trust also makes the completed sites available to local schools for special educational projects. Our 'Stories by Rudyard Kipling' program at Naulakha, for example, allows hundreds of school children every year to hear the *Just So Stories* where they were first told by Kipling to his daughter, Josephine.

One of our most exciting challenges is the 571-acre Scott Farm which abuts the 55-acre Naulakha property and which we have owned since 1995. Scott Farm has long been known for the quality of the apples from its 60-acre orchard. Landmark USA has broadened the appeal by adding over 70 varieties of heirloom apples and converting to low-spray, ecologically grown apples. We have also planted pears, plums, raspberries, gooseberries, grapes, and blueberries. The farm's Sugarhouse and Dutton Farmhouse have been repaired and converted into Landmarks.

Americans who would like to help the Landmark Trust USA to rescue neglected historic sites in the United States should contact our office in Vermont. There are many types of charitable donation with substantial tax benefits and our staff would be pleased to provide information and assistance. Your donation can help you minimise your tax burden while you support the conservation of historic resources for future generations.

Landmark Trust USA, Inc.
707 Kipling Road
Dummerston, Vermont, USA 05301
Telephone 802-254-6868
Fax 802-257-7783
Email info@landmarktrustusa.org
Websites www.landmarktrustusa.org
www.scottfarmvermont.com

Board of Directors
Mr John Doncaster
Mr Michael Lehan
Mr Albert Hunker
Mr David Tansey
Mrs Jane Booth, Secretary
Mr James Berkman
Mrs McKey Berkman
Mrs Bland Banwell
Mr Gene Walsh

Staff
Mr David Tansey, Executive Director
Ms Kelly Carlin
Mr Ezekiel Goodband
Mr Thomas Kuralt

Scott Farm, Dummerston, Vermont

Amos Brown House

Whitingham, Vermont

For up to 6 people
Gas stove
Garden and grounds
Adjacent parking

The Amos Brown House of 1802 is the oldest house in Whitingham, Vermont, less than a mile north of the Massachusetts border. While the area at the time must have been heavily forested, Amos Brown chose to build his home in brick which was fabricated on site. Designed with elements of the Federal style, the first style of the new American republic, the house also retained features that were common from the seventeenth century in New England.

The farm prospered and in the 1870s the house was expanded with the addition of a summer kitchen and pantry, porch, woodshed, chicken coop, barn and 4-seater outhouse, all of which remain virtually unchanged. Despite the fact that by this date Vermont had been nearly deforested for sheep farming, these additions were constructed in wood.

By the late nineteenth century the Amos Brown House began to decline, following the trend of agriculture in New England and in the 1930s farming at this site ceased. Soon afterwards this farm became the charterhouse of Carthusian monks, a contemplative order founded in France. For nearly 20 years the monks lived in shacks in the woods and held services and prepared meals in the house. An interesting reminder of their presence is a nearly complete set of the stations of the cross in ornate plaster relief with French inscriptions. These have been conserved and are now mounted in the woodshed.

Landmark USA acquired the property in 2000 from the local historical society who found the project beyond their means. Over two years we reversed the extensive deterioration and damage caused by neglect and ill-considered repairs. Visitors can now enjoy the humble beauty of the farmhouse and serenity of our 30 acres.

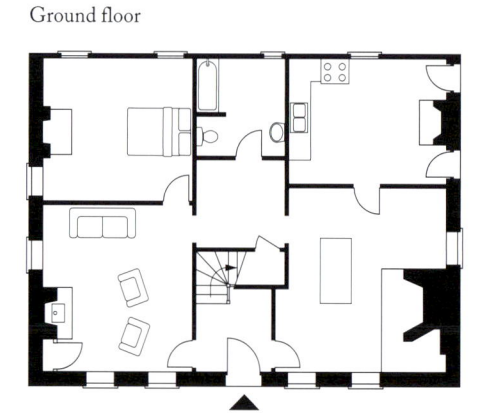

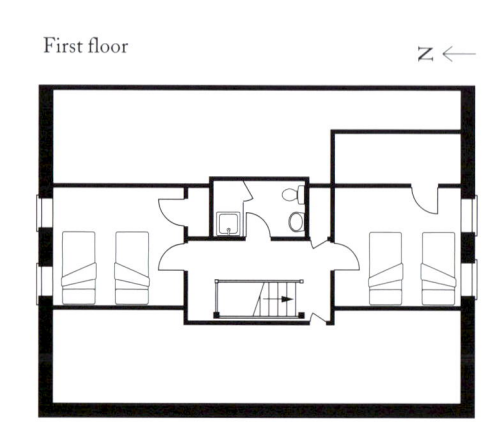

Ground floor

First floor

The Dutton Farmhouse

Dummerston, Vermont

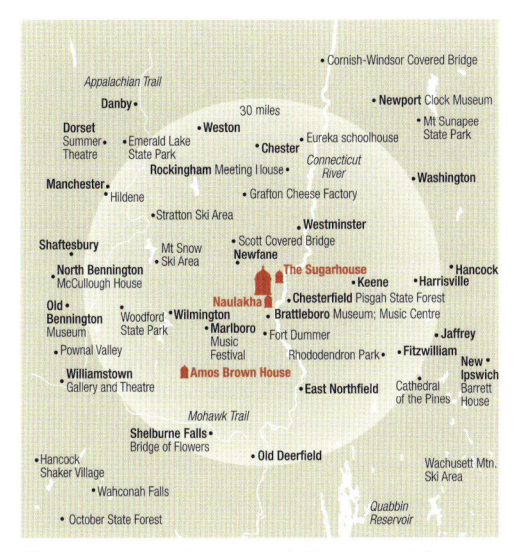

For up to 8 people
Gas stove
Extensive grounds

Adjacent parking
Access to clay tennis
court at Naulakha

The Dutton Farmhouse sits near the top of a hill and offers a broad vista eastward over the apple orchards of Scott Farm in the foreground and, beyond, the Connecticut River valley and Mount Monadnock 35 miles away. It lies near the centre of the Scott Farm with its 571 acres, four farmhouses and six barns, most generously given to Landmark USA by Fred Holbrook, a well known apple grower who wished to see his farm preserved.

The main house was built by Asa Dutton around 1840 in Greek Revival style and it sits proudly on a granite plinth. A mile down the road is another prominent farmhouse, built by Asa's brother. The brothers chose exceptionally beautiful sites and both featured large clapboarded barns; unfortunately the Asa Dutton barn burned down in the 1980s.

While investigating the structure of the Dutton Farmhouse, we discovered that the rear wing, although constructed of older components, was brought to the site later by Dutton. So, too, were the very unusual Federal style decorations in the front parlour; the cornice with carved palm trees, stylised seashells and geometric elements came from an earlier house.

By the time we acquired this house, it had served as seasonal housing for apple pickers for over 30 years, lying empty and neglected most of the time. For a house of such high quality in such a beautiful location, this was indeed a strange fate but it had, at least, prevented extreme alterations.

The Dutton Farmhouse presents the finest of Vermont. Not a single house can be seen across a view of many miles, yet music festivals, ski areas, and beautiful towns are nearby. Visitors will, however, find the charm of exploring Scott Farm just as alluring as these attractions of civilization.

Ground floor

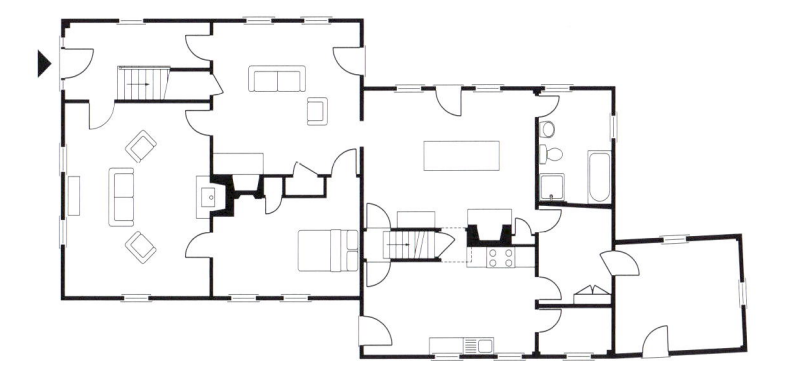

First floor

www.landmarktrust.org.uk 227

Naulakha

Brattleboro, Vermont

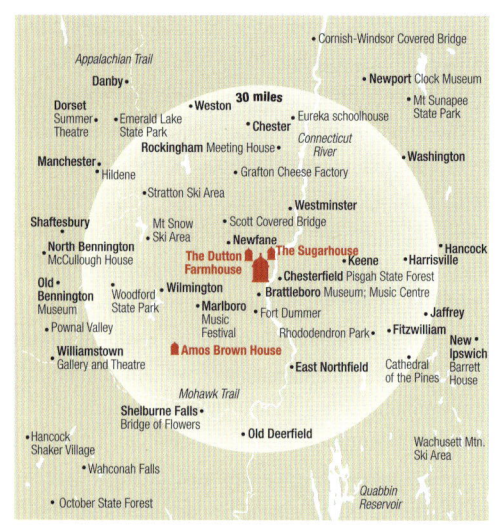

For up to 8 people
Gas fire
Garden and grounds
Clay tennis court
Adjacent parking

In 1892 Rudyard Kipling and his new wife, Caroline, arrived in Vermont to stay with her family near Brattleboro. He was captivated by this new country and resolved to settle there permanently. He bought 11 acres of gently sloping pasture, and over the next winter supervised the building of a house, which he called Naulakha, the jewel beyond price.

The plans for Naulakha were drawn by H. R. Marshall, but Kipling saw its design as very much his own. He called it a ship, with his study at the bow. Here he could write in closely guarded privacy, with direct access to a verandah and flower garden. The main point of the house was the view, across woods and farmland to distant hills. Each room must enjoy this, making the house long and thin.

The Kiplings' ideal of a remote creative life in Vermont did not prosper. They left Naulakha in 1896 and circumstances and new directions made this an abandonment for good. By 1902, already living at Bateman's in Sussex, they were desperate to sell their American home, with much of its furniture. It was bought by a friend, Miss Cabot, and soon afterwards descended to the Holbrook family, from whom we bought it. In their gentle care the house kept a strong sense of its builder, and such small alterations as they made, we have now reversed. Many of the rooms thus remain exactly as Kipling knew them, including the study in which he wrote *The Jungle Books* and *Captains Courageous*.

Naulakha shows us a different Kipling to Bateman's. Here he was unharnessed by a romantic sense of history: each mark he made was his alone. And Vermont, with its forests and lakes, its quiet villages and unhurried life, summer music festivals and winter skiing, is as captivating as it was a century ago.

228 The Landmark Trust Handbook

Rudyard Kipling in the Library.

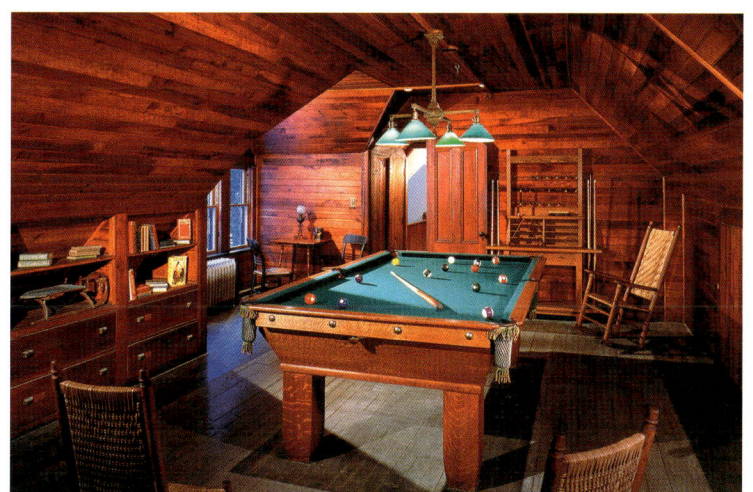

First floor

Ground floor

The Sugarhouse

Dummerston, Vermont

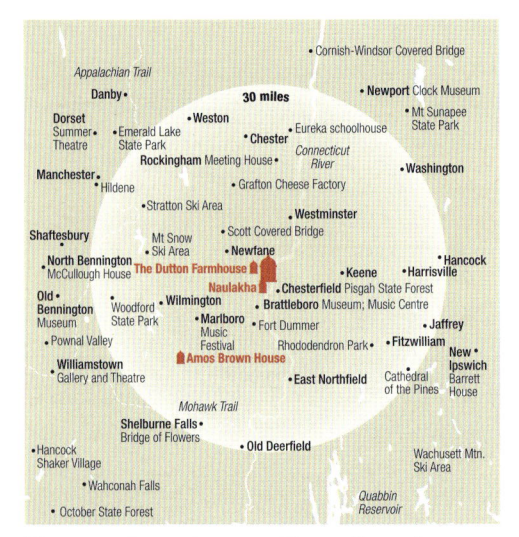

For up to 2 people
Gas stove
Extensive grounds
Adjacent parking

Dogs allowed
Access to clay tennis court at Naulakha

Maple sugaring goes back many centuries in this part of North America. Native Americans were the first to recognise this gift of the forest and early settlers quickly learned the delight of 'Indian molasses', an early term for maple syrup. Benjamin Rush, a signer of the Declaration of Independence, wrote in a letter to Thomas Jefferson, 'The gift of the sugar maple trees is from a benevolent Providence'.

Our Sugarhouse dates from around 1900, although almost certainly it replaced another. It takes 40 gallons of sap to produce one gallon of maple syrup, a process which requires a great deal of boiling over large, intense fires. Sugarhouses were, therefore, prone to burning down, so that few early ones now survive. The very steep slate roof on our Sugarhouse is perhaps responsible for its survival by protecting it from flying sparks.

The eccentric shape of the building was perfectly suited to syrup making: long and narrow for the evaporator pan and tall with a monitor roof to allow the escape of steam. The room once used for the storage of sap buckets is now the bedroom while the bathroom is tucked into the woodshed.

Rudyard Kipling, who lived a short distance down the road, may well have been a customer of Scott Farm. He is known to have developed a taste for maple syrup on his pancakes and he did sign the Scott Farm guest book. Records reveal that Scott Farm was producing syrup by 1845 and, in the 1920s, it became one of the first to adopt mail-order marketing, soon shipping its syrup worldwide. 50 years later syrup production here ended and the Sugarhouse was converted to housing for farm workers.

The Sugarhouse is set back from the road up its own driveway flanked by stone walls.

From the logbook
Everything you need, nothing you don't – the Sugarhouse was the perfect place to ring in the New Year.

Ground floor

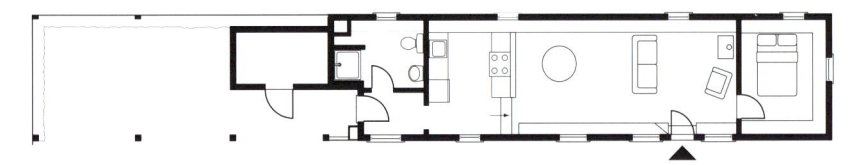

People

Royal Patron
His Royal Highness, The Prince of Wales, KG, KT

Founder
Sir John Smith CH, CBE (1923–2007)

Trustees
Martin Drury CBE (Chairman), Malcolm Airs, Richard Collins, Hugh Cookson, John de Trafford, Alec Hamilton, Victoria Mitchell, Barry Sealey CBE

Director
Peter Pearce

Shottesbrooke
Katie Arber, Joan Belcher, Catherine Brown, Rebecca Brown, David Dawson, Alastair Dick-Cleland, Lynne Dunning, Patricia Eriksson, Louise Evans, Yvonne Foord, Sue Gardiner, Anna Gordon, Bruce Hall, Geraldine Heywood, Emma Hillier, Diana Joel, Barbara Jotham, Johanna Lee, Valerie Lord, Angela McKersie, Linda McLean, Salma Mehdi, Alice Meynell, Linda Millard, Marilyn Noble, Elizabeth Nolan, James Norman, Victoria O'Keeffe, Katherine Oakes, Carole Paton, Joan Portsmouth, Trisha Pottinger, Joanna Reece, Gavin Robinson, Emma Seymour, Mark Sharratt, Caroline Stanford, Marguerite Thomson, Simon Verdon, Dawn Waterman, Sheila Wilkinson

Furnishings, Decorations, Books
Willa Bailey, Valerie Charlton, John Evetts, Sarah Fletcher, Mark Harris, Sandor Korik, Charles Morgan, Lady Smith OBE, Mark Smitten, Jake Wright

Building Works
John Brown, Carl Dowding, Reg Lo-Vel

Regional Property Managers
Susan Bladon, Ann Callan, Ruth Davies, Marilyn Donohue, Rebekah Foxley, Lyn Francis, Lorella Graham, Isobel Kelly, Cy Neil, Diana Newton, Jo Quinby, Pamela Reed, Geof Salt, Shirley Stewart

Crownhill Fort
Donna Bourne, Paul Hickford, Samantha Lanchbery, Terry Rowe

Lundy and MS Oldenburg
Lisa Bailey, Jack Bater, Zoe Bignell, Eric Blacker, Tom Carr, Robert Cheetham, Tania Cheetham, Ian Clark, Tracey Crump, Nigel Dalby, Aaron Davis, Alan Daw, Lesley Dixon Chatfield, Christopher Dubber, Frank Dunbar, Glyn Eager, John-Paul Faramus, Maria Faramus, Christopher Flower, Emily Francis, Patrizia Fursdon, Roger Fursdon, Derek Green, Paul Gyurgyak, Jacqueline Hewitt, Aiden Keenan, Stuart Leavy, Lee Miles, Emma Parnell, Luke Parnell, Emmie Perham, Carl Perrin, Carl Pimlott, Stephen Roberts, Julie Saunders, Nicola Saunders, Grant Sherman, Brian Slade, Lyndsey Slade, Rebecca Smythe, Shelley Southon, Liz Stafford, Glyn Sturtivant, Reginald Tuffin, Jeremy Waller, Keith Ward, Thomas Welch, Julie Welsh, Kevin Welsh, Sophie Wheatley, Duncan Withall

Volunteers and Helpers
Donald Amlot, Mavis Fleetwood

Friends of Landmark
Anne Purser, Janice Waterman

Principal Housekeepers and Gardeners
Nancy Agger, Helen Angus, Barbara Askew, Jill Avis, Patricia Back, Dorothy Baker, Frederic Baldry, Margaret Baldry, Karen Ballantyne, Marion Barker, Doreen Barnett, Rosemary Bates, Irene Batt, Brigette Baxter, Daniel Baxter, Glyn Baxter, Matthew Beecroft, Barbara Begley, Jean Bennett, Sasha Bennetts, Christine Bennion, Giovanna Bett, Antony Bevan, Christine Biggart, Roslynn Bishop, Barry Blackwell, Linda Blackwell, Marion Blaker, Elaine Blatchford, Judith Blyth, Kenneth Bowe, Barbara Bowen, Christian Bowers, Penny Bowers, Anna Boyd, Rosalind Boyd, Debra Briggs, Sarah Briggs, Christine Brown, Fiona Brown, Jayne Brown, Paula Bruce, Chantal Buchanan, Caroline Buckley, Zoe Burch, Kim Burgess, Brian Buxton, Raymond Callan, Margaret Cameron, Dugald Campbell, John Caplen-Newman, Pat Caplen-Newman, David Carr, Elizabeth Carr, Layann Carroll, Marion Chandler, Adele Charlton, Charles Chatfield, Elizabeth Chatfield, Dorothy Christmas, Tina Clancey, Elizabeth Clark, Julie Clegg, Chloe Clifford, Jennifer Clifford, Christopher Cole, Wendy Cole, Claire Coleman, Jayde Collett, Alan Collier, Karen Connolly, Marlene Coombes, Linda Coulter, Roy Cousens, Linda Crombie, Chris Crook, Colin Croucher, Karen Curtis, Martyn Dack, Daniel Davies, Elizabeth Davies, Lesley Davies, Laura Dawkins, Amanda Dawson, Louise Delaney, Peter Denman, Ian Dennis, Andrew Dick, Bridget Dodsworth, Edward Donohue, Susan Doody, Patricia Dunworth, Gillian Edwards, Gerwyn Edwards, Claire Elcock, Jane Elson, Sally Enefer-Kemp, Valerie Evans, Carol Everitt, Diane Farrington, Jill Faulkner, Jonathan Few, Tracey Few, Jacqueline Field, Mary Fisher, Frances Flavell, Ray Forey, Michael Foxley, Rae Francis, Rosemary Francis, Shirley Francis, Nicola Frankland, Mary Fraser, Thomas Fraser, Andrea Gainfort, Elizabeth Gamble, Nicholas Gamble, Louise Genner, Brian George, Wendy Gibbs, Dorothy Gibson, Caroline Gilder, David Gilfoyle, Rita Gillingham, Linda Glanville, Lee Glenister, Samantha Glenister, Sonya Glenister, Pam Gray, Dorothy Green, Sarah Griffiths, Virginia Grosvenor, Michael Guest, Wendy Guest, Julia Hally, Jane Hamper, Antonia Harding, Maureen Harrington, Charlotte Harris, Eric Harris, Nigel Hart, Angela Hartley, James Hartley, Katherine Haspineall, Brian Hatcher, Druscilla Hatcher, Julie Hawker, Shawen Hayman, Helen Hayward, Carol Hellier, Susan Hicks, Patricia Hindmarch, Angela Holman, Andrea Hopkins, Linda Horner, Anthony Howells, Patricia Howells, Dorothy Hubball, Monica Hurst, Christine Jago, Malcolm Jago, Glenys James, Jack Jarman, Lynne Jeffers, Denis Jevon, Nicky Jevon, Brenda Johnson, Dorothy Johnson, Dorothy Jones, Janet Jones, Peter Jones, Jacqueline Jordan, Julian Jordan, Ruth Jordan, Christina Kay, Christine Keeler, Tracy Keeler, Claire Keen, Kate Kelland, Roderick Kelland, Penny Keogh, Bridget Kingston, Susan Knight, Susan Lake, Christine Lamb, Pamela Laurie, Joanne Lavender, Mary Lavender, Gillian Lawrence, Gill Lawson, Beryl Lawton, Barbara Leaning, Daisy Letch, Amanda Lewis, David Lewis, Beverley Lipp, Angela Little, Pearl Llewellyn, Patricia Lloyd, Sarah Luton, Kirsty Mable, Georgina MacArthur, Katherine Mackay, Susan MacKay, Alexandra Mackinnon, Pauline Malpas, Margaret Manley, Michael Manley, Louise Marchent, Margaret Martin, Rieta Mawson, Joan McDermott, Rosanne McGugan, Katrina McKay, Sandra McKerrall, William McKirdy, Anthony McTaggart, Judith McTaggart, Bridget Mellor, Alan Mews, Johnathan Miller, Eileen Miller, Janet Mills, Jonathan Milne, Alison Miners, James Mitchell, Zhoe Mitchell, Isabella Moore, Thomas Morgan, Kerry Moule, Lee Moule, Mary Muir, Lesley Munday, Reginald Myring, Heather Newham, Ron Newton, Dianne Ninnmey, Ian Ogden, Yvonne Ogden, Aimee Olde, Alison Olde, Lucy Olde, Sarah Oldham, Pierre Orr, Janet Pain, Victoria Palmer, John Parry, Carole Parsons, Maureen Patterson, William Patterson, Jane Pearce, Michele Pearce-Authers, Paula Peck, Lydia Pemberton, Roger Pengilly, Christopher Penner, Penelope Perrott, Rita Peters, Caroline Phillips, Hollie Phillips, Marie Phillips, Sharon Phillips, Cynthia Plowright, May Povey, Rhodie Povey, Terry Povey, Gillian Powell, John Poyner, Janice Preston, Margaret Price, Rosemary Price, Angela Puddu, Barry Purple, Ann Quinby, Terence Quinby, Julia Quinell, Helen Randles, Lauren Reid, Karen Richardson, Lynne Rickard, Peter Rickard, Gina Roberts, Gwyneth Roberts, Sheila Roberts, Mary Robertson, Evelyn Robinson, Sally-Anne Robinson, Sue Robinson, Mary Roche, Helen Rogerson, Ian Rogerson, Julie Rotherham, Jennifer Roshier, Christine Rudd, Christine Ryder, Pauline Salt, Sara Sampson, Julie Sanderson, Valerie Sandford, Linda Sargeant, Wendy Sargeant, Lynne Seymour, Natasha Sharman, David Shepherd, Gillian Shepherd, Jennifer Skelding, Paula Skinner, Carol Slade, Mervyn Slade, Gillian Smith, Helen Smith, Karen Smith, Patricia Smith, Pauline Smith, Ted Smith, Brenda Sore, Tony Sore, Andrew Spalton, Jeanette Spalton, Carolyn Sparrow, Anne Speirs, Robert Sperrin, Susan Springett, Francis Steele, Teresa Steele, Stephanie Stenhouse, Gabrielle Stephens, Fred Stephenson, James Stewart, Julie Storey, Rosemary Stowell, Jan Swannick, Nick Syrett, Sarah Syrett, Julie Tee, Toni Tee, Janet Thomas, Francis Thomson, Sarah Thomson, Julia Thornton, Jennifer Timms, Peter Trim, Sonja Trim, Julie Turnham, Christine Vincent, Anne Von Broen, Clare Waby, Tracey Wain, Brenda Walford, Joan Walker, Deborah Wallace, Luana Wallace, David Wallis, Philippa Wallis, Dawn Ward, Peter Warwick, Amanda Wason, Stuart Webster, Lucie West, Carol West, Claire Wheeler, Joanna White, Lionel White, Stephen Whiteley, Amanda Williams, Claire Williams, Eirlys Williams, Joanna Wilson, Susan Winsor, Sarah Winter-Wright, Shirley Woodward, Susan Wright, Angela Wyatt, Geoff Wyness, Valerie Wyness, Esther Yarnold, Alistair Young

In addition we gratefully acknowledge the voluntary help of numerous relatives and friends of the Landmark staff throughout the country.

Acknowledgements

Photographers
Front Cover by Angus Bremner
David Alexander, R Allenby-Pratt, Stuart Andrews, Katie Arber, Archive Photography, Kelvin Barber, Paul Barker, Constance Barrett, Nigel Bonsor, Clive Boursnell, Derry Brabbs, Angus Bremner, Doug Brown, Country Life Picture Library/Paul Barker, Country Life Picture Library/June Buck, M Campbell Cole, Carlo Contini, Martin Charles, Christopher Dalton, James O Davies, Louise Evans, Mike Foxley, Derek Green, Paul Gummer, P Douglas Hamilton, Janine Hall, Nicolette Hallett, Barry Hamilton, Richard Hayman, Andy Hendry, Ross Hoddinott, Keith Hunter, Gareth Ireland, Aldo Jacovelli, James Kerr, Tim Key, PS Kristensen, Reg Lo-Vel, Peter Mauss/Esto, F Magonio, John Miller, David Morgan, James Morris, Gary Moyse, Katherine Oakes, Lee Pengelly, Gavin Robinson, Geof Salt, Mark Sharratt, Nigel Shuttleworth, Caroline Stanford, Ian Sumner, David Tansey, Jonathan Thompson, V&A Images (Victoria and Albert Museum), Tom Valentine, Chris Warde-Jones, Paul Watson, Matthew Weinreb, John Wilkie, Harry Williams, George Wright

We have credited those photographers whose work has been identified or labelled and we apologise to those who have not been recorded as a result.

Maps
The location maps were drawn by Michael Robinson and other site maps by Desmond Thomas.

The map of Lundy is based on Ordnance Survey mapping with the permission of the Controller of Her Majesty's Office © Crown Copyright; Licence Number MC100018629.

Plans
The plans were drawn by John Hewitt, based on original plans by Michael Fleetwood.

© The Landmark Trust 2008
ISBN: 978-0-9533124-6-7

The Handbook is as accurate as possible at the time of going to print. We cannot be held liable for any inaccuracies that may arise.

Designed originally by Atelier Works
23rd edition by Third Millenium Publishing
Printed by Clifford Press
Printed on chemical free paper from sustainable forestry.

Twenty-third edition
Published September 2008

The Landmark Trust
Shottesbrooke
Maidenhead
Berkshire SL6 3SW
United Kingdom

Charity registered in England & Wales 243312
and Scotland SC039205

Ways to Get Involved

The Landmark Trust is a building preservation charity and as such depends on your support to maintain existing Landmarks and rescue buildings at risk.

Stay
There is no better way to get involved than by staying in one of our properties. By living in these unique buildings for just a short while, you will feel completely surrounded by history while contributing towards the cost of its ongoing maintenance.

Visit
We run a number of Open Days each year. At these everyone can visit and learn about the building's history and restoration. Admission is free and leaflets detailing the building's history are available, for both adults and children.

A Patrons' visit to Astley Castle in Warwickshire.

To book please visit:
www.landmarktrust.org.uk
or telephone **01628 825925**
Overseas **+44 1628 825925**
Email **bookings@landmarktrust.org.uk**

Donate
By making a donation of any size, you will be helping us rescue and restore buildings of architectural and historic importance for all to enjoy, and to create future Landmarks. Donations can be made by post, telephone, and online.

Remembering Landmark in your will
For many people, remembering charities in their will is a natural extension of the support they have shown in their lifetime. In Landmark's case, it can also be an expression of appreciation for the many wonderful Landmark experiences they have had. If you would like to receive our legacy guide, please contact the Development Office.

Friends of the Landmark Trust
The Landmark Friends are enthusiasts who support our work and enjoy visiting and staying in Landmarks, as well as meeting other Friends. The annual subscription to become a Landmark Friend is £50 per person or just £40 if you opt to pay by Direct Debit. Life membership costs £500.

Patrons of the Landmark Trust
Patrons are invited to bespoke events around the country, including an annual opportunity to meet the Director. They also receive booking privileges, including for new Landmarks. The annual donation is a minimum of £1,000 or from as little as £83 per month by Direct Debit. Life Patronage is £10,000 and Joint Patronage £15,000.

Project Guardians
For a single donation of £6,000 you can become a Project Guardian. In return for this crucial support, we are delighted to offer a number of benefits to allow close involvement with the many dimensions of the rescue and repair of your chosen building. You will have the opportunity to see how Landmark goes about raising the required funds, finalises the restoration scheme and be able to follow the restoration process from start to finish.

Cavendish Hall was bequeathed to the Landmark Trust by Pamela Matthews who wished it to have a secure future.

Development Office telephone
01628 825920

Website **www.landmarktrust.org.uk**
Email **fundraising@landmarktrust.org.uk**

Charity registered in England & Wales 243312 and Scotland SC039205

Great Value Landmarks

Landmarks offer great value for money all year round especially when you fully occupy them. Choose from over 180 historic places throughout Britain and in Italy, accommodating from one to 16 people. You will discover follies, castles, towers, banqueting houses, cottages and many other historic buildings, in which you can stay. Below are just a few examples of properties to suit a range of budgets.

Under £15 per person per night

Tangy Mill
Argyll and Bute
A week in January for just £8 pppn

Tangy Mill was built in about 1820, to serve the big arable farms on the west side of Kintyre. Much of the mill machinery is still in position and amongst it you live and sleep. Tangy Mill stands in beautiful remote surroundings on the north bank of the Tangy Burn, near the point where it enters the sea.

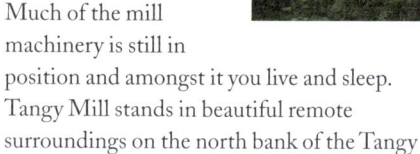

St Mary's Lane
Gloucestershire
A week in May from £15 pppn

Built in the eighteenth century for the framework knitters or stocking makers of Tewkesbury, this terraced cottage is light and cheerful, the upper floor looking out over the marvellous roofscape of Tewkesbury. St Mary's Lane is a quiet side street, a short walk from Tewkesbury Abbey.

2nd Floor, Egyptian House
Cornwall
A week in November from £10 pppn

The Egyptian House is part of a rare and noble survivor of a style that enjoyed a vogue after Napoleon's campaign in Egypt of 1798. It was built in Penzance in 1835 as a museum and geological repository and now is let as three Landmark flats.

Under £30 per person per night

Fort Clonque
Alderney
Christmas break – 7 nights £28 pppn

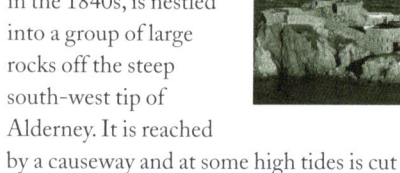

This dramatic fort, built in the 1840s, is nestled into a group of large rocks off the steep south-west tip of Alderney. It is reached by a causeway and at some high tides is cut off from the mainland. The rest of Alderney is extremely pleasant, the island being just small enough to explore on foot, or by bicycle, and in the centre is St Anne, a very pretty little town, English with a hint of France.

Obriss Farm
Kent
A week in June from £27 pppn

Obriss Farm, surrounded by traditional byres, a stable and a smokehouse, has a field pattern not changed since 1840. Sitting on the lower slopes of Toys Hill, looking south over the Weald, it is a convenient distance from London but feels unexpectedly peaceful in this busy part of the country.

Crownhill Fort
Devon
A week in July from £26 pppn

Built in the 1860s to protect Plymouth from attack by land and sea, Crownhill Fort is one of only two large works of its kind to survive in good condition in the country. You stay in the Officers' Quarters and have a free run of the Fort once the gates close for the evening.

Under £50 per person per night

Kingswear Castle
Devon
A 4 night midweek break in March from £48 pppn

Built in 1502 to support Dartmouth Castle on the opposite shore, Kingswear Castle almost stands on the water's edge. From the windows and the roof platform you can look across to Dartmouth or down the rocky coast with its woods of maritime pine and out to sea.

The Grange
Kent
A week break in August from £42 pppn

Augustus Pugin built The Grange in 1843 to live in with his family. He designed it to live out his idea of life in a medieval, Catholic community, in buildings executed in the Gothic style of so-called pointed architecture. To stay here offers a unique chance to step into Pugin's colourful and idiosyncratic world.

Ascog
Argyll and Bute
New Year for 5 nights, both for under £50 pppn

Ascog lies in large and secluded grounds on the sheltered east coast of the Isle of Bute. Ascog House is a seventeenth-century Laird's house, while Meikle Ascog is a nineteenth-century villa, which reflects the logical and inventive personality who built it.

Booking Conditions

General
1. Your booking must be for holiday purposes only. The property must not be used for gatherings, such as weddings or parties (except on Lundy, by prior written permission) or for business purposes (except by prior special arrangement).
2. The property will not be available before 4pm on the first day of your booking and you must leave before 10am on your last day.
3. Excluding babies in cots, the number of people occupying the property and its grounds must not exceed the number shown in the Price List and on the Landmark Trust website. Except on Lundy, you may invite an additional two guests to visit you during your stay, however they must not stay overnight.
4. You may bring up to two dogs to properties where dogs are allowed (except on Lundy where dogs are not permitted except assistance dogs). They must be kept off the furniture and under proper control. No other pets are permitted.
5. No fireworks shall be taken onto, or let off from the property.
6. Whilst the information in our Handbook, Price List and website is correct at the time of publishing, we reserve the right to change any of the prices, services, or other particulars contained in published information at any time before we enter into a contract with you.

Contract and warranties
7. Once we have accepted your booking and payment, a contract has been entered into, which includes these conditions, and those set out in the documents 'Staying in Landmarks' and 'Staying on Lundy', as appropriate, and such contract is governed by English law. Payment of all required amounts when they are due is of the essence of the contract.
8. When you make a booking you warrant that you are over 18 years old and accept full responsibility for all persons who will use the property during the period booked and you have read all the Terms & Conditions.
9. In the case of buildings we let on behalf of others (The Roslin and Hampton Court properties, Wolveton Gatehouse, Gargunnock House, Hole Cottage, Oxenford Gatehouse and Sant'Antonio), your contract is with the owner, for whom we act as agent, and is otherwise upon these Terms & Conditions.

Bookings
10. Reservation requests received by email from the Landmark Trust website will be held for four days. If we are unable to contact you by telephone and take payment within four days of receiving your reservation request, your reservation will lapse. Provisional bookings made by telephone will remain firm provided we receive the amount due within the period agreed at the time of booking (usually four days).
11. If your stay starts within three months of the date you make your booking, you are required to pay the total price at the time of booking.
12. If your stay starts more than three months from the date you make the booking, you are required to pay a deposit of one third of the cost of your stay (or £100 per booking, if greater) at the time of booking.
13. Camping on Lundy must be paid for in full at the time of booking. Under 18s must be accompanied on the campsite by a responsible adult.
14. If prices have not yet been fixed for the period booked, then the deposit is one third (or £100 per booking, if greater) of the current price for an equivalent period (not necessarily the same dates). Please note: the deposit secures only the booking and not the price. In some cases prices may change considerably. The price will not alter if you pay in full at the time of booking (we may make specific exceptions to this).
15. Bookings must be for our normal booking periods and will not be for fewer than three days (two days on Lundy) or for more than three weeks. In the case of bookings for more than one week, we provide linen and towels but no cleaning for each successive week, but will only remake beds with the new linen if you ask for this one month before your holiday.
16. If you pay a deposit, the balance must be received at least three months before the beginning of the period booked. We do not undertake to remind you and if we do not receive the balance when due, we shall, with regret, cancel your booking and you will lose your deposit.

Payments
17. We accept Maestro (issued in the UK), Delta, Visa, MasterCard, direct transfer and sterling cheques drawn on a UK bank. Cheques should be made payable to the Landmark Trust except for Lundy stays and boat/helicopter tickets which should be payable to The Lundy Company Ltd. All payments must be in sterling. Only one voucher issued with a Handbook can be used as part payment for any booking.

Loss or damage
18. When you book, you agree to indemnify us against all loss and damage arising (including more than normally and reasonably anticipated amounts of cleaning) directly or indirectly to the property and its contents from any deliberate or negligent act or omission by yourself, or any person or animal accompanying you, and, without limitation of the foregoing to pay us forthwith upon written demand our costs in making good any such loss and damage and cleaning. Where we have to make a claim for the cost of extra cleaning and putting right damage, the amount involved is generally in the order of £250.

Problems during your stay
19. If you have any issues concerning the property during your stay you should notify the Regional Property Manager (whose name and telephone number appears in the information sent with the confirmation of your booking and in the Information and Advice folder) as soon as possible. The Landmark Trust will not normally make any refunds in respect of complaints made after the customer's departure from the property if the customer did not make the complaint or problem known to the local contact during the stay. In considering any complaint we will take into account whether we have been given the opportunity to investigate it and the chance to put matters right.

Cancellation
20. If you cancel a booking for any reason, you must notify us in writing by email, fax or by post only. The following cancellation charges will apply:

- **More than 90 days before start date:** Your deposit
- **89 to 60 days before start date:** 50% of the total rental
- **59 to 30 days before start date:** 75% of the total rental
- **29 days or less to start date:** 90% of the total rental
- **On start date or early departure:** 100% of total rental

For camping bookings there will be no refund for bookings worth £45 or less. For camping bookings worth over £45 the above charges apply. In addition, you will be responsible for any travel costs incurred by you in relation to the booking. We do not operate a cancellation insurance scheme and strongly recommend that you ensure that you have your own appropriate cover. We will charge a fee of £45 to re-instate any cancelled booking.

21. We can in some cases transfer bookings to a new date or building (but in the case of buildings we let for others, we can only transfer the date) for a charge of £45 for each property booked, plus any additional rent, at the rate set in the current Price List or on the Landmark Trust website, provided this is requested no fewer than three months before the start of the holiday. If there is a surplus we will hold that against a future booking and will not refund it.
22. We may cancel a booking at any time before the date on which it begins. We would expect to do this only for essential building work or for some other reason unforeseen by us at the time your booking was accepted. In this unlikely event we shall refund in full all money received by us for the booking, but will not have any liability beyond this, and, without limitation of the foregoing, we will not have any liability for travel costs incurred by you in relation to the booking.
23. We accept no liability for any works or activity of any sort occurring on any premises adjoining or neighbouring our property, nor shall we be responsible for making any enquiries about the likelihood of, or providing any information to you about, any such works or activity.

Access
24. Anyone with our authority may have access during your stay. This is unlikely to happen, but if it does, we will give you as much warning as we can. There will be no need for you to stay in, since our Housekeeper can accompany the visitor.

Lundy
25. If we cannot transport you to Lundy either by boat or helicopter at the beginning of your stay, and you have bought from us either a boat or helicopter ticket we will refund the rent you have paid for each night until you reach the island. If we cannot transport you from Lundy at the end of your stay and you have bought from us a boat or helicopter ticket we will cover the cost of each extra night's accommodation on Lundy. If we offer you a sailing or helicopter flight to or from Lundy but you refuse it, we reserve the right to change your accommodation and/or to charge for it.

VAT
26. Our prices include VAT where appropriate. If VAT rates change, we reserve the right to amend our prices accordingly.

Limitation of Liability
27. Our liability to you and those accompanying you at the property is strictly limited to direct loss up to the amount paid by you on booking but this does not apply to our liability for:
    a) death or personal injury caused by our negligence;
    b) fraud or fraudulent misrepresentation on our part;
    c) anything else for which liability may not at law be excluded.

    We shall not be liable to you at all for any indirect or consequential loss, whether caused by negligence, breach of contract or otherwise.

28. We reserve the right to terminate a booking at any time if these conditions are not met in full.

Privacy policy
We promise that any information you give us will only be used for the purposes of the Landmark Trust. If you wish to opt out of particular types of mailing in the future please call us on 01628 825920, write to us or send an email to dataprotection@landmarktrust.org.uk, giving your full name and postcode.
To view our full Privacy Policy please see our website at www.landmarktrust.org.uk.

29 May to 4 Jun	5 June to 16 July		17 Jul to 27 Aug	28 Aug to 3 Sep		4 Sep to 8 Oct	9 Oct to 28 Oct		29 Oct to 28 Nov			29 Nov to 22 Dec			23 Dec to 29 Dec	30 Dec to 2 Jan	Beds	Sleeps	Property
	Per night*	Weekly	Weekly	Per night*	Weekly	Per night*	Per night*	Weekly	Short Stays		Weekly	Short Stays		Weeks	Xmas	New Year			
Start Sat 7 nights			Start Sat 7 nights						Start Fri 3 nights	Start Mon 4 nights	Start Fri or Mon 7 nights	Start Fri 3 nights	Start Mon 4 nights	Start Fri or Mon 7 nights	Start Thur 7 nights	Start Thur 4 nights			
1160	141	966	1224	163	1084	127	105	722	300	249	480	282	235	453	838	792	VI VIII	14	The Barn
873	110	757	911	125	833	103	82	562	289	240	462	273	227	437	632	596	T D	4	Bramble Villa East
812	102	700	852	117	780	96	76	520	262	218	419	246	204	396	594	561	T D	4	Bramble Villa West
																			The Castle
761	97	662	798	106	708	90	75	518	250	207	400	236	196	378	550	519	D	2	Castle Cottage
660	84	571	685	95	630	73	66	449	228	190	365	216	179	345	479	450	T	2	Castle Keep East
545	70	480	567	78	518	64	54	369	179	149	288	169	141	271	395	374	D	2	Castle Keep North
821	104	713	854	117	781	96	76	524	275	229	440	259	216	416	593	561	2T	4	Castle Keep South
1437	180	1237	1497	201	1341	168	128	881	431	358	690	405	338	651	1041	982	S T D	5	Government House
1089	137	938	1133	156	1039	128	102	699	344	285	551	324	271	519	789	743	T B	4	Hanmers
2714	330	2264	2831	380	2536	297	245	1682	681	567	1092	643	535	1030	1966	1854	2S 3T 2D	12	Millcombe House
808	102	699	839	116	773	95	80	546	269	224	432	254	212	408	584	552	T	2	Old House North
1268	160	1096	1326	178	1185	150	116	795	396	330	637	374	312	600	920	869	S T D	5	Old House South
																			The Old Light
307	40	269	323	45	297	37	31	212	110	93	177	104	86	168	223	210	(S)	1	Old Light Cottage
969	123	839	1014	139	925	114	91	620	308	258	493	290	241	466	700	667	2S T	4	Old Light Lower
1185	149	1021	1235	166	1104	139	107	736	373	310	598	351	294	563	856	808	S 2T	5	Old Light Upper
702	90	612	728	100	668	82	70	483	236	196	378	224	186	357	505	478	D	2	The Old School
1148	144	994	1199	164	1095	165	110	750	385	322	618	364	303	583	831	785	S T D	5	The Quarters
308	40	269	324	45	298	37	31	213	112	93	179	104	88	168	223	212	(S)	1	Radio Room
758	96	659	793	108	721	91	75	515	258	213	410	242	202	387	551	521	(S) T	3	St John's, Big
624	80	547	651	89	591	73	62	426	202	170	327	194	159	309	451	425	T	2	St John's, Little
1000	126	861	1043	143	957	116	101	693	328	274	526	309	258	496	726	684	S T	3	Square Cottage
1045	132	907	1092	149	996	123	99	676	336	280	539	318	263	508	756	713	T D	4	Stoneycroft
748	95	655	782	107	714	89	70	484	254	211	408	240	200	384	542	511	2 B	4	Tibbetts
10	11		11	12		11	9												Camping (per person per day)

Rock climbing

Some of the country's best sea cliff climbs are to be found on the island. There are however, some climbing restrictions during the nesting season, from 1 April – 31 July. You must let us know when you book if you wish to climb.

Group bookings

We usually welcome large groups to stay on the island, and can normally provide meals for them in the Tavern. Accommodation will be provided in a combination of different properties, according to the level of comfort you require. Please note that stag and hen parties are not permitted.

Please speak to the Lundy Shore Office on 01271 863636 about these arrangements.

Facilities

- Bath
- Shower
- Shower over bath
- Small outside WC adjoining property
- Awkward stairs
- Fire or stove
- Simply and practically furnished
- Furnished to a higher level of comfort
- Within the village
- A short walk from the village
- A distance from the village

Bed Arrangements

- S   Single room
- T   Twin room
- D   Double room
- VI   Rooms with 6 beds
- VIII   Rooms with 8 beds
- B   Bunk beds
- ( )   Bed or beds in a living room

Further Information

Sleeps column
For example: 4 + 2 beds shows that two of the beds are not part of the main building or are of lesser status than the other available beds. Call the Booking Office for clarification.

*Minimum 2 nights

Lundy

Prices shown are per property for the period stated and not per person

Property	Sleeps	Beds	Facilities	18 Jan to 11 Feb			12 Feb to 14 Feb	15 Feb to 18 Feb	19 Feb to 21 Mar			22 Mar to 26 Mar	27 Mar to 2 Apr		3 Apr to 16 Apr		17 Apr to 28 May	
				Short Stays		Weekly			Short Stays		Weekly		Per night*	Weekly	Per night*	Weekly	Per night*	Weekly
				Start Fri 3 nights	Start Mon 4 nights	Start Fri or Mon 7 nights	Start Fri 3 nights	Start Mon 4 nights	Start Fri 3 nights	Start Mon 4 nights	Start Fri or Mon 7 nights	Start Mon 5 nights						
The Barn	14	VI VIII		272	228	437	408	307	354	296	569	296	84	580	117	806	106	760
Bramble Villa East	4	T D		261	218	420	387	294	340	284	545	284	80	556	103	708	92	653
Bramble Villa West	4	T D		241	201	388	362	273	315	263	510	266	75	520	97	666	87	621
The Castle																		
Castle Cottage	2	D		230	191	369	338	258	299	249	479	249	72	489	91	616	80	576
Castle Keep East	2	T		209	175	337	311	235	273	227	438	227	66	446	78	538	70	499
Castle Keep North	2	D		164	136	263	241	184	213	177	340	177	51	346	65	441	58	412
Castle Keep South	4	2T		247	205	398	366	278	321	268	514	268	76	525	96	659	88	626
Government House	5	S T D		385	321	620	566	433	501	418	804	418	119	820	169	1155	151	1078
Hanmers	4	T B		312	260	503	464	352	407	339	652	339	97	665	128	876	115	824
Millcombe House	12	2S 3T 2D		618	515	991	904	695	801	667	1288	667	192	1313	277	1895	247	1769
Old House North	2	T		242	201	387	359	272	316	262	505	262	74	515	95	651	86	615
Old House South	5	S T D		362	303	583	537	408	472	392	757	392	112	772	150	1027	134	958
The Old Light																		
Old Light Cottage	1	(S)		99	82	157	121	110	128	106	205	106	30	209	37	253	34	242
Old Light Lower	4	2S T		285	238	458	427	322	371	310	596	310	89	608	114	785	102	730
Old Light Upper	5	S 2T		333	278	536	499	376	434	362	696	362	104	711	139	955	126	901
The Old School	2	D		216	180	348	318	245	281	235	452	235	67	460	82	565	75	535
The Quarters	5	S T D		343	286	550	508	386	446	372	714	372	106	729	135	931	121	861
Radio Room	1	(S)		99	82	158	120	112	128	106	206	106	31	210	38	254	34	243
St John's, Big	3	(S) T		230	188	369	338	259	297	248	478	248	71	488	91	622	81	583
St John's, Little	2	T		186	156	299	274	208	244	202	389	202	58	396	74	506	65	469
Square Cottage	3	S T		298	247	478	445	334	386	322	621	322	92	632	116	802	106	761
Stoneycroft	4	T D		312	260	501	467	352	407	338	651	338	96	664	123	847	110	788
Tibbetts	4	2B		228	190	366	340	256	296	246	474	246	70	483	89	608	79	570
Camping (per person per day)			x4										9		9		9	

General Notes

Before you leave
We will send you more detailed information about the journey, giving guidance on sailings, luggage allowances, convenient hotels at the ports, parking and an advance shopping order form.

On arrival on Lundy
Entry to the building you are staying in should not be expected before 4pm, to allow time for it to be cleaned before you arrive. Both the Tavern and the shop will be open on arrival of *MS Oldenburg* or helicopter.

Facilities
All properties have water, electricity (except Tibbetts), gas and drainage. Lundy being an island, water supplies may be restricted at times and electricity will not usually be available after midnight. There are no televisions, radios or telephones in the properties, but there is a pay phone in the Tavern.

Beds and linen
One set of sheets and pillowcases and one hand and one bath towel per bed per week are included in the price (except for The Barn, where you can hire them at the extra charge of £17 per bed). You must not exceed the maximum number of people shown in the Price List for each building.

Dogs
Lundy is a working farm with large numbers of ewes and lambs at certain times of the year. For this reason we cannot allow you to bring dogs (except assistance dogs) when travelling to, or staying on, the island.

Diving
Lundy is England's only statutory Marine Nature Reserve. Diving numbers are strictly controlled. It is essential that you book the diving facilities at the same time as you book your accommodation, or you will not be able to use them. A charge of £15 per person will be made for transporting diving equipment to Lundy via *MS Oldenburg*.

2010 Lundy Transport Timetable

By Helicopter	Depart Hartland Point	Arrive Hartland Point
January 2010		
18 Mon	1100	1400
22 Fri	1100	1400
25 Mon	1100	1400
29 Fri	1100	1400
February		
1 Mon	1100	1400
5 Fri	1100	1400
8 Mon	1100	1400
12 Fri	1100	1400
15 Mon	1100	1400
19 Fri	1100	1400
22 Mon	1100	1400
26 Fri	1100	1400
March		
1 Mon	1100	1400
5 Fri	1100	1400
8 Mon	1100	1400
12 Fri	1100	1400
15 Mon	1100	1400
19 Fri	1100	1400
22 Mon	1100	1400

By MS Oldenburg	Depart Bideford	Depart Ilfracombe	Arrive Ilfracombe	Arrive Bideford
March				
27 Sat		1000	1800	
30 Tue		1000	1800	
April				
1 Thu		1000		1930
3 Sat	0900			2015
6 Tue		1000	1800	
8 Thu		1000	1800	
10 Sat		1000	1800	
13 Tue		1000	1800	
15 Thu		1000		1830
17 Sat	0815			1930
20 Tue	0930		1800	
22 Thu		1000	1800	
24 Sat		1000	1800	
27 Tue		1000	1800	
29 Thu		1000		1830
May				
1 Sat	0815			1930
3 Mon	0900			2030
5 Wed		1000	1830	
8 Sat		1000	1830	
11 Tue		1000	1830	
13 Thu		1000		1830
15 Sat	0800			1830
18 Tue	0900			2030
20 Thu		1000	1830	
22 Sat		1000	1830	
25 Tue		1000	1830	
27 Thu		1000		1830
29 Sat	0800			1830
June				
1 Tue	0900			2030
3 Thu	0930		1830	
5 Sat		1000	1830	
8 Tue		1000	1830	
10 Thu		1000	1830	
12 Sat		1000		1830
15 Tue	0830			1930
17 Thu	0900		1830	

By MS Oldenburg	Depart Bideford	Depart Ilfracombe	Arrive Ilfracombe	Arrive Bideford
19 Sat		1000	1830	
22 Tue		1000	1830	
24 Thu		1000	1830	
26 Sat		1000		1830
29 Tue	0830			1930
July				
1 Thu	0900			2030
3 Sat	1000		1830	
6 Tue		1000	1830	
7 Wed		1000	1830	
8 Thu		1000	1830	
10 Sat		1000	1830	
13 Tue		1000		1900
14 Wed	0830			1930
15 Thu	0900			2000
17 Sat		1500	1400	
20 Tue		1000	1830	
21 Wed		1000	1830	
22 Thu		1000	1830	
24 Sat		1500	1400	
27 Tue		1000		1830
28 Wed	0830			1900
29 Thu	0830			1930
31 Sat		1500	1400	
August				
3 Tue		1000	1830	
4 Wed		1000	1830	
5 Thu		1000	1830	
7 Sat		1500	1400	
10 Tue		1000		1830
11 Wed	0800			1830
12 Thu	0830			1900
14 Sat		1500	1400	
17 Tue		1000	1830	
18 Wed		1000	1830	
19 Thu		1000	1830	
21 Sat		1500	1400	
24 Tue		1000	1830	
25 Wed		1000		1830
26 Thu	0800			1830
28 Sat		1500	1400	
31 Tue	0900		1830	
September				
2 Thu		1000	1800	
4 Sat		1000	1800	
7 Tue		1000	1800	
9 Thu		1000		1830
11 Sat	0830			1930
14 Tue	0930		1800	
16 Thu		1000	1800	
18 Sat		1000	1800	
21 Tue		1000	1800	
23 Thu		1000		1800
25 Sat	0800			1830
28 Tue	0830			2000
30 Thu	0930		1800	
October				
2 Sat		1000	1800	
5 Tue		1000	1800	
7 Thu		1000	1800	
9 Sat		1000		1830
12 Tue	0900			2030
14 Thu	1000		1800	
16 Sat		1000	1800	
19 Tue		1000	1800	
21 Thu		1000	1800	
23 Sat		1000		1830
26 Tue	0800			1930

By Helicopter	Depart Hartland Point	Arrive Hartland Point
October		
29 Fri	1100	1400
November		
1 Mon	1100	1400
5 Fri	1100	1400
8 Mon	1100	1400
12 Fri	1100	1400
15 Mon	1100	1400
19 Fri	1100	1400
22 Mon	1100	1400
26 Fri	1100	1400
29 Mon	1100	1400
December		
3 Fri	1100	1400
6 Mon	1100	1400
10 Fri	1100	1400
13 Mon	1100	1400
17 Fri	1100	1400
20 Mon	1100	1400
23 Thu	1100	1400
30 Thu	1100	1400
January 2011		
3 Mon		1400

Guide to what you could see on Lundy

- Sika deer sightings
- Birds of prey sightings
- Many migrating birds
- Carpets of spring flowers
- Sightings of Puffin
- Sightings of grey seals
- Soay sheep
- Soay lambs
- Interesting seashore life
- Rhododendron in flower
- Heather in flower
- Lundy Cabbage in flower
- Basking shark sightings
- Thrift and Sea Campion

Transport is subject to weather conditions. Some sailings do not return to the same port from which they departed.

Lundy

View from Castle Cottage, Lundy

Getting to Lundy
See 2010 transport timetable, facing page.
Between 27 March and 26 October 2010 the island ship, *MS Oldenburg*, sails from Bideford and Ilfracombe, weather permitting. From 18 January 2010 – 22 March 2010 and 29 October 2010 – 3 January 2011 a helicopter service is operated between Hartland Point and Lundy. Visitors staying on Lundy will require return transport tickets, which should be purchased no later than 14 days prior to travel.

Payment for accommodation on the island does not entitle you to transport to the island. Please be aware that there are weight restrictions on the luggage taken to Lundy, 20kg per person on *MS Oldenburg* and 10kg per person on the helicopter. No single piece of luggage should weigh more than 15kg for either service and we reserve the right to refuse to transport luggage over this weight. Excess baggage will be charged.

Passages can be secured only by buying a ticket, which should be done when your final payment is due (usually three months before your departure). If you do not wish to travel on a day when transport is provided, it may be possible for you (usually at greater cost) to charter suitable boats in Bideford or Ilfracombe, or a helicopter. We can provide further details. The start and end dates of your booking must correspond with the sailing or the helicopter timetable. If you do not arrive on *MS Oldenburg*, we will charge you for carrying your luggage to and from the top of the island. Our Lundy Shore Office is always delighted to answer queries, or help with any particular requirements you may have. The telephone number is 01271 863636. They can be contacted between 9am and 5pm Monday to Friday.

Bed and breakfast
This may be available at short notice, using an unoccupied building. To book please telephone the Lundy Shore Office on 01271 863636, not more than two weeks before your visit. Breakfast is provided in the Tavern. There are facilities for making coffee and tea in your property. The price is £40 a night for a single room and £60 for a twin room. Between 17 July – 3 September 2010 this will be £48 and £75 respectively.

Cancellations
Please see our booking conditions on page 18.

Travelling by *MS Oldenburg*
27 March 2010 – 26 October 2010
Return tickets cost £56 for adults, £28 for children under 16 and £9 for babies and children under four. The journey to or from Lundy usually takes less than two hours. The ship's departure time from Lundy will be posted on the Tavern notice-board at least 24 hours before the sailing. Some sailings return you to a different port from that which you departed. Please refer to the sailing timetable. When the coach/transport link is required between the ports of Ilfracombe and Bideford, we are happy to co-ordinate this service if you let us know on your return journey aboard *MS Oldenburg*.

Cancelled sailings
Like any other sea journey, the crossing to Lundy is subject to sea and weather conditions and sometimes we are unable to sail to or from the island on the planned day. If this happens we will arrange for a local helicopter operator to take you to or from the island at a subsidised price of £25 for adults and children under 16, provided that flying conditions and helicopter availability allow it and that you have paid for a passage on *MS Oldenburg*. Babies under two go free.

Travelling by helicopter
18 January 2010 – 22 March 2010 and
29 October 2010 – 3 January 2011
Return tickets cost £95 for adults, £50 for children under 16 and no charge for babies under two. The helicopter leaves from Hartland Point, about 20 miles west of Bideford. The journey to or from Lundy takes approximately seven minutes. It is important that you arrive at Hartland Point to check in in plenty of time. The helicopter usually seats seven passengers and you will be allocated to one of several flights that day at check in. This may mean that your departure or arrival time will be later than shown in the timetable. Parking is available at Hartland Point, for which a small charge will be made.

Further information on Lundy is available in a free illustrated colour brochure. Please contact the Booking Office for a copy.

The Friends of Lundy
Many of those who visit Lundy are keen to help the islanders preserve this unique environment. The Friends' subscription is spent on protecting and conserving Lundy's natural beauty. The individual annual subscription is £24, couples £30, families £36. Friends receive a discount on *MS Oldenburg* and winter helicopter fares each time they travel to the island, and a discount on accommodation booked within 14 days of departure. They also receive Landmark's Spring and Autumn Newsletters and their own annual Newsletter giving details of life on the island, its fauna and flora.

Lundy Shore Office, The Quay, Bideford, Devon EX39 2LY

Tel **01271 863636 (sales and enquiries)**
Tel **01237 470074 (administration)**
Tel **01237 431831 (island)**
Website **www.lundyisland.co.uk**
Email **info@lundyisland.co.uk**

Booking Office telephone
01628 825925
Overseas **+44 1628 825925**

Website **www.landmarktrust.org.uk**
Email **bookings@landmarktrust.org.uk**

30 Apr to 3 May	4 May to 6 May	7 May to 27 May			28 May to 31 May	1 Jun to 3 Jun	4 Jun to 8 Jul			9 Jul to 26 Aug			27 Aug to 30 Aug	31 Aug to 2 Sep	3 Sep to 28 Oct			29 Oct to 19 Dec			20 Dec to 22 Dec	23 Dec to 29 Dec	30 Dec to 3 Jan		
May BH		Short Stays		Weeks	Spr BH		Short Stays		Weeks	Short Stays		Weeks	Aug BH		Short Stays		Weeks	Short Stays		Weeks	Xmas	New Year			
Start Fri 4 nights	Start Tues 3 nights	Start Fri 3 nights	Start Mon 4 nights	Start Fri or Mon 7 nights	Start Fri 4 nights	Start Tues 3 nights	Start Fri 3 nights	Start Mon 4 nights	Start Fri or Mon 7 nights	Start Fri 3 nights	Start Mon 4 nights	Start Fri or Mon 7 nights	Start Fri 4 nights	Start Tues 3 nights	Start Fri 3 nights	Start Mon 4 nights	Start Fri or Mon 7 nights	Start Fri 3 nights	Start Mon 4 nights	Start Fri or Mon 7 nights	Start Mon 3 nights	Start Thurs 7 nights	Start Thurs 5 nights	Sleeps	Property
766	302	714	401	892	920	443	719	421	911	918	781	1359	974	556	772	438	968	523	279	641	251	1350	1231	5	Silverton Park Stables
1073	423	998	561	1249	1288	620	1006	589	1276	1285	1093	1902	1363	779	1081	613	1355	732	391	898	352	1890	1724	7	
1379	544	1285	721	1605	1656	797	1293	757	1641	1652	1405	2445	1752	999	1390	788	1742	941	503	1155	453	2430	2217	9	
1685	665	1571	882	1962	2024	974	1581	926	2005	2019	1718	2989	2142	1223	1699	963	2129	1150	614	1411	553	2970	2709	11	
2145	846	1999	1122	2497	2576	1240	2012	1178	2552	2569	2186	3804	2726	1557	2162	1226	2710	1463	782	1796	704	3780	3448	14	

19 Jun to 30 Jul		31 Jul to 3 Sep		4 Sep to 8 Oct		9 Oct to 29 Oct		30 Oct to 19 Nov		20 Nov to 22 Dec		23 Dec to 29 Dec	30 Dec to 3 Jan		
Per Night*	Weeks	Per Night*	Weeks	Per Night*	Weeks	Per Night*	Weeks	Per Night*	Weeks	Per Night*	Weeks	Xmas	New Year		
												Start Thurs 7 nights	Start Thurs 5 nights	Sleeps	Property
350	1819	338	1754	351	1819	358	1855	298	1545	263	1366	1559	1487	2 + 4	Casa Guidi
360	1873	351	1827	489	2517	496	2555	366	1886	293	1526	1825	1800	3 + 1	Piazza di Spagna
n/a	3966	n/a	3707	n/a	3732	673	3498	402	2074	311	1604	2624	2849	12	Sant'Antonio
813	4229	801	4166	807	4192	710	3696	433	2255	339	1756	2900	2900	16	Villa Saraceno

Bed Arrangements

- S Single room
- T Twin room
- D Double room
- II Triple room
- IV Room with 4 beds
- B Bunk beds
- ( ) Bed or beds in a living room
- u Beds in unheated room – only recommended for summer use

Further Information

))) Visitors to this property have noted that the background level of noise is higher than might be expected; this may be due to location or other factors beyond our control.

Sleeps column

For example: 4 + 2 beds shows that two of the beds are not part of the main building or are of lesser status than the other available beds. Call the Booking Office for clarification.

Silverton Park Stables

Due to the layout of the bedrooms, we are able to offer the building to groups smaller than the full capacity. Future bookings are filling up but for a limited period Landmark is keen to offer the chance for smaller groups to experience Silverton Park Stables.

Silverton is available for groups of 5, 7, 9, 10, 11 or 14 people. You will have the building to yourselves and any additional bedrooms will be closed off.

Prices shown are per property for the period stated and not per person

Property	Sleeps	Beds	Facilities	4 Jan to 7 Feb			8 Feb to 28 Mar			29 Mar to 31 Mar	1 Apr to 5 Apr	6 Apr to 8 Apr	9 Apr to 15 Apr			16 Apr to 29 Apr		
				Short Stays		Weeks	Short Stays		Weeks	Easter			Short Stays		Weeks	Short Stays		Weeks
				Start Fri 3 nights	Start Mon 4 nights	Start Fri or Mon 7 nights	Start Fri 3 nights	Start Mon 4 nights	Start Fri or Mon 7 nights	Start Mon 3 nights	Start Thurs 5 nights	Start Tues 3 nights	Start Fri 3 nights	Start Mon 4 nights	Start Fri or Mon 7 nights	Start Fri 3 nights	Start Mon 4 nights	Start Fri or Mon 7 nights
Silverton Park Stables	5	S T D	🛁x2 🍽️ 📷 🔥 ❋ S	482	229	569	653	363	813	273	958	427	769	439	966	687	391	863
	7	S T 2D	🛁x2 🚿 🍽️ 📷 🔥 ❋ S	675	320	796	914	509	1138	382	1342	598	1077	614	1353	962	548	1208
	9	3S T 2D	🛁x3 🍽️ 📷 🔥 ❋ S	868	411	1023	1175	654	1463	491	1725	769	1385	789	1740	1236	705	1553
	11	3S T 3D	🛁x3 🚿 🍽️ 📷 🔥 ❋ S	1061	503	1251	1436	799	1788	599	2108	940	1692	965	2126	1511	861	1898
	14	3S T 3D III	🛁x3 🚿 🛁 📷 🔥 ❋ S	1350	640	1592	1828	1017	2276	763	2683	1196	2154	1228	2706	1923	1096	2415

Italy (note booking periods are different from British Landmarks)

Bookings for Italian properties can start on any day of the week, except at Sant'Antonio between 8 May and 8 October where weekly bookings only start on a Saturday.

Prices shown are per property for the period stated and not per person

Property	Sleeps	Beds	Facilities	4 Jan to 5 Feb		6 Feb to 19 Mar		20 Mar to 31 Mar		1 Apr to 5 Apr	6 Apr to 7 May		8 May to 18 June	
				Per Night*	Weeks	Per Night*	Weeks	Per Night*	Weeks	Easter Start Thurs 5 nights	Per Night*	Weeks	Per Night*	Weeks
Casa Guidi	2+4	T D B	🚿x3 🅿️ 🐕 📶	239	1236	321	1665	352	1826	1798	363	1883	378	1971
Piazza di Spagna	3+1	S (S) D	🚿 🅿️ 🐕 📶	291	1511	379	1975	453	2356	2484	469	2440	464	2416
Sant'Antonio	12	4T 2D	🛁x3 🚿x2 🍽️ 📷 🔥 ❋ 🐕	n/a	n/a	402	2074	650	3354	3171	747	3884	n/a	4081
Villa Saraceno	16	2S 2T 3D IV	🛁x3 🚿x4 🍽️x2 📷 🔥 ❋	300	1559	404	2099	734	3695	3778	864	4497	870	4525

*Price per night, starting on any day of the week, minimum 3 nights.

Facilities

- 🛁 Bath
- 🚿 Shower
- 🛁 Shower over bath
- 🍽️ Dishwasher
- 📷 Washing machine
- S Washing machine shared between Landmarks
- 🔥 Fire or stove
- Awkward stairs
- ❋ Open grounds, garden or terrace or yard
- 🅿️ Parking may be difficult
- Cot not available
- 🐕 Dogs not allowed
- Remote property or isolated location

30 Apr to 3 May	4 May to 6 May	7 May to 27 May	28 May to 31 May	1 Jun to 3 Jun	4 Jun to 8 Jul	9 Jul to 26 Aug	27 Aug to 30 Aug	31 Aug to 2 Sep	3 Sep to 28 Oct	29 Oct to 19 Dec	20 Dec to 22 Dec	23 Dec to 29 Dec	30 Dec to 3 Jan	Sleeps	Property
May BH	Short Stays	Weeks	Spr BH	Short Stays	Weeks	Short Stays	Weeks	Aug BH	Short Stays	Weeks	Short Stays	Weeks	Xmas	New Year		
Start Fri 4 nights	Start Tues 3 nights	Start Fri 3 nights	Start Mon 4 nights	Start Fri or Mon 7 nights	Start Fri 4 nights	Start Tues 3 nights	Start Fri 3 nights	Start Mon 4 nights	Start Fri or Mon 7 nights	Start Fri 4 nights	Start Tues 3 nights	Start Fri 3 nights	Start Mon 4 nights	Start Fri or Mon 7 nights	Start Fri 3 nights	Start Mon 4 nights	Start Fri or Mon 7 nights	Start Mon 3 nights	Start Thurs 7 nights	Start Thurs 5 nights		

May BH	Short Stays	Weeks	Spr BH	Short Stays	Weeks	Short Stays	Weeks	Aug BH	Short Stays	Weeks	Short Stays	Weeks	Xmas	New Year	Sleeps	Property
																Rhiwddolion
353	168	303	220	418	422	272	334	241	460	460	390	680	488	278	330	240	456	213	144	286	128	559	554	2 + 1	Ty Capel
459	211	389	281	543	540	339	434	312	604	607	517	910	645	367	417	305	585	262	182	360	166	716	710	4	Ty Coch
349	161	294	215	407	408	273	323	233	445	445	381	661	472	271	319	234	442	206	144	280	128	524	521	2	Ty Uchaf
638	323	539	428	774	693	473	615	442	846	751	641	1114	797	456	577	464	833	387	294	545	259	865	859	2	Robin Hood's Hut
																Roslin
631	310	533	408	753	713	470	654	428	866	836	796	1306	936	562	524	413	750	307	222	423	196	1074	1167	6	Collegehill House
1060	516	897	684	1265	1245	876	1131	811	1554	1593	1354	2358	1698	964	957	740	1358	607	446	842	394	1941	2027	7	Rosslyn Castle
583	299	499	396	716	642	433	569	409	782	697	593	1032	739	422	535	431	773	358	272	504	240	809	821	2	The Ruin
1242	516	1034	685	1375	1356	782	1086	729	1452	1333	1133	1973	1421	816	1142	769	1529	855	525	1104	468	2133	2084	8	Sackville House
																Saddell
880	394	663	522	960	961	703	788	683	1192	1488	1266	2231	1610	910	707	559	1025	340	258	484	232	1523	1608	4	Cul na Shee
813	411	733	546	1036	929	797	880	754	1324	1504	1279	2254	1595	907	726	586	1063	331	251	471	228	1541	1642	5	Ferryman's Cottage
1329	594	1043	787	1482	1590	1088	1524	1095	2121	2232	1899	3346	2368	1346	1018	786	1461	619	442	859	394	3170	2805	8	Saddell Castle
1837	854	1512	1133	2142	2480	1590	1977	1477	2798	3195	2718	4790	3389	1918	1519	1148	2160	883	643	1236	567	3174	4060	13	Saddell House
463	233	392	309	568	505	342	398	326	586	607	519	912	646	368	420	332	609	187	142	266	132	814	868	4	Saddell Lodge
994	429	715	568	1039	1305	742	988	710	1375	1724	1466	2584	1830	1041	773	620	1128	378	288	539	265	1671	1781	6	Shore Cottage
350	163	295	217	410	349	218	270	204	379	320	273	474	340	192	307	231	430	202	144	277	129	608	566	4	St Mary's Lane
384	177	323	237	448	449	300	355	256	490	490	419	727	519	298	351	257	486	227	158	308	141	576	573	2	St Winifred's Well
1109	543	1005	720	1380	1293	816	1018	719	1390	1262	1073	1868	1331	737	1066	750	1453	766	498	1011	450	2329	2238	8	Shelwick Court
754	359	638	471	887	846	596	742	558	1040	1079	918	1598	1145	652	692	516	966	395	279	539	246	1099	1069	3 + 2	Shute Gatehouse
																Shuttleworth Estate
581	309	547	412	767	679	443	543	413	765	642	545	950	679	384	568	444	810	407	294	561	259	736	731	4	Keeper's Cottage
552	294	520	391	729	645	424	516	393	727	610	518	902	648	367	545	426	777	387	279	533	246	700	695	2	Queen Anne's SH*
Can be booked for 5–14 people. See page 12–13 for further details.															5–14	Silverton Park Stables
625	306	527	407	757	866	535	710	540	1013	940	892	1484	1049	632	571	438	817	411	295	572	266	1819	1610	7	South Street
517	273	467	363	664	557	371	454	377	665	458	378	669	480	269	505	396	721	388	292	544	260	840	798	2	The Steward's House
584	287	492	380	698	637	423	492	399	713	845	721	1253	893	511	536	416	762	325	239	451	211	1103	1040	6	Stockwell Farm
1023	497	865	659	1219	1114	728	980	703	1346	1369	1164	2026	1452	829	939	723	1330	642	468	888	413	1609	1598	4	Stogursey Castle
411	204	375	269	515	460	295	377	283	527	399	339	590	424	241	407	293	560	288	193	384	170	554	548	2	Stoker's Cottage
505	279	442	371	650	569	410	446	370	653	560	475	828	593	339	471	368	671	320	236	445	208	729	697	2	Swarkestone Pavilion
517	263	434	343	629	729	528	649	461	899	898	763	1345	948	539	472	377	688	256	192	363	169	884	942	6	Tangy Mill
798	374	665	496	929	848	552	676	526	962	816	695	1209	867	489	713	538	1001	510	364	699	331	1461	1460	4 + 2	Tixall Gatehouse
459	231	399	303	562	499	329	402	321	578	493	419	730	524	298	407	340	598	271	202	378	181	695	650	2	The Tower, Canons Ashby
658	307	556	407	780	763	519	680	482	941	914	779	1371	971	552	597	448	846	335	244	469	215	998	982	4 + 2	Tower Hill
713	382	671	507	942	831	548	666	508	939	786	668	1163	837	476	702	551	1002	506	367	698	323	909	902	5	Warden Abbey
766	424	715	560	1020	922	620	741	599	1072	768	624	1114	802	427	753	623	1101	584	447	825	399	1088	1026	4	The Wardrobe
1575	560	1209	743	1562	1587	957	1366	982	1878	2073	1764	3070	2198	1250	1300	781	1665	896	507	1122	447	2753	2639	8	West Blockhouse
1207	572	1075	759	1467	1385	838	1084	796	1504	1376	1171	2038	1461	831	1162	827	1591	829	562	1113	501	2305	2209	8	The White House
495	250	423	334	606	558	368	457	344	641	639	543	946	673	386	436	370	645	275	202	382	179	794	779	2	Whiteford Temple
1258	523	1064	692	1405	1376	767	1077	726	1442	1418	1207	2100	1505	856	1155	755	1528	795	519	1051	458	2083	1979	6	Wilmington Priory
948	459	802	614	1133	1032	678	847	637	1187	1212	1031	1794	1285	732	870	640	1208	628	430	846	379	1674	1667	6	Wolveton Gatehouse
1637	689	1385	913	1838	1785	998	1348	965	1850	2003	1703	2965	2124	1214	1456	974	1944	1062	649	1369	573	2886	2749	8	Woodsford Castle
1476	608	1236	809	1636	1604	850	1210	871	1665	1743	1484	2582	1849	1047	1306	855	1729	1007	603	1288	537	2544	2279	8	Woodspring Priory
3032	1196	2825	1586	3529	3639	1735	2817	1650	3574	3631	3090	5377	3834	2126	2996	1699	3756	2068	1105	2538	975	5291	4826	15	Wortham Manor

Bed Arrangements

- S   Single room
- T   Twin room
- D   Double room
- III Triple room
- IV Room with 4 beds
- B   Bunk beds
- ( ) Bed or beds in a living room
- u   Beds in unheated room – only recommended for summer use

Further Information

H Landmark for hardier visitors. These are equipped as any other Landmarks and are of the same (sometimes greater) architectural and historic interest, but they may be colder or damper.

S Some rooms (including bedrooms or bathrooms) must be reached from outside the main accommodation.

))) Visitors to this property have noted that the background level of noise is higher than might be expected; this may be due to location or other factors beyond our control.

Sleeps column
For example: 4 + 2 beds shows that two of the beds are not part of the main building or are of lesser status than the other available beds. Call the Booking Office for clarification.

Rhiwddolion – Wortham Manor

Prices shown are per property for the period stated and not per person

Property	Sleeps	Beds	Facilities	4 Jan to 7 Feb Short Stays Start Fri 3 nights	4 Jan to 7 Feb Short Stays Start Mon 4 nights	4 Jan to 7 Feb Weeks Start Fri or Mon 7 nights	8 Feb to 28 Mar Short Stays Start Fri 3 nights	8 Feb to 28 Mar Short Stays Start Mon 4 nights	8 Feb to 28 Mar Weeks Start Fri or Mon 7 nights	29 Mar to 31 Mar Start Mon 3 nights	1 Apr to 5 Apr Easter Start Thurs 5 nights	6 Apr to 8 Apr Start Tues 3 nights	9 Apr to 15 Apr Short Stays Start Fri 3 nights	9 Apr to 15 Apr Short Stays Start Mon 4 nights	9 Apr to 15 Apr Weeks Start Fri or Mon 7 nights	16 Apr to 29 Apr Short Stays Start Fri 3 nights	16 Apr to 29 Apr Short Stays Start Mon 4 nights	16 Apr to 29 Apr Weeks Start Fri or Mon 7 nights
Rhiwddolion																		
Ty Capel	2 + 1	III		184	126	248	273	198	377	149	461	234	328	241	455	293	214	406
Ty Coch	4	T D		245	167	334	347	251	484	190	607	304	421	308	590	376	274	527
Ty Uchaf	2	D		177	121	238	266	194	368	145	446	229	315	235	440	281	210	393
Robin Hood's Hut	2	D		340	251	473	461	358	655	265	852	455	577	466	834	515	416	745
Roslin																		
Collegehill House	6	2T D		264	194	366	332	248	464	186	1012	451	542	422	771	484	366	680
Rosslyn Castle	7	S 2T D		556	401	766	801	608	1127	447	1595	732	964	750	1371	861	669	1224
The Ruin	2	D		317	235	442	436	339	620	254	789	422	534	431	772	477	385	690
Sackville House	8	2S 2T D		770	460	984	907	574	1185	422	1499	755	1141	766	1526	1019	681	1360
Saddell																		
Cul na Shee	4	T D		297	220	419	541	426	783	319	1278	556	708	568	1034	632	507	923
Ferryman's Cottage	5	S T D		286	212	403	540	420	778	312	1392	598	684	550	999	611	479	883
Saddell Castle	8	2S 2T D		560	394	773	812	604	1147	451	2165	848	1134	866	1620	1012	766	1440
Saddell House	13	S 4T 2D		708	504	982	1189	888	1682	656	3347	1284	1516	1148	2158	1354	995	1903
Saddell Lodge	4	T D		162	120	228	317	248	458	184	774	335	385	309	562	343	276	501
Shore Cottage	6	2T D		325	245	462	591	463	854	344	1383	609	774	624	1132	691	554	1008
St Mary's Lane	4	2T		168	116	227	256	186	354	140	447	236	319	237	445	285	214	399
St Winifred's Well	2	(T)		195	133	262	293	213	405	160	491	252	347	259	484	309	231	432
Shelwick Court	8	2S 2T D		729	449	942	919	625	1235	462	1386	805	1113	810	1538	994	702	1357
Shute Gatehouse	3 + 2	S D Bu		354	239	474	581	426	806	319	1099	508	690	519	967	616	461	862
Shuttleworth Estate																		
Keeper's Cottage	4	T D		372	260	506	496	368	691	276	738	439	586	424	808	523	379	722
Queen Anne's SH*	2	(D)		355	249	483	476	353	663	265	702	417	556	402	766	496	359	684
Silverton Park Stables	5–14	3S T 3D III		Can be booked for 5–14 people. See page 12–13 for further details.														
South Street	7	S 2T D		360	258	501	425	317	601	234	1068	435	568	446	821	507	398	733
The Steward's House	2	T		338	251	471	421	327	598	244	593	388	479	374	682	428	334	610
Stockwell Farm	6	2T D		279	197	381	396	303	559	227	873	429	538	420	766	480	375	684
Stogursey Castle	4	T D		587	415	802	788	594	1106	446	1306	709	937	726	1330	837	645	1186
Stoker's Cottage	2	D		271	181	361	344	244	471	183	506	288	393	295	550	351	263	491
Swarkestone Pavilion	2	(D)		249	202	361	397	305	562	228	597	360	470	370	672	419	330	599
Tangy Mill	6	2T D		227	163	316	318	246	457	184	879	359	472	378	689	422	336	614
Tixall Gatehouse	4 + 2	2Su T D		479	327	645	608	449	846	337	933	549	712	539	1001	635	479	891
The Tower, Canons Ashby	2	D		232	180	330	341	255	477	191	534	327	429	332	609	383	298	545
Tower Hill	4 + 2	T D B		277	206	391	449	359	654	269	944	440	596	441	840	532	396	752
Warden Abbey	5	D III		463	327	632	609	454	850	335	912	545	725	528	1002	647	467	891
The Wardrobe	4	T D		471	323	635	631	468	879	351	931	584	749	591	1072	669	528	958
West Blockhouse	8	3T D		772	412	947	1098	648	1397	486	1967	795	1307	815	1698	1167	724	1513
The White House	8	2S 2T D		767	503	1016	965	673	1310	495	1526	833	1165	832	1598	1041	739	1424
Whiteford Temple	2	D		227	158	308	375	298	538	220	641	357	448	362	648	399	323	578
Wilmington Priory	6	2T D		664	441	884	946	600	1237	448	1392	751	1149	755	1523	1026	674	1360
Wolveton Gatehouse	6	2T D		544	364	726	722	526	998	389	1189	669	862	670	1226	770	598	1094
Woodsford Castle	8	4S T D		920	546	1173	1240	805	1636	595	1958	974	1490	995	1988	1330	889	1775
Woodspring Priory	8	3T D		886	518	1123	1114	678	1434	508	1744	864	1342	876	1774	1198	782	1584
Wortham Manor	15	S 4T 3D		1909	905	2251	2558	1424	3186	1068	3792	1689	3043	1735	3822	2717	1549	3413

Facilities

- Bath
- Shower
- Shower over bath
- Dishwasher
- Washing machine
- Washing machine shared between Landmarks
- Fire or stove
- Awkward stairs
- Open grounds, garden or terrace or yard
- Parking may be difficult
- Cot not available
- Dogs not allowed
- Remote property or isolated location

* Denotes a new Landmark

30 Apr to 3 May	4 May to 6 May	7 May to 27 May			28 May to 31 May	1 Jun to 3 Jun	4 Jun to 8 Jul			9 Jul to 26 Aug			27 Aug to 30 Aug	31 Aug to 2 Sep	3 Sep to 28 Oct			29 Oct to 19 Dec			20 Dec to 22 Dec	23 Dec to 29 Dec	30 Dec to 3 Jan	Sleeps	Property
May BH		Short Stays		Weeks	Spr BH		Short Stays		Weeks	Short Stays		Weeks	Aug BH		Short Stays		Weeks	Short Stays		Weeks	Xmas	New Year			
Start Fri 4 nights	Start Tues 3 nights	Start Fri 3 nights	Start Mon 4 nights	Start Fri or Mon 7 nights	Start Fri 4 nights	Start Tues 3 nights	Start Fri 3 nights	Start Mon 4 nights	Start Fri or Mon 7 nights	Start Fri 3 nights	Start Mon 4 nights	Start Fri or Mon 7 nights	Start Fri 4 nights	Start Tues 3 nights	Start Fri 3 nights	Start Mon 4 nights	Start Fri or Mon 7 nights	Start Fri 3 nights	Start Mon 4 nights	Start Fri or Mon 7 nights	Start Mon 3 nights	Start Thurs 7 nights	Start Thurs 5 nights		
																									Lower Porthmeor
820	384	694	510	975	963	699	896	646	1249	1243	1058	1864	1319	754	708	561	1028	369	264	513	233	1330	1285	5	Arra Venton
702	330	593	437	834	818	594	830	597	1156	1087	925	1630	1155	659	647	481	914	299	209	411	184	1276	1261	4	The Captain's House
681	319	574	424	808	783	577	837	601	1165	1099	936	1648	1166	666	624	464	881	292	206	403	181	1277	1272	4	The Farmhouse
1372	683	1162	911	1658	1494	1007	1374	992	1893	1739	1481	2576	1845	1241	1251	994	1796	856	611	1174	539	1845	1831	4	Luttrell's Tower
507	252	463	332	636	568	364	465	349	651	493	418	729	523	298	502	362	691	355	238	474	210	684	676	2	Lynch Lodge
453	210	384	280	538	516	340	440	319	615	562	478	842	599	342	374	278	528	226	160	313	143	645	643	4	The Mackintosh Building
692	351	584	463	838	752	511	611	479	872	806	685	1193	855	488	637	468	884	418	319	590	284	910	901	4	Maesyronen Chapel
740	384	626	510	909	809	578	658	544	962	969	824	1434	1028	585	692	564	1005	495	388	706	345	1657	1500	8	Manor Farm
915	476	770	633	1122	993	695	770	659	1143	1425	1212	2110	1511	859	819	667	1189	569	424	794	374	1523	1436	5	Margells
764	401	676	534	968	869	590	645	530	940	655	553	966	696	395	735	624	1087	547	539	869	476	1193	1067	4	Marshal Wade's House
1026	482	867	640	1206	1116	708	870	665	1228	1160	985	1716	1229	702	933	658	1273	683	483	933	426	1311	1301	4	Martello Tower
697	349	605	463	854	778	511	636	460	877	814	693	1206	859	488	641	479	896	461	329	632	290	990	950	5	Methwold Old Vicarage
1048	532	884	707	1273	1201	830	1102	792	1515	1775	1509	2627	1882	1069	950	748	1358	646	493	911	435	1967	1820	7	Monkton Old Hall
1089	551	919	729	1335	1171	815	1052	764	1471	1382	1176	2072	1466	831	1002	793	1454	598	457	855	403	2046	1865	7	Morpeth Castle
406	199	345	262	486	445	290	344	273	494	433	368	641	459	258	341	272	490	244	194	350	173	616	538	2 + 2	The Music Room
																									New Inn
553	264	475	348	658	614	394	488	372	688	752	610	1114	795	454	517	358	700	374	236	488	219	1043	1006	5	The Cottage
515	244	443	324	614	570	356	441	336	622	682	579	1009	724	412	480	329	647	351	222	458	198	936	899	2 + 2	High End
539	255	463	339	642	597	376	466	355	657	711	604	1052	750	428	502	344	677	371	235	485	207	979	942	4	Low End
408	304	396	302	558	492	366	419	316	588	702	589	1033	737	419	442	316	622	227	173	320	156	712	690	2	Nicolle Tower
415	195	351	259	488	452	285	356	272	502	434	369	642	460	262	383	282	532	260	184	355	168	608	585	4	North Street
734	367	621	486	886	797	537	657	506	930	899	764	1330	953	545	669	502	937	514	384	718	339	1286	1247	5	Obriss Farm
																									Old Campden House
897	425	731	563	1035	935	622	872	705	1262	1222	1039	1809	1290	732	874	736	1288	511	383	715	338	1335	1324	4 + 2	East Banqueting House
681	321	554	428	786	709	469	658	532	952	913	775	1350	973	559	693	585	1022	505	379	707	334	1320	1310	2 + 2	West Banqueting House
712	359	601	475	861	775	526	605	500	884	806	686	1194	855	489	652	521	938	416	317	586	282	1081	1056	5	The Old Hall
1437	713	1222	948	1736	1575	1052	1234	998	1786	1428	1216	2115	1516	870	1208	947	1724	876	653	1223	582	2067	2040	6	The Old Parsonage
856	413	723	547	1029	989	679	895	643	1246	1249	1061	1871	1324	753	790	599	1125	425	308	594	275	1497	1596	8	Old Place of Monreith
918	401	758	532	1032	977	586	833	634	1174	1158	985	1714	1228	702	879	654	1226	644	434	862	391	1535	1494	4	Oxenford Gatehouse*
576	281	503	373	701	625	382	572	410	786	739	631	1096	786	447	528	392	736	364	258	498	232	938	916	4	Parish House
597	310	508	410	734	656	464	573	427	800	775	658	1146	821	464	547	442	791	336	248	467	221	913	889	5	Paxton's Tower Lodge
548	280	499	365	691	619	380	499	380	703	606	515	897	642	368	536	396	746	367	258	499	230	1003	990	4	Peake's House
																									Peppercombe
649	309	545	411	775	719	505	729	524	1016	970	867	1488	1082	617	594	451	846	351	254	491	224	813	808	3	Bridge Cottage
865	412	727	548	1033	958	673	972	699	1354	1293	1156	1984	1442	823	792	601	1128	468	339	654	299	1084	1077	2 + 2	Castle Bungalow
355	181	300	242	434	386	265	318	248	453	366	308	539	386	219	321	237	446	219	164	306	148	530	513	2	Peters Tower
587	309	530	410	752	671	456	571	457	822	656	560	973	697	397	591	473	851	337	253	472	224	819	780	2	The Pigsty
775	379	655	505	928	809	535	740	524	1011	960	817	1422	1019	579	701	544	996	353	249	482	220	1142	1119	4	The Pineapple
602	276	517	366	706	666	403	529	380	727	702	598	1040	745	425	557	397	763	262	176	350	158	837	813	4	Plas Uchaf
526	266	443	351	635	572	387	476	363	671	640	543	946	679	387	483	363	677	339	257	477	229	896	849	4	Poultry Cottage
619	313	523	414	750	652	447	587	414	801	755	643	1118	802	456	556	450	805	373	296	535	261	1075	1024	5	The Priest's House
950	645	859	856	1372	1065	908	905	870	1420	880	855	1388	993	595	945	946	1513	815	788	1282	695	1485	1112	6	Princelet Street
746	373	616	496	890	752	512	627	520	918	797	678	1180	842	483	665	539	963	502	376	702	332	947	913	2	The Prospect Tower
601	315	525	419	755	723	528	672	479	921	879	748	1302	929	515	564	449	810	342	256	478	235	1048	1024	4	Purton Green

Bed Arrangements

- S Single room
- T Twin room
- D Double room
- Ⅱ Triple room
- V Room with 4 beds
- 3 Bunk beds
- ( ) Bed or beds in a living room
- u Beds in unheated room – only recommended for summer use

Further Information

H Landmark for hardier visitors. These are equipped as any other Landmarks and are of the same (sometimes greater) architectural and historic interest, but they may be colder or damper.

S Some rooms (including bedrooms or bathrooms) must be reached from outside the main accommodation.

))) Visitors to this property have noted that the background level of noise is higher than might be expected; this may be due to location or other factors beyond our control.

Sleeps column
For example: 4 + 2 beds shows that two of the beds are not part of the main building or are of lesser status than the other available beds. Call the Booking Office for clarification.

Lower Porthmeor – Purton Green

Prices shown are per property for the period stated and not per person

Property	Sleeps	Beds	Facilities	4 Jan to 7 Feb Short Stays Start Fri 3 nights	4 Jan to 7 Feb Short Stays Start Mon 4 nights	4 Jan to 7 Feb Weeks Start Fri or Mon 7 nights	8 Feb to 28 Mar Short Stays Start Fri 3 nights	8 Feb to 28 Mar Short Stays Start Mon 4 nights	8 Feb to 28 Mar Weeks Start Fri or Mon 7 nights	29 Mar to 31 Mar Start Fri 3 nights	1 Apr to 5 Apr Easter Start Thurs 5 nights	6 Apr to 8 Apr Start Tues 3 nights	9 Apr to 15 Apr Short Stays Start Fri 3 nights	9 Apr to 15 Apr Short Stays Start Mon 4 nights	9 Apr to 15 Apr Weeks Start Fri or Mon 7 nights	16 Apr to 29 Apr Short Stays Start Fri 3 nights	16 Apr to 29 Apr Short Stays Start Mon 4 nights	16 Apr to 29 Apr Weeks Start Fri or Mon 7 nights
Lower Porthmeor																		
Arra Venton	5	S T D		336	227	456	599	436	838	327	1231	549	750	562	1063	670	499	947
The Captain's House	4	T D		251	167	339	530	385	741	283	1048	467	642	471	902	573	418	803
The Farmhouse	4	T D		245	168	335	513	372	717	278	1010	451	619	459	873	553	410	780
Luttrell's Tower	4	T D		775	523	1038	1062	828	1512	621	1792	976	1240	997	1790	1107	890	1598
Lynch Lodge	2	D		334	224	446	425	301	581	226	625	355	485	364	679	433	325	606
The Mackintosh Building	4	T D		195	134	266	311	221	431	162	611	296	411	305	580	367	272	518
Maesyronen Chapel	4	T D		360	266	501	537	419	765	313	834	496	630	505	908	562	451	810
Manor Farm	8	2S 2T D		436	331	614	568	461	823	342	1044	603	693	575	1014	619	498	894
Margells	5	S T D		526	377	722	681	552	986	408	1398	683	838	698	1229	748	626	1099
Marshal Wade's House	4	T D		503	372	699	617	485	882	364	909	574	729	587	1053	651	521	938
Martello Tower	4	2T		617	421	830	793	581	1099	434	1163	684	927	699	1301	828	625	1162
Methwold Old Vicarage	5	S T D		399	282	545	493	366	687	273	797	491	655	497	922	585	441	821
Monkton Old Hall	7	S 2T D		579	422	801	805	635	1152	477	1506	760	956	778	1387	854	691	1236
Morpeth Castle	7	S 2T D		546	396	763	824	648	1192	484	1494	786	1000	802	1460	893	709	1298
The Music Room	2 + 2	T D		208	165	298	300	234	427	176	504	286	360	285	516	321	253	459
New Inn																		
The Cottage	5	S T D		349	213	450	437	292	583	217	746	388	533	396	743	476	345	657
High End	2 + 2	D B		324	197	417	407	275	546	206	675	352	484	360	675	432	321	602
Low End	4	T D		330	199	423	428	287	572	216	708	369	507	376	706	453	336	631
Nicolle Tower	2	D		170	130	240	293	223	413	170	752	309	428	326	603	382	293	540
North Street	4	T D		221	163	307	323	223	437	167	513	293	381	284	532	341	253	475
Obriss Farm	5	S T D		505	367	698	606	464	856	348	901	520	669	531	960	597	475	858
Old Campden House																		
East Banqueting House	4 + 2	T Tu D		448	334	626	490	381	697	371	1125	592	764	599	1090	682	533	972
West Banqueting House	2 + 2	T D		443	330	618	485	377	690	283	849	446	578	454	826	516	405	737
The Old Hall	5	D III		354	260	491	542	426	774	314	827	508	646	520	933	577	464	833
The Old Parsonage	6	2T D		874	628	1202	1115	839	1563	629	1595	1011	1317	1032	1879	1176	922	1678
Old Place of Monreith	8	2T 2D		362	258	502	615	461	872	349	1279	587	781	599	1118	697	535	998
Oxenford Gatehouse*	4	T D		589	392	785	670	463	906	347	1114	562	808	574	1106	721	512	986
Parish House	4	T D		324	219	434	412	323	588	238	793	399	540	397	750	483	354	670
Paxton's Tower Lodge	5	D III		313	226	431	432	345	622	261	818	438	550	449	799	491	401	714
Peake's House	4	T D		332	224	445	435	316	601	237	734	395	546	405	761	487	362	679
Peppercombe																		
Bridge Cottage	3	S D		305	213	420	494	368	699	272	1018	440	591	449	842	528	401	752
Castle Bungalow	2 + 2	D B		407	284	560	659	491	932	362	1357	587	788	598	1123	704	534	1003
Peters Tower	2	B		199	150	279	268	213	385	160	437	256	322	263	468	288	236	419
The Pigsty	2	D		284	207	393	459	354	650	265	693	449	572	458	824	511	407	734
The Pineapple	4	T D		323	219	434	558	426	787	319	1035	535	702	547	999	627	491	894
Plas Uchaf	4	T D		225	147	298	430	295	580	222	729	391	552	398	760	493	355	678
Poultry Cottage	4	2S D		281	203	387	398	315	570	232	701	377	481	385	693	430	342	618
The Priest's House	5	S T D		318	269	470	435	336	617	248	842	449	571	458	823	510	405	732
Princelet Street	6	2T D		723	679	1122	838	838	1341	628	1170	881	940	949	1511	839	834	1338
The Prospect Tower	2	D		469	347	653	575	450	820	337	854	531	679	543	978	606	485	873
Purton Green	4	T D		318	221	431	436	346	626	261	955	446	556	441	798	496	394	712

Facilities

- Bath
- Dishwasher
- Fire or stove
- Parking may be difficult
- Remote property or isolated location
- Shower
- Washing machine
- Awkward stairs
- Cot not available
- Shower over bath
- Washing machine shared between Landmarks
- Open grounds, garden or terrace or yard
- Dogs not allowed

* Denotes a new Landmark

	30 Apr to 3 May	4 May to 6 May	7 May to 27 May		28 May to 31 May	1 Jun to 3 Jun	4 Jun to 8 Jul		9 Jul to 26 Aug		27 Aug to 30 Aug	31 Aug to 2 Sep	3 Sep to 28 Oct		29 Oct to 19 Dec		20 Dec to 22 Dec	23 Dec to 29 Dec	30 Dec to 3 Jan		
	May BH	Short Stays	Short Stays	Weeks	Spr BH	Short Stays	Short Stays	Weeks	Short Stays	Weeks	Aug BH	Short Stays	Short Stays	Weeks	Short Stays	Weeks	Xmas		New Year	Sleeps	Property
	Start Fri 4 nights	Start Tues 3 nights	Start Fri 3 nights	Start Mon 4 nights	Start Fri or Mon 7 nights	Start Fri 4 nights	Start Tues 3 nights	Start Fri 3 nights	Start Mon 4 nights	Start Fri or Mon 7 nights	Start Fri 3 nights	Start Mon 4 nights	Start Fri or Mon 7 nights	Start Fri 4 nights	Start Tues 3 nights	Start Fri 3 nights	Start Mon 4 nights	Start Fri or Mon 7 nights	Start Fri 3 nights	Start Mon 4 nights	Start Fri or Mon 7 nights	Start Mon 3 nights	Start Thurs 7 nights	Start Thurs 5 nights		
912	433	774	574	1078	1001	631	862	624	1189	1152	979	1705	1226	705	816	628	1155	553	502	844	443	1371	1362	4	Culloden Tower
678	335	570	445	812	741	544	674	485	927	958	816	1419	1017	579	613	489	882	292	223	412	199	1014	959	4	Danescombe Mine
913	410	770	546	1053	993	604	791	571	1090	1026	945	1577	1124	670	844	603	1158	481	331	650	297	1443	1429	6	Dolbelydr
495	232	418	310	582	552	382	499	360	687	590	502	874	629	360	455	340	636	294	208	402	185	818	797	4	Edale Mill
																									The Egyptian House
407	188	344	250	481	441	269	344	263	492	475	405	713	506	291	361	266	508	215	148	294	133	590	540	3	First Floor
396	185	334	245	469	432	274	348	265	497	509	432	762	536	306	344	258	488	207	146	286	130	646	600	4	Second Floor
432	202	365	268	513	472	296	376	290	539	522	443	782	551	317	376	280	531	221	156	305	142	659	612	4	Third Floor
1293	529	1091	701	1434	1365	767	1121	700	1457	1191	912	1682	1201	773	1142	777	1535	854	672	1221	602	2462	2216	10	Elton House
																									Endsleigh
917	462	776	613	1111	1001	728	955	685	1312	1271	1080	1881	1348	767	832	661	1194	442	336	622	297	1504	1490	5	Pond Cottage
741	369	626	490	893	832	592	843	606	1159	1041	885	1541	1111	638	677	540	974	389	296	548	267	1227	1164	2+2	Swiss Cottage
1170	546	989	725	1371	1277	844	1164	842	1605	1677	1427	2483	1780	1017	1059	786	1476	781	551	1066	491	2064	2004	6	Field House
1699	931	1402	1068	2001	1983	1256	1733	1301	2458	2706	2303	4057	2549	1641	1284	979	1833	1100	837	1569	753	2533	2492	13	Fort Clonque
831	338	694	448	914	901	495	716	513	983	991	842	1466	1046	598	752	488	992	558	337	716	298	1186	1127	2+2	Fox Hall
872	441	738	585	1072	972	655	1076	782	1505	1319	1122	1977	1400	800	763	595	1100	382	300	552	265	1360	1348	4	Frenchman's Creek
825	413	693	549	994	891	607	702	575	1022	945	805	1400	1003	573	752	590	1074	543	411	763	366	1128	1087	4	Freston Tower
2514	1081	2104	1431	2863	2605	1636	2266	1650	3172	2616	2224	3920	2773	1508	2238	1522	3046	1423	923	1900	815	4795	5009	16	Gargunnock House
504	257	437	342	623	559	376	472	364	669	571	486	846	606	345	478	381	687	296	221	414	197	684	666	2	Glenmalloch Lodge
3234	1612	2766	2137	3922	3316	2201	3303	2439	4594	3460	2943	5122	3764	2151	3006	2209	4172	1913	1529	2754	1362	5759	4892	12	Goddards
1089	544	920	723	1314	1184	798	1021	749	1416	1148	978	1701	1219	696	994	774	1414	685	470	924	415	1593	1582	4	Gothic Temple
460	263	381	350	585	506	424	388	363	601	640	544	947	676	388	419	380	639	273	253	421	224	858	903	4	The Grammar School
1449	663	1185	881	1653	1541	886	1335	993	1862	1573	1338	2329	1661	949	1269	877	1749	951	668	1295	598	2768	2688	8	The Grange
1661	620	1402	817	1775	1806	935	1457	1012	1975	2073	1763	3069	2199	1256	1517	896	1930	1185	629	1451	555	2909	2733	9	Gurney Manor
																									Hampton Court Palace
1271	707	1074	936	1608	1382	1032	1230	970	1760	1571	1335	2325	1667	1027	1182	948	1704	915	783	1358	691	2489	2477	6	Fish Court
1536	850	1300	1129	1943	1672	1247	1525	1171	2157	2079	1769	3078	2173	1273	1433	1177	2088	1038	864	1522	770	3095	2837	8	The Georgian House
673	338	577	449	821	746	502	666	479	916	904	768	1338	963	546	610	477	870	271	205	381	182	992	1036	6	The Hill House
810	444	763	590	1082	984	659	776	627	1122	908	774	1346	964	545	825	646	1177	588	436	819	385	1354	1342	2+2	Hole Cottage
579	291	487	385	698	629	427	491	405	717	582	517	879	645	261	517	419	749	378	283	529	250	727	703	2	Houghton West Lodge
630	318	537	418	764	691	464	548	445	794	648	552	960	685	393	584	458	834	415	313	582	279	874	872	4	The House of Correction
1351	635	1142	844	1609	1470	933	1329	956	1851	1819	1548	2727	1929	1102	1234	877	1746	738	525	1023	473	2139	2095	8	Howthwaite
938	448	793	595	1110	1020	653	779	589	1094	953	811	1411	1011	574	853	621	1179	612	416	822	367	1468	1394	6	Ingestre Pavilion
567	278	482	368	680	619	408	488	388	700	597	509	885	633	364	514	392	725	363	265	502	235	835	830	4	Iron Bridge House
1426	677	1206	898	1683	1553	993	1495	1157	2122	1921	1632	2842	2037	1164	1192	897	1671	685	485	936	428	1928	1883	4	Kingswear Castle
733	339	620	450	856	798	500	689	495	947	877	746	1298	935	532	661	490	921	363	255	494	227	1028	1020	5	Knowle Hill
786	382	669	508	942	844	542	694	500	955	975	828	1442	1034	585	708	542	998	516	379	716	348	1362	1274	6	Langley Gatehouse
757	396	672	525	958	867	578	672	549	977	859	732	1273	910	520	710	570	1024	488	344	666	309	1041	1012	4	Laughton Place
602	281	509	373	706	656	413	589	426	812	710	604	1051	749	429	552	406	766	365	257	498	231	1032	996	4	Lengthsman's Cottage
																									Lettaford
469	203	398	268	533	518	333	415	296	569	558	499	846	624	355	431	295	581	264	189	362	167	670	657	2	The Chapel
867	411	733	546	1036	945	641	858	615	1193	1135	965	1701	1203	685	792	568	1102	470	334	651	298	1766	1666	7	Higher Lettaford
673	341	569	453	828	772	538	716	524	1004	985	838	1477	1045	495	591	477	865	372	285	532	254	1279	1273	5	Sanders
604	301	517	399	733	665	442	619	451	856	799	680	1183	848	485	580	450	824	244	185	343	163	562	543	2+2	The Library
588	274	496	363	687	640	397	565	408	778	688	587	1020	731	415	536	395	745	354	248	482	224	1002	966	4	Lock Cottage

Bed Arrangements

- S Single room
- T Twin room
- D Double room
- II Triple room
- V Room with 4 beds
- B Bunk beds
- ( ) Bed or beds in a living room
- u Beds in unheated room – only recommended for summer use

Further Information

H Landmark for hardier visitors. These are equipped as any other Landmarks and are of the same (sometimes greater) architectural and historic interest, but they may be colder or damper.

S Some rooms (including bedrooms or bathrooms) must be reached from outside the main accommodation.

))) Visitors to this property have noted that the background level of noise is higher than might be expected; this may be due to location or other factors beyond our control.

Sleeps column
For example: 4 + 2 beds shows that two of the beds are not part of the main building or are of lesser status than the other available beds. Call the Booking Office for clarification.

Culloden Tower – Lock Cottage

Prices shown are per property for the period stated and not per person

Property	Sleeps	Beds	Facilities	4 Jan to 7 Feb Short Stays Start Fri 3 nights	4 Jan to 7 Feb Short Stays Start Mon 4 nights	4 Jan to 7 Feb Weeks Start Fri or Mon 7 nights	8 Feb to 28 Mar Short Stays Start Fri 3 nights	8 Feb to 28 Mar Short Stays Start Mon 4 nights	8 Feb to 28 Mar Weeks Start Fri or Mon 7 nights	29 Mar to 31 Mar Start Mon 3 nights	1 Apr to 5 Apr Easter Start Thurs 5 nights	6 Apr to 8 Apr Start Tues 3 nights	9 Apr to 15 Apr Short Stays Start Fri 3 nights	9 Apr to 15 Apr Short Stays Start Mon 4 nights	9 Apr to 15 Apr Weeks Start Fri or Mon 7 nights	16 Apr to 29 Apr Short Stays Start Fri 3 nights	16 Apr to 29 Apr Short Stays Start Mon 4 nights	16 Apr to 29 Apr Weeks Start Fri or Mon 7 nights
Culloden Tower	4	T D		509	476	788	713	522	988	390	1190	615	840	621	1169	750	552	1042
Danescombe Mine	4	T D		258	186	355	479	367	677	275	932	477	605	487	874	540	435	780
Dolbelydr	6	2T D		409	284	554	679	473	922	352	1194	593	836	594	1144	746	528	1019
Edale Mill	4	T D		269	182	361	369	265	507	199	713	344	452	337	631	404	301	564
The Egyptian House																		
First Floor	3	S T		171	156	265	265	193	371	143	505	270	374	276	527	334	248	471
Second Floor	4	T D		180	176	288	262	187	364	140	497	267	365	272	516	326	243	461
Third Floor	4	T D		189	192	309	287	205	399	153	545	292	399	299	565	358	265	505
Elton House	10	2S 3T D		788	552	1072	1003	676	1343	504	1609	900	1178	807	1588	1052	721	1418
Endsleigh																		
Pond Cottage	5	S T D		377	278	524	690	541	985	398	1276	654	829	668	1198	740	599	1071
Swiss Cottage	2 + 2	D B		329	245	459	568	445	810	334	1064	527	671	536	966	599	481	864
Field House	6	2T D		724	496	976	877	635	1210	477	1611	775	1061	792	1482	948	710	1326
Fort Clonque	13	5T III		881	812	1371	877	685	1265	514	2583	873	1191	907	1699	1063	810	1517
Fox Hall	2 + 2	T (D)		527	315	674	609	380	791	281	991	482	757	492	999	676	437	890
Frenchman's Creek	4	T D		362	267	509	634	519	934	387	1321	626	794	638	1160	709	570	1036
Freston Tower	4	T D		504	368	698	639	499	910	373	943	589	749	599	1078	669	536	964
Gargunnock House	16	5T 3D		1149	753	1541	1809	1211	2446	895	3239	1484	2110	1440	2876	1884	1325	2599
Glenmalloch Lodge	2	(D)		257	188	356	386	298	547	224	617	365	470	375	676	420	335	604
Goddards	12	4S 2T 2D		1615	1348	2370	2519	1823	3474	1367	4007	2285	2975	2298	4218	2657	2052	3767
Gothic Temple	4	2D		617	448	852	789	580	1095	433	1282	773	991	790	1425	885	705	1272
The Grammar School	4	T D		229	198	342	354	314	534	235	708	379	422	388	648	377	347	579
The Grange	8	2T 2D		882	608	1192	1110	805	1532	601	2021	960	1316	984	1840	1175	879	1643
Gurney Manor	9	S 2T 2D		1053	524	1262	1280	729	1607	547	2072	909	1513	884	1918	1351	789	1712
Hampton Court Palace																		
Fish Court	6	2S T D		759	648	1126	969	839	1446	629	1694	987	1184	1046	1784	1057	939	1597
The Georgian House	8	2S 2T D		912	753	1332	1155	994	1719	760	2102	1202	1435	1267	2162	1281	1137	1934
The Hill House	6	2T D		237	170	326	437	337	619	247	957	499	617	487	883	551	437	790
Hole Cottage	2 + 2	D B		526	378	723	699	536	988	402	1034	640	829	652	1185	740	577	1054
Houghton West Lodge	2	D		327	242	455	449	350	639	261	665	409	527	419	757	470	376	677
The House of Correction	4	T D		346	280	501	475	377	682	278	805	502	582	463	836	520	411	745
Howthwaite	8	2T 2D		638	397	838	1046	766	1468	575	1746	905	1230	923	1744	1098	824	1557
Ingestre Pavilion	6	2T D		551	362	730	667	477	915	362	1108	662	854	630	1187	763	562	1060
Iron Bridge House	4	T D		318	242	448	433	333	613	247	741	424	523	408	744	467	363	664
Kingswear Castle	4	T D		696	468	931	1042	764	1445	573	1836	955	1308	994	1842	1168	888	1645
Knowle Hill	5	S T D		325	205	424	503	359	690	269	950	488	673	499	938	601	441	834
Langley Gatehouse	6	2T D		477	335	650	566	427	794	315	1067	547	725	559	1027	647	494	913
Laughton Place	4	2T		413	278	553	586	430	813	322	903	571	735	583	1054	657	520	942
Lengthsman's Cottage	4	T D		338	231	455	463	336	639	252	875	435	550	411	769	491	365	685
Lettaford																		
The Chapel	2	(T)		230	162	314	320	218	430	163	608	286	427	292	575	381	260	513
Higher Lettaford	7	S T 2D		384	265	526	581	427	816	314	1176	665	792	601	1128	707	534	1005
Sanders	5	S T D		322	233	450	476	372	687	274	981	488	618	499	905	552	443	806
The Library	2 + 2	Tu D		281	218	399	454	346	640	260	822	443	553	434	790	494	389	706
Lock Cottage	4	T D		329	225	443	449	326	620	246	844	420	531	397	742	474	356	664

Facilities

- Bath
- Shower
- Shower over bath
- Dishwasher
- Washing machine
- Washing machine shared between Landmarks
- Fire or stove
- Awkward stairs
- Open grounds, garden or terrace or yard
- Parking may be difficult
- Cot not available
- Dogs not allowed
- Remote property or isolated location
- * Denotes a new Landmark

30 Apr to 3 May	4 May to 6 May	7 May to 27 May		28 May to 31 May	1 Jun to 3 Jun	4 Jun to 8 Jul			9 Jul to 26 Aug			27 Aug to 30 Aug	31 Aug to 2 Sep	3 Sep to 28 Oct			29 Oct to 19 Dec			20 Dec to 22 Dec	23 Dec to 29 Dec	30 Dec to 3 Jan	Sleeps	Property
May BH		Short Stays	Weeks	Spr BH		Short Stays		Weeks	Short Stays		Weeks	Aug BH		Short Stays		Weeks	Short Stays		Weeks	Xmas	New Year			
Start Fri 4 nights	Start Tues 3 nights	Start Fri 3 nights	Start Mon 4 nights	Start Fri or Mon 7 nights	Start Fri 4 nights	Start Tues 3 nights	Start Fri 3 nights	Start Mon 4 nights	Start Fri or Mon 7 nights	Start Fri 3 nights	Start Mon 4 nights	Start Fri or Mon 7 nights	Start Fri 4 nights	Start Tues 3 nights	Start Fri 3 nights	Start Mon 4 nights	Start Fri or Mon 7 nights	Start Fri 3 nights	Start Mon 4 nights	Start Fri or Mon 7 nights	Start Mon 3 nights	Start Thurs 7 nights	Start Thurs 5 nights		
572	297	513	394	726	615	433	538	449	790	534	455	791	563	322	571	454	820	392	288	544	257	720	702	2	Abbey Gatehouse
762	370	646	492	910	833	542	692	510	962	939	798	1390	914	476	709	526	981	430	332	610	293	1262	1226	8	Alton Station
618	309	520	410	744	644	451	522	432	763	591	503	875	627	359	540	445	788	415	322	590	284	853	804	2	The Ancient House
848	412	691	546	1002	904	618	799	570	1109	1282	1090	1921	1361	778	708	562	1029	485	365	689	319	1348	1308	5	Anderton House
957	466	809	615	1139	1043	679	840	634	1179	1148	979	1702	1220	698	844	621	1172	606	446	842	394	1324	1276	2 + 2	Appleton Water Tower
																									Ascog
929	415	747	551	1051	991	678	921	661	1281	1397	1187	2093	1481	837	875	640	1227	412	299	576	264	2006	2074	7 + 2	Ascog House
1008	465	834	617	1175	1074	693	951	685	1325	1470	1250	2203	1560	869	902	672	1275	461	326	637	288	2071	2098	10	Meikle Ascog
2117	904	1790	1199	2391	2305	1319	1986	1384	2696	2701	2297	3998	2865	1596	1853	1234	2470	1141	746	1510	658	3976	3725	13	Auchinleck House
664	347	560	459	815	737	514	652	492	915	839	712	1241	887	508	600	494	875	407	315	578	278	993	984	2 + 2	The Banqueting House
621	308	535	410	756	688	453	540	427	774	628	535	930	667	381	573	406	783	393	286	543	252	801	774	2	The Bath House
670	321	579	427	805	749	471	634	469	882	881	750	1305	935	528	628	441	855	319	228	438	203	1131	1118	5	Bath Tower
886	425	747	562	1047	960	616	876	652	1222	1148	977	1700	1223	695	799	607	1125	544	396	752	349	1442	1419	5	Beamsley Hospital
755	381	632	506	910	814	564	664	550	971	901	768	1335	952	546	691	545	989	513	390	722	344	1152	1021	4	Beckford's Tower
867	450	742	597	1085	946	658	831	697	1238	1311	1116	1966	1391	795	774	650	1153	374	290	538	256	1464	1358	4	Brinkburn Mill
867	421	727	556	1039	932	612	832	597	1157	1062	904	1592	1127	638	788	603	1127	563	417	794	379	1465	1364	6	Bromfield Priory GH
448	234	388	311	559	498	342	369	299	534	529	451	784	562	321	417	321	590	282	205	390	185	764	750	5	Calverley Old Hall
788	376	663	503	942	899	608	792	579	1111	1148	978	1722	1219	693	723	549	1030	457	331	638	295	1749	1517	7	Castle of Park
597	308	503	409	730	649	450	590	425	812	710	604	1051	752	431	542	443	788	247	191	350	169	1009	992	2 + 2	Causeway House
2458	1225	2102	1624	2981	2520	1673	2510	1854	3491	2630	2237	3893	2861	1635	2285	1679	3171	1454	1162	2093	1035	4377	3718	12	Cavendish Hall*
524	292	461	385	677	592	426	516	399	732	631	538	935	673	384	497	392	711	309	246	444	219	856	845	2 + 2	Cawood Castle
655	330	540	437	782	696	480	527	405	746	603	513	893	651	393	575	449	819	388	304	554	268	901	883	2	The Château
570	265	479	350	663	663	427	587	422	807	785	669	1163	834	478	523	383	725	288	204	394	180	976	950	4	Church Cottage
709	354	585	471	846	714	486	596	494	872	757	644	1121	799	459	632	512	915	477	357	667	315	911	867	2	Clavell Tower
																									Cloth Fair
745	499	678	663	1073	872	754	696	672	1094	637	614	998	809	462	714	713	1142	629	593	978	523	876	809	2	43 Cloth Fair
918	623	829	827	1325	1030	884	841	875	1373	927	790	1374	1041	591	920	922	1474	788	762	1240	672	1160	1076	4	45a Cloth Fair
1403	662	1186	878	1651	1527	975	1229	916	1716	1524	1422	2357	1771	1008	1285	926	1769	905	629	1227	555	2077	2044	6	Clytha Castle
597	277	505	370	709	734	523	701	505	977	982	835	1472	1040	592	569	418	799	279	197	386	176	1113	1096	5	The College
																									Coombe
738	354	623	468	884	869	652	773	589	1103	1305	1110	1956	1385	791	701	553	1016	330	239	461	215	1353	1333	4	The Carpenter's Shop
552	265	467	350	662	651	484	583	444	832	1043	887	1563	1106	632	521	413	757	247	177	343	158	1082	1061	4	Chapel Cottage
724	348	612	461	869	856	625	760	580	1085	1308	1113	1961	1388	792	672	532	975	314	227	438	202	1318	1294	6	Coombe Corner
720	349	612	463	871	839	634	752	574	1074	1260	1072	1889	1335	759	673	536	979	360	262	504	235	1211	1190	2 + 2	Ford Cottage
695	333	587	441	833	813	609	722	550	1030	1231	1048	1846	1306	743	642	507	931	320	228	444	205	1224	1203	5	1 Hawkers Cottages
781	374	658	498	936	909	684	829	633	1184	1396	1188	2093	1482	842	727	570	1051	344	252	483	224	1402	1380	6	2 Hawkers Cottages
624	307	528	399	751	724	540	644	491	919	1119	953	1678	1188	676	583	461	846	293	212	409	189	1225	1205	4	1 Mill House
520	249	443	332	620	619	462	524	398	738	910	775	1348	966	549	488	382	696	237	172	327	158	999	973	3	2 Mill House
676	331	569	441	808	732	491	579	465	835	733	624	1086	778	444	622	485	886	390	284	539	256	871	825	3	Coop House
842	404	710	534	995	912	585	832	619	1161	1091	928	1615	1162	660	759	577	1069	517	376	714	332	1370	1348	5	Cowside*
767	375	647	495	914	834	544	645	468	890	984	838	1458	1045	591	693	532	980	502	364	693	331	1407	1316	8	Crownhill Fort

Bed Arrangements

- Single room
- Twin room
- Double room
- l Triple room
- / Room with 4 beds
- Bunk beds
- ( ) Bed or beds in a living room
- u Beds in unheated room – only recommended for summer use

Further Information

H Landmark for hardier visitors. These are equipped as any other Landmarks and are of the same (sometimes greater) architectural and historic interest, but they may be colder or damper.

S Some rooms (including bedrooms or bathrooms) must be reached from outside the main accommodation.

))) Visitors to this property have noted that the background level of noise is higher than might be expected; this may be due to location or other factors beyond our control.

Sleeps column
For example: 4 + 2 beds shows that two of the beds are not part of the main building or are of lesser status than the other available beds. Call the Booking Office for clarification.

Landmarks in Britain

Abbey Gatehouse – Crownhill Fort

Prices shown are per property for the period stated and not per person

Property	Sleeps	Beds	Facilities	4 Jan to 7 Feb Short Stays Start Fri 3 nights	4 Jan to 7 Feb Short Stays Start Mon 4 nights	4 Jan to 7 Feb Weeks Start Fri or Mon 7 nights	8 Feb to 28 Mar Short Stays Start Fri 3 nights	8 Feb to 28 Mar Short Stays Start Mon 4 nights	8 Feb to 28 Mar Weeks Start Fri or Mon 7 nights	29 Mar to 31 Mar Start Mon 3 nights	1 Apr to 5 Apr Easter Start Thurs 5 nights	6 Apr to 8 Apr Start Tues 3 nights	9 Apr to 15 Apr Short Stays Start Fri 3 nights	9 Apr to 15 Apr Short Stays Start Mon 4 nights	9 Apr to 15 Apr Weeks Start Fri or Mon 7 nights	16 Apr to 29 Apr Short Stays Start Fri 3 nights	16 Apr to 29 Apr Short Stays Start Mon 4 nights	16 Apr to 29 Apr Weeks Start Fri or Mon 7 nights
Abbey Gatehouse	2	T		330	260	472	486	354	672	265	692	419	550	429	783	491	383	699
Alton Station	8	2T 2D	H S	367	281	518	592	451	834	336	978	545	697	541	990	622	480	882
The Ancient House	2	D		374	290	531	465	362	662	272	691	436	558	438	797	498	391	711
Anderton House	5	S T D		445	328	626	569	432	811	324	1135	615	702	559	1021	627	499	912
Appleton Water Tower	2 + 2	T (D)	H	541	405	757	720	543	1010	407	1172	656	870	672	1234	777	601	1102
Ascog																		
Ascog House	7 + 2	S 3T D	x3 S	349	243	480	612	447	858	329	1329	648	776	584	1102	693	501	967
Meikle Ascog	10	2S 2T 2D	x2	391	267	533	643	474	905	348	1384	678	801	609	1142	716	544	1021
Auchinleck House	13	S 4T 2D	x4 x2	958	633	1273	1516	979	1996	719	2752	1279	1822	1240	2450	1627	1113	2192
The Banqueting House	2 + 2	(T) D		353	268	497	457	349	645	263	930	491	602	502	883	538	449	790
The Bath House	2	(D)		364	248	490	477	360	670	270	752	489	575	448	818	513	399	730
Bath Tower	5	D III		273	164	350	499	360	687	268	872	465	631	470	881	564	415	783
Beamsley Hospital	5	S T D		453	317	616	665	491	925	369	1254	597	805	615	1136	719	549	1014
Beckford's Tower	4	T D		473	347	656	588	461	839	346	929	544	690	556	997	616	494	888
Brinkburn Mill	4	T D		357	267	505	680	545	992	407	1334	638	790	651	1167	705	581	1042
Bromfield Priory GH	6	2T D		544	380	748	653	487	923	358	1163	596	793	608	1135	708	540	1011
Calverley Old Hall	5	S T D		238	172	328	354	261	492	196	593	332	415	341	605	370	304	539
Castle of Park	7	S 2T D	x3	396	276	544	594	443	840	326	1230	544	714	544	1019	637	488	911
Causeway House	2 + 2	Tu D	H	193	145	270	361	298	527	224	810	433	537	442	783	479	399	702
Cavendish Hall*	12	3T 3D	x2	1227	1024	1801	1914	1385	2640	1039	3045	1737	2261	1746	3206	2019	1560	2863
Cawood Castle	2 + 2	T (D)		285	221	405	392	317	567	234	652	410	464	393	686	414	351	612
The Château	2	D		358	267	499	477	363	672	272	723	454	584	476	848	522	425	758
Church Cottage	4	T D		231	171	322	437	318	604	238	803	374	510	382	714	456	341	638
Clavell Tower	2	D	H	446	330	620	546	428	779	320	811	504	645	516	929	576	461	829
Cloth Fair																		
43 Cloth Fair	2	T		607	553	928	706	686	1114	505	924	706	744	742	1189	664	643	1046
45a Cloth Fair	4	2S D		717	669	1109	834	811	1298	608	1159	873	929	940	1495	830	806	1309
Clytha Castle	6	T 2D	H	796	527	1058	1068	779	1478	585	1675	943	1282	963	1796	1144	856	1598
The College	5	S T D		220	152	301	367	269	515	198	965	412	569	420	801	508	360	703
Coombe																		
The Carpenter's Shop	4	T D		276	194	381	518	390	735	287	1268	535	692	530	990	618	473	884
Chapel Cottage	4	2S D		208	145	286	385	288	545	215	942	399	517	397	740	462	354	661
Coombe Corner	6	2S T D		261	182	359	499	374	707	281	1259	522	676	517	966	604	464	865
Ford Cottage	2 + 2	D B		305	212	415	504	379	715	281	1227	526	683	523	977	610	465	871
1 Hawkers Cottages	5	S T D	x2	266	185	365	481	357	679	268	1203	503	656	499	936	586	443	833
2 Hawkers Cottages	6	2T D		301	207	411	546	405	770	301	1361	566	736	564	1053	657	501	938
1 Mill House	4	T D		248	173	341	436	325	616	241	1005	453	585	450	838	522	402	748
2 Mill House	3	S D		204	142	277	371	275	517	203	820	377	490	374	691	437	334	617
Coop House	3	S D		345	250	476	510	394	723	290	768	463	611	480	873	546	429	780
Cowside*	5	S T D		430	301	585	632	466	879	351	1191	567	765	584	1079	683	522	963
Crownhill Fort	8	T D IV	x2	463	315	622	567	418	788	313	1030	545	697	540	990	622	483	884

Facilities

- Bath
- Shower
- Shower over bath
- Dishwasher
- Washing machine
- Washing machine shared between Landmarks
- Fire or stove
- Awkward stairs
- Open grounds, garden or terrace or yard
- Parking may be difficult
- Cot not available
- Dogs not allowed
- Remote property or isolated location

* Denotes a new Landmark

Booking

Bookings can be made and availability checked on our **website** or by telephoning the Landmark Booking Office on **01628 825925**. We can answer your questions and suggest alternatives if your first choice is not available.

The Booking Office is normally open:
Monday to Friday 9am–6pm
Saturday 10am–4pm
Sunday 10am–4pm (January only)

We are closed on Sundays (apart from in January) and public holidays. In 2010 we are open from Saturday 2 January.

To ensure the widest possible choice of Landmarks, we recommend early booking as some buildings book up a long time in advance. It is always worth checking the website or telephoning the Booking Office to check late availability.

Booking periods
Short stay bookings*
Short stays can either be **weekends** (three nights, Friday night to Monday morning) or **midweeks** (four nights, Monday night to Friday morning).

Weekly bookings
We take bookings for weeks throughout the year. You can choose to start the week on either a Monday or a Friday, subject to availability.

Lundy bookings
Stays on Lundy are governed by sailing and helicopter dates. Where a daily rate is shown you can book any length of stay (minimum two nights), but the start and end dates of your booking must correspond with the sailing or helicopter timetable.

Easter, Bank Holidays, Christmas and New Year*
The Easter weekend, both May Bank Holidays and the August Bank Holiday are let as five nights, four nights and four nights respectively. The length of midweek stays either side of these periods are shown in this Price List and on the website. Christmas 2010 will be seven nights. New Year 2010/11 will be five nights.

*Different arrangements apply for Italy (see pages 12–13) and Lundy (see pages 14–17).

Short notice bookings
If you book within one week of the start of your stay (or two weeks for Lundy), we may be able to vary the start date and length of stay (minimum three nights). During your stay, you can extend your booking if the building is still unlet.

How to book
Bookings can be made via our website or by telephoning the Booking Office. If the Landmark you want is available, you can secure it at once with a debit or credit card payment by telephone. We are currently unable to take payment on our website and in booking online you are making a provisional booking, which will be confirmed once payment has been received. We can hold your booking for a short period until we receive your payment. If we have not received the correct amount within the agreed time, this provisional booking will lapse.

Payment
If you book **more than three months before your stay**, you can choose to pay a deposit of one third of the full amount (minimum £100) with the balance of the cost due three months before your holiday. If booking for a future year you can guarantee the price by paying in full at the time of booking. If you book **fewer than three months before your stay**, your payment must be for the full amount. We accept Maestro (issued in the UK), Delta, Visa, MasterCard, direct transfer and sterling cheques drawn on a UK bank. All payments must be in sterling.

Cancellation
If you have to cancel for any reason you will be liable for a cancellation charge (see booking condition 20, on page 18). We strongly recommend that you take out your own insurance cover.

Bookings for future years
From 2 January 2010 we can accept bookings as far ahead as the end of 2012, except for Landmarks close to venues for the 2012 Olympics which will be released at a later date. For further information please contact the Booking Office. Prices for 2011 and 2012 will not have been fixed when you book. In this case, the deposit is one third (or £100 per booking if greater) of the current price for an equivalent period (not necessarily the same dates). Please note the deposit secures only the booking and not the price. In some cases prices may change considerably. The price will not alter if you pay in full at the time of booking (we may make specific exceptions to this). Lundy sailing and helicopter times may also change. Please see booking condition 14, on page 18 for further details.

Booking conditions
All bookings are on the terms set out on page 18. For the most up to date prices and information on Landmark buildings, please check our website. This Price List is accurate at 8 December 2009 and prices may change at any point. We cannot be held liable for any inaccuracies which might arise.

To book please visit:
www.landmarktrust.org.uk
or telephone **01628 825925**

Overseas **+44 (0)1628 825925**
Office **01628 825920**

Email **bookings@landmarktrust.org.uk**

Causeway House, Northumberland

Landmark Holidays

There are 190 historic buildings available to stay in through the Landmark Trust – follies, castles, towers, banqueting houses, cottages and many other unusual buildings. Full details of each can be found on our website or in the latest edition of the Landmark Trust Handbook. This Price List should be read in conjunction with one of these.

Staying in Landmarks
All our buildings are remarkable in some way and some are positively eccentric. We make each Landmark as practical and comfortable as we can without damaging its character. All have bathrooms and well-equipped kitchens, some now including microwaves. Larger buildings have dishwashers, freezers, and some have washing machines too. As a matter of philosophy, we do not provide televisions or telephones.

You may, especially in the country, come across natural intrusions like insects from time to time. Some Landmarks have awkward stairs or other oddities; all have the patina of age. The Handbook, website and this Price List provide further details, as can the Booking Office, whose staff are familiar with all our buildings.

Heating
Landmarks are let all year round and every building has heating, including where possible, an open fire or stove. All electricity, gas and oil are included in the rent. Energy costs are a significant and rising proportion of our running costs, so please use heating appropriately. Heating is usually switched off between mid-May and mid-September. Where there are open fires or stoves, we do not provide wood or coal, but this can usually be obtained locally.

Historic buildings can rarely be entirely draught-proofed without spoiling their character. A few Landmarks are difficult to heat due to their construction or exposed location and others have rooms that must be reached from outside the main accommodation. These are marked with an **H** or an **S** in the facilities column. We suggest you bring extra jumpers or hot water bottles to those marked **H**.

Linen
Linen and towels are included. The beds will be made up with sheets and blankets (duvets on bunks) and pillowcases when you arrive, except in The Barn on Lundy. We provide one hand and one bath towel per bed per week.

Front cover: Ingestre Pavilion, Staffordshire

Babies
Most Landmarks have a cot, which is suitable for children up to two years of age. (We provide a mattress but not bedding for this.)

Visitors with special requirements
Our Booking Office can offer advice on buildings suitable for the less mobile or those with specific disabilities. We are also able to provide information in alternative formats. In all cases we will endeavour to make available sufficient information to ensure that you enjoy your stay.

Fire alarms
Landmarks are fitted with audible smoke alarms. If you, or a member of your party, are hard of hearing then please make alternative arrangements.

Health and safety
Our buildings were made to the standards of earlier ages, often without the intention that they should be lived in. Consequently, you may encounter features that reflect their particular characters but deserve due care and attention, particularly for the young, elderly, less mobile or visually impaired. Examples of these are steps worn with age or with narrow treads, uneven surfaces, low ceilings and beams, unexpected drops and changes of level, and (by modern standards) low or absent lighting. In all cases we have sought to make a sensible compromise between due regard for safety and the careful retention of the fabric of each building, which makes it an interesting place to stay. We ask you to appreciate and use the building with this understanding. Please read the information sent with your booking confirmation and the Information & Advice folder on arrival, and familiarise yourself with the building, its surroundings and safety instructions.

Extra guests
The number staying at the property and its grounds (excluding babies in cots) must not exceed the number shown in the Price List. You may invite an additional two guests to visit you during your stay, however, they must not stay overnight.

Appleton Water Tower, Suffolk

Dogs
Up to two really well-behaved dogs are welcome, except where the Price List and website say otherwise. Assistance dogs are welcome at all buildings, but please inform us when booking.

Car-free holidays
The Booking Office can offer advice on which buildings are suitable for those without a car and there are some suggestions on our website. These buildings can be reached using public transport and shops and/or restaurants will be within walking distance.

Smoking
We would prefer you not to smoke in our buildings but in all cases please avoid smoking in bedrooms, including where a bed is located in a living room. Some buildings have specific conditions which prohibit smoking – please ask the Booking Office for details.

Arrival and departure
Our Housekeeper will clean and prepare your Landmark which will be available from 4pm on your day of arrival. You must leave before 10am on your last day to allow the building to be prepared for the next Landmarkers. Your stay will not be disturbed (except in emergencies or by prior arrangement).

The Landmark Trust
Price List 2010